5 LANGUAGE
VISUAL DICTIONARY

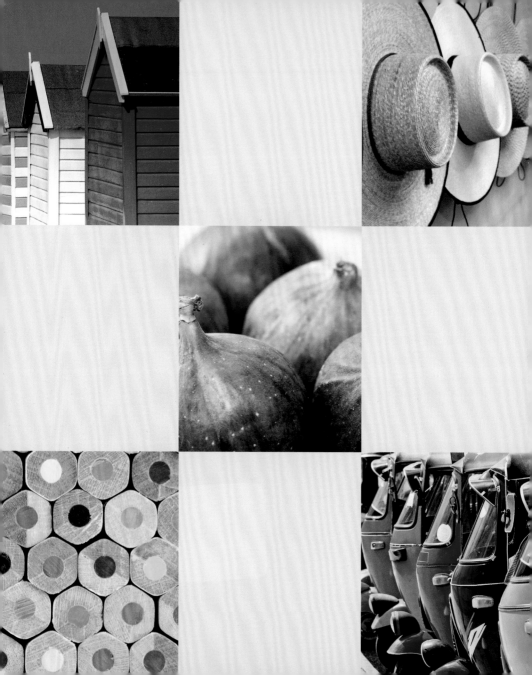

5 LANGUAGE
VISUAL DICTIONARY

2020 Edition

Managing Editor Christine Stroyan
Managing Art Editor Anna Hall
Editors Arpita Dasgupta, Priyanjali Narain
Assistant Editor Ishita Jha
DTP Designer Anita Yadav
Jacket Designer Suhita Dharamjit
Managing Jackets Editor Saloni Singh
Jacket Design Development Manager Sophia MTT
Senior Managing Editor Rohan Sinha
Managing Art Editor Sudakshina Basu
Preproduction Manager Balwant Singh
Production Manager Pankaj Sharma
Publisher Liz Wheeler
Art Director Karen Self
Publishing Director Jonathan Metcalf

First Edition

Senior Editor Angeles Gavira
Senior Art Editor Ina Stradins
US Editors Margaret Parrish, Christine Heilman
DTP Designer Rajen Shah
Production Controller Melanie Dowland
Picture Researcher Anna Grapes
Managing Art Editor Phil Ormerod

Designed for Dorling Kindersley by WaltonCreative.com
Art Editor Colin Walton, assisted by Tracy Musson
Designers Peter Radcliffe, Earl Neish, Ann Cannings
Picture Research Marissa Keating

Language content for Dorling Kindersley by
g-and-w publishing

Translation and editing by Ana Bremón, Renate Betson,
Marc Vitale, Christine Arthur

This American Edition, 2020
First American Edition, 2003
Published in the United States by DK Publishing
1450 Broadway, Suite 801, New York, NY 10018

Copyright © 2003, 2016, 2020 Dorling Kindersley Limited
DK, a Division of Penguin Random House LLC
20 21 22 23 24 10 9 8 7 6 5 4 3 2 1
001–316704–Apr/2020

A catalog record for this book
is available from the Library of Congress.
ISBN 978-1-4654-9103-9

DK books are available at special discounts when purchased in bulk for
sales promotions, premiums, fund-raising, or educational use.
For details, contact: DK Publishing Special Markets,
1450 Broadway, Suite 801, New York, NY 10018.
SpecialSales@dk.com

Printed and bound in China

A WORLD OF IDEAS:
SEE ALL THERE IS TO KNOW

www.dk.com

contents
table des matières
Inhalt
contenido
sommario

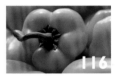

about the dictionary

The use of pictures is proven to aid understanding and the retention of information. Working on this principle, this highly-illustrated multilingual dictionary presents a large range of useful current vocabulary in five European languages.

The dictionary is divided thematically and covers most aspects of the everyday world in detail, from the restaurant to the gym, the home to the workplace, outer space to the animal kingdom. You will also find additional words and phrases for conversational use and for extending your vocabulary.

This is an essential reference tool for anyone interested in languages – practical, stimulating, and easy-to-use.

A few things to note

The five languages are always presented in the same order – English, French, German, Spanish, and Italian.

Other than in English, nouns are given with their definite articles reflecting the gender (masculine, feminine, or neuter) and number (singular or plural), for example:

seed almonds
la graine les amandes
der Samen die Mandeln
la semilla las almendras
il seme le mandorle

Verbs are indicated by a *(v)* after the English, for example:

harvest *(v)* • récolter • ernten
• recolectar • raccogliere

Each language also has its own index at the back of the book. Here you can look up a word in any of the five languages and be referred to the page number(s) where it appears. The gender is shown using the following abbreviations:

m = masculine
f = feminine
n = neuter

à propos du dictionnaire

Il est bien connu que les illustrations nous aident à comprendre et retenir l'information. Fondé sur ce principe, ce dictionnaire multilingue richement illustré présente un large éventail de vocabulaire courant et utile dans cinq langues européennes.

Le dictionnaire est divisé de façon thématique et couvre en détail la plupart des aspects du monde quotidien, du restaurant au gymnase, de la maison au lieu de travail, de l'espace au monde animal. Vous y trouverez également des mots et expressions supplémentaires pour la conversation et pour enrichir votre vocabulaire.

Il s'agit d'un outil de référence essentiel pour tous ceux qui s'intéressent aux langues – pratique, stimulant et d'emploi facile.

Quelques points à noter

Les cinq langues sont toujours présentées dans le même ordre – anglais, français, allemand, espagnol et italien.

Sauf en anglais, les noms sont donnés avec leurs articles définis qui indiquent leur genre (masculin, féminin ou neutre) et leur nombre (singulier ou pluriel):

seed almonds
la graine les amandes
der Samen die Mandeln
la semilla las almendras
il seme le mandorle

Les verbes sont indiqués par un *(v)* après l'anglais, par exemple:

harvest *(v)* • récolter • ernten
• recolectar • raccogliere

Chaque langue a également son propre index à la fin du livre. Vous pourrez y vérifier un mot dans n'importe laquelle des cinq langues et vous serez renvoyé au(x) numéro(s) de(s) page(s) où il figure. Le genre est indiqué par les abréviations suivantes:

m = masculin
f = féminin
n = neutre

über das Wörterbuch

Bilder helfen erwiesenermaßen, Informationen zu verstehen und zu behalten. Dieses mehrsprachige Wörterbuch enthält eine Fülle von Illustrationen und präsentiert gleichzeitig ein umfangreiches aktuelles Vokabular in fünf europäischen Sprachen.

Das Wörterbuch ist thematisch gegliedert und behandelt eingehend die meisten Bereiche des heutigen Alltags, vom Restaurant und Fitnesscenter, Heim und Arbeitsplatz bis zum Tierreich und Weltraum. Es enthält außerdem Wörter und Redewendungen, die für die Unterhaltung nützlich sind und das Vokabular erweitern.

Dies ist ein wichtiges Nachschlagewerk für jeden, der sich für Sprachen interessiert – es ist praktisch, anregend und leicht zu benutzen.

Einige Anmerkungen

Die fünf Sprachen werden immer in der gleichen Reihenfolge aufgeführt – Englisch, Französisch, Deutsch, Spanisch und Italienisch.

Außer für Englisch werden Substantive mit den bestimmten Artikeln, die das Geschlecht (Maskulinum, Femininum oder Neutrum) und den Numerus (Singular oder Plural) ausdrücken, angegeben, zum Beispiel:

seed almonds
la graine les amandes
der Samen die Mandeln
la semilla las almendras
il seme le mandorle

Die Verben sind durch ein *(v)* nach dem englischen Wort gekennzeichnet:

harvest *(v)* • récolter • ernten
• recolectar • raccogliere

Am Ende des Buchs befinden sich Register für jede Sprache. Sie können dort ein Wort in einer der fünf Sprachen und die jeweilige Seitenzahl nachsehen. Die Geschlechtsangabe erfolgt mit folgenden Abkürzungen:

m = Maskulinum
f = Femininum
n = Neutrum

sobre el diccionario

Está comprobado que el empleo de fotografías ayuda a la comprensión y a la retención de información. Basados en este principio, este diccionario plurilingüe y altamente ilustrado exhibe un amplio registro de vocabulario útil y actual en cinco idiomas europeos.

El diccionario aparece dividido según su temática y abarca la mayoría de los aspectos del mundo cotidiano con detalle, desde el restaurante al gimnasio, la casa al lugar de trabajo, el espacio al reino animal. Encontrará también palabras y frases adicionales para su uso en conversación y para ampliar su vocabulario.

Este diccionario es un instrumento de referencia esencial para todo aquél que esté interesado en los idiomas; es práctico, estimulante y fácil de usar.

Algunos puntos a observar

Los cinco idiomas se presentan siempre en el mismo orden: inglés, francés, alemán, español e italiano.

A excepción del inglés, los sustantivos se muestran con sus artículos definidos reflejando el género (masculino, femenino o neutro) y el número (singular/plural):

seed	almonds
la graine	les amandes
der Samen	die Mandeln
la semilla	las almendras
il seme	le mandorle

Los verbos se indican con una *(v)* después del inglés:

harvest *(v)* • récolter • ernten • recolectar • raccogliere

Cada idioma tiene su propio índice. Aquí podrá mirar una palabra en cualquiera de los cinco idiomas y se le indicará el número de la página donde aparece. El género se indica utilizando las siguientes abreviaturas:

m = masculino

f = femenino

n = neutro

informazioni sul dizionario

È dimostrato che l'uso di immagini aiuta a capire e memorizzare le informazioni. Applicando tale principio, abbiamo realizzato questo dizionario multilingue, corredato da numerosissime illustrazioni, che presenta un ampio ventaglio di vocaboli utili in cinque lingue europee.

Il dizionario è diviso in vari argomenti ed esamina dettagliatamente molti aspetti del mondo moderno, dal ristorante alla palestra, dalla casa all'ufficio, dallo spazio al regno animale. L'opera contiene inoltre frasi e vocaboli utili per conversare e per estendere il proprio vocabolario.

È un'opera di consultazione essenziale per tutti gli appassionati delle lingue – pratica, stimolante e facile da usare.

Indicazioni

Le cinque lingue vengono presentate sempre nello stesso ordine: inglese, francese, tedesco, spagnolo e italiano.

In tutte le lingue, tranne l'inglese, i sostantivi vengono riportati con il relativo articolo determinativo, che indica il genere (maschile, femminile o neutro) e il numero (singolare o plurale), come ad esempio:

seed	almonds
la graine	les amandes
der Samen	die Mandeln
la semilla	las almendras
il seme	le mandorle

I verbi sono contraddistinti da una *(v)* dopo il vocabolo inglese, come ad esempio:

harvest *(v)* • récolter • ernten • recolectar • raccogliere

Alla fine del libro ogni lingua ha inoltre il proprio indice, che consente di cercare un vocabolo in una qualsiasi delle cinque lingue e di trovare il rimando alla pagina che gli corrisponde. Il genere è indicato dalle seguenti abbreviazioni:

m = maschile

f = femminile

n = neutro

free audio app

The audio app contains all the words and phrases in the book, spoken by native speakers in English and four European languages, making it easier to learn important vocabulary and improve your pronunciation.

how to use the audio app

• Search for "DK Visual Dictionary" in your chosen app store and download the free app on your smartphone or tablet.
• Open the app and scan the barcode (or enter the ISBN) on the back of your book to unlock your Visual Dictionary in the Library.
• Download the audio files for your book.
• Enter a page number, then scroll up and down through the list to find a word or phrase.
• Tap a word to hear it.
• Swipe left or right to view the previous or next page.
• Tap the star icon to add words to your Favorites.

application audio gratuite

L'application audio contient tous les mots et les phrases du livre, prononcés en cinq langues européennes par des natifs des deux langues, afin de faciliter la maîtrise d'un vocabulaire essentiel, et aider à améliorer la prononciation.

comment utiliser l'application audio?

• Faites une recherche pour "DK Visual Dictionary" depuis votre app store préféré et téléchargez l'application gratuite sur votre smartphone ou tablette.
• Ouvrez l'application et scannez le code-barres (ou insérez le numéro ISBN) au verso du livre pour déverrouiller le Dictionnaire Visuel dans la Bibliothèque.
• Téléchargez les fichiers audio qui correspondent à votre livre.
• Saisissez un numéro de page et faites défiler la liste pour trouver des mots ou phrases.
• Appuyez sur un mot pour écouter la prononciation.
• Glissez vers la gauche ou la droite pour parcourir les pages.
• Appuyez sur l'icône étoile pour ajouter des mots à vos Favoris.

Kostenlose Audio-App

Die Audio-App enthält alle Begriffe und Redewendungen aus dem Buch, gesprochen von Muttersprachlern in fünf europäischen Sprachen. Das Anhören der Wörter erleichtert das Lernen von wichtigen Vokabeln und das Verbessern Ihrer eigenen Aussprache.

So funktioniert die Audio-App

• Laden Sie sich die kostenlose App auf Ihr Smartphone oder Tablet vom App-Store Ihres Betriebssystems, indem Sie nach „DK Visual Dictionary" suchen.
• Öffnen Sie die App und scannen Sie den Barcode oder geben Sie die ISBN ein (siehe Rückseite Ihres Buchs), um Ihr Visuelles Wörterbuch in der Bibliothek freizuschalten.
• Laden Sie sich die Audio-Daten für Ihr Buch herunter.
• Geben Sie eine Seitenzahl ein, scrollen Sie anschließend in der Wörterliste nach oben oder unten, um einen Begriff oder eine Redewendung zu finden.
• Tippen Sie auf ein Wort, um es sich anzuhören.
• Wischen Sie nach links oder rechts, um sich die vorige oder nächste Seite anzusehen.
• Tippen Sie auf den Stern, um Wörter zu Ihren Favoriten hinzuzufügen.

app de audio gratuita

Esta app de audio incluye todas las palabras y frases del libro, leídas por hablantes nativos tanto de cinco idiomas europeos, para facilitar el aprendizaje de vocabulario importante y mejorar la pronunciación.

app audio gratuita

L' app audio include tutte le parole e le frasi presenti nel libro. Grazie all'impiego di madrelingua in cinque lingue europee, ti aiuta ad arricchire il vocabolario e a migliorare la pronuncia.

DK VISUAL DICTIONARY

cómo utilizar la app de audio

• Puedes descargar la app de forma gratuita directamente en tu teléfono o tableta. Simplemente busca «DK Visual Dictionary» en la tienda de apps de tu elección.
• Para desbloquear el contenido del Diccionario Visual correspondiente en la Biblioteca, abre la app y escanea el código de barras que se encuentra en la contracubierta del libro (alternativamente también puedes introducir el ISBN del libro).
• Descarga los archivos de audio del libro.
• Para escuchar una palabra o frase, introduce el número de página y navega por la lista desplazándote de arriba abajo hasta encontrar la palabra o frase que quieras escuchar.
• Para escuchar una palabra, pulsa sobre ella.
• Para acceder al contenido de la página anterior o siguiente, simplemente pulsa a izquierda o derecha.
• Para añadir una palabra a la lista de Favoritos, pulsa sobre el icono de la estrella.

Come utilizzare l'app audio

• Cerca "Dizionario Visuale DK" sul tuo store preferito e scarica l'applicazione gratuita su smartphone o tablet.
• Apri l'applicazione e scansiona il codice a barre (oppure inserisci il codice ISBN) sul retro del libro per sbloccare il Dizionario Visuale nella Biblioteca.
• Scarica i file audio corrispondenti al libro che stai utilizzando.
•Inserisci il numero di una pagina, poi scorri lungo la lista per trovare la parola o la frase che stai cercando.
• Tocca un vocabolo per ascoltarne la pronuncia.
• Scorri le pagine verso destra o sinistra per visualizzare la pagina precendente o quella sucessiva.
• Tocca l'icona della stella per aggiungere la parola ai Preferiti.

people
les gens
die Menschen
la gente
le persone

body • le corps • der Körper • el cuerpo • il corpo

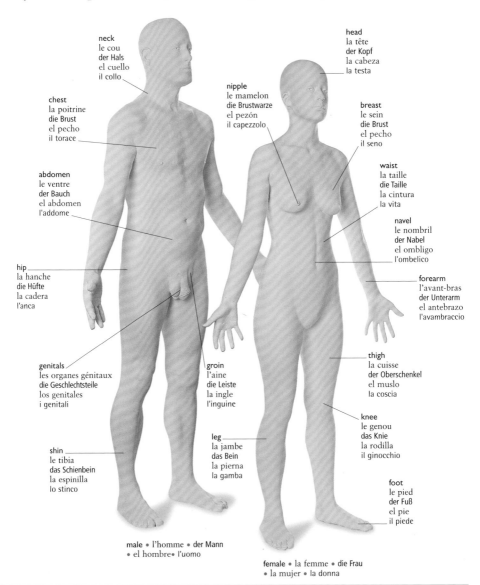

neck
le cou
der Hals
el cuello
il collo

head
la tête
der Kopf
la cabeza
la testa

nipple
le mamelon
die Brustwarze
el pezón
il capezzolo

chest
la poitrine
die Brust
el pecho
il torace

breast
le sein
die Brust
el pecho
il seno

abdomen
le ventre
der Bauch
el abdomen
l'addome

waist
la taille
die Taille
la cintura
la vita

navel
le nombril
der Nabel
el ombligo
l'ombelico

hip
la hanche
die Hüfte
la cadera
l'anca

forearm
l'avant-bras
der Unterarm
el antebrazo
l'avambraccio

genitals
les organes génitaux
die Geschlechtsteile
los genitales
i genitali

groin
l'aine
die Leiste
la ingle
l'inguine

thigh
la cuisse
der Oberschenkel
el muslo
la coscia

knee
le genou
das Knie
la rodilla
il ginocchio

shin
le tibia
das Schienbein
la espinilla
lo stinco

leg
la jambe
das Bein
la pierna
la gamba

foot
le pied
der Fuß
el pie
il piede

male • l'homme • der Mann
• el hombre• l'uomo

female • la femme • die Frau
• la mujer • la donna

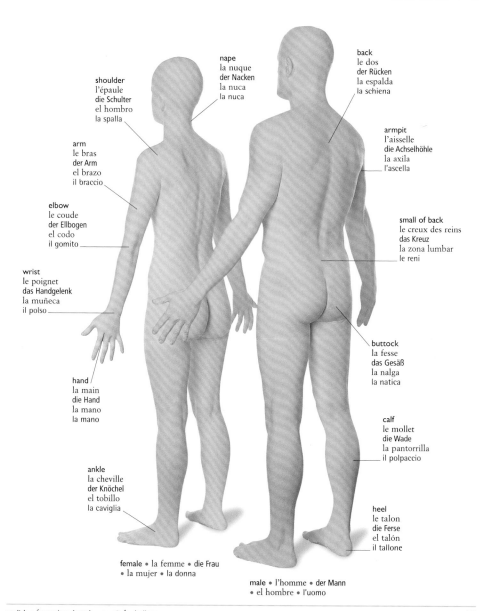

nape
la nuque
der Nacken
la nuca
la nuca

back
le dos
der Rücken
la espalda
la schiena

shoulder
l'épaule
die Schulter
el hombro
la spalla

armpit
l'aisselle
die Achselhöhle
la axila
l'ascella

arm
le bras
der Arm
el brazo
il braccio

elbow
le coude
der Ellbogen
el codo
il gomito

small of back
le creux des reins
das Kreuz
la zona lumbar
le reni

wrist
le poignet
das Handgelenk
la muñeca
il polso

buttock
la fesse
das Gesäß
la nalga
la natica

hand
la main
die Hand
la mano
la mano

calf
le mollet
die Wade
la pantorrilla
il polpaccio

ankle
la cheville
der Knöchel
el tobillo
la caviglia

heel
le talon
die Ferse
el talón
il tallone

female • la femme • die Frau
• la mujer • la donna

male • l'homme • der Mann
• el hombre • l'uomo

face • le visage • das Gesicht • la cara • la faccia

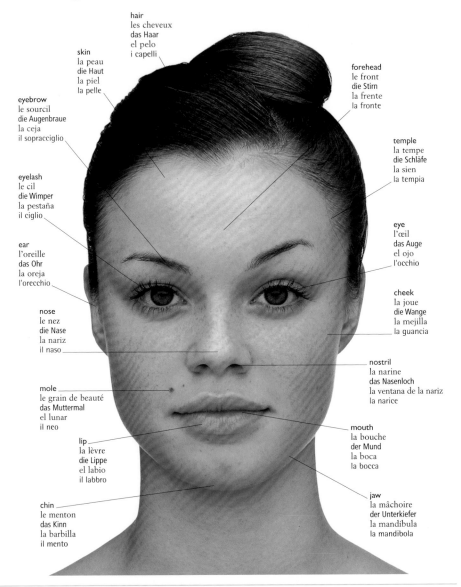

hair
les cheveux
das Haar
el pelo
i capelli

skin
la peau
die Haut
la piel
la pelle

forehead
le front
die Stirn
la frente
la fronte

eyebrow
le sourcil
die Augenbraue
la ceja
il sopracciglio

temple
la tempe
die Schläfe
la sien
la tempia

eyelash
le cil
die Wimper
la pestaña
il ciglio

eye
l'œil
das Auge
el ojo
l'occhio

ear
l'oreille
das Ohr
la oreja
l'orecchio

cheek
la joue
die Wange
la mejilla
la guancia

nose
le nez
die Nase
la nariz
il naso

nostril
la narine
das Nasenloch
la ventana de la nariz
la narice

mole
le grain de beauté
das Muttermal
el lunar
il neo

mouth
la bouche
der Mund
la boca
la bocca

lip
la lèvre
die Lippe
el labio
il labbro

jaw
la mâchoire
der Unterkiefer
la mandibula
la mandibola

chin
le menton
das Kinn
la barbilla
il mento

wrinkle • la ride • die Falte
• la arruga • la ruga

freckle • la tache de rousseur
• die Sommersprosse • la peca
• la lentiggine

pore • le pore • die Pore
• el poro • il poro

dimple • la fossette
• das Grübchen • el hoyuelo
• la fossetta

hand • la main • die Hand • la mano • la mano

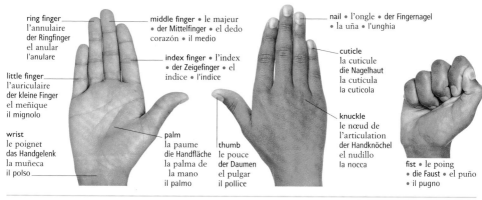

ring finger
l'annulaire
der Ringfinger
el anular
l'anulare

middle finger • le majeur
• der Mittelfinger • el dedo
corazón • il medio

index finger • l'index
• der Zeigefinger • el
indice • l'indice

little finger
l'auriculaire
der kleine Finger
el meñique
il mignolo

nail • l'ongle • der Fingernagel
• la uña • l'unghia

cuticle
la cuticule
die Nagelhaut
la cutícula
la cuticola

knuckle
le nœud de
l'articulation
der Handknöchel
el nudillo
la nocca

wrist
le poignet
das Handgelenk
la muñeca
il polso

palm
la paume
die Handfläche
la palma de
la mano
il palmo

thumb
le pouce
der Daumen
el pulgar
il pollice

fist • le poing
• die Faust • el puño
• il pugno

foot • le pied • der Fuß • el pie • il piede

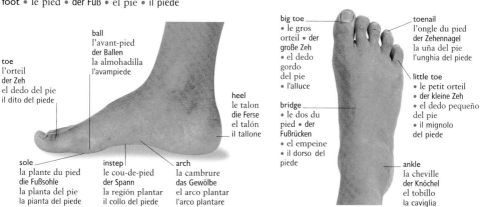

ball
l'avant-pied
der Ballen
la almohadilla
l'avampiede

toe
l'orteil
der Zeh
el dedo del pie
il dito del piede

big toe
• le gros
orteil • der
große Zeh
• el dedo
gordo
del pie
• l'alluce

toenail
l'ongle du pied
der Zehennagel
la uña del pie
l'unghia del piede

heel
le talon
die Ferse
el talón
il tallone

bridge
• le dos du
pied • der
Fußrücken
• el empeine
• il dorso del
piede

little toe
• le petit orteil
• der kleine Zeh
• el dedo pequeño
del pie
• il mignolo
del piede

sole
la plante du pied
die Fußsohle
la planta del pie
la pianta del piede

instep
le cou-de-pied
der Spann
la región plantar
il collo del piede

arch
la cambrure
das Gewölbe
el arco plantar
l'arco plantare

ankle
la cheville
der Knöchel
el tobillo
la caviglia

muscles • les muscles • die Muskeln • los músculos • i muscoli

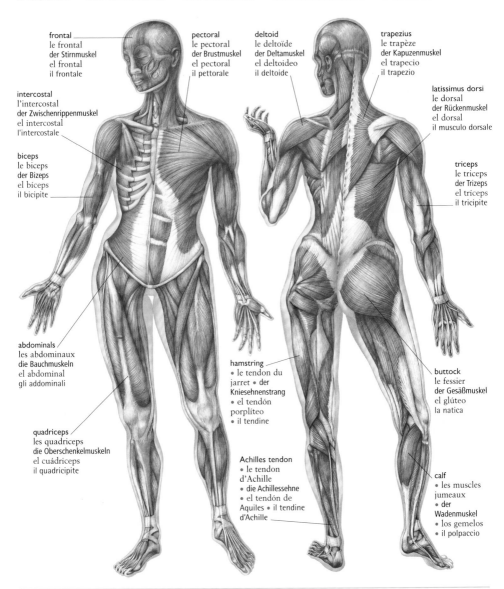

frontal
le frontal
der Stirnmuskel
el frontal
il frontale

pectoral
le pectoral
der Brustmuskel
el pectoral
il pettorale

deltoid
le deltoïde
der Deltamuskel
el deltoideo
il deltoide

trapezius
le trapèze
der Kapuzenmuskel
el trapecio
il trapezio

intercostal
l'intercostal
der Zwischenrippenmuskel
el intercostal
l'intercostale

latissimus dorsi
le dorsal
der Rückenmuskel
el dorsal
il musculo dorsale

biceps
le biceps
der Bizeps
el bíceps
il bicipite

triceps
le triceps
der Trizeps
el tríceps
il tricipite

abdominals
les abdominaux
die Bauchmuskeln
el abdominal
gli addominali

hamstring
• le tendon du
jarret • der
Kniesehnenstrang
• el tendón
porpliteo
• il tendine

buttock
le fessier
der Gesäßmuskel
el glúteo
la natica

quadriceps
les quadriceps
die Oberschenkelmuskeln
el cuádriceps
il quadricipite

Achilles tendon
• le tendon
d'Achille
• die Achillessehne
• el tendón de
Aquiles • il tendine
d'Achille

calf
• les muscles
jumeaux
• der
Wadenmuskel
• los gemelos
• il polpaccio

skeleton • le squelette • das Skelett • el esqueleto • lo scheletro

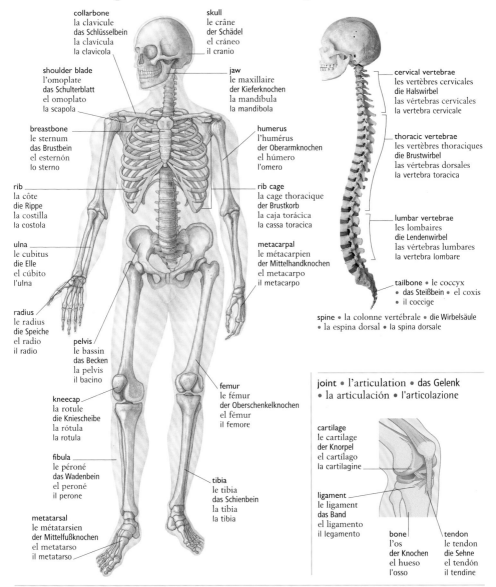

collarbone
la clavicule
das Schlüsselbein
la clavícula
la clavicola

skull
le crâne
der Schädel
el cráneo
il cranio

shoulder blade
l'omoplate
das Schulterblatt
el omoplato
la scapola

jaw
le maxillaire
der Kieferknochen
la mandíbula
la mandibola

breastbone
le sternum
das Brustbein
el esternón
lo sterno

humerus
l'humérus
der Oberarmknochen
el húmero
l'omero

rib
la côte
die Rippe
la costilla
la costola

rib cage
la cage thoracique
der Brustkorb
la caja torácica
la cassa toracica

ulna
le cubitus
die Elle
el cúbito
l'ulna

metacarpal
le métacarpien
der Mittelhandknochen
el metacarpo
il metacarpo

radius
le radius
die Speiche
el radio
il radio

pelvis
le bassin
das Becken
la pelvis
il bacino

kneecap
la rotule
die Kniescheibe
la rótula
la rotula

femur
le fémur
der Oberschenkelknochen
el fémur
il femore

fibula
le péroné
das Wadenbein
el peroné
il perone

tibia
le tibia
das Schienbein
la tibia
la tibia

metatarsal
le métatarsien
der Mittelfußknochen
el metatarso
il metatarso

cervical vertebrae
les vertèbres cervicales
die Halswirbel
las vértebras cervicales
la vertebra cervicale

thoracic vertebrae
les vertèbres thoraciques
die Brustwirbel
las vértebras dorsales
la vertebra toracica

lumbar vertebrae
les lombaires
die Lendenwirbel
las vértebras lumbares
la vertebra lombare

tailbone • le coccyx
• das Steißbein • el coxis
• il coccige

spine • la colonne vertébrale • die Wirbelsäule
• la espina dorsal • la spina dorsale

joint • l'articulation • das Gelenk • la articulación • l'articolazione

cartilage
le cartilage
der Knorpel
el cartílago
la cartilagine

ligament
le ligament
das Band
el ligamento
il legamento

bone
l'os
der Knochen
el hueso
l'osso

tendon
le tendon
die Sehne
el tendón
il tendine

internal organs • les organes internes • die inneren Organe • los órganos internos • gli organi interni

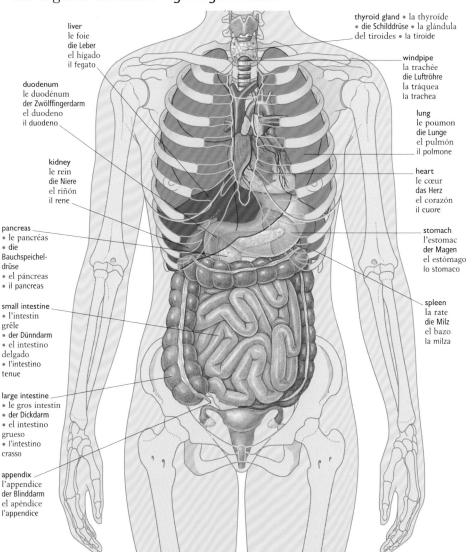

thyroid gland • la thyroïde • die Schilddrüse • la glándula del tiroides • la tiroide

liver
le foie
die Leber
el hígado
il fegato

windpipe
la trachée
die Luftröhre
la tráquea
la trachea

duodenum
le duodénum
der Zwölffingerdarm
el duodeno
il duodeno

lung
le poumon
die Lunge
el pulmón
il polmone

kidney
le rein
die Niere
el riñón
il rene

heart
le cœur
das Herz
el corazón
il cuore

pancreas
• le pancréas
• die Bauchspeicheldrüse
• el páncreas
• il pancreas

stomach
l'estomac
der Magen
el estómago
lo stomaco

small intestine
• l'intestin grêle
• der Dünndarm
• el intestino delgado
• l'intestino tenue

spleen
la rate
die Milz
el bazo
la milza

large intestine
• le gros intestin
• der Dickdarm
• el intestino grueso
• l'intestino crasso

appendix
l'appendice
der Blinddarm
el apéndice
l'appendice

head • la tête • der Kopf • la cabeza • la testa

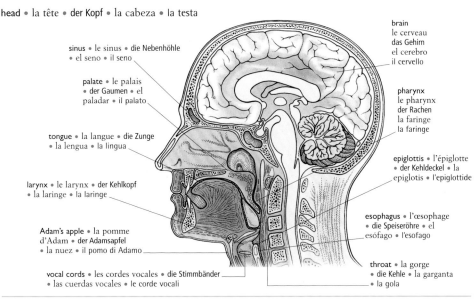

sinus • le sinus • die Nebenhöhle • el seno • il seno

palate • le palais • der Gaumen • el paladar • il palato

tongue • la langue • die Zunge • la lengua • la lingua

larynx • le larynx • der Kehlkopf • la laringe • la laringe

Adam's apple • la pomme d'Adam • der Adamsapfel • la nuez • il pomo di Adamo

vocal cords • les cordes vocales • die Stimmbänder • las cuerdas vocales • le corde vocali

brain • le cerveau • das Gehirn • el cerebro • il cervello

pharynx • le pharynx • der Rachen • la faringe • la faringe

epiglottis • l'épiglotte • der Kehldeckel • la epiglotis • l'epiglottide

esophagus • l'œsophage • die Speiseröhre • el esófago • l'esofago

throat • la gorge • die Kehle • la garganta • la gola

body systems • les systèmes du corps • die Körpersysteme • los sistemas • i sistemi organici

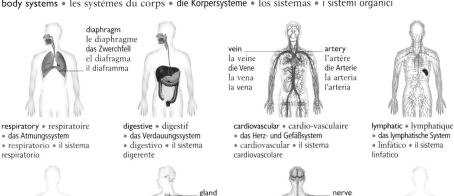

diaphragm • le diaphragme • das Zwerchfell • el diafragma • il diaframma

respiratory • respiratoire • das Atmungssystem • respiratorio • il sistema respiratorio

digestive • digestif • das Verdauungssystem • digestivo • il sistema digerente

vein • la veine • die Vene • la vena • la vena

artery • l'artère • die Arterie • la arteria • l'arteria

cardiovascular • cardio-vasculaire • das Herz- und Gefäßsystem • cardiovascular • il sistema cardiovascolare

lymphatic • lymphatique • das lymphatische System • linfático • il sistema linfatico

urinary • urinaire • das Harnsystem • urinario • il sistema urinario

gland • la glande • die Drüse • la glándula • la ghiandola

endocrine • endocrine • das endokrine System • endocrino • il sistema endocrino

nerve • le nerf • der Nerv • el nervio • il nervo

nervous • nerveux • das Nervensystem • nervioso • il sistema nervoso

reproductive • reproducteur • das Fortpflanzungssystem • reproductor • il sistema riproduttivo

reproductive organs • les organes de reproduction • die Fortpflanzungsorgane • los órganos reproductores • gli organi riproduttivi

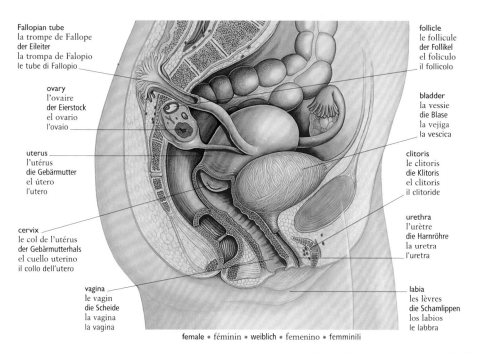

Fallopian tube
la trompe de Fallope
der Eileiter
la trompa de Falopio
le tube di Fallopio

ovary
l'ovaire
der Eierstock
el ovario
l'ovaio

uterus
l'utérus
die Gebärmutter
el útero
l'utero

cervix
le col de l'utérus
der Gebärmutterhals
el cuello uterino
il collo dell'utero

vagina
le vagin
die Scheide
la vagina
la vagina

follicle
le follicule
der Follikel
el folículo
il follicolo

bladder
la vessie
die Blase
la vejiga
la vescica

clitoris
le clitoris
die Klitoris
el clítoris
il clitoride

urethra
l'urètre
die Harnröhre
la uretra
l'uretra

labia
les lèvres
die Schamlippen
los labios
le labbra

female • féminin • weiblich • femenino • femminili

reproduction • la reproduction • die Fortpflanzung • la reproducción • la riproduzione

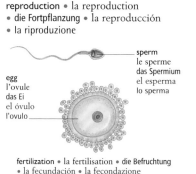

sperm
le sperme
das Spermium
el esperma
lo sperma

egg
l'ovule
das Ei
el óvulo
l'ovulo

fertilization • la fertilisation • die Befruchtung • la fecundación • la fecondazione

hormone	impotent	menstruation
l'hormone	impuissant	les règles
das Hormon	impotent	die Menstruation
la hormona	impotente	la menstruación
l'ormone	impotente	la mestruazione
ovulation	fertile	intercourse
l'ovulation	fécond	les rapports sexuels
der Eisprung	fruchtbar	der Geschlechtsverkehr
la ovulación	fértil	el coito
l'ovulazione	fecondo	il coito
infertile	conceive	sexually transmitted disease
stérile	concevoir	la maladie sexuellement transmissible
steril	empfangen	die Geschlechtskrankheit
estéril	concebir	la enfermedad de transmisión sexual
sterile	concepire	la malattia venerea

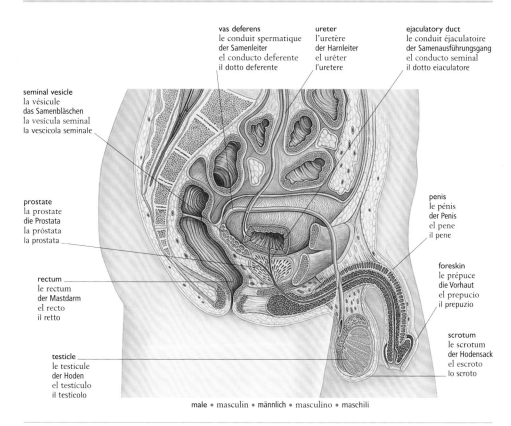

vas deferens
le conduit spermatique
der Samenleiter
el conducto deferente
il dotto deferente

ureter
l'uretère
der Harnleiter
el uréter
l'uretere

ejaculatory duct
le conduit éjaculatoire
der Samenausführungsgang
el conducto seminal
il dotto eiaculatore

seminal vesicle
la vésicule
das Samenbläschen
la vesícula seminal
la vescicola seminale

prostate
la prostate
die Prostata
la próstata
la prostata

rectum
le rectum
der Mastdarm
el recto
il retto

testicle
le testicule
der Hoden
el testículo
il testicolo

penis
le pénis
der Penis
el pene
il pene

foreskin
le prépuce
die Vorhaut
el prepucio
il prepuzio

scrotum
le scrotum
der Hodensack
el escroto
lo scroto

male • masculin • männlich • masculino • maschili

contraception • la contraception • die Empfängnisverhütung • la anticoncepción • la contraccezione

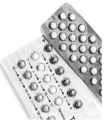

cervical cap
la cape cervicale
das Pessar
el anillo cervical
il pessario

diaphragm
le diaphragme
das Diaphragma
el diafragma
il diaframma

condom
le condom
das Kondom
el condón
il preservativo

IUD
le stérilet
die Spirale
el dispositivo intrauterino DIU
la spirale intrauterina

pill
la pilule
die Pille
la píldora
la pillola

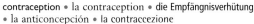

family • la famille • die Familie • la familia • la famiglia

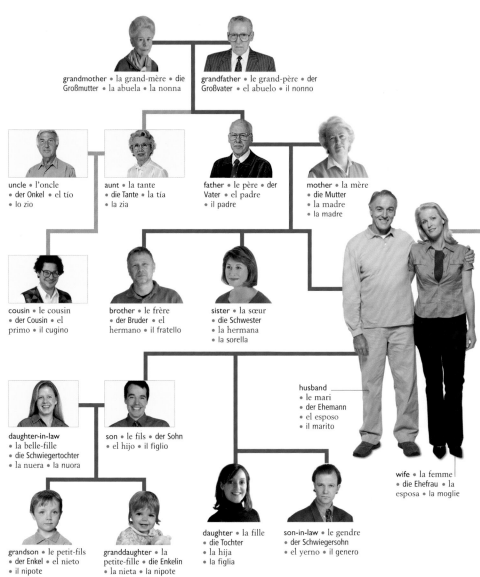

grandmother • la grand-mère • die Großmutter • la abuela • la nonna

grandfather • le grand-père • der Großvater • el abuelo • il nonno

uncle • l'oncle • der Onkel • el tío • lo zio

aunt • la tante • die Tante • la tía • la zia

father • le père • der Vater • el padre • il padre

mother • la mère • die Mutter • la madre • la madre

cousin • le cousin • der Cousin • el primo • il cugino

brother • le frère • der Bruder • el hermano • il fratello

sister • la sœur • die Schwester • la hermana • la sorella

husband • le mari • der Ehemann • el esposo • il marito

daughter-in-law • la belle-fille • die Schwiegertochter • la nuera • la nuora

son • le fils • der Sohn • el hijo • il figlio

wife • la femme • die Ehefrau • la esposa • la moglie

grandson • le petit-fils • der Enkel • el nieto • il nipote

granddaughter • la petite-fille • die Enkelin • la nieta • la nipote

daughter • la fille • die Tochter • la hija • la figlia

son-in-law • le gendre • der Schwiegersohn • el yerno • il genero

relatives	parents	grandchildren	stepmother	stepson	generation
les parents	les parents	les petits-enfants	la belle-mère	le beau-fils	la génération
die Verwandten	die Eltern	die Enkelkinder	die Stiefmutter	der Stiefsohn	die Generation
los parientes	los padres	los nietos	la madrastra	el hijastro	la generación
i parenti	i genitori	i nipoti	la matrigna	il figliastro	la generazione

grandparents	children	stepfather	stepdaughter	partner	twins
les grands-parents	les enfants	le beau-père	la belle-fille	le/la partenaire	les jumeaux
die Großeltern	die Kinder	der Stiefvater	die Stieftochter	der Partner/die Partnerin	die Zwillinge
los abuelos	los niños	el padrastro	la hijastra	el/la compañero/-a	los gemelos
i nonni	i bambini	il patrigno	la figliastra	il/la compagno/-a	i gemelli

mother-in-law
• la belle-mère
• die Schwiegermutter
• la suegra • la suocera

father-in-law
• le beau-père
• der Schwiegervater
• el suegro • il suocero

stages • les stades • die Stadien • las etapas • le fasi

baby • le bébé
• das Baby • el
bebé • il bimbo

child • l'enfant
• das Kind • el
niño • il bambino

brother-in-law
• le beau-frère
• der Schwager • el
cuñado • il cognato

sister-in-law
• la belle-sœur • die
Schwägerin • la cuñada
• la cognata

boy • le garçon
• der Junge • el
niño • il ragazzo

girl • la fille • das
Mädchen • la niña
• la ragazza

niece • la nièce
• die Nichte • la
sobrina • la nipote

nephew • le neveu
• der Neffe • el
sobrino • il nipote

Mrs.
Madame
Frau
Señora
Signora

teenager • l'adolescent
• die Jugendliche
• la adolescente
• l'adolescente

adult • l'adulte • der
Erwachsene • el adulto
• l'adulto

titles • les titres • die Anreden • los tratamientos • gli appellativi

Mr.
Monsieur
Herr
Señor
Signore

Miss/Ms.
Mademoiselle
Fräulein
Señorita
Signorina

man • l'homme
• der Mann • el
hombre • l'uomo

woman • la femme
• die Frau • la mujer
• la donna

relationships • les relations • die Beziehungen • las relaciones • i rapporti

assistant
l'assistante
die Assistentin
la ayudante
l'assistente

manager
le chef
der Chef
el jefe
il capo

business partner
l'associée
die Geschäftspartnerin
la socia
la partner di affari

employer
l'employeur
die Arbeitgeberin
el empresario
il datore di lavoro

employee
l'employée
der Arbeitnehmer
la empleada
la dipendente

colleague
le collègue
der Kollege
el compañero
il collega

office • le bureau • das Büro • la oficina • l'ufficio

neighbor • la voisine • der Nachbarin • la vecina • la vicina

friend • l'ami • der Freund • el amigo • l'amico

acquaintance • la connaissance • der Bekannte • el conocido • il conoscente

pen pal • le correspondant • der Brieffreund • el amigo por correspondencia • l'amico di penna

boyfriend
le petit ami
der Freund
el novio
il ragazzo

girlfriend
la petite amie
die Freundin
la novia
la ragazza

fiancé
le fiancé
der Verlobte
el prometido
il fidanzato

fiancée
la fiancée
die Verlobte
la prometida
la fidanzata

couple • le couple • das Paar • la pareja • la coppia

engaged couple • les fiancés • die Verlobten • la pareja prometida • i fidanzati

emotions • les émotions • die Gefühle • las emociones • le emozioni

smile
le sourire
das Lächeln
la sonrisa
il sorriso

happy • heureuse • glücklich
• contenta • felice

sad • triste • traurig
• triste • triste

excited • excitée • begeistert
• entusiasmada • entusiasta

bored • ennuyé • gelangweilt
• aburrido • annoiato

surprised • surpris
• überrascht • sorprendido
• sorpreso

scared • effrayée
• erschrocken • asustado
• spaventata

frown • le froncement
de sourcils • das
Stirnrunzeln • el
ceño fruncido
• aggrottare le
sopracciglia

angry • fâchée • verärgert
• enfadada • arrabiata

confused • désorientée
• verwirrt • confundida
• confusa

worried • inquiète • besorgt
• preocupada • preoccupata

nervous • nerveuse • nervös
• nerviosa • nervosa

proud • fiers • stolz
• orgullosos • fieri

confident • confiante
• selbstsicher • segura de
sí misma • sicura di sé

embarrassed • gênée
• verlegen • avergonada
• imbarazzata

shy • timide • schüchtern
• timida • timida

upset	laugh (v)	sigh (v)	shout (v)
contrarié	rire	soupirer	crier
aufgebracht	lachen	seufzen	schreien
triste	reír	suspirar	gritar
adirato	ridere	sospirare	gridare
shocked	cry (v)	faint (v)	yawn (v)
choqué	pleurer	s'évanouir	bâiller
schockiert	weinen	in Ohnmacht fallen	gähnen
horrorizado	llorar	desmayarse	bostezar
scioccato	piangere	svenire	sbadigliare

life events • les événements de la vie • die Ereignisse des Lebens • los acontecimientos de una vida • gli avvenimenti della vita

be born (v) • naître • geboren werden • nacer • nascere

start school (v) • commencer à l'école • zur Schule kommen • empezar el colegio • iniziare la scuola

make friends (v) • se faire des amis • sich anfreunden • hacer amigos • fare amicizia

graduate (v) • obtenir sa licence • graduieren • licenciarse • laurearsi

get a job (v) • trouver un emploi • eine Stelle bekommen • conseguir un trabajo • trovare un lavoro

fall in love (v) • tomber amoureux • sich verlieben • enamorarse • innamorarsi

get married (v) • se marier • heiraten • casarse • sposarsi

have a baby (v) • avoir un bébé • ein Baby bekommen • tener un hijo • avere un bambino

wedding • le mariage • die Hochzeit • la boda • il matrimonio

christening
le baptême
die Taufe
el bautizo
il battesimo

bar mitzvah
la bar-mitsvah
die Bar-Mizwa
el bar mitzvah
il bar mitzvah

anniversary
l'anniversaire de mariage
der Hochzeitstag
el aniversario
l'anniverario

emigrate (v)
émigrer
emigrieren
emigrar
emigrare

retire (v)
prendre sa retraite
in den Ruhestand treten
jubilarse
andare in pensione

die (v)
mourir
sterben
morir
morire

make a will (v)
faire son testament
sein Testament machen
hacer testamento
fare testamento

birth certificate
l'acte de naissance
die Geburtsurkunde
la partida de nacimiento
il certificato di nascita

wedding reception
le repas de noces
die Hochzeitsfeier
la celebración de la boda
il ricevimento nuziale

honeymoon
le voyage de noces
die Hochzeitsreise
la luna de miel
il viaggio di nozze

divorce • le divorce • die Scheidung • el divorcio • il divorzio

funeral • l'enterrement • das Begräbnis • el funeral • il funerale

celebrations • les fêtes • die Feiern • las celebraciones • le celebrazioni

festivals • les fêtes • die Feste • las fiestas • le feste

birthday party
la fête
die Geburtstagsfeier
la fiesta de cumpleaños
la festa di compleanno

card
la carte
die Karte
la tarjeta
il biglietto d'auguri

present
le cadeau
das Geschenk
el regalo
il regalo

birthday • l'anniversaire • der Geburtstag • el cumpleaños • il compleanno

das Geschenk
el regalo
il regalo

Christmas • Noël • das Weihnachten • la Navidad • il Natale

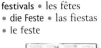

Passover • la Pâque (juives) • das Passah • la Pascua judía • la Pasqua ebraica

New Year • le Nouvel An • das Neujahr • el Año Nuevo • il Capodanno

carnival • le carnaval • der Karneval • el carnaval • il carnevale

procession
le défilé
der Umzug
el desfile
la processione

Ramadan • le Ramadan • der Ramadan • el Ramadán • il Ramadan

ribbon
le ruban
das Band
la cinta
il nastro

Thanksgiving • la fête de Thanksgiving • das Erntedankfest • el día de Acción de Gracias • il Giorno del Ringraziamento

Easter • Pâques • das Ostern • la Semana Santa • la Pasqua

Halloween • Halloween • das Halloween • el día de Halloween • la Festa di Halloween

Diwali • Diwali • das Diwali • el Diwali • il Diwali

appearance
l'apparence
die äußere Erscheinung
el aspecto
l'aspetto

children's clothing • les vêtements d'enfants • die Kinderkleidung • la ropa de niño • gli abiti per il bambino

baby • le bébé • das Baby • el bebé • il bimbo

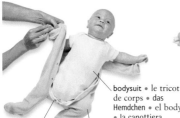

snowsuit • la combinaison de neige • der Schneeanzug • el buzo • la tutina da neve

bodysuit • le tricot de corps • das Hemdchen • el body • la canottiera

snap
le bouton-pression
der Druckknopf
el corchete
il bottone automatico

onesie • la grenouillère • der Strampelanzug • el pelele con pies • la tutina

sleeper • le pyjama • der Schlafanzug • el pijama enterizo • il pigiamino

romper • la combinaison-short • der Spielanzug • el pelele sin pies • il pagliacetto

bib • le bavoir • das Lätzchen • el babero • il bavaglino

mittens • les moufles • die Babyhandschuhe • las manoplas • i guanti

booties • les chaussons • die Babyschuhe • los patucos • le scarpette

cloth diaper • la couche éponge • die Stoffwindel • el pañal de felpa • il pannolino di spugna

disposable diaper • la couche jetable • die Wegwerfwindel • el pañal desechable • il pannolino usa e getta

plastic pants • la culotte en plastique • das Gummihöschen • las braguitas de plástico • le mutande di plastica

---

toddler • le petit enfant • das Kleinkind • el niño pequeño • il bambino piccolo

T-shirt
le t-shirt
das T-Shirt
la camiseta
la maglietta

overalls • la salopette • die Latzhose • los panatalones con peto • la salopette

sun hat • le chapeau de soleil • der Sonnenhut • el gorro para el sol • il cappello per il sole

apron • le tablier • die Schürze • el delantal • il grembiulino

shorts • le bermuda • die Shorts • los pantalones cortos • i pantaloncini

skirt
la jupe
der Rock
la falda
la gonna

---

child • l'enfant • das Kind • el niño • il bambino

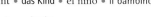

dress • la robe • das Kleid • el vestido • il vestito

hood
la capuche
die Kapuze
la capucha
il cappuccio

jeans • le jean • die Jeans • los pantalones vaqueros • i jeans

sandals
les sandales
die Sandalen
las sandalias
i sandali

backpack
le sac à dos
der Rucksack
la mochila
lo zaino

toggle
le bouton
der Knebelknopf
la muletilla
l'olivetta

scarf
l'écharpe
der Schal
la bufanda
la sciarpa

parka
l'anorak
der Anorak
el chaquetón
l'eskimo

rain boots
• les bottes de caoutchouc • die Gummistiefel • las botas de agua • le galosce

summer • l'été • der Sommer • el verano • l'estate

raincoat • l'imperméable • der Regenmantel • el impermeable • l'impermeabile

fall • l'automne • der Herbst • el otoño • l'autunno

duffel coat • le duffel-coat • der Dufflecoat • la trenca • il montgomery

winter • l'hiver • der Winter • el invierno • l'inverno

bathrobe
la robe de chambre
der Morgenrock
la bata
la vestaglia

logo
le logo
das Logo
el logotipo
il logo

athletic shoes
les baskets
die Sportschuhe
las zapatillas de deporte
le scarpe da ginnastica

nightgown
la chemise de nuit
das Nachthemd
el camisón
la camicia da notte

slippers
les pantoufles
die Hausschuhe
las pantuflas
le pantofole

soccer uniform • la tenue de foot • der Fußballdress • el uniforme del equipo • la tenuta da calcio

jogging suit • le survêtement • der Trainingsanzug • el chándal • la tuta

leggings • les leggings • die Leggings • las mallas • il pantacollant

natural fiber la fibre naturelle die Naturfaser la fibra natural la fibra naturale	Is it machine washable? C'est lavable en machine? Ist es waschmaschinenfest? ¿Se puede lavar a máquina? È lavabile in lavatrice?
synthetic synthétique synthetisch sintético sintetico	Will this fit a two-year-old? C'est la bonne taille pour deux ans? Passt das einem Zweijährigen? ¿Le valdrá esto a un niño de dos años? È la taglia giusta per un bambino di due anni?

nightwear • les vêtements de nuit • die Nachtwäsche • la ropa para dormir • gli indumenti per la notte

men's clothing • les vêtements pour hommes • die Herrenkleidung • la ropa de caballero • l'abbigliamento da uomo

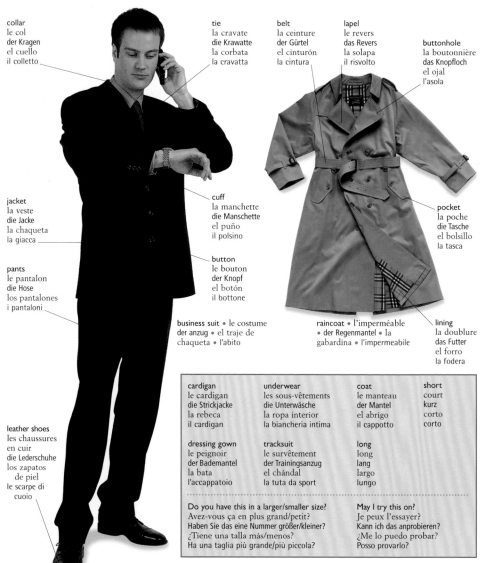

collar
le col
der Kragen
el cuello
il colletto

tie
la cravate
die Krawatte
la corbata
la cravatta

belt
la ceinture
der Gürtel
el cinturón
la cintura

lapel
le revers
das Revers
la solapa
il risvolto

buttonhole
la boutonnière
das Knopfloch
el ojal
l'asola

jacket
la veste
die Jacke
la chaqueta
la giacca

cuff
la manchette
die Manschette
el puño
il polsino

pocket
la poche
die Tasche
el bolsillo
la tasca

pants
le pantalon
die Hose
los pantalones
i pantaloni

button
le bouton
der Knopf
el botón
il bottone

business suit • le costume
der anzug • el traje de
chaqueta • l'abito

raincoat • l'imperméable
• der Regenmantel • la
gabardina • l'impermeabile

lining
la doublure
das Futter
el forro
la fodera

leather shoes
les chaussures
en cuir
die Lederschuhe
los zapatos
de piel
le scarpe di
cuoio

cardigan	underwear	coat	short
le cardigan	les sous-vêtements	le manteau	court
die Strickjacke	die Unterwäsche	der Mantel	kurz
la rebeca	la ropa interior	el abrigo	corto
il cardigan	la biancheria intima	il cappotto	corto
dressing gown	tracksuit	long	
le peignoir	le survêtement	long	
der Bademantel	der Trainingsanzug	lang	
la bata	el chándal	largo	
l'accappatoio	la tuta da sport	lungo	

Do you have this in a larger/smaller size?
Avez-vous ça en plus grand/petit?
Haben Sie das eine Nummer größer/kleiner?
¿Tiene una talla más/menos?
Ha una taglia più grande/più piccola?

May I try this on?
Je peux l'essayer?
Kann ich das anprobieren?
¿Me lo puedo probar?
Posso provarlo?

blazer • le blazer • der Blazer • la chaqueta • il blazer

sport coat • la veste de sport • das Sportjackett • la americana sport • la giacca sportiva

vest • le gilet • die Weste • el chaleco • il gilet

V-neck
l'encolure en V
der V-Ausschnitt
el cuello de pico
il collo a V

crew neck
le col rond
der runde Ausschnitt
el cuello redondo
il girocollo

T-shirt
le t-shirt
das T-Shirt
la camiseta
la maglietta

parka • l'anorak • der Anorak • el chaquetón • il giaccone

sweatshirt • le sweat-shirt • das Sweatshirt • la sudadera • la felpa

shirt • la chemise • das Hemd • la camisa • la camicia

jeans
le jean
die Jeans
los tejanos
i jeans

sweater • le pullover • der Pullover • el jersey • il maglione

pajamas • le pyjama • der Schlafanzug • el pijama • il pigiama

undershirt • le tricot de corps • das Unterhemd • la camiseta de tirantes • la canottiera

casual wear • les vêtements sport • die Freizeitkleidung • la ropa casual • il casual

shorts • le short • die Shorts • los pantalones cortos • i calzoncini

briefs • le slip • der Slip • los calzoncillos • lo slip

boxer shorts • le caleçon • die Boxershorts • los calzoncillos de pata • i boxer

socks • les chaussettes • die Socken • los calcetines • i calzini

women's clothing • les vêtements pour femmes • die Damenkleidung • la ropa de señora • l'abbigliamento da donna

jacket
la veste
die Jacke
la chaqueta
la giacca

strapless
sans bretelles
trägerlos
sin tirantes
senza spalline

seam
la couture
die Naht
la costura
la cucitura

sleeveless
sans manches
ärmellos
sin mangas
senza maniche

sleeve
la manche
der Ärmel
la manga
la manica

ankle length
long
knöchellang
largo
alla caviglia

evening dress • la robe du soir • das Abendkleid • el traje de noche • l'abito da sera

dress • la robe • das Kleid • el vestido • il vestito

skirt
la jupe
der Rock
la falda
la gonna

blouse
le chemisier
die Bluse
la blusa
la camicetta

hem
l'ourlet
der Saum
el dobladillo
l'orlo

knee length
à genou
knielang
hasta la rodilla
al ginocchio

pants
le pantalon
die Hose
los pantalones
i pantaloni

shoes
les chaussures
die Schuhe
los zapatos
le scarpe

formal • habillé • formell • formal • formale

casual • décontracté • leger • sport • casual

lingerie • la lingerie • die Unterwäsche • la lencería • la biancheria intima

strap
la bretelle
der Träger
el tirante
la spallina

robe • le peignoir
• der Morgenmantel
• la bata • la vestaglia

slip • le caraco
• der Unterrock
• la combinación
• la sottoveste

camisole • la camisole
• das Mieder • la
camisola • il corpetto

garter strips
la jarretelle
der Strumpfhalter
las ligas
i reggicalze

bustier • la guêpière
• das Bustier • el
corsé con liguero
• il bustino

stocking • le bas
• der Strumpf • la
media • la calza

panty hose • le collant
• die Strumpfhose • las
medias • il collant

bra • le soutien-gorge
• der Büstenhalter
• el sujetador
• il reggiseno

panties • le slip
der Slip • las bragas
• lo slip

nightgown • la
chemise de nuit
• das Nachthemd
• el camisón
• la camicia da notte

wedding • le mariage • die Hochzeit • la boda • il matrimonio

lace
la dentelle
die Spitze
el encaje
il pizzo

veil
le voile
der Schleier
el velo
il velo

bouquet
le bouquet
das Bukett
el ramo de flores
il bouquet

train
la traîne
die Schleppe
la cola
lo strascico

wedding dress • la robe de mariée
• das Hochzeitskleid • el vestido de novia
• l'abito da sposa

corset	tailored
le corset	ajusté
das Korsett	gut geschnitten
el corsé	sastre
il busto	attillato
garter	halter neck
la jarretière	dos-nu
das Strumpfband	rückenfrei
la liga	al cuello y con los
la giarrettiera	hombros al aire
	scollo all'Americana
shoulder pad	
l'épaulette	sports bra
das Schulterpolster	le soutien-gorge sport
la hombrera	der Sport-BH
la spallina	el sujetador deportivo
	il reggiseno sportivo
waistband	
la ceinture	underwire
der Rockbund	à armature
la cinturilla	mit Formbügeln
il girovita	con aros
	con armatura

accessories • les accessoires • die Accessoires • los accesorios • gli accessori

buckle
la boucle
die Gürtelschnalle
la hebilla
la fibbia

handle
le manche
der Griff
el asa
il manico

cap • la casquette • die Mütze • la gorra • il berretto

hat • le chapeau • der Hut • el sombrero • il cappello

scarf • le foulard • der Schal • el pañuelo • la sciarpa

belt • la ceinture • der Gürtel • el cinturón • la cintura

tiepin • l'épingle de cravate • die Krawattennadel • el alfiler de corbata • il fermacravatta

tip
la pointe
die Spitze
la punta
la punta

handkerchief • le mouchoir • das Taschentuch • el pañuelo • il fazzoletto

bow tie • le nœud papillon • die Fliege • la pajarita • la farfalla

gloves • les gants • die Handschuhe • los guantes • i guanti

umbrella • le parapluie • der Regenschirm • el paraguas • l'ombrello

jewelry • les bijoux • der Schmuck • las joyas • i gioielli

strand of pearls
le rang de perles
die Perlenkette
el collar de perlas
il filo di perle

pendant • le pendentif • der Anhänger • el colgante • il pendaglio

brooch • la broche • die Brosche • el broche • la spilla

cuff links • le bouton de manchette • der Manschettenknopf • el gemelo • il gemello

link
le maillon
das Glied
el eslabón
la maglia

clasp
le fermoir
der Verschluss
el cierre
il fermaglio

earrings • la boucle d'oreille • der Ohrring • el pendiente • l'orecchino

ring
la bague
der Ring
el anillo
l'anello

stone
la pierre
der Edelstein
la piedra
la pietra

necklace
le collier
die Halskette
el collar
la collana

watch • la montre • die Armbanduhr • el reloj • l'orologio da polso

bracelet • le bracelet • das Armband • la pulsera • il bracciale

chain • la chaîne • die Kette • la cadena • la collana

jewelry box • la boîte à bijoux • der Schmuckkasten • el joyero • il cofanetto portagioie

bags • les sacs • die Taschen • los bolsos • le borse

clasp
le fermoir
der Verschluss
el cierre
la cinghia

shoulder strap
la bretelle
der Schulterriemen
la correa
la bretella

handles
les poignées
die Griffe
las asas
i manici

wallet • le portefeuille • die Brieftasche • la cartera • il portafoglio

change purse • le porte-monnaie • das Portemonnaie • el monedero • il portamonete

shoulder bag • le sac à bandoulière • die Umhängetasche • el bolso • la borsa a tracolla

duffel bag • le fourre-tout • die Reisetasche • la bolsa de viaje • la borsa da viaggio

briefcase • la serviette • die Aktentasche • el maletín • la cartella

handbag • le sac à main • die Handtasche • el bolso de mano • la borsetta

backpack • le sac à dos • der Rucksack • la mochila • lo zaino

shoes • les chaussures • die Schuhe • los zapatos • le scarpe

eyelet
l'œillet
die Öse
el ojal
l'occhiello

lace
le lacet
der Schnürsenkel
el cordón
il laccio

tongue
la languette
die Zunge
la lengüeta
la lingua

sole
la semelle
die Sohle
la suela
la suola

heel
le talon
der Absatz
el tacón
il tacco

hiking boot • le pataugas • der Wanderschuh • la bota de trekking • la scarpa da trekking

sneaker • la basket • der Sportschuh • la zapatilla deportiva • la scarpa da ginnastica

lace-up • la chaussure lacée • der Schnürschuh • el zapato de cordoneras • la scarpa con i lacci

boot • la botte • der Stiefel • la bota • lo stivale

flip-flop • la tong • die Strandsandale • la chancla • l'infradito

dress shoe • la chaussure de cuir • der Lederschuh • el zapato de caballero • la scarpa da uomo

high-heeled shoe
la chaussure à talon
der Schuh mit hohem Absatz
el zapato de tacón
la scarpa con il tacco alto

wedge • la chaussure compensée • der Keilschuh • la cuña • la zeppa

sandal
la sandale
die Sandale
la sandalia
il sandalo

slip-on
le mocassin
der Slipper
el mocasín
il mocassino

pump
la ballerine
der Ballerina
la bailarina
la ballerina

hair • les cheveux • das Haar • el pelo • i capelli

comb
le peigne
der Kamm
el peine
il pettine

comb (v) • peigner • kämmen
• peinar • pettinare

brush
la brosse
die Haarbürste
el cepillo
la spazzola

brush (v) • brosser • bürsten
• cepillar • spazzolare

rinse (v) • rincer • ausspülen
• enjuagar • sciacquare

hairdresser
la coiffeuse
die Friseurin
la peluquera
la parrucchiera

sink
le lavabo
das Waschbecken
el lavabo
il lavandino

client
la cliente
die Kundin
la clienta
la cliente

wash (v) • laver • waschen • lavar • lavare

cut (v) • couper • schneiden
• cortar • tagliare

robe
le peignoir
der Frisierumhang
la bata
il grembiule

blow-dry (v) • sécher • föhnen
• secar con el secador
• asciugare con il fon

set (v) • faire une mise en
plis • legen • marcar
• mettere in piega

---

accessories • les accessoires • die Frisierartikel • los accesorios • gli accessori

blow-dryer • le
sèche-cheveux
• der Föhn
• el secador
• l'asciugacapelli

shampoo • le shampoing
• das Shampoo • el
champú • lo shampoo

conditioner • l'après-
shampoing • die Haarspülung
• el suavizante • il balsamo

gel • le gel
• das Haargel
• el gel • il gel

hairspray • la laque
• das Haarspray
• la laca • la lacca

curling iron
le fer à friser
der Lockenstab
las tenacillas
l'arricciacapelli

scissors • les ciseaux
• die Schere • las
tijeras • le forbici

headband • le serre-tête
• der Haarreif • la diadema
• il cerchietto

hair straightener • le fer
à lisser • der Haarglätter
• la plancha de pelo
• la piastra per capelli

bobby pins • la pince à
cheveux • die Haarklammer
• la horquilla • la forcina

styles • les coiffures • die Frisuren • los estilos • le acconciature

ponytail • la queue de cheval • **der Pferdeschwanz** • la cola de caballo • la coda di cavallo

braid • la natte • **der Zopf** • la trenza • la treccia

French twist • le rouleau • **die Hochfrisur** • el moño francés • la piega alla francese

bun • le chignon • **der Haarknoten** • el moño • la crocchia

pigtails • les couettes • **die Schwänzchen** • las coletas • i codini

bob • au carré • **der Bubikopf** • la melena • il caschetto

crop • la coupe courte • **der Kurzhaarschnitt** • el pelo corto • l'acconciatura corta

curly • frisé • **lockig** • rizado • ricci

perm • la permanente • **die Dauerwelle** • la permanente • la permanente

straight • raide • **glatt** • lacio • lisci

roots
les racines
die Wurzeln
las raíces
le radici

highlights • les reflets • **die Strähnen** • los reflejos • i colpi di sole

bald • chauve • **kahl** • calvo • calvo

wig • la perruque • **die Perücke** • la peluca • la parrucca

hairband	greasy
l'élastique pour cheveux	gras
das Haarband	fettig
la goma del pelo	graso
l'elastico	grasso
trim (v)	dry
rafraîchir	sec
nachschneiden	trocken
cortar las puntas	seco
spuntare	secco
barber	normal
le coiffeur	normal
der Herrenfriseur	normal
el barbero	normal
il barbiere	normale
dandruff	scalp
les pellicules	le cuir chevelu
die Schuppen	die Kopfhaut
la caspa	el cuero cabelludo
la forfora	il cuoio capelluto
split ends	straighten (v)
les fourches	décrêper
der Haarspliss	glätten
las puntas abiertas	alisar
le doppie punte	lisciare

colors • les couleurs • die Haarfarben • los colores • i colori

blonde • blond • **blond** • rubio • biondo

brunette • châtain • **brünett** • castaño • bruno

auburn • auburn • **rotbraun** • rojizo • castano

red • roux • **rot** • pelirrojo • rosso

black • noir • **schwarz** • negro • nero

gray • gris • **grau** • gris • grigio

white • blanc • **weiß** • blanco • bianco

dyed • teint • **gefärbt** • teñido • tinto

beauty • la beauté • die Schönheit • la belleza • la bellezza

hair dye
la teinture de cheveux
das Haarfärbemittel
el tinte para el pelo
la tintura per capelli

eye shadow
le fard à paupières
der Lidschatten
la sombra de ojos
l'ombretto

mascara
le mascara
die Wimperntusche
el rímel
il mascara

eyeliner
l'eye-liner
der Eyeliner
el lápiz de ojos
la matita per gli occhi

blush
le fard à joues
das Puderrouge
el colorete
il fard

foundation
le fond de teint
die Grundierung
el maquillaje de fondo
il fondotinta

lipstick
le rouge à lèvres
der Lippenstift
el pinta labios
il rossetto

makeup • le maquillage • das Make-up
• el maquillaje • il trucco

eyebrow pencil • le crayon à sourcils • der Augenbrauenstift
• el lápiz de cejas • la matita per le sopracciglia

eyebrow brush • la brosse à
sourcils • das Brauenbürstchen
• el cepillo para las cejas
• la spazzolina per le sopracciglia

tweezers • la pince à épiler
• die Pinzette • las pinzas
• le pinzette

lip gloss • le brillant à lèvres
• das Lipgloss • el brillo de
labios • il luicidalabbra

lip brush • le pinceau à lèvres
• der Lippenpinsel • el pincel
de labios • il pennello per
le labbra

lip liner • le crayon à lèvres • der Lippenkonturenstift
• el lápiz de labios • la matita per le labbra

brush • le pinceau • der
Puderpinsel • la brocha
• il pennello

concealer • le correcteur
• der Korrekturstift • el lápiz
corrector • il correttore

face powder
la poudre
der Gesichtspuder
los polvos compactos
la cipria

mirror
le miroir
der Spiegel
el espejo
lo specchio

powder puff
la houppette
die Puderquaste
la borla
il piumino

compact • le poudrier • die Puderdose • la polvera • il portacipria

english • français • deutsch • español • italiano

beauty treatments • les soins de beauté • die Schönheitsbehandlungen • los tratamientos de belleza • i trattamenti di bellezza

face mask • le masque de beauté • die Gesichtsmaske • la mascarilla • la maschera di bellezza

sunbed • le lit U.V. • die Sonnenbank • la cama de rayos ultravioletas • il lettino solare

facial • le soin du visage • die Gesichtsbehandlung • la limpieza de cutis • il trattamento per il viso

exfoliate (v) • exfolier • Peeling machen • exfoliar • esfoliare

wax • l'épilation • die Enthaarung • la depilación a la cera • la depilazione

pedicure • la pédicurie • die Pediküre • la pedicura • la pedicure

toiletries • les accessoires de toilette • die Toilettenartikel • los artículos de tocador • gli articoli da toilette

cleanser • le démaquillant • der Reiniger • la leche limpiadora • il latte detergente

toner • le tonique • das Gesichtswasser • el tónico • la lozione tonificante

moisturizer • la crème hydratante • die Feuchtigkeitscreme • la crema hidratante • la crema idratante

self-tanning lotion • l'autobronzant • die Selbstbräunungscreme • la crema autobronceadora • la crema autoabbronzante

perfume le parfum das Parfum el perfúme il profumo

eau de toilette • l'eau de toilette • das Eau de Toilette • el agua de colonia • l'acqua di colonia

manicure • la manicure • die Maniküre • la manicura • la manicure

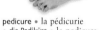

nail polish remover le dissolvant der Nagellackentferner el quitaesmalte l'acetone

nail file • la lime à ongles • die Nagelfeile • la lima de uñas • la limetta

nail polish • le vernis à ongles • der Nagellack • el esmalte de uñas • lo smalto per unghie

nail scissors • les ciseaux à ongles • die Nagelschere • las tijeras de uñas • le forbicine per le unghie

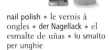

nail clippers le coupe-ongles der Nagelknipser el cortaúñas il tagliaunghie

complexion	oily	tan
le teint	gras	le bronzage
der Teint	fettig	die Sonnenbräune
el cutis	graso	el bronceado
la carnagione	grasso	l'abbronzatura
fair	sensitive	tattoo
clair	sensible	le tatouage
hell	empfindlich	die Tätowierung
claro	sensible	el tatuaje
chiaro	sensibile	il tatuaggio
dark	hypoallergenic	antiwrinkle
foncé	hypoallergénique	antirides
dunkel	hypoallergen	Antifalten-
moreno	hipoalergénico	antiarrugas
scuro	ipoallergenico	antirughe
dry	shade	cotton balls
sec	le ton	les boules de coton
trocken	der Farbton	die Wattebällchen
seco	el tono	las bolas de algodón
secco	la tonalità	i batuffoli di ovatta

health
la santé
die Gesundheit
la salud
la salute

illness • la maladie • die Krankheit • la enfermedad • la malattia

headache • le mal de tête • die Kopfschmerzen • el dolor de cabeza • il mal di testa

nosebleed • le saignement de nez • das Nasenbluten • la hemorragia nasal • l'epistassi

cough • la toux • der Husten • la tos • la tosse

fever • la fièvre • das Fieber • la fiebre • la febbre

inhaler
l'inhalateur
der Inhalationsapparat
el inhalador
l'inalatore

sneeze • l'éternuement • das Niesen • el estornudo • lo starnuto

cold • le rhume • die Erkältung • el resfriado • il raffreddore

flu • la grippe • die Grippe • la gripe • l'influenza

asthma • l'asthme • das Asthma • el asma • l'asma

cramps • les crampes • die Krämpfe • los calambres • i crampi

nausea • la nausée • die Übelkeit • la náusea • la nausea

chicken pox • la varicelle • die Windpocken • la varicela • la varicella

rash • l'éruption • der Hautausschlag • el sarpullido • lo sfogo

heart attack	diabetes	eczema	chill	vomit (v)	diarrhea
la crise cardiaque	le diabète	l'eczéma	le refroidissement	vomir	la diarrhée
der Herzinfarkt	die Zuckerkrankheit	das Ekzem	die Verkühlung	sich übergeben	der Durchfall
el infarto de miocardio	la diabetes	el eccema	el resfriado	vomitar	la diarrea
l'infarto	il diabete	l'eczema	l'infreddatura	vomitare	la diarrea
stroke	hay fever	infection	stomachache	epilepsy	measles
l'attaque	le rhume des foins	l'infection	le mal d'estomac	l'épilepsie	la rougeole
der Schlaganfall	der Heuschnupfen	die Infektion	die Magenschmerzen	die Epilepsie	die Masern
el derrame cerebral	la fiebre del heno	la infección	el dolor de estómago	la epilepsia	el sarampión
l'apoplessia	il reffredore da fieno	l'infezione	il mal di stomaco	l'epilessia	il morbillo
blood pressure	allergy	virus	faint (v)	migraine	mumps
la tension	l'allergie	le virus	s'évanouir	la migraine	les oreillons
der Blutdruck	die Allergie	der Virus	in Ohnmacht fallen	die Migräne	der Mumps
la tensión arterial	la alergia	el virus	desmayarse	la jaqueca	las paperas
la pressione sanguina	l'allergia	il virus	svenire	l'emicrania	gli orecchioni

doctor • le médecin • der Arzt • el médico • il medico

consultation • la consultation • die Konsultation • la consulta • la visita

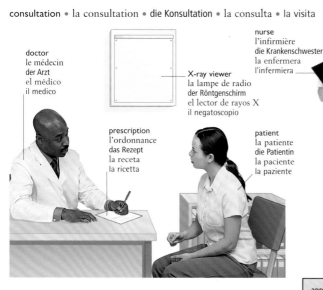

doctor
le médecin
der Arzt
el médico
il medico

X-ray viewer
la lampe de radio
der Röntgenschirm
el lector de rayos X
il negatoscopio

nurse
l'infirmière
die Krankenschwester
la enfermera
l'infermiera

prescription
l'ordonnance
das Rezept
la receta
la ricetta

patient
la patiente
die Patientin
la paciente
la paziente

scale • la
balance • die
Personenwaage
• la báscula
• la bilancia

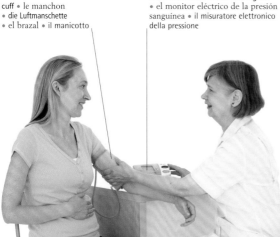

cuff • le manchon
• die Luftmanschette
• el brazal • il manicotto

electric blood pressure monitor
• le tensiomètre électronique
• das Elektrisches Blutdruckmessgerät
• el monitor eléctrico de la presión
sanguinea • il misuratore elettronico
della pressione

appointment
le rendez-vous
der Termin
la cita
l'appuntamento

medical examination
l'examen médical
die Untersuchung
el examen médico
la visita medica

doctor's office
le cabinet
das Sprechzimmer
la consulta
l'ambulatorio

vaccination
l'inoculation
die Impfung
la inoculación
l'inoculazione

waiting room
la salle d'attente
der Wartezimmer
la sala de espera
la sala d'attesa

thermometer
le thermomètre
das Thermometer
el termómetro
il termometro

I need to see a doctor.
J'ai besoin de voir un médecin.
Ich muss einen Arzt sprechen.
Necesito ver a un médico.
Ho bisogno di vedere un medico.

It hurts here.
J'ai mal ici.
Es tut hier weh.
Me duele aquí.
Ho un dolore qui.

injury • la blessure • die Verletzung • la lesión • la ferita

sling
l'écharpe
die Schlinge
el cabestrillo
la fascia a tracolla

neck brace
la minerve
die Halskrawatte
el collarín
il collare

sprain • l'entorse • die Verstauchung • la torcedura • la slogatura

fracture • la fracture • die Fraktur • la fractura • la frattura

whiplash • le coup du lapin • das Schleudertrauma • el tirón en el cuello • il colpo di frusta

cut • la coupure • der Schnitt • el corte • il taglio

graze • l'écorchure • die Abschürfung • el arañazo • la sbucciatura

bruise • la contusion • der blaue Fleck • el hematoma • il livido

splinter • l'écharde • der Splitter • la astilla • la scheggia

sunburn • le coup de soleil • der Sonnenbrand • la quemadura de sol • la scottatura

burn • la brûlure • die Brandwunde • la quemadura • l'ustione

bite • la morsure • der Biss • el mordisco • il morso

sting • la piqûre • der Stich • la picadura • la puntura

accident l'accident der Unfall el accidente l'incidente	hemorrhage l'hémorragie die Blutung la hemorragia l'emorragia	concussion la commotion cérébrale die Gehirnerschütterung la conmoció cerebral la commozione cerebrale	Will he/she be all right? Est-ce qu'il/elle va se remettre? Wird er/sie es gut überstehen? ¿Se pondrá bien? Si rimetterà?
emergency l'urgence der Notfall la urgencia l'emergenza	blister l'ampoule die Blase la ampolla la vescica	head injury le traumatisme crânien die Kopfverletzung la lesión en la cabeza la ferita alla testa	Please call an ambulance. Appelez une ambulance s'il vous plaît. Rufen Sie bitte einen Krankenwagen. Por favor llame a una ambulancia. Chiami un'ambulanza, per favore.
wound la blessure die Wunde la herida la ferita	poisoning l'empoisonnement die Vergiftung el envenenamiento l'avvelenamento	electric shock le choc électrique der elektrische Schlag la descarga eléctrica la scossa elettrica	Where does it hurt? Où avez-vous mal? Wo haben Sie Schmerzen? ¿Dónde le duele? Dove le fa male?

first aid • les premiers secours • die erste Hilfe • los primeros auxilios • il pronto soccorso

ointment • la pommade • die Salbe • la pomada • la pomata

adhesive bandage • le pansement • das Pflaster • la tirita • il cerotto

safety pin
l'épingle de sûreté
die Sicherheitsnadel
el imperdible
la spilla da balia

bandage
le bandage
die Bandage
la venda
la benda

painkillers
les analgésiques
die Schmerztabletten
los analgésicos
gli antidolorifici

antiseptic wipe
la serviette antiseptique
das Desinfektionstuch
la toallita antiséptica
la salvietta antisettica

tweezers
la pince fine
die Pinzette
las pinzas
la pinzetta

scissors
les ciseaux
die Schere
las tijeras
le forbici

antiseptic
l'antiseptique
das Antiseptikum
el desinfectante
il disinfettante

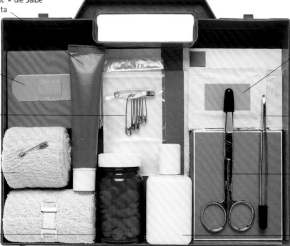

first-aid kit • la trousse de premiers secours • der Erste-Hilfe-Kasten • el botiquín • la cassetta di pronto soccorso

gauze • la gaze • die Gaze • la gasa • la garza

dressing • le pansement • der Verband • el vendaje • la bendatura

splint • l'attelle • die Schiene • la tablilla • la stecca

adhesive tape
le sparadrap
das Leukoplast
el esparadrapo
il nastro adesivo

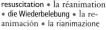

resuscitation • la réanimation • die Wiederbelebung • la re-animación • la rianimazione

shock	pulse	choke (v)	Can you help?
le choc	le pouls	étouffer	Est-ce que vous pouvez m'aider?
der Schock	der Puls	ersticken	Können Sie mir helfen?
el shock	el pulso	ahogarse	¿Me puede ayudar?
lo shock	le pulsazione	soffocare	Può aiutarmi?
unconscious	breathing	sterile	Do you know first aid?
sans connaissance	la respiration	stérile	Pouvez-vous donner les soins d'urgence?
bewusstlos	die Atmung	steril	Beherrschen Sie die Erste Hilfe?
inconsciente	la respiración	estéril	¿Sabe primeros auxilios?
privo di sensi	la respirazione	sterile	Sa dare pronto soccorso?

hospital • l'hôpital • das Krankenhaus • el hospital • l'ospedale

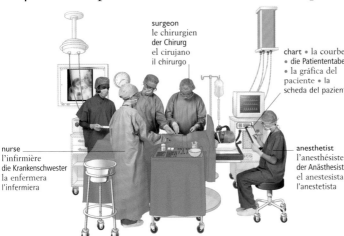

surgeon
le chirurgien
der Chirurg
el cirujano
il chirurgo

chart • la courbe
• die Patiententabelle
• la gráfica del
paciente • la
scheda del paziente

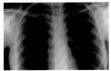

blood test • l'analyse de
sang • die Blutuntersuchung
• el análisis de sangre
• l'analisi del sangue

nurse
l'infirmière
die Krankenschwester
la enfermera
l'infermiera

anesthetist
l'anesthésiste
der Anästhesist
el anestesista
l'anestetista

injection • l'injection
• die Spritze • la inyección
• l'iniezione

operating room • la salle d'opération • der Operationssaal
• el quirófano • la sala operatoria

gurney • le chariot • die
fahrbare Liege • la camilla
• la lettiga

call button • le bouton d'appel
• der Rufknopf • el timbre
• il pulsante di chiamata

X-ray • la radio • die
Röntgenaufnahme • la
radiografía • la radiografia

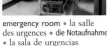

emergency room • la salle
des urgences • die Notaufnahme
• la sala de urgencias
• il pronto soccorso

ward • la salle
• das Patientenzimmer
• la planta • il reparto

wheelchair • la chaise
roulante • der Rollstuhl
• la silla de ruedas
• la sedia a rotelle

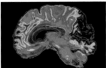

scan • la scanographie
• sad CT-Bild • la ecografia
• l'ecografia

operation	discharged	visiting hours	maternity ward	intensive care unit	
l'opération	renvoyé	les heures de visite	la maternité	le service de soins intensifs	
die Operation	entlassen	die Besuchszeiten	die Entbindungsstation	die Intensivstation	
la operación	dado de alta	las horas de visita	la sala de maternidad	la unidad de cuidados intensivos	
l'operazione	dimesso	l'orario delle visite	il reparto maternità	il reparto di cura intensiva	
admitted	clinic	children's ward	private room	outpatient	
admis	la clinique	la pédiatrie	la chambre privée	le malade en consultation externe	
aufgenommen	die Klinik	die Kinderstation	das Privatzimmer	der ambulante Patient	
ingresado	la clínica	la sala de pediatría	la habitación privada	el paciente externo	
ricoverato	la clinica	il reparto pediatrico	la camera privata	il paziente ambulatoriale	

departments • les services • die Abteilungen • los servicios • i reparti

ENT • l'O.R.L.
• die HNO-Abteilung
• la otorrinolaringología
• l'otorinolaringologia

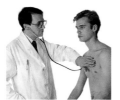

cardiology • la cardiologie
• die Kardiologie • la
cardiologia • la cardiologia

orthopedics • l'orthopédie
• die Orthopädie • la
ortopedia • l'ortopedia

gynecology • la gynécologie
• die Gynäkologie • la
ginecología • la ginecologia

physiotherapy • la
kinésithérapie • die
Physiotherapie • la fisioterapia
• la fisioterapia

dermatology • la dermatologie
• die Dermatologie • la
dermatología • la dermatologia

pediatrics • la pédiatrie
• die Kinderheilkunde • la
pediatría • la pediatria

radiology • la radiologie
• die Radiologie • la radiología
• la radiologia

surgery • la chirurgie
• die Chirurgie • la cirugía
• la chirurgia

maternity • la maternité
• die Entbindungsstation • la
maternidad • la maternità

psychiatry • la psychiatrie
• die Psychiatrie • la
psiquiatría • la psichiatria

ophthalmology
• l'ophtalmologie
• die Augenheilkunde • la
oftalmología • l'oftalmologia

neurology	urology	plastic surgery	pathology	result
la neurologie	l'urologie	la chirurgie esthétique	la pathologie	le résultat
die Neurologie	die Urologie	die plastische Chirurgie	die Pathologie	das Ergebnis
la neurología	la urología	la cirugía plástica	la patología	el resultado
la neurologia	l'urologia	la chirurgia plastica	la patologia	il risultato
oncology	endocrinology	referral	test	specialist
l'oncologie	l'endocrinologie	l'orientation d'un patient	l'analyse	le spécialiste
die Onkologie	die Endokrinologie	die Überweisung	die Untersuchung	der Facharzt
la oncología	la endocrinología	el volante	el análisis	el especialista
l'oncologia	l'endocrinologia	la richiesta di visita specialista	l'analisi	lo specialista

dentist • le dentiste • der Zahnarzt • el dentista • il dentista

tooth • la dent • der Zahn • el diente
• il dente

checkup • la visite de contrôle • der Check-up
• la revisión • il controllo

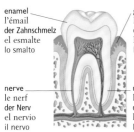

enamel
l'émail
der Zahnschmelz
el esmalte
lo smalto

gum
la gencive
das Zahnfleisch
la encía
la gengiva

nerve
le nerf
der Nerv
el nervio
il nervo

root
la racine
die Zahnwurzel
la raíz
la radice

premolar
la prémolaire
der vordere
 Backenzahn
el premolar
il premolare

incisor
l'incisive
der Schneidezahn
el incisivo
l'incisivo

molar
la molaire
der Backenzahn
la muela
il molare

canine
la canine
der Eckzahn
el colmillo
il canino

reflector
• la lampe
• die Behandlungs-
lampe • el foco
• la lampada

probe
la sonde
die Sonde
la sonda
la sonda

apron • le bavoir
• die Behandlungsschürze
• el delantal • il
bavaglio

sink
le crachoir
das Spuckbecken
el lavabo
la sputacchiera

dentist's chair
le fauteuil de dentiste
der Patientenstuhl
el sillón del dentista
la poltrona da dentista

toothache la rage de dents die Zahnschmerzen el dolor de muelas il mal di denti	drill la fraise der Bohrer el torno del dentista il trapano
plaque la plaque der Zahnbelag la placa bacteriana la placca	dental floss le fil dentaire die Zahnseide el hilo dental il filo interdentale
decay la carie die Karies la caries la carie	extraction l'extraction die Extraktion la extracción l'estrazione
filling le plombage die Zahnfüllung el empaste l'otturazione	crown la couronne die Krone la corona la corona

floss (v) • utiliser le
fil dentaire • mit
Zahnseide reinigen
• usar el hilo dental
• usare il filo dentale

brush (v) • brosser
• bürsten • cepillarse
los dientes • spazzolare

braces • l'appareil
dentaire • die
Zahnspange • el
aparato corrector
• l'apparecchio correttore

dental X-ray • la radio
dentaire • die Röntgen-
aufnahme • los rayos
x dentales • la radio-
grafia dentale

X-ray film • la radio
• das Röntgenbild
• la radiografía
• la radiografia

dentures • le dentier
• die Zahnprothese
• la dentadura
postiza • la dentiera

optometrist • l'opticien • der Augenoptiker • el óptico • l'oculista

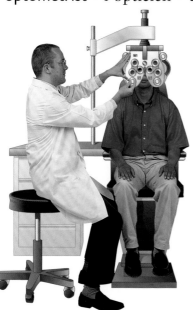

case
l'etui
das Futteral
la funda
la custodia

lens
le verre
das Glas
el cristal
la lente

frame
la monture
das Brillengestell
la montura
la montatura

glasses • les lunettes • die Brille
• las gafas • gli occhiali

sunglasses • les lunettes de soleil
• die Sonnenbrille • las gafas de sol
• gli occhiali da sole

cleaning fluid
la solution nettoyante
das Reinigungsmittel
el líquido limpiador
la soluzione per la pulizia

disinfectant solution
la solution désinfectante
das Desinfektionsmittel
la solución desinfectante
la soluzione disinfettante

lens case
• l'étui à lentilles
• der Kontaktlinsenbehälter
• el estuche para las
lentillas • la custodia
per le lenti

eye test • l'examen de la vue • der Sehtest
• el examen de ojos • l'esame della vista

contact lenses • les lentilles de contact • die Kontaktlinsen
• las lentes de contacto • le lenti a contatto

eye • l'œil • das Auge • el ojo • l'occhio

eyebrow
le sourcil
die Augenbraue
la ceja
il sopracciglio

pupil
la pupille
die Pupille
la pupila
la pupilla

lens
le cristallin
die Linse
el cristalino
il cristallino

cornea • la cornée
• die Hornhaut • la
córnea • la cornea

eyelid
la paupière
das Lid
el párpado
la palpebra

eyelash
le cil
die Wimper
la pestaña
il ciglio

iris • l'iris • die Iris
• el iris • l'iride

retina
la rétine
die Netzhaut
la retina
la retina

optic nerve
le nerf optique
der Sehnerv
el nervio óptico
il nervo ottico

vision	astigmatism
la vue	l'astigmatisme
die Sehkraft	der Astigmatismus
la vista	el astigmatismo
la vista	l'astigmatismo
diopter	farsighted
la dioptrie	la presbytie
die Dioptrie	die Weitsichtigkeit
la dioptría	la hipermetropía
la diottria	la presbiopia
tear	nearsighted
la larme	la myopie
die Träne	die Kurzsichtigkeit
la lágrima	la miopía
la lacrima	la miopia
cataract	bifocal
la cataracte	bifocal
der graue Star	Bifokal-
la catarata	bifocal
la cataratta	bifocale

pregnancy • la grossesse • die Schwangerschaft • el embarazo • la gravidanza

scan
l'échographie
die Ultraschallaufnahme
la ecografía
l'ecografia

pregnancy test • le test de grossesse • der Schwangerschaftstest • la prueba del embarazo • il test di gravidanza

umbilical cord
le cordon ombilical
die Nabelschnur
el cordón umbilical
il cordone ombelicale

placenta
le placenta
die Plazenta
la placenta
la placenta

cervix
le col de l'utérus
der Gebärmutterhals
el cuello uterino
la cervice

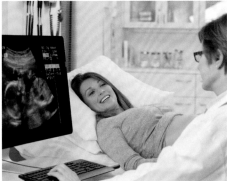

uterus
l'utérus
die Gebärmutter
el útero
l'utero

ultrasound • les ultrasons • der Ultraschall • el ultrasonido • l'ultrasuono

fetus • le fœtus • der Fötus • el feto • il feto

ovulation l'ovulation der Eisprung la ovulación l'ovulazione	**prenatal** prénatal vorgeburtlich prenatal prenatale	**amniotic fluid** le liquide amniotique das Fruchtwasser el líquido amniótico il liquido amniotico	**dilation** la dilatation die Erweiterung la dilatación la dilatazione	**stitches** les points de suture die Naht los puntos i punti	**breech birth** l'accouchement par le siège die Steißgeburt el parto de nalgas il parto podalico
conception la conception die Empfängnis la concepción la concepimento	**trimester** le trimestre das Trimester el trimestre il trimestre	**amniocentesis** l'amniocentèse die Amniozentese la amniocentesis l'amniocentesi	**epidural** la péridurale die Periduralanästhesie la epidural l'epidurale	**delivery** l'accouchement die Entbindung el parto il parto	**premature** prématuré vorzeitig prematuro prematuro
pregnant enceinte schwanger embarazada incinta	**embryo** l'embryon der Embryo el embrión l'embrione	**contraction** la contraction die Wehe la contracción la contrazione	**cesarean section** la césarienne der Kaiserschnitt la cesárea il taglio cesareo	**birth** la naissance die Geburt el nacimiento la nascita	**gynecologist** le gynécologue der Gynäkologe el ginecólogo il ginecologo
expecting enceinte schwanger encinta in stato interessante	**womb** l'utérus die Gebärmutter la matriz l'utero	**break water** *(v)* perdre les eaux das Fruchtwasser geht ab romper aguas rompere le acque	**episiotomy** l'épisiotomie der Dammschnitt la episiotomía l'episiotomia	**miscarriage** la fausse couche die Fehlgeburt el aborto espontáneo l'aborto spontaneo	**obstetrician** l'obstétricien der Geburtshelfer el tocólogo l'ostetrico

childbirth • la naissance • die Geburt • el parto • il parto

drip • la perfusion
• die Tropf • el gotero
• la flebo

catheter
le cathéter
der Katheter
el catéter
il catetere

monitor
le moniteur
der Monitor
el monitor
il monitor

midwife
la sage-femme
die Hebamme
la comadrona
l'ostetrica

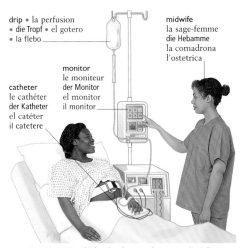

induce labor (v) • déclencher l'accouchement • die Geburt
einleiten • provocar el parto • indurre il travaglio

forceps • le forceps
• die Geburtszange
• los fórceps • il forcipe

suction cup • la ventouse
• die Saugglocke • la ventosa
• la ventosa

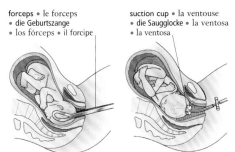

assisted delivery • l'accouchement assisté • die assistierte
Entbindung • el parto asistido • il parto assistito

identity tag • le bracelet d'identité
• das Erkennungsetikett • la pulsera de
identificación • la targhetta d'identità

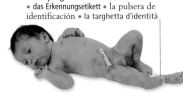

newborn baby • le nouveau-né • das Neugeborene • el recién
nacido • il neonato

incubator • la couveuse • der Brutkasten
• la incubadora • l'incubatrice

birth weight • le poids de naissance • das
Geburtsgewicht • el peso al nacer • il peso alla nascita

---

nursing • l'allaitement • das Stillen • la lactancia
• l'allattamento

breast pump • la pompe à lait
• die Brustpumpe • el sacaleches
• la pompa tiralatte

nursing bra • le soutien-
gorge d'allaitement
• der Stillbüstenhalter
• el sujetador para la
lactancia • il reggiseno
da allattamento

breastfeed (v) • donner le
sein • stillen • dar el pecho
• allattare al seno

nursing pads • les coussinets
• die Einlagen • los discos
protectores • le coppe

alternative therapy • les thérapies alternatives • die Alternativtherapien • las terapias alternativas • le terapie alternative

yoga pose
la posture de yoga
die Yoga-Haltung
la postura de yoga
la posizione yoga

massage • le massage
• die Massage • el masaje
• il massaggio

mat
le tapis
die Matte
la colchoneta
il tappetino

shiatsu • le shiatsu
• das Shiatsu • el shiatsu
• lo shiatsu

yoga • le yoga • das Yoga • el yoga • lo yoga

chiropractic • la chiropractie
• die Chiropraktik • la
quiropráctica • la chiropratica

osteopathy • l'ostéopathie
• die Osteopathie • la
osteopatía • l'osteopatia

reflexology • la réflexiologie
• die Reflexzonenmassage • la
reflexología • la riflessologia

meditation • la méditation
• die Meditation • la
meditación • la meditazione

english • français • deutsch • español • italiano

counselor • le conseiller
• der Berater • el terapeuta
• l'assistente socio-psicologico

group therapy • la thérapie de groupe • die Gruppentherapie
• la terapia di gruppo • la terapia di gruppo

reiki • le reiki • das Reiki
• el reiki • il reiki

ayurveda • la médecine
ayurvédique • das Ayurveda • la
ayurveda • la medicina aiurvedica

acupuncture • l'acuponcture
• die Akupunktur • la
acupuntura • l'agopuntura

• hypnotherapy
• l'hypnothérapie
• die Hypnotherapie • la
hipnoterapia • l'ipnositerapia

essential oils • les huiles
essentielles • die ätherischen
Öle • los aceites esenciales
• gli oli essenziali

herbalism • l'herboristerie
• die Kräuterheilkunde • el
herbolario • la fitoterapia

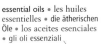

aromatherapy • l'aromathérapie
• die Aromatherapie • la
aromaterapia • l'aromaterapia

homeopathy • l'homéopathie
• die Homöopathie • la
homeopatía • l'omeopatia

acupressure • l'acupression
• die Akupressur • la
acupresión •l'agopressione

therapist • la thérapeute • die Therapeutin
• la terapeuta • la terapista

psychotherapy • la psychothérapie
• die Psychotherapie • la
psicoterapia • la psicoterapia

crystal healing	naturopathy	relaxation	herb
la guérison par cristaux	la naturopathie	la relaxation	l'herbe
die Kristalltherapie	die Naturheilkunde	die Entspannung	das Heilkraut
la cristaloterapia	la naturopatía	la relajación	la hierba
la cristalloterapia	la naturopatia	il rilassamento	l'erba
supplement	hydrotherapy	stress	feng shui
le supplément	l'hydrothérapie	le stress	le feng shui
das Nahrungsergänzungsmittel	die Wasserbe handlung	der Stress	das Feng Shui
el suplemento	la hidroterapia	el estrés	el feng shui
l'integratore alimentare	l'idroterapia	lo stress	il feng shui

home
la maison
das Haus
la casa
la casa

house • la maison • das Haus • la casa • la casa

roof
le toit
das Dach
el tejado
il tetto

gutter
la gouttière
die Dachrinne
el canalón
la grondaia

chimney
la cheminée
der Schornstein
la chimenea
il camino

dormer window
le chien assis
das Mansardenfenster
la ventana de la buhardilla
l'abbaino

shingle
la tuile
der Dachziegel
la teja
la tegola

wall
le mur
die Mauer
la pared
il muro

eaves
l'avant-toit
der Dachvorsprung
el alero
la gronda

shutter
le volet
der Fensterladen
la contraventana
la persiana

porch
le porche
das Vordach
el porche
il portico

window
la fenêtre
das Fenster
la ventana
la finestra

addition
l'agrandissement
der Anbau
la ampliación
l'annesso

path
l'allée
der Weg
el camino
il viottolo

front door
la porte d'entrée
die Haustür
la puerta principal
il portone

single-family	townhouse	garage	floor	burglar alarm	rent (v)
individuelle	la maison de deux étages	le garage	l'étage	l'alarme	louer
das Einzelhaus	das Stadthaus	die Garage	das Stockwerk	die Alarmanlage	mieten
la casa particular	la vivienda urbana	el garaje	el piso	la alarma antirrobo	alquilar
unifamiliare	la casa di città	il garage	il piano	l'allarme antifurto	affittare
duplex	bungalow	attic	courtyard	mailbox	rent
mitoyenne	la pavillon	le grenier	la cour	la boîte aux lettres	le loyer
Doppelhaus	der Bungalow	der Dachboden	der Hof	der Briefkasten	die Miete
adosado por un lado	la vivienda de una planta	el ático	el patio	el buzón	el alquiler
bifamiliare	il bungalow	la soffitta	il cortile	la cassetta per le lettere	l'affitto
row house	basement	room	porch light	landlord	tenant
attenante	le sous-sol	la chambre	la lampe d'entrée	le propriétaire	le locataire
Reihenhaus	das Kellergeschoss	das Zimmer	die Haustürlampe	der Vermieter	der Mieter
la casa adosado	el sótano	la habitación	la luz del porche	el propietario	el inquilino
a schiera	il seminterrato	la stanza	la luce del portico	il padrone di casa	l'inquilino

entrance • l'entrée • der Eingang • la entrada • l'ingresso

hand rail
la main courante
der Handlauf
el pasamanos
il corrimano

landing
le palier
der Treppenabsatz
el descansillo
il pianerottolo

banister
la rampe
das Treppengeländer
la barandilla
la ringhiera

staircase
l'escalier
die Treppe
la escalera
la scala

foyer • le vestibule • die Diele • el vestíbulo • l'entrata

apartment • l'appartement
• die Wohnung • el piso
• l'appartamento

balcony • le balcon
• der Balkon • el balcón
• il balcone

apartment buildings • l'immeuble
• der Wohnblock • el edificio
• il caseggiato

intercom • l'interphone
• die Sprechanlage • el interfono
• il citofono

elevator • l'ascenseur
• der Fahrstuhl • el ascensor
• l'ascensore

doorbell • la sonnette
• die Türklingel • el timbre
• il campanello

doormat • le paillasson
• der Fußabtreter • el felpudo
• lo zerbino

door knocker • le marteau
de porte • der Türklopfer
• la aldaba • il battente

key • la clef • der Schlüssel
• la llave • la chiave

door chain • la chaîne de
sûreté • die Türkette
• la cadena • la catenella

lock • la serrure • das
Schloss • la cerradura
• la serratura

bolt • le verrou • der
Türriegel • el cerrojo
• il chiavistello

internal systems • les systèmes domestiques • die Hausanschlüsse • las instalaciones internas • i sistemi interni

blade • l'aile • der Flügel • el aspa • la pala

fan • le ventilateur • der Ventilator • el ventilador • il ventilatore

radiator • le radiateur • der Heizkörper • el radiador • il calorifero

space heater • l'appareil de chauffage • der Heizofen • la estufa • la stufa

convector heater • le convecteur • der Heizlüfter • el calentador de convección • il termoventilatore

electricity • l'électricité • die Elektrizität • la electricidad • l'elettricità

neutral • neutre • neutral • neutro • neutro

ground • la mise à la terre • die Erdung • la toma de tierra • la messa a terra

pin • la broche • der Pol • la clavija • il polo

live • sous tension • geladen • con corriente • in tensione

energy-saving bulb • l'ampoule basse consommation • die Energiesparbirne • la bombilla de ahorro de energía • la lampadina a risparmio energetico

plug • la prise • der Stecker • el enchufe • la spina

wires • les fils • die Leitung • los cables • i fili

voltage	fuse	outlet	direct current	transformer
la tension	le fusible	la prise de courant	le courant continu	le transformateur
die Spannung	die Sicherung	die Steckdose	der Gleichstrom	der Transformator
el voltaje	el fusible	el enchufe	la corriente continua	el transformador
la tensione	il fusibile	la presa	la corrente continua	il trasformatore
amp	fuse box	switch	electric meter	household current
l'ampère	la boîte à fusibles	l'interrupteur	le compteur d'électricité	le réseau d'électricité
das Ampère	der Sicherungskasten	der Schalter	der Stromzähler	das Stromnetz
el amperio	la caja de los fusibles	el interruptor	el contador de la luz	el suministro de electricidad
l'ampere	la valvoliera	l'interruttore	il contatore di corrente	la rete elettrica
power	generator	alternating current	power outage	
le courant	la génératrice	le courant alternatif	la coupure de courant	
der Strom	der Generator	der Wechselstrom	der Stromausfall	
la corrriente eléctrica	el generador	la corriente alterna	el corte de luz	
l'elettricità	il generatore	la corrente alternata	l'interruzione di corrente	

plumbing • la plomberie • die Sanitärtechnik • la fontanería • l'impianto idraulico

sink • l'évier • die Spüle • el fregador • l'acquaio

inlet • l'arrivée • die Zuleitung • la toma • l'entrata

pressure valve • la soupape de sûreté • das Sicherheitsventil • la válvula de la presión • la valvola di sicurezza

overflow pipe • le trop-plein • der Überlauf • el tubo de desagüe • il tubo di troppopieno

water chamber • la chambre d'eau • der Wasserraum • el tanque del agua • il serbatoio dell'acqua

thermostat • le thermostat • der Thermostat • el termostato • il termostato

burner • le brûleur à gaz • der Gasbrenner • el quemador • il bruciatore a gas

outlet • la sortie • der Auslass • la salida • l'uscita

insulation • l'isolation • die Isolierung • el aislamiento • l'isolamento

tank • le réservoir • der Kessel • el tanque • il serbatoio

drain valve • le robinet de purge • der Ablasshahn • la llave del desagüe • il rubinetto di scarico

heating element • la résistance • das Heizelement • la resistencia • l'elemento riscaldante

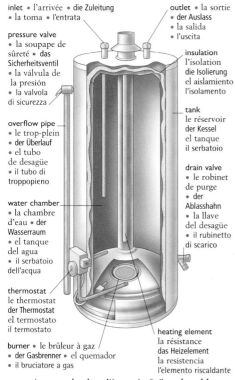

water heater • la chaudière • der Boiler • la caldera • lo scaldaacqua

faucet • le robinet • der Hahn • el grifo • il rubinetto

supply pipe • la conduite d'amenée • die Zuleitung • la toma del agua • il tubo dell'acqua

waste disposal unit • le broyeur d'ordures • der Müllschlucker • el triturador de basuras • il macinatore di rifiuti

lever • la manette • der Hebel • la palanca • la leva

gasket • le joint • die Dichtung • la junta • la guarnizione

shutoff valve • le robinet de sectionnement • der Absperrhahn • la llave de paso • il rubinetto di arresto

drain • le tuyau d'écoulement • der Abfluss • el desagüe • lo scolo

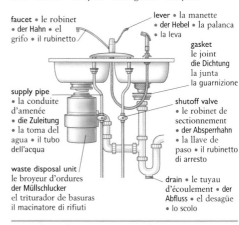

toilet • les toilettes • die Toilette • el wáter • il water

float ball • le flotteur • der Schwimmer • el flotador • il galleggiante

seat • le siège • der Toilettensitz • la tapa • il sedile

bowl • la cuvette • das Becken • la taza • la tazza

tank • la chasse-d'eau • der Spülkasten • la cisterna • la cassetta

waste pipe • le tuyau d'écoulement • das Abflussrohr • el desagüe • il tubo di scolo

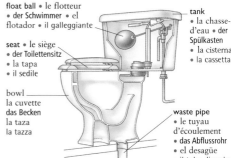

waste disposal • l'enlèvement de déchets • die Abfallentsorgung • la eliminación de desechos • lo smaltimento dei rifiuti

bottle • la bouteille • die Flasche • la botella • la bottiglia

pedal • la pédale • der Trethebel • el pedal • il pedale

lid • le couvercle • der Deckel • la tapa • il coperchio

recycling bin • la boîte à déchets recyclables • der Recyclingbehälter • el cubo para reciclar • il contenitore di riciclaggio

trash can • la poubelle • der Abfalleimer • el cubo de la basura • la pattumiera

sorting unit • la boîte de tri • die Abfallsortiereinheit • el armario para clasificar la basura • l'unità di smistamento

organic waste • les déchets bios • der Bio-Abfall • los desperdicios orgánicos • i rifiuti organici

living room • le salon • das Wohnzimmer • el cuarto de estar • il salotto

wall light
l'applique
die Wandlampe
el aplique
l'applique

fireplace
la cheminée
der Kamin
la chimenea
il caminetto

ceiling
le plafond
die Decke
el techo
il soffitto

vase
le vase
die Vase
el jarrón
il vaso

pillow
le coussin
das Sofakissen
el cojín
il cuscino

lamp
la lampe
die Lampe
la lámpara
la lampada

coffee table
la table basse
der Couchtisch
la mesa de café
il tavolino

sofa
le canapé
das Sofa
el sofá
il divano

floor
le sol
der Fußboden
el suelo
il pavimento

english • français • deutsch • español • italiano

frame
le cadre
der Bilderrahmen
el marco
la cornice

curtain • le rideau • der
Vorhang • la cortina
• la tenda

sheer curtain • le brise-bise
• die Gardine • el visillo
• la tendina

Venetian blind • le store vénitien
• die Jalousie • el estor de
láminas • la veneziana

roller shade • le store
• das Rollo • el estor
• l'avvolgibile

painting
le tableau
das Gemälde
el cuadro
il quadro

molding • la moulure
• der Stuck • la moldura
• la cornice

armchair • le fauteuil
• der Sessel • el sillón
• la poltrona

bookshelf
la bibliothèque
das Bücherregal
la estantería
la libreria

sofa bed
le canapé-lit
die Bettcouch
el sofá-cama
il divano letto

rug
le tapis
der Teppich
la alfombra
il tappeto

study • le bureau • das Arbeitszimmer • el despacho • lo studio

dining room • la salle à manger • das Esszimmer • el comedor • la sala da pranzo

pepper
le poivre
der Pfeffer
la pimienta
il pepe

salt
le sel
das Salz
la sal
il sale

table
la table
der Tisch
la mesa
il tavolo

crockery
la vaisselle
das Geschirr
la vajilla
i piatti

cutlery
les couverts
das Besteck
los cubiertos
le posate

chair
la chaise
der Stuhl
la silla
la sedia

back
le dossier
die Lehne
el respaldo
lo schienale

seat
le siège
die Sitzfläche
el asiento
il sedile

leg
le pied
das Bein
la pata
la gamba

set the table (v)	placemat	lunch	full	host	Can I have some more, please?
mettre la table	le set de table	le déjeuner	rassasié	l'hôte	Puis-je en reprendre un peu, s'il
den Tisch decken	das Set	das Mittagessen	satt	der Gastgeber	vous plaît?
poner la mesa	el mantel individual	la comida	lleno	el anfitrión	Könnte ich bitte noch ein bisschen haben?
apparecchiare	il set da tavola	il pranzo	sazio	il padrone di casa	¿Puedo repetir, por favor?
					Posso averne ancora, per favore?
serve (v)	tablecloth	dinner	portion	hostess	I've had enough, thank you.
servir	la nappe	le dîner	la portion	l'hôtesse	Non merci, j'en ai eu assez.
servieren	die Tischdecke	das Abendessen	die Portion	die Gastgeberin	Ich bin satt, danke.
servir	el mantel	la cena	la ración	la anfitriona	Estoy lleno, gracias.
servire	la tovaglia	la cena	la porzione	la padrona di casa	Sono sazio, grazie.
eat (v)	breakfast	hungry	meal	guest	That was delicious.
manger	le petit déjeuner	(avoir) faim	le repas	l'invité	C'était délicieux.
essen	das Frühstück	hungrig	die Mahlzeit	der Gast	Das war lecker.
comer	el desayuno	hambriento	la comida	el invitado	Estaba buenísimo.
mangiare	la colazione	affamato	il pasto	l'ospite	Era squisito.

crockery and cutlery • la vaisselle et les couverts • das Geschirr und das Besteck
• la vajilla y los cubiertos • le stoviglie e le posate

teaspoon • la cuiller
à café • der Teelöffel
• la cucharilla de
café • il cucchiaino

mug • la grande
tasse • der Becher
• la taza • la tazza

coffee cup • la tasse
à café • die Kaffeetasse
• la taza de café
• la tazzina da caffè

teacup • la tasse à thé
• die Teetasse • la taza
de té • la tazza da tè

plate • l'assiette
• der Teller • el plato
• il piatto

bowl • le bol • die
Schüssel • el bol
• la ciotola

wine glass • le verre à vin
• das Weinglas • la copa de
vino • il calice da vino

tumbler
le verre
das Wasserglas
el vaso
il bicchiere

French press • la cafetière
• die Cafetière • la cafetera
de émbolo • la caffettiera

teapot • la théière
• die Teekanne • la
tetera • la teiera

pitcher • le pot
• der Krug • la
jarra • la brocca

eggcup • le coquetier
• der Eierbecher • la
huevera • il portauovo

glassware • la verrerie
• die Glaswaren • la
cristalería • la cristalleria

napkin ring
le rond de serviette
der Serviettenring
el servilletero
il portatovagliolo

side plate
l'assiette à dessert
der Beilagenteller
el plato del pan
il piattino

dinner plate
l'assiette plate
der Essteller
el plato llano
il piatto piano

soup bowl
l'assiette à soupe
der Suppenteller
el plato sopero
il piatto fondo

soup spoon • la cuiller à
soupe • der Suppenlöffel
• la cuchara sopera • il
cucchiaio da minestra

napkin
la serviette
die Serviette
la servilleta
il tovagliolo

fork • la fourchette
• die Gabel • el tenedor
• la forchetta

spoon
la cuiller
der Löffel
la cuchara
il cucchiaio

knife
le couteau
das Messer
el cuchillo
il coltello

place setting • le couvert • das Gedeck • el lugar en la mesa • il coperto

kitchen • la cuisine • die Küche • la cocina • la cucina

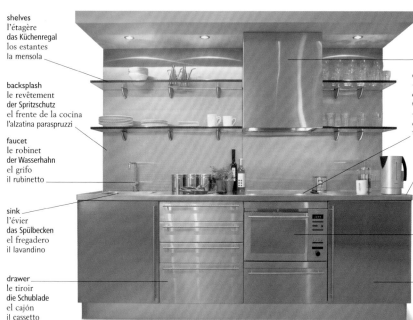

shelves
l'étagère
das Küchenregal
los estantes
la mensola

backsplash
le revêtement
der Spritzschutz
el frente de la cocina
l'alzatina paraspruzzi

faucet
le robinet
der Wasserhahn
el grifo
il rubinetto

sink
l'évier
das Spülbecken
el fregadero
il lavandino

drawer
le tiroir
die Schublade
el cajón
il cassetto

ventilation hood
la hotte
der Dunstabzug
el extractor
la cappa

ceramic stovetop
• la table de cuisson
céramique • das
Glaskeramikkochfeld
• la placa vitro-
cerámica • il
fornello di ceramica

countertop
• le plan de
travail • die
Arbeitsfläche
• la encimera
• il piano di
lavoro

oven • le four
• der Backofen
• el horno
• il forno

cabinet
le placard
der Küchenschrank
el armario
l'armadietto

appliances • les appareils ménagers • die Küchengeräte • los electrodomésticos • gli elettrodomestici

mixing bowl
le bol du mixeur
die Mixerschüssel
el cuenco mezclador
il recipiente

blade
la lame
das Messer
la cuchilla
la lama

lid
le couvercle
der Deckel
la tapa
il coperchio

microwave oven • le micro-ondes
• die Mikrowelle • el horno
microondas • il forno a microonde

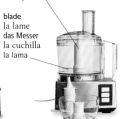

electric kettle • la
bouilloire électrique
• der Wasserkocher • el
hervidor • il bollitore

toaster • le grille-
pain • der Toaster
• el tostador • il
tostapane

food processor • le robot
ménager • die
Küchenmaschine • el robot
de cocina • il tritatutto

blender • le mixeur
• der Mixer • la
licuadora • il frullatore

dishwasher • le lave-
vaisselle • die Spülmaschine
• el friegaplatos • la
lavastoviglie

ice maker
• le freezer
• das Eisfach
• la máquina de los cubitos
• il freezer

freezer
le congélateur
das Gefrierfach
el congelador
il congelatore

refrigerator
le réfrigérateur
der Kühlschrank
el frigorífico
il frigorifero

shelf
la clayette
der Rost
el estante
la mensola

crisper • le bac à légumes
• das Gemüsefach
• el cajón de las verduras
• il cassetto per la verdura

stovetop	**freeze (v)**
la table de cuisson	congeler
das Kochfeld	einfrieren
la placa	congelar
il piano di cottura	congelare
draining board	**defrost (v)**
l'égouttoir	décongeler
das Abtropfbrett	auftauen
el escurridor	descongelar
lo scolapiatti	scongelare
burner	**steam (v)**
le brûleur	cuire à la vapeur
der Brenner	dämpfen
el quemador	cocer al vapor
il fornello	cuocere al vapore
garbage can	**sauté (v)**
la poubelle	faire sauter
der Mülleimer	anbraten
el cubo de basura	saltear
la pattumiera	rosolare

side-by-side refrigerator • le réfrigérateur-congélateur • der Gefrier-Kühlschrank • el frigorífico congelador • il frigocongelatore

cooking • la cuisine • das Kochen • cocinar • cucinare

peel (v) • éplucher
• schälen • pelar
• sbucciare

slice (v) • couper
• schneiden • cortar
• affettare

grate (v) • râper
• reiben • rallar
• grattugiare

pour (v) • verser
• gießen • echar
• versare

mix (v) • mélanger
• verrühren • mezclar
• mescolare

whisk (v) • battre
• schlagen • batir
• sbattere

boil (v) • bouillir
• kochen • hervir
• bollire

fry (v) • frire
• braten • freír
• friggere

roll (v) • étaler au rouleau
• ausrollen • extender con el rodillo • spianare

stir (v) • remuer
• rühren • remover
• rimestare

simmer (v) • mijoter
• köcheln lassen
• cocer a fuego lento
• cuocere a fuoco lento

poach (v) • pocher
• pochieren • escalfar
• affogare

bake (v) • cuire au four • backen • cocer al horno • cuocere al forno

roast (v) • rôtir
• braten • asar
• arrostire

broil (v) • griller
• grillen • asar a la parrilla • cuocere alla griglia

kitchenware • les ustensiles de cuisine • die Küchengeräte • los utensilios de cocina • gli utensili da cucina

cutting board
la planche à hacher
das Schneidebrett
la tabla para cortar
il tagliere

bread knife • le couteau
à pain • das Brotmesser
• el cuchillo de sierra
• il coltello da pane

kitchen knife
le couteau de cuisine
das Küchenmesser
el cuchillo de cocina
il coltello da cucina

cleaver • le fendoir
• das Hackmesser
• el hacha de cocina
• la mannaia

knife sharpener
• l'aiguisoir • der Messerschärfer • el afilador
• l'affilacoltelli

meat tenderizer
• l'attendrisseur • der
Fleischklopfer • el mazo
de cocina • il martello

skewer • la broche • der Spieß • el pincho
• lo spiedino

pestle
• le pilon
• der Stößel
• la mano
de mortero
• il pestello

peeler • l'épluche-
légume • der Schäler
• el mondador
• il pelapatate

apple corer
le vide-pomme
der Apfelstecher
el descorazonador
il cavatorsoli

grater • la râpe • die
Reibe • el rallador
• la grattugia

mortar • le mortier
• der Mörser • el
mortero • il mortaio

masher • le presse-
purée • der Kartoffel-
stampfer • el mazo
para puré de patatas
• lo schiacciapatate

can opener • l'ouvre-
boîte • der Dosenöffner
• el abrelatas
• l'apriscatole

bottle opener
l'ouvre-bouteille
der Flaschenöffner
el abrebotellas
l'apribottiglie

garlic press
le presse-ail
die Knoblauchpresse
el prensaajos
lo spremiaglio

serving spoon
• la cuiller à servir
• der Servierlöffel • la
cuchara de servir • il
cucchiaio da portata

slotted spatula • la pelle à
poisson • der Pfannenwender
• la pala • la paletta forata

colander • la
passoire • das Sieb
• el escurridor
• lo scolapasta

spatula • la spatule
• der Teigschaber • la
espátula • la spatola

wooden spoon • la
cuiller en bois • der
Holzlöffel • la cuchara
de madera • il
cucchiaio di legno

slotted spoon
l'écumoire
der Schaumlöffel
la espumadera
la schiumarola

ladle • la louche
• der Schöpflöffel • el
cucharón • il mestolo

carving fork • la fourchette à découper
• die Tranchiergabel • el tenedor para
trinchar • il forchettone

ice-cream scoop • la cuiller
à glace • der Portionierer
• la cuchara para helado
• il cucchiaio dosatore

whisk • le fouet
• der Schneebesen
• el batidor de
varillas • la frusta

sieve • la passoire
• das Sieb • el colador
• il colino

lid • le couvercle • der Deckel • la tapa • il coperchio

nonstick • anti-adhérent • antihaftbeschichtet • antiadherente • antiaderente

frying pan • la poêle • die Bratpfanne • la sartén • la padella

saucepan • la casserole • der Kochtopf • el cazo • la pentola

grill pan • le gril • die Grillpfanne • la parrilla • la padella per grigliare

wok • le wok • der Wok • el wok • il wok

earthenware dish • le fait-tout • der Schmortopf • la cazuela de barro • la casseruola di terracotta

glass • en verre • Glas- • de cristal • di vetro

ovenproof • allant au four • feuerfest • resistente al horno • pirofilo

mixing bowl • le grand bol • die Rührschüssel • el cuenco • la scodella

soufflé dish • le moule à soufflé • die Souffléform • el molde para suflé • lo stampo per soufflé

gratin dish • le plat à gratin • die Auflaufform • la fuente para gratinar • il piatto da gratin

ramekin • le ramequin • das Auflaufförmchen • el molde individual • lo stampo

casserole dish • la cocotte • die Kasserolle • la cazuela • la casseruola

baking cakes • la pâtisserie • das Kuchenbacken • la repostería • la cottura dei dolci

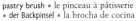

scale • la balance • die Haushaltswaage • la báscula de cocina • la bilancia

measuring cup • le verre mesureur • der Messbecher • la jarra graduada • il misurino

cake pan • le moule à gâteaux • die Kuchenform • el molde para bizcocho • lo stampo per dolci

pie pan • la tourtière • die Biskuitform • el molde redondo • lo stampo per torte

quiche pan • le moule à tarte • die Obstkuchenform • la flanera • lo stampo per flan

pastry brush • le pinceau à pâtisserie • der Backpinsel • la brocha de cocina • il pennello da cucina

rolling pin • le rouleau pâtissier • das Nudelholz • el rodillo de cocina • il matterello

piping bag • la poche à douille • der Spritzbeutel • la manga pastelera • la tasca da pasticciere

muffin pan • le moule à muffins • die Muffinform • el molde para magdalenas • la teglia per pasticcini

cookie sheet la plaque à gâteaux das Kuchenblech la bandeja de horno la piastra del forno

cooling rack • la grille de refroidissement • das Abkühlgitter • la rejilla • la gratella

oven mitt • le gant isolant • der Topfhandschuh • la manopla de cocina • il guanto da forno

apron • le tablier • die Schürze • el delantal • il grembiule

bedroom • la chambre • das Schlafzimmer • el dormitorio • la camera da letto

wardrobe
l'armoire
der Kleiderschrank
el armario
l'armadio

bedside lamp
la lampe de chevet
die Nachttischlampe
la lámpara de la mesilla
l'abat-jour

headboard
la tête de lit
das Kopfende
el cabecero
la testata

nightstand
la table de nuit
der Nachttisch
la mesilla de noche
il comodino

chest of drawers
la commode
die Kommode
la cómoda
il cassettone

drawer
le tiroir
die Schublade
el cajón
il cassetto

bed
le lit
das Bett
la cama
il letto

mattress
le matelas
die Matratze
el colchón
il materasso

bedspread
le couvre-lit
die Tagesdecke
la colcha
il copriletto

pillow
l'oreiller
das Kopfkissen
la almohada
il guanciale

hot-water bottle
• la bouillotte • die Wärmflasche • la bolsa de agua caliente • la borsa calda

clock radio • le radio-réveil • der Radiowecker • la radio despertador • la radiosveglia

alarm clock • le réveil • der Wecker • el reloj despertador • la sveglia

box of tissues • la boîte de kleenex • die Papiertaschentuchschachtel • la caja de pañuelos de desechables • la scatola di fazzolettini

coat hanger • le cintre • der Kleiderbügel • la percha • la gruccia

bed linen • le linge de lit • die Bettwäsche • la ropa de cama • la biancheria da letto

mirror
le miroir
der Spiegel
el espejo
lo specchio

dressing table
la coiffeuse
der Frisiertisch
el tocador
la toeletta

floor
le sol
der Fußboden
el suelo
il pavimento

pillowcase
la taie d'oreiller
der Kissenbezug
la funda de la almohada
la federa

sheet
le drap
das Bettlaken
la sábana
il lenzuolo

dust ruffle
la frange de lit
der Volant
el cubrecanapé
il volant

comforter
la couette
die Bettdecke
el edredón
il piumone

quilt
l'édredon
die Steppdecke
la colcha
la trapunta

blanket
la couverture
die Decke
la manta
la coperta

twin bed	footboard	insomnia	wake up (v)	set the alarm (v)
le lit simple	le pied de lit	l'insomnie	se réveiller	mettre le réveil
das Einzelbett	das Fußende	die Schlaflosigkeit	aufwachen	den Wecker stellen
la cama individual	el pie de la cama	el insomnio	despertarse	poner el despertador
il letto singolo	i piedi del letto	l'insonnia	svegliarsi	mettere la sveglia
full bed	bedspring	go to bed (v)	get up (v)	snore (v)
le grand lit	le sommier	se coucher	se lever	ronfler
das Doppelbett	der Sprungrahmen	ins Bett gehen	aufstehen	schnarchen
la cama de matrimonio	el somier	acostarse	levantarse	roncar
il letto matrimoniale	le molle del letto	andare a letto	alzarsi	russare
electric blanket	carpet	go to sleep (v)	make the bed (v)	closet
la couverture chauffante	le tapis	s'endormir	faire le lit	l'armoire encastrée
die Heizdecke	der Teppich	einschlafen	das Bett machen	der Einbauschrank
la manta eléctrica	la moqueta	dormirse	hacer la cama	el armario empotrado
la termocoperta	il tappeto	addormentarsi	fare il letto	l'armadio a muro

bathroom • la salle de bain • das Badezimmer • el cuarto de baño • la stanza da bagno

towel rack
le porte-serviettes
der Handtuchhalter
el toallero
il portasciugamani

shower door
la porte de douche
die Duschtür
la puerta de la ducha
la porta della doccia

cold faucet
le robinet d'eau froide
der Kaltwasserhahn
el grifo de agua fría
il rubinetto dell'acqua fredda

hot faucet
le robinet d'eau chaude
der Heißwasserhahn
el grifo de agua caliente
il rubinetto dell'acqua calda

shower head
le pommeau de douche
der Duschkopf
la alcachofa de la ducha
il soffione della doccia

sink
le lavabo
das Waschbecken
el lavabo
il lavandino

shower
la douche
die Dusche
la ducha
la doccia

plug
la bonde
der Stöpsel
el tapón
il tappo

drain
le tuyau d'écoulement
der Abfluss
el desagüe
lo scolo

toilet seat
le siège des toilettes
der Toilettensitz
la tapa del wáter
il sedile

bathtub • la baignoire
• die Badewanne • la bañera
• la vasca

toilet
les toilettes
die Toilette
el wáter
il water

bidet • le bidet • das Bidet
• el bidé • il bidè

toilet brush
la brosse
die Toilettenbürste
la escobilla del wáter
la spazzola da water

---

medicine cabinet
l'armoire à pharmacie
die Hausapotheke
el armario de las medicinas
l'armadietto dei medicinali

bath mat
le tapis de bain
die Badematte
la alfombrilla de baño
lo scendibagno

dental hygiene • l'hygiène dentaire • die Zahnpflege
• la higiene dental • l'igiene dentale

toilet paper
le rouleau de papier hygiénique
die Rolle Toilettenpapier
el rollo de papel higiénico
la carta igienica

shower curtain
le rideau de douche
der Duschvorhang
la cortina de ducha
la tenda da doccia

toothbrush • la brosse à
dents • die Zahnbürste
• el cepillo de dientes
• lo spazzolino da denti

dental floss
le fil dentaire
die Zahnseide
el hilo dental
il filo interdentale

take a shower *(v)*
prendre une douche
duschen
darse una ducha
farsi la doccia

take a bath *(v)*
prendre un bain
baden
darse un baño
farsi il bagno

toothpaste • le dentifrice
• die Zahnpasta • la pasta
de dientes • il dentifricio

mouthwash • l'eau dentifrice
• das Mundwasser • el
enjuague bucal • il collutorio

---

sponge • l'éponge • der Schwamm • la esponja • la spugna

pumice stone • la pierre ponce • der Bimsstein • la piedra pómez • la pomice

back brush • la brosse pour le dos • die Rückenbürste • el cepillo para la espalda • la spazzola

deodorant • le déodorant • das Deo • el desodorante • il deodorante

soap dish
le porte-savon
die Seifenschale
la jabonera
il portasapone

shower gel
le gel douche
das Duschgel
el gel de ducha
la docciaschiuma

soap • le savon • die Seife • el jabón • il sapone

face cream • la crème pour le visage • die Gesichtscreme • la crema para la cara • la crema per il viso

bubble bath • le bain moussant • das Schaumbad • el gel de baño • il bagnoschiuma

hand towel
la serviette
das Handtuch
la toalla de lavabo
l'asciugamano piccolo

bath towel
la serviette de bain
das Badetuch
la toalla de baño
l'asciugamano grande

towels • les serviettes • die Handtücher • las toallas • gli asciugamani

body lotion • la lotion pour le corps • die Körperlotion • la leche del cuerpo • la lozione per il corpo

talcum powder • le talc • der Körperpuder • los polvos de talco • il talco

bathrobe • le peignoir • der Bademantel • el albornoz • l'accappatoio

shaving • le rasage • das Rasieren • el afeitado • la rasatura

electric razor
le rasoir électrique
der Elektrorasierer
la maquinilla eléctrica
il rasoio elettrico

razor blade
la lame de rasoir
die Rasierklinge
la hoja de afeitar
la lametta

shaving foam • la mousse à raser • der Rasierschaum • la espuma de afeitar • la schiuma da barba

disposable razor • le rasoir jetable • der Einwegrasierer • la cuchilla de afeitar desechable • il rasoio monouso

aftershave • l'after-shave • das Rasierwasser • el aftershave • il dopobarba

nursery • la chambre d'enfants • das Kinderzimmer • la habitación de los niños • la camera dei bambini

baby care • les soins de bébé • die Säuglingspflege • el cuidado del bebé • l'igiene dei bambini

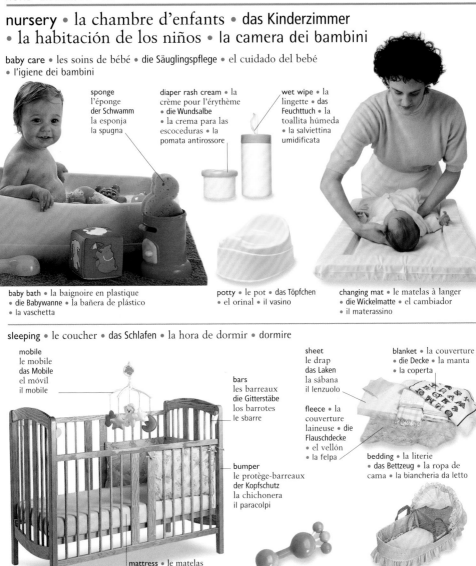

sponge
l'éponge
der Schwamm
la esponja
la spugna

diaper rash cream • la crème pour l'érythème • die Wundsalbe • la crema para las escoceduras • la pomata antirossore

wet wipe • la lingette • das Feuchttuch • la toallita húmeda • la salviettina umidificata

baby bath • la baignoire en plastique • die Babywanne • la bañera de plástico • la vaschetta

potty • le pot • das Töpfchen • el orinal • il vasino

changing mat • le matelas à langer • die Wickelmatte • el cambiador • il materassino

---

sleeping • le coucher • das Schlafen • la hora de dormir • dormire

mobile
le mobile
das Mobile
el móvil
il mobile

bars
les barreaux
die Gitterstäbe
los barrotes
le sbarre

sheet
le drap
das Laken
la sábana
il lenzuolo

blanket • la couverture • die Decke • la manta • la coperta

fleece • la couverture laineuse • die Flauschdecke • el vellón • la felpa

bumper
le protège-barreaux
der Kopfschutz
la chichonera
il paracolpi

bedding • la literie • das Bettzeug • la ropa de cama • la biancheria da letto

mattress • le matelas • die Matratze • el colchón • il materasso

rattle • le hochet • die Rassel • el sonajero • il sonaglio

bassinet • le moïse • das Körbchen • el moisés • il portabebè

crib • le lit d'enfant • das Kinderbett • la cuna • il lettino

playing • le jeu • das Spielen • los juegos • il gioco

doll • la poupée
• die Puppe • la muñeca
• la bambola

stuffed toy • le jouet en
peluche • das Kuscheltier
• el muñeco de peluche
• il peluche

dollhouse • la maison de
poupée • das Puppenhaus
• la casa de muñecas
• la casa delle bambole

playhouse • la maison
pliante • das Spielhaus
• la casa de juguete
• la casa da gioco

teddy bear • l'ours en
peluche • der Teddy
• el oso de peluche
• l'orsacchiotto

toy	ball
le jouet	la balle
das Spielzeug	der Ball
el juguete	la pelota
il giocattolo	la palla

toy basket • le panier à jouets
• der Spielzeugkorb • el cesto de los
juguetes • il cesto dei giocattoli

playpen • le parc • der Laufstall
• el parque • il box

safety • la sécurité • die Sicherheit • la seguridad • la sicurezza

child lock • la serrure de
sécurité • die Kindersicherung
• el cierre de seguridad • il
fermo di sicurezza

baby monitor • le moniteur
• das Babyphon
• el escuchabebés
• l'interfono

stair gate • la barrière
d'escalier • das Treppengitter
• la barrera de seguridad
• lo sbarramento

eating • le manger • das Essen • la comida • il pasto

going out • la sortie • das Ausgehen • el paseo • la passeggiata

hood
la capote
das Verdeck
la capota
la capote

high chair • la chaise haute
• der Kinderstuhl • la trona
• il seggiolone

stroller • la poussette
• der Sportwagen • la silleta
de paseo • il passeggino

baby carriage • le landau
• der Kinderwagen
• el cochecito
de niños • la carrozzina

nipple • la tétine
• der Sauger • la tetina
• la tettarella

drinking cup
la tasse
die Schnabeltasse
la taza
la tazza per bere

diaper
la couche
die Windel
el pañal
il pannolino

bottle • le biberon
• die Babyflasche • el
biberón • il biberon

carrier • le couffin
• das Tragebettchen • el
capazo • la culla portatile

diaper bag • le sac
• die Babytasche • la bolsa del
bebé • la borsa per il cambio

baby sling • le porte-bébé
• die Babytrage • la mochila
de bebé • il marsupio

utility room • la buanderie • der Haushaltsraum • el lavadero • la lavanderia

laundry • le linge • die Wäsche • la colada • il bucato

dirty laundry
le linge sale
die schmutzige Wäsche
la ropa sucia
i panni sporchi

clean clothes
le linge propre
die saubere Wäsche
la ropa limpia
i vestiti puliti

laundry basket • le panier à linge • der Wäschekorb • el cesto de la colada • il cesto della biancheria da lavare

washing machine • le lave-linge • die Waschmaschine • la lavadora • la lavatrice

washer-dryer • le lave-linge séchant • der Waschtrockner • la lavadora secadora • la lavasciuga

tumble dryer • le sèche-linge • der Trockner • la secadora • l'asciugabiancheria

clothespin
la pince à linge
die Wäscheklammer
la pinza para la ropa
la molletta

clothesline
la corde à linge
die Wäscheleine
la cuerda para tender la ropa
la corda per il bucato

iron • le fer à repasser • das Bügeleisen • la plancha • il ferro da stiro

dry (v) • sécher • trocknen • secar • asciugare

ironing board • la planche à repasser • das Bügelbrett • la tabla de la plancha • l'asse da stiro

load (v)	spin (v)	iron (v)	How do I operate the washing machine?
charger	essorer	repasser	Comment fonctionne le lave-linge?
füllen	schleudern	bügeln	Wie benutze ich die Waschmaschine?
cargar	centrifugar	planchar	¿Cómo funciona la lavadora?
caricare	centrifugare	stirare	Come funziona la lavatrice?
rinse (v)	spin dryer	fabric softener	What is the setting for colors/whites?
rincer	l'essoreuse	l'assouplissant pour	Quel est le programme pour les couleurs/le blanc?
spülen	die Wäscheschleuder	le linge	Welches Programm nehme ich für farbige/weiße Wäsche?
aclarar	la centrifugadora	der Weichspüler	¿Cuál es el programa para la ropa de color/blanca?
sciacquare	la centrifuga	el suavizante	Qual è il programma per i tessuti colorati/bianchi?
		l'ammorbidente	

cleaning equipment • l'équipement d'entretien • die Reinigungsartikel • el equipo de limpieza • gli accessori per la pulizia

suction hose • le tuyau flexible • der Saugschlauch • el tubo de la aspiradora • il tubo di aspirazione

brush
la balayette
der Handfeger
el cepillo
la spazzola

dustpan • la pelle • das Kehrblech • el recogedor • la paletta

bleach • l'eau de Javel • das Reinigungsmittel • la lejía • la candeggina

bucket
le seau
der Eimer
el cubo
il secchio

powder
la poudre
das Waschpulver
en polvo
la polvere

liquid
le liquide
der Flüssigreiniger
líquido
liquido

dust cloth
le chiffon
das Staubtuch
el trapo del polvo
lo spolverino

vacuum cleaner • l'aspirateur • der Staubsauger • la aspiradora • l'aspirapolvere

mop • le balai laveur • der Mopp • la fregona • la scopa lavapavimenti

detergent • le détergent • das Waschmittel • el detergente • il detersivo

polish • la cire • die Politur • la cera • la cera

activities • les activités • die Tätigkeiten • las acciones • le attività

clean (v) • nettoyer • putzen • limpiar • pulire

wash (v) • laver • spülen • fregar • lavare

wipe (v) • essuyer • wischen • pasar la bayeta • pulire

scrub (v) • laver à la brosse • schrubben • restregar • fregare

scrape (v) • racler • kratzen • raspar • raschiare

broom
le balai
der Besen
la escoba
la scopa

sweep (v) • balayer • fegen • barrer • spazzare

dust (v) • épousseter • Staub wischen • limpiar el polvo • spolverare

polish (v) • cirer • polieren • sacar brillo • lucidare

workshop • l'atelier • die Heimwerkstatt • el taller • il laboratorio

chuck
le mandrin
das Bohrfutter
el cabezal
il mandrino

drill bit
la mèche
der Bohrer
la broca
la punta

battery pack
la pile
der Akku
la batería
la batteria

jigsaw • la scie sauteuse • die Stichsäge • la sierra de vaivén • il gattuccio

cordless drill • la perceuse rechargeable • der Akkuschrauber Batteriebetrieb • el taladro inalámbrico • il trapano ricaricabile

electric drill • la perceuse électrique • die Elektrische Bohrmaschine • el taladro eléctrico • il trapano elettrico

glue gun • le pistolet à colle • die Klebepistole • la pistola para encolar • la pistola per colla

clamp • le serre-joint • die Zwinge • la abrazadera • il morsetto

blade • la lame • das Sägeblatt • la cuchilla • la lama

vise • l'étau • der Schraubstock • el torno de banco • la morsa

sander • la ponceuse • die Schleifmaschine • la lijadora • la levigatrice

circular saw • la scie circulaire • die Kreissäge • la sierra circular • la sega circolare

workbench • l'établi • die Werkbank • el banco de trabajo • il banco da lavoro

wood glue
la colle à bois
der Holzleim
la cola de carpintero
la colla da legno

tool rack
• le porte-outils
• das Werkzeuggestell
• el organizador de las herramientas
• la rastrelliera per gli arnesi

router
la défonceuse
die Oberfräse
la rebajadora
la contornitrice

bit brace
le vilebrequin
die Bohrwinde
el taladro manual
il girabacchino

wood shavings
les copeaux
die Holzspäne
las virutas de madera
i trucioli

extension cord
la rallonge
das Verlängerungskabel
el alargador
la prolunga

english • français • deutsch • español • italiano

techniques • les techniques • die Techniken • las técnicas • le tecniche

cut (v) • découper • schneiden • cortar • tagliare

saw (v) • scier • sägen • serrar • segare

drill (v) • percer • bohren • taladrar • forare

hammer (v) • marteler • hämmern • clavar • martellare

solder
la soudure
der Lötzinn
el hilo de estaño
la lega per saldatura

plane (v) • raboter • hobeln • alisar • piallare

turn (v) • tourner • drechseln • tornear • tornire

carve (v) • sculpter • schnitzen • tallar • incidere

solder (v) • souder • löten • soldar • saldare

materials • les matériaux • die Materialien • los materiales • i materiali

MDF
le médium
die MDF-Platte
el tablero de densidad media
l'MDF

hardwood
le bois dur
das Hartholz
la madera noble
il legno duro

wire
le fil de fer
der Draht
el alambre
il filo

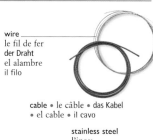

plywood
le contreplaqué
das Sperrholz
el contrachapado
il compensato

cable • le câble • das Kabel • el cable • il cavo

particle board
l'aggloméré
das Spanholz
el aglomerado
il truciolato

varnish
le vernis
der Lack
el barniz
la lacca

stainless steel
l'inox
der rostfreie Stahl
el acero inoxidable
l'acciaio inossidabile

hardboard • l'isorel • die Hartfaserplatte • el cartón madera • la masonite

wood stain • la couleur pour bois • die Beize • el tinte para madera • il mordente per legno

galvanized
galvanisé
galvanisiert
galvanizado
zincato

softwood • le bois tendre • das Weichholz • la madera de pino • il legno dolce

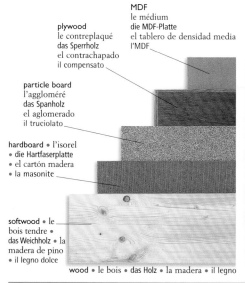

metal • le métal • das Metall • el metal • il metallo

wood • le bois • das Holz • la madera • il legno

toolbox • la boîte à outils • der Werkzeugkasten • la caja de las herramientas • la scatola degli attrezzi

wrench
la clef
der Schraubenschlüssel
la llave de boca
la chiave

adjustable wrench
• la clef à molette
• der verstellbare Schraubenschlüssel • la llave inglesa
• la chiave regolabile

hammer • le marteau
• der Hammer • el martillo
• il martello

needle-nose pliers • la pince plate
• die Flachzange • las tenazas de
alambre • le pinze ad ago

socket wrench • la clef à pipe • der Steckschlüssel
• la llave de tubo • la chiave a tubo

screwdriver bits
• les embouts de
tournevis • die
Schraubenziehereinsätze
• los cabezales de
destornillador • le
punte per cacciavite

screwdriver
le tournevis
der Schraubenzieher
el destornillador
il cacciavite

level
le niveau
die Wasserwaage
el nivel
la livella

washer
le joint
die Unterlegscheibe
la arandela
la rondella

nut
l'écrou
die Mutter
la tuerca
il dado

tape measure • le mètre • das
Metermaß • la cinta métrica
• il metro

utility
knife • le cutter
• das Tapeziermesser
• el cúter • il
coltello da pacchi

bull-nose pliers • la pince universelle
• die Kombinationszange • los alicates
• le pinze tonde

socket • la douille • der Steckschlüsseleinsatz
• el encaje • la bussola

Allen wrench • la clef • der
Schlüssel • la llave • la chiave

---

drill bits • les forets • die Bohrer • las brocas • le punte

metal bit • le foret à métaux
• der Metallbohrer • la broca para
metal • la punta per metalli

flat wood bit • le foret à bois plat
• der Flachholzbohrer • la broca para
madera • la punta piana per legno

reamer
l'alésoir
die Reibahle
el escariador
l'alesatore

phillips screwdriver • le tournevis cruciforme
• der Kreuzschlitzschraubenzieher • el
destornillador de estrella • il cacciavite a croce

head • la tête
• der Nagelkopf • la
cabeza • la testa

security bit
le foret de sécurité
der Sicherheitsbohrer
la broca de seguridad
la punta di sicurezza

nail • le clou • der
Nagel • el clavo
• il chiodo

carpentry bits
• les forets à bois
• die Holzbohrer
• las brocas para
madera • le punte
da falegnameria

masonry bit
le foret de maçonnerie
der Mauerwerkbohrer
la broca de albañilería
la punta per muratura

screw • la vis • die
Schraube • el tornillo
• la vite

wire strippers • la pince à dénuder • die Abisolierzange • el pelacables • la pinza spelafilo

wire cutters • la pince coupante • der Drahtschneider • el cortaalambres • la pinza tagliafilo

soldering iron le fer à souder der Lötkolben el soldador il saldatoio

electrical tape le ruban isolant das Isolierband la cinta aislante il nastro isolante

craft knife le scalpel das Skalpell el escalpelo il bisturi

fretsaw • la scie à chantourner • die Laubsäge • la sierra de calar • la sega da traforo

solder la soudure der Lötzinn el soldadura le lega per saldatura

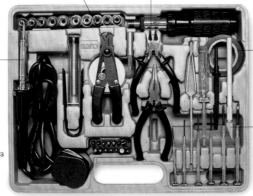

tenon saw • la scie à dosseret • die Profilsäge • el serrucho de costilla • la sega per tenoni

safety goggles • les lunettes de sécurité • die Schutzbrille • las gafas de seguridad • gli occhiali protettivi

plane • le rabot • der Hobel • el cepillo • la pialla

handsaw • la scie égoïne • der Fuchsschwanz • el serrucho • il seghetto

miter block • la boîte à onglets • die Gehrungslade • la caja para cortar en inglete • la cassetta guidalama per ugnature

hacksaw • la scie à métaux • die Metallsäge • la sierra para metales • il seghetto per metalli

hand drill • la perceuse manuelle • der Handbohrer • el taladro manual • il trapano manuale

steel wool • la paille de fer • die Stahlwolle • la lana de acero • la lana d'acciaio

wrench • la clef serre-tube • die Rohrzange • las tenazas • la chiave inglese

sandpaper • le papier de verre • das Schmirgelpapier • el papel de lija • la carta vetrata

chisel • le burin • der Stechbeitel • el formón • lo scalpello

plunger • la ventouse • die Saugglocke • el desatascador • lo sturalavandini

whetstone • la pierre à aiguiser • der Wetzstahl • la piedra afiladora • l'affilatore

file • la lime • die Feile • la lima • la lima

pipe cutter • le coupe-tube • der Rohrab-schneider • el cortatuberías • il tagliatubi

decorating • la décoration • das Tapezieren • la decoración • la decorazione

scissors • les ciseaux • die Tapezierschere • las tijeras • le forbici

utility knife • le cutter • das Tapeziermesser • el cúter • il coltello da pacchi

plumb line • le fil à plomb • das Senkblei • la cuerda de plomada • il filo a piombo

scraper • le grattoir • der Spachtel • el raspador • la spatola

decorator
le tapissier décorateur
der Tapezierer
el pintor
il decoratore

wallpaper
le papier peint
die Tapete
el papel pintado
la carta di parati

stepladder
l'escabeau
die Trittleiter
la escalera de mano
la scaletta

wallpaper brush
• la brosse à tapisser
• die Tapezierbürste
• la brocha de empapelador
• la spazzola

pasting table
la table à encoller
der Tapeziertisch
la mesa de encolar
il tavolo da lavoro

pasting brush
la brosse à encoller
die Kleisterbürste
la brocha de encolar
il pennello da colla

wallpaper paste • la colle à tapisser • der Tapetenkleister • la cola para empapelar • la colla da parati

bucket
le seau
der Eimer
el cubo
il secchio

wallpaper (v) • tapisser • tapezieren • empapelar • tappezzare

strip (v) • décoller • abziehen • arrancar • staccare

fill (v) • mastiquer • spachteln • rellenar • stuccare

sand (v) • poncer • schmirgeln • lijar • scartavetrare

plaster (v) • plâtrer • verputzen • enyesar • intonacare

hang (v) • poser • anbringen • empapelar • incollare

tile (v) • carreler • kacheln • alicatar • piastrellare

roller
le rouleau
der Roller
el rodillo
il rullo

paint tray • le bac à peinture • die Wanne • la bandeja para la pintura • la vaschetta per la vernice

paint • la peinture • die Farbe • la pintura • la vernice

brush
la brosse
die Streichbürste
la brosse
il pennello

paint can
le pot de peinture
der Farbtopf
la lata de pintura
il barattolo di vernice

sponge • l'éponge
• der Schwamm
• la esponja
• la spugna

masking tape • le papier cache • das Abdeckband • la cinta adhesiva protectora • il nastro adesivo coprente

sandpaper • le papier de verre
• das Schmirgelpapier
• el papel de lija
• la carta vetrata

coveralls
le bleu de travail
der Overall
el mono
la tuta

turpentine
la térébenthine
das Terpentin
la trementina
la trementina

drop cloth
la couverture de protection
das Abdecktuch
el protector
il telo di protezione

filler • le mastic • die Spachtelmasse • la masilla • lo stucco

paint thinner • le white-spirit • das Verdünner • el aguarrás • l'acquaragia

paint (v) • peindre • anstreichen • pintar • dipingere

plaster	gloss	embossed paper	undercoat	sealant
le plâtre	brillant	le papier gaufré	la couche de fond	l'enduit
der Gips	Glanz-	das Relieftapete	die Grundierung	das Versiegelungsmittel
el yeso	con brillo	el papel estampado en relieve	la primera mano	el sellante
l'intonaco	lucido	la carta a rilievo	la mano di fondo	il sigillante
varnish	matte	lining paper	topcoat	solvent
le vernis	mat	le papier d'apprêt	la dernière couche	le solvant
der Lack	matt	das Einsatzpapier	der Deckanstrich	das Lösungsmittel
el barniz	mate	el papel de apresto	la última mano	el disolvente
la vernice trasparente	opaco	la carta di fondo	la mano finale	il solvente
latex paint	stencil	primer	preservative	grout
la peinture mate	le pochoir	l'apprêt	l'agent de conservation	le mastic
die Emulsionsfarbe	die Schablone	die Grundfarbe	der Schutzanstrich	der Fugenkitt
la pintura al agua	la plantilla	la imprimación	el conservante	el cemento blanco
la pittura	lo stampino	la vernice di base	il conservante	la malta

garden • le jardin • der Garten • el jardín • il giardino

garden styles • les styles de jardin • die Gartentypen • los estilos de jardín • i tipi di giardino

patio garden • le patio • der Patiogarten • la terraza ajardinada • il giardino a patio

formal garden • le jardin à la française • der architektonische Garten • el jardín clásico • il giardino all'italiana

cottage garden • le jardin paysan • der Bauerngarten • el jardín campestre • il giardino all'inglese

herb garden • le jardin d'herbes aromatiques • der Kräutergarten • el jardín de plantas herbáceas • il giardino di erbe

roof garden • le jardin sur le toit • der Dachgarten • el jardín en la azotea • il giardino pensile

rock garden • la rocaille • der Steingarten • la rocalla • il giardino il pietra

courtyard • la cour • der Hof • el patio • il cortile

water garden • le jardin d'eau • der Wassergarten • el jardín acuático • il giardino acquatico

garden features • les ornements de jardin • die Gartenornamente • los adornos para el jardín • gli ornamenti per il giardino

hanging basket • le panier suspendu • die Blumenampel • la cesta colgante • il cesto sospeso

trellis • le treillis • das Spalier • la espaldera • il graticcio

arbor • la pergola • die Pergola • la pérgola • la pergola

paving
le pavé
die Platten
la terraza
la pavimentazione

path
l'allée
der Weg
el camino
il sentiero

compost pile
le tas de compost
der Komposthaufen
el compost
la concimaia

soil • le sol • der
Boden • la tierra
• il terreno

gate
le portail
das Tor
la puerta
il cancello

flowerbed
le parterre
das Blumenbeet
el parterre
l'aiuola

topsoil • la terre • die
Erde • la capa superior
de la tierra • lo strato
superficiale

sand • le sable
• der Sand • la arena
• la sabbia

shed
la cabane
der Schuppen
el cobertizo
il capanno

chalk • la chaux • der
Kalk • la creta • il calcare

greenhouse
la serre
das Gewächshaus
el invernadero
la serra

lawn
la pelouse
der Rasen
el césped
il prato

fence
la clôture
der Zaun
la valla
il recinto

pond
le bassin
der Teich
el estanque
lo stagno

hedge
la haie
die Hecke
el seto
la siepe

silt • le limon
• der Schluff • el
cieno • il limo

arch
l'arceau
der Bogen
el arco
l'arco

vegetable garden
le potager
der Gemüsegarten
el huerto
l'orto

herbaceous border
la bordure de plantes herbacées
die Staudenrabatte
el arriate de plantas herbáceas
il bordo erbaceo

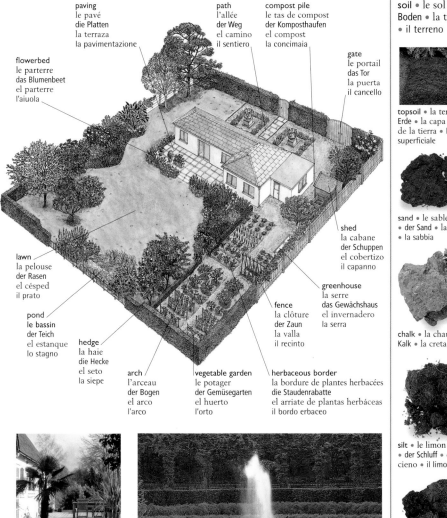

clay • l'argile • der
Lehm • la arcilla
• l'argilla

deck • les planches • die
Planken • el entarimado
• il tavolato

fountain • la fontaine • der Springbrunnen • la fuente • la fontana

garden plants • les plantes de jardin • die Gartenpflanzen • las plantas de jardín • le piante da giardino

types of plants • les genres de plantes • die Pflanzenarten • los tipos de plantas • i tipi di piante

annual • annuel • einjährig
• anual • annuale

biennial • bisannuel
• zweijährig • bienal
• biennale

perennial • vivace • mehrjährig
• perenne • perenne

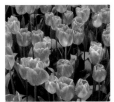

bulb • le bulbe • die Zwiebel
• el bulbo • il bulbo

fern • la fougère • der Farn
• el helecho • la felce

cattail • le jonc • die Binse
• el junco • il giunco

bamboo • le bambou
• der Bambus • el bambú
• il bambù

weeds • les mauvaises
herbes • das Unkraut • las
malas hierbas • le erbacce

herb • l'herbe • das Kraut
• la hierba • l'erba aromatica

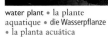

water plant • la plante
aquatique • die Wasserpflanze
• la planta acuática
• la pianta acquatica

tree • l'arbre • der Baum
• el árbol • l'albero

palm • le palmier
• die Palme • la palmera
• la palma

conifer • le conifère
• der Nadelbaum • la conífera
• la conifera

evergreen • à feuilles
persistantes • immergrün
• de hoja perenne
• sempreverde

deciduous • à feuilles
caduques • der Laubbaum
• de hoja caduca • a foglie
caduche

topiary • la topiaire • der Formschnitt • las plantas podadas con formas • l'arte topiaria

alpine • la plante alpestre • die Alpenpflanze • la planta alpestre • le piante da roccia

succulent • la plante grasse • die Fettpflanze • la planta suculenta • la pianta grassa

cactus • le cactus • der Kaktus • el cactus • il cactus

potted plant • la plante en pot • die Topfpflanze • la planta de maceta • la pianta da vaso

shade plant • la plante d'ombre • die Schattenpflanze • la planta de sombra • la pianta d'ombra

climber
la plante grimpante
die Kletterpflanze
la planta trepadora
il rampicante

flowering shrub
l'arbuste à fleurs
der Zierstrauch
el arbusto de flor
l'arbusto da fiore

ground cover
• la couverture du sol • der Bodendecker • la planta para cubrir suelo • la pianta copriterreno

creeper
la plante rampante
die Kriechpflanze
la planta trepadora
la pianta strisciante

ornamental
ornemental
die Zierpflanze
ornamental
ornamentale

grass
l'herbe
das Gras
el césped
l'erba

garden tools • les outils de jardin • die Gartengeräte • las herramientas de jardinería • gli attrezzi da giardino

compost • le terreau
• die Komposterde
• el abono compuesto
• il terriccio

lawn rake
le balai à gazon
der Laubrechen
el rastrillo para el césped
la scopa di ferro

seeds • les graines
• die Samen • las
semillas • i semi

bone meal • la cendre
d'os • die Knochenasche
• la harina de huesos
• la farina di ossa

shovel • la
bêche • der
Spaten • la pala
• la vanga

fork • la fourche
• die Mistgabel
• la horca
• la forca

long-handled shears • la
grande cisaille • die Schere
• la podadera de mango
largo • le forbici tagliabordi

rake • le râteau
• der Rechen
• el rastrillo
• il rastrello

hoe • la houe
• die Hacke
• la azada
• la zappa

gravel • le gravier
• der Kies • la grava
• la ghiaia

grass bag
le sac à herbe
der Grasfangsack
la bolsa para la hierba
il raccoglierba

motor
le moteur
der Motor
el motor
il motore

handle
le bras
der Griff
el asa
il manico

gardening basket • le panier de
jardinier • der Gartenkorb • la
cesta de jardinero • il cestello

shield
l'écran de protection
der Schutz
el protector
la protezione

stand
le support
der Ständer
el soporte
il sostegno

trimmer • la tondeuse
• der Schneider • el
guarnecedor • il tagliabordi

lawnmower • la tondeuse
à gazon • der Rasenmäher
• el cortacésped • il tosaerba

wheelbarrow • la brouette
• der Schubkarren • la carretilla
• la carriola

hand fork • la petite fourche • die Handgabel • la horquilla • la forca

trowel • le déplantoir • die Pflanzschaufel • la pala pequeña • la paletta

blade
la lame
die Klinger
la hoja
la lama

shears • la cisaille • die Heckenschere • la cizalla • le forbici da giardino

handsaw • la scie à main • die Handsäge • la sierra de mano • la sega

pruners • le sécateur • die Gartenschere • las tijeras de podar • la cesoia

seed tray • le germoir • der Setzkasten • el semillero • il semenzaio

pesticide
le pesticide
das Pestizid
el pesticida
il pesticida

gardening gloves
les gants de jardinage
die Gartenhandschuhe
los guantes de jardín
i guanti da giardinaggio

twine
la ficelle
der Zwirn
el hilo de bramante
il refe

labels
les étiquettes
die Pflanzenschildchen
las etiquetas
le etichette

twist ties
les attaches
die Befestigungen
el alambre
le fettucce

canes
les cannes
die Gartenstöcke
las cañas
le canne

ring ties
les anneaux
die Ringbefestigungen
las anillas
gli anelli

sieve
le tamis
das Sieb
la criba
il setaccio

plant pot
le pot à fleurs
der Blumentopf
la maceta
il vaso da fiori

rubber boots • les bottes • die Gummistiefel • las botas de goma • le galosce

watering • l'arrosage • Gießen • el riego • l'annaffiatura

nozzle
le jet
die Düse
la boquilla
il becco

sprinkler • l'arroseur • der Rasensprenger • el aspersor • l'irrigatore

spray bottle • le vaporisateur • die Spritzflasche • el pulverizador • il diffusore

watering can
l'arrosoir
die Gießkanne
la regadera
l'annaffiatoio

hose
le tuyau d'arrosage
der Gartenschlauch
la manguera
la pompa da giardino

spray • la pomme • die Brause • la alcachofa • la rosa

hose reel • le dévidoir de tuyau • der Schlauchwagen • el enrollador de manguera • l'avvolgitubo

gardening • le jardinage • die Gartenarbeit • la jardinería • il giardinaggio

lawn
la pelouse
der Rasen
el césped
il prato

flowerbed
le parterre
das Blumenbeet
el parterre
l'aiuola

lawnmower
la tondeuse
der Rasenmäher
el cortacésped
il tosaerba

hedge
la haie
die Hecke
el seto
la siepe

stake
le tuteur
die Stange
la estaca
il tutore

mow (v) • tondre • mähen • cortar el césped • tagliare l'erba

sod (v) • gazonner • mit Rasen bedecken • poner césped • ricoprire di zolle erbose

spike (v) • piquer • stechen • hacer agujeros con la horquilla • inforcare

rake (v) • ratisser • harken • rastrillar • rastrellare

trim (v) • tailler • stutzen • podar • spuntare

dig (v) • bêcher • graben • cavar • scavare

sow (v) • semer • säen • sembrar • seminare

top-dress (v) • fumer en surface • mit Kopfdünger düngen • abonar en la superficie • concimare a spandimento

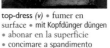

water (v) • arroser • gießen • regar • annaffiare

cane
la canne
der Stock
la caña
la canna

train (v) • palisser
• hochbinden • guiar
• far crescere

deadhead (v) • enlever les
fleurs fanées • ausputzen
• quitar las flores muertas
• togliere i fiori appassiti

spray (v) • asperger • sprühen
• rociar • spruzzare

cutting
la bouture
der Ableger
el esqueje
la propaggine

graft (v) • greffer • pfropfen
• injertar • innestare

propagate (v) • propager
• vermehren • propagar
• propagare

prune (v) • élaguer
• beschneiden • podar
• potare

stake (v) • mettre un tuteur
• stützen • apuntalar
• legare a un tutore

transplant (v) • transplanter
• umpflanzen • transplantar
• trapiantare

weed (v) • désherber • jäten
• escardar • sradicare
le erbacce

mulch (v) • pailler • mulchen
• cubrir la tierra • pacciamare

harvest (v) • récolter • ernten
• cosechar • raccogliere

cultivate (v)	landscape (v)	fertilize (v)	sift (v)	organic	seedling	subsoil
cultiver	dessiner	fertiliser	tamiser	biologique	le semis	le sous-sol
züchten	gestalten	düngen	sieben	biodynamisch	der Sämling	der Untergrund
cultivar	diseñar	abonar	cribar	biológico	el plantón	el subsuelo
coltivare	architettare	concimare	setacciare	biologico	il semenzale	il sottosuolo
tend (v)	pot (v)	pick (v)	aerate (v)	drainage	fertilizer	weedkiller
soigner	mettre en pot	cueillir	retourner	le drainage	l'engrais	l'herbicide
hegen	eintopfen	pflücken	auflockern	die Entwässerung	der Dünger	der Unkrautvernichter
cuidar	plantar en tiesto	coger	airear	el drenaje	el abono	el herbicida
curare	invasare	cogliere	aerare	il prosciugamento	il concime	il diserbante

services
les services
die Dienstleistungen
los servicios
i servizi

emergency services • les services d'urgence • die Notdienste • los servicios de emergencia • i servizi di emergenza

ambulance • l'ambulance • der Krankenwagen • la ambulancia • l'ambulanza

stretcher
le brancard
die Tragbahre
la camilla
la barella

ambulance • l'ambulance • der Rettungsdienst
• la ambulancia • l'ambulanza

paramedic • l'infirmier du SAMU • der
Rettungssanitäter • el ambulancero • il paramedico

police • la police • die Polizei • la policía • la polizia

badge
le badge
die Kennmarke
la placa
il distintivo

uniform
l'uniforme
die Uniform
el uniforme
l'uniforme

lights
les feux
das Licht
las luces
le luci

siren
la sirène
die Sirene
la sirena
la sirena

police car • la voiture de police
• das Polizeiauto • el coche de policía
• l'auto della polizia

police station • le poste
de police • die Polizeiwache
• la estación de policía
• la stazione di polizia

nightstick
la matraque
der Gummiknüppel
la porra
il manganello

gun
le pistolet
die Pistole
la pistola
la pistola

handcuffs
les menottes
die Handschellen
las esposas
le manette

police officer • le policier • der Polizist
• el agente de policía • il poliziotto

captain	burglary	complaint	arrest
l'inspecteur	le cambriolage	la plainte	l'arrestation
der Inspektor	der Einbruchdiebstahl	die Anzeige	die Festnahme
el inspector	el robo	la denuncia	el arresto
il commissario	il furto	la denuncia	l'arresto
detective	assault	investigation	cell
l'officier de police	l'agression	l'enquête	la cellule
der Kriminalbeamte	die Körperverletzung	die Ermittlung	die Polizeizelle
el detective	la agresión	la investigación	la celda
l'investigatore	l'aggressione	l'indagine	la cella
crime	fingerprint	suspect	charge
le crime	les empreintes	le suspect	l'accusation
das Verbrechen	der Fingerabdruck	der Verdächtige	die Anklage
el crimen	la huella dactilar	el sospechoso	el cargo
il reato	l'impronta digitale	il sospetto	l'accusa

fire department • les pompiers • die Feuerwehr • los bomberos • i vigili del fuoco

helmet • la casque
• der Schutzhelm • el
casco • il casco

smoke
la fumée
der Rauch
el humo
il fumo

hose
le tuyau
der Schlauch
la manguera
l'idrante

basket
la nacelle
der Auslegerkorb
la cesta
la gabbia

water jet
le jet d'eau
der Wasserstrahl
el chorro de agua
il getto d'acqua

firefighters • les
sapeurs-pompiers
• die Feuerwehrleute
• los bomberos
• i vigili del fuoco

boom
la flèche
der Ausleger
el brazo
il braccio

ladder
l'échelle
die Leiter
la escalera
la scala

cab
la cabine
die Fahrerkabine
la cabina
la cabina

fire • l'incendie • der Brand • el incendio • l'incendio

fire station • le caserne de
pompiers • die Feuerwache
• el parque de bomberos
• la caserma dei vigili del fuoco

fire escape • l'escalier de
secours • die Feuertreppe
• la salida de incendios
• la scala di sicurezza

fire engine • la voiture de pompiers • das Löschfahrzeug
• el coche de bomberos • l'autopompa

smoke alarm • le
détecteur de fumée
• der Rauchmelder
• el detector de humo
• l'allarme antifumo

fire alarm • l'avertisseur
d'incendie • der
Feuermelder • la alarma
contra incendios
• l'allarme antincendio

ax • la hache • das
Beil • el hacha • l'ascia

fire extinguisher
• l'extincteur • der
Feuerlöscher • el
extintor • l'estintore

hydrant • la borne
d'incendie • der
Hydrant • la boca
de agua • l'idrante

I need the police/fire department/ambulance.	There's a fire at…	There's been an accident.	Call the police!
La police/les pompiers/une ambulance, s'il vous plaît.	Il y a un incendie à…	Il y a eu un accident.	Appelez la police!
Die Polizei/die Feuerwehr/einen Krankenwagen, bitte.	Es brennt in…	Es ist ein Unfall passiert.	Rufen Sie die Polizei!
Necesito la policía/los bomberos/una ambulancia.	Hay un incendio en…	Ha habido un accidente.	¡Llame a la policía!
Ho bisogno della polizia/dei vigili del fuoco/di un'ambulanza.	C'è un incendio a…	C'è stato un incidente.	Chiamate la polizia!

bank • la banque • die Bank • el banco • la banca

customer
le client
der Kunde
el cliente
il cliente

window
le guichet
der Schalter
la ventanilla
lo sportello

teller
le caissier
der Kassierer
el cajero
il cassiere

brochures
les dépliants
die Broschüren
los folletos
i dèpliants

counter
le comptoir
der Schalter
el mostrador
il banco

deposit slips
les fiches de versement
die Einzahlungsscheine
las hojas de ingreso
i moduli di versamento

debit card
la carte bancaire
die EC-Karte
la tarjeta de débito
la carta di debito

stub
le talon
der Stammabschnitt
la matriz
la matrice

account number
le numéro de compte
die Kontonummer
el número de cuenta
il numero di conto

signature
la signature
die Unterschrift
la firma
la firma

amount
le montant
der Betrag
la cantidad
l'importo

check
le chèque
der Scheck
el cheque
l'assegno

branch manager
• le directeur d'agence
• der Filialleiter • el director
de banco • il direttore

credit card • la carte de
crédit • die Kreditkarte
• la tarjeta de crédito
• la carta di credito

checkbook • le carnet de chèques
• das Scheckheft • el talonario de
cheques • il libretto degli assegni

savings l'épargne die Spareinlagen los ahorros i risparmi	mortgage l'hypothèque die Hypothek la hipoteca l'ipoteca	payment le paiement die Zahlung el pago il pagamento	deposit *(v)* verser einzahlen ingresar versare	checking account le compte courant das Girokonto la cuenta corriente il conto corrente
tax l'impôt die Steuer los impuestos l'imposta	overdraft le découvert die Kontoüberziehung el descubierto lo scoperto	automatic payment le prélèvement der Einzugsauftrag la domiciliación bancaria l'addebito diretto	bank transfer le virement bancaire die Banküberweisung la transferencia bancaria il bonifico	savings account le compte d'épargne das Sparkonto la cuenta de ahorros il conto di risparmio
loan le prêt das Darlehen el préstamo il prestito	interest rate le taux d'intérêt der Zinssatz el tipo de interés il tasso d'interesse	withdrawal slip la fiche de retrait das Abhebungsformular la hoja de reintegro il modulo di prelievo	bank charge les frais bancaire die Überweisung la comisión bancaria la commissione bancaria	PIN le code secret der PIN-Code el pin il pin

coin
la pièce
die Münze
la moneda
la moneta

bill
le billet
der Schein
el billete
la banconota

screen
l'écran
der Bildschirm
la pantalla
lo schermo

keypad
le clavier
das Tastenfeld
el teclado
la tastiera

card reader
la fente
der Kartenschlitz
la ranura de la tarjeta
la fessura per la carta

money • l'argent • das Geld
• el dinero • il denaro

ATM • le distributeur • der Geldautomat
• el cajero automático • il bancomat

foreign currency • les devises étrangères • die ausländische Währung • las divisas • la valuta estera

traveller's check
le traveller
der Reisescheck
el cheque de viaje
il travel cheque

currency exchange • le bureau de change
• die Wechselstube • la oficina de cambio
• l'ufficio di cambio

exchange rate
le taux de change
der Wechselkurs
el tipo de cambio
il tasso di cambio

finance • la finance • die Geldwirtschaft • las finanzas • la finanza

share price
le prix des actions
der Aktienpreis
el valor de las acciones
il corso per azione

stockbroker
l'agent de la bourse
der Börsenmakler
el agente de bolsa
il broker

financial advisor • la conseillère
financière • die Finanzberaterin
• la asesora financiera
• la consulente finanziaria

stock exchange • la bourse • die Börse
• la bolsa de valores • la borsa valori

cash (v)
encaisser
einlösen
cobrar
incassare

denomination
la valeur
der Nennwert
el valor nominal
la denominazione

commission
la commission
die Provision
la comisión
la commissione

investment
l'investissement
die Kapitalanlage
la inversión
l'investimento

stocks
les titres
die Wertpapiere
las acciones
i titoli

shares
les actions
die Aktien
las acciones
le azioni

dividends
les dividendes
die Gewinnanteile
los dividendos
i dividendi

accountant
le comptable
der Buchhalter
el contable
il contabile

portfolio
le portefeuille
das Portefeuille
la cartera
il portafoglio

equity
l'action
das Eigenkapital
el patrimonio neto
il capitale netto

Can I change this please?
Est-ce que je peux changer ça, s'il vous plaît?
Könnte ich das bitte wechseln?
¿Podría cambiar esto por favor?
Posso cambiare questo?

What's today's exchange rate?
Quel est le taux de change aujourd'hui?
Wie ist der heutige Wechselkurs?
¿A cuánto está el cambio hoy?
Qual è il tasso di cambio oggi?

communications • les communications • die Kommunikation • las comunicaciones • le comunicazioni

postal worker
le postier
der Postbeamte
el empleado de correos
l'impiegato delle poste

window
le guichet
der Schalter
la ventanilla
lo sportello

scale
la balance
die Waage
la báscula
la bilancia

counter
le guichet
der Schalter
el mostrador
il banco

post office • la poste • die Post • la oficina de correos • l'ufficio postale

postmark
le tampon de la poste
der Poststempel
el matasellos
il timbro postale

stamp
le timbre
die Briefmarke
el sello
il francobollo

address
l'adresse
die Adresse
la dirección
l'indirizzo

zip code
le code postal
die Postleitzahl
el código postal
il codice di avviamento postale

envelope • l'enveloppe • der Umschlag • el sobre • la busta

mail carrier • le facteur
• der Briefträger • el cartero
• il postino

letter	return address	delivery	fragile	do not bend (v)
la lettre	l'expéditeur	la distribution	fragile	ne pas plier
der Brief	der Absender	die Zustellung	zerbrechlich	nicht falten
la carta	el remite	el reparto	frágil	no doblar
la lettera	il mittente	la consegna	fragile	non piegare
by airmail	signature	postage	mailbag	this way up
par avion	la signature	le tarif d'affranchissement	le sac postal	dessus
per Luftpost	die Unterschrift	die Portokosten	der Postsack	oben
por avión	la firma	el franqueo	la saca postal	hacia arriba
posta aerea	la firma	l'affrancatura	il sacco postale	alto
registered mail	pickup	money order	telegram	
l'envoi en recommandé	la levée	le mandat postal	le télégramme	
das Einschreiben	die Leerung	die Postanweisung	das Telegramm	
el correo certificado	la recogida	el giro postal	el telegrama	
la posta raccomandata	la levata della posta	il vaglia postale	il telegramma	

mailbox • la boîte aux lettres • der Briefkasten • el buzón • la buca delle lettere

letter slot • la boîte aux lettres • der Hausbriefkasten • el buzón • la cassetta delle lettere

package • le colis • das Paket • el paquete • il pacco

courier • le service de messagerie • der Kurierdienst • el mensajero • il corriere

telephone • le téléphone • das Telefon • el teléfono • il telefono

handset
le combiné
der Hörer
el auricular
il ricevitore

base station
la base
die Basisstation
la base
la base

answering machine
le répondeur
der Anrufbeantworter
el contestador automático
la segreteria telefonica

phone booth
la cabine téléphonique
die Telefonzelle
la cabina telefónica
la cabina telefonica

cordless phone • le téléphone sans fil • das schnurlose Telefon • el teléfono inalámbrico • il telefono senza fili

receiver
le combiné
der Hörer
el auricular
il ricevitore

keypad
le clavier
das Tastenfeld
el teclado
la tastiera

coin return
les pièces rendues
die Münzrückgabe
las monedas devueltas
la restituzione monete

smartphone • le smartphone • das Smartphone • el teléfono inteligente • lo smartphone

cell phone • le portable • das Handy • el teléfono móvil • il telefonino

payphone
• le téléphone public • der Münzfernsprecher • el teléfono público • il telefono pubblico

app l'appli die App la aplicación l'app	answer (v) répondre abheben • contestar rispondere	operator le téléphoniste die Vermittlung el operador il centralino	directory assistance les renseignements die Auskunft la información telefónica le informazioni telefoniche	Can you give me the number for...? Pouvez-vous me donner le numéro pour…? Können Sie mir die Nummer für…geben? ¿Me podría dar el número de…? Può darmi il numero per...?
passcode le mot de passe das Passwort la clave de acceso il codice d'accesso	text (SMS) le SMS die SMS el mensaje de texto (SMS) il messaggio (SMS)	busy occupé besetzt comunicando occupato	reverse change call le P.C.V das R-Gespräch a cobro revertido la chiamata a carico del destinatario	What is the area code for...? Quel est l'indicatif pour...? Was ist die Vorwahl für…? ¿Cuál es el prefigode de larga distancia para llamar a…? Qual è il prefisso per...?
dial (v) composer wählen marcar comporre	voice message le message vocal die Sprachmitteilung el mensaje de voz il messaggio vocale	disconnected coupé unterbrochen apagado interrotto		Text me! Envoie-moi un SMS! Schick mir eine SMS! ¡Mándame un mensaje de texto! Mandami un SMS!

hotel • l'hôtel • das Hotel • el hotel • l'albergo

lobby • le hall • die Empfangshalle • el vestíbulo • l'ingresso

guest
le client
der Gast
el huésped
l'ospite

room key
la clef de la chambre
der Zimmerschlüssel
la llave de la habitación
la chiave della camera

messages
les messages
die Nachrichten
los mensajes
i messaggi

pigeonhole
le casier
das Fach
la casilla
la casilla

receptionist
la réceptionniste
die Empfangsdame
la recepcionista
l'addetta alla ricezione

register
le registre
das Gästebuch
el registro
il registro

counter
le comptoir
der Schalter
el mostrador
il banco

reception • la réception • der Empfang • la recepción • la ricezione

luggage
les bagages
das Gepäck
el equipaje
il bagaglio

cart
le diable
der Kofferkuli
el carrito
il carrello

porter • le porteur • der Page
• el botones • il facchino

elevator • l'ascenseur • der Fahrstuhl
• el ascensor • l'ascensore

room number • le numéro de
chambre • die Zimmernummer
• el número de la habitación
• il numero della camera

rooms • les chambres • die Zimmer • los habitaciones • le camere

single room • la chambre
simple • das Einzelzimmer
• la habitación individual
• la camera singola

double room • la chambre
double • das Doppelzimmer
• la habitación doble
• la camera doppia

twin room • la chambre à
deux lits • das Zweibettzimmer
• la habitación con dos
camas individuales
• la camera a due letti

private bathroom
la salle de bain privée
das Privatbadezimmer
el cuarto de baño privado
il bagno privato

services • les services • die Dienstleistungen • los servicios • i servizi

breakfast tray • le plateau à petit déjeuner • das Frühstückstablett • la bandeja del desayuno • il vassoio della colazione

maid service • le service de ménage • die Zimmerreinigung • el servicio de limpieza • il servizio di pulizia

laundry service • le service de blanchisserie • der Wäschedienst • el servicio de lavandería • il servizio di lavanderia

room service • le service d'étage • der Zimmerservice • el servicio de habitaciones • il servizio in camera

minibar • le minibar • die Minibar • el minibar • il minibar

restaurant • le restaurant • das Restaurant • el restaurante • il ristorante

gym • la salle de sport • der Fitnessraum • el gimnasio • la palestra

swimming pool • la piscine • das Schwimmbad • la piscina • la piscina

all meals included	Do you have any vacancies?	I'd like a room for three nights.
la pension complète	Avez-vous une chambre de libre?	Je voudrais une chambre pour trois nuits.
die Vollpension	Haben Sie ein Zimmer frei?	Ich möchte ein Zimmer für drei Nächte.
la pensión completa	¿Tiene alguna habitación libre?	Quiero una habitación para tres noches.
la pensione completa	Avete una camera libera?	Vorrei una camera per tre notti.
some meals included	I have a reservation.	What is the charge per night?
la demi-pension	J'ai une réservation.	C'est combien par nuit?
die Halbpension	Ich habe ein Zimmer reserviert.	Was kostet das Zimmer pro Nacht?
la media pensión	Tengo una reserva.	¿Cuánto cuesta la habitación por día?
la mezza pensione	Ho una prenotazione.	Quanto costa la camera a notte?
bed and breakfast	I'd like a single room.	When do I have to check out?
la chambre avec le petit déjeuner	Je voudrais une chambre simple.	Quand est-ce que je dois quitter la chambre?
die Übernachtung mit Frühstück	Ich möchte ein Einzelzimmer.	Wann muss ich das Zimmer räumen?
la habitación con desayuno incluido	Quiero una habitación individual.	¿Cuándo tengo que dejar la habitación?
la pensione con colazione	Vorrei una camera singola	Quando devo lasciare la stanza?

shopping
les courses
der Einkauf
las compras
gli acquisti

shopping center • le centre commercial • das Einkaufszentrum • el centro comercial • il centro commerciale

atrium
l'atrium
das Atrium
el atrio
l'atrio

sign
l'enseigne
das Schild
el letrero
l'insegna

elevator
l'ascenseur
der Fahrstuhl
el ascensor
l'ascensore

third floor
le deuxième étage
die zweite Etage
la segunda planta
il secondo piano

second floor
le premier étage
die erste Etage
la primera planta
il primo piano

escalator
l'escalier
    mécanique
die Rolltreppe
la escalera
    mecánica
la scala mobile

ground floor
le rez-de-chaussée
das Erdgeschoss
la planta baja
il piano terra

customer
le client
der Kunde
el cliente
il cliente

children's department le rayon enfants die Kinderabteilung la sección de niños il reparto bambini	customer services le service après-vente der Kundendienst el servicio al cliente l'assistenza ai clienti	fitting rooms les cabines d'essayage die Anprobe los probadores i camerini	How much is this? C'est combien? Was kostet das? ¿Cuánto cuesta esto? Quanto costa questo?
luggage department le rayon bagages die Gepäckabteilung la sección de equipajes il reparto bagagli	store directory le guide die Anzeigetafel el directorio la guida al negozio	baby changing room les soins de bébés der Wickelraum el cuarto para cambiar a los bebés il spazio con fasciatoio	May I exchange this? Est-ce que je peux changer ça? Kann ich das umtauschen? ¿Puedo cambiar esto? Posso cambiare questo?
shoe department le rayon chaussures die Schuhabteilung la sección de zapatería il reparto calzature	salesclerk le vendeur der Verkäufer el dependiente il commesso	restroom les toilettes die Toiletten los aseos le toilettes	

department store • le grand magasin • das Kaufhaus • los grandes almacenes • il grande magazzino

menswear • les vêtements pour hommes • die Herrenbekleidung • la ropa de caballero • l'abbigliamento da uomo

womenswear • les vêtements pour femmes • die Damenoberbekleidung • la ropa de señora • l'abbigliamento da donna

lingerie • la lingerie • die Damenwäsche • la lencería • la biancheria intima

perfumes • la parfumerie • die Parfümerie • la perfumería • la profumeria

cosmetics • la beauté • die Schönheitspflege • los productos de belleza • la comesi

linens • le linge de maison • die Haushaltswäsche • la ropa de hogar • la biancheria

home furnishings • l'ameublement • die Möbel • el mobiliario para el hogar • l'arredamento per la casa

notions • la mercerie • die Kurzwaren • la mercería • la merceria

kitchenware • la vaisselle • die Küchengeräte • el menaje de hogar • gli articoli da cucina

china • la porcelaine • das Porzellan • la porcelana • la porcellana

• electronics • l'électroménager • die Elektroartikel • los aparatos eléctronicos • gli articoli elettronici

lighting • l'éclairage • die Lampen • la iluminación • l'illuminazione

sportswear • les articles de sport • die Sportartikel • los artículos deportivos • gli articoli sportivi

toys • les jouets • die Spielwaren • la juguetería • i giocattoli

stationery • la papeterie • die Scheibwaren • la papelería • la cancelleria

groceries • l'alimentation • die Lebensmittelabteilung • el super-mercado • il reparto alimentari

supermarket • le supermarché • der Supermarkt • el supermercado • il supermercato

aisle • l'allée • der
Gang • el pasillo
• la corsia

shelf • l'étagère
• das Warenregal • el
estante • lo scaffale

conveyor belt
le tapis roulant
das Laufband
la cinta transportadora
il nastro convogliatore

checker
le caissier
der Kassierer
el cajero
il cassiere

specials
les promotions
die Angebote
las ofertas
le offerte

checkout • la caisse • die Kasse • la caja • la cassa

customer
le client
der Kunde
el cliente
il cliente

cash register
la caisse
die Kasse
la caja
la cassa

shopping bag
la sac à provisions
die Einkaufstasche
la bolsa de la compra
la busta della spesa

groceries
les provisions
die Lebensmittel
la compra
la spesa

handle
l'anse
der Henkel
el asa
il manico

bar code • le code barres
• der Strichcode • el código
de barras • il codice a barre

grocery cart • le caddie • der
Einkaufswagen • el carro • il carrello

basket • le panier • der
Einkaufskorb • la cesta • il cestino

scanner • le lecteur optique • der
Scanner • el escáner • il lettore ottico

bakery • la boulangerie
• die Backwaren
• la panadería
• la panetteria

dairy • la crémerie
• die Milchprodukte
• los lácteos
• i latticini

breakfast cereals
les céréales
die Getreideflocken
los cereales
i cereali da colazione

canned food
les conserves
die Konserven
las conservas
lo scatolame

candy • la confiserie
• die Süßwaren • los
golosinas • i dolci

vegetables • les
légumes • das Gemüse
• la verdura
• la verdura

fruit • les fruits
• das Obst • la fruta
• la frutta

meat and poultry • la
viande et la volaille
• das Fleisch und das
Geflügel • la carne y las
aves • la carne e il pollame

fish • le poisson
• der Fisch • el
pescado • il pesce

deli • la charcuterie
• die Feinkost
• los comestibles
finos • la salumeria

frozen food • les
produits surgelés
• die Tiefkühlkost
• los congelados
• i surgelati

prepared food
• les plats cuisinés
• die Fertiggerichte
• los platos preparados
• i precotti

drinks • les boissons
• die Getränke • las
bebidas • le bibite

household products
• les produits d'entretien
• die Haushaltswaren
• los productos de
limpieza • i casalinghi

toiletries • les articles
de toilette • die
Toilettenartikel • los
artículos de aseo
• gli articoli da toilette

baby products • les
articles pour bébés
• die Babyprodukte • los
artículos para el bebé
• i prodotti per bambini

electrical goods
l'électroménager
die Elektroartikel
los electrodomésticos
gli articoli elettrici

pet food • la nourriture
pour animaux • das
Tierfutter • la comida
para animales • il cibo
per animali

magazines • les magazines • die Zeitschriften
• las revistas • le riviste

drugstore • les plantes médicinales • die Apotheke • la farmacia • la farmacia

dental care
le soins dentaires
die Zahnpflege
el cuidado dental
i prodotti per i denti

feminine hygiene
l'hygiène féminine
die Monatshygiene
la higiene femenina
l'igiene femminile

deodorants
les déodorants
die Deos
los desodorantes
i deodoranti

vitamins
les vitamines
die Vitamintabletten
las vitaminas
le vitamine

pharmacy
l'officine
die Arzneiausgabe
el dispensario
il dispensario

pharmacist
le pharmacien
der Apotheker
el farmacéutico
il farmacista

cough medicine
le médicament pour la toux
das Hustenmedikament
el jarabe para la tos
la medicina per la tosse

herbal remedies
les plantes médicinales
das Kräuterheilmittel
los remedios de herbolario
i rimedi fitoterapici

skin care
les soins de la peau
die Hautpflege
el cuidado de la piel
i prodotti per la pelle

aftersun lotion
• l'après-soleil
• die After-Sun-
Lotion • la crema
para después del
sol• il doposole

sunscreen • l'écran solaire
• die Sonnenschutzcreme • la
crema protectora • la crema
schermo

sunblock • l'écran total
• der Sonnenblock • la
crema protectora total
• la crema schermo totale

insect repellent • le produit anti-
insecte • das Insektenschutzmittel
• el repelente de insectos
• l'insettifugo

wet wipe • la lingette humide
• das Reinigungstuch • la toallita
húmeda • la salviettina
umidificata

tissue • le kleenex • das
Papiertaschentuch • el pañuelo
de papel • il fazzolettino

sanitary napkin • la serviette
hygiénique • die Damenbinde
• la compresa • l'assorbente

tampon • le tampon
• der Tampon • el tampón
• il tampone

panty liner • le protège-slip
• die Slipeinlage • el salvaslip
• i salvaslip

measuring spoon
la cuiller pour mesurer
der Messlöffel
la cuchara medidora
il cucchiaio dosatore

instructions
le mode d'emploi
die Gebrauchsanweisung
el modo de empleo
le istruzioni

capsule • la gélule
• die Kapsel • la cápsula
• la capsula

pill • la pilule • die Tablette
• la pildora • la compressa

syrup • le sirop • der Saft
• el jarabe • lo sciroppo

inhaler • l'inhalateur
• der Inhalierstift • el inhalador
• l'inalatore

cream • la crème • die Creme
• la crema • la pomata

ointment • la pommade • die
Salbe • la pomada • l'unguento

gel • le gel • das Gel • el gel
• il gel

suppository • le suppositoire
• das Zäpfchen • el supositorio
• la supposta

dropper
le compte-gouttes
der Tropfer
el cuentagotas
il contagocce

needle
l'aiguille
die Nadel
la aguja
l'ago

drops • les gouttes • die
Tropfen • las gotas • le gocce

syringe • la seringue
• die Spritze • la jeringuilla
• la siringa

spray • le spray • das Spray
• el spray • lo spray

powder • la poudre
• der Puder • los polvos
• la polvere

iron le fer das Eisen el hierro il ferro	multivitamins le médicament multivitamine das Multivitaminmittel el complejo vitamínico la multivitamina	disposable jetable Wegwerf- desechable monouso	medicine le médicament das Medikament el medicamento la medicina	painkiller l'analgésique das Schmerzmittel el analgésico l'antidolorifico
calcium le calcium das Kalzium el calcio il calcio	side effects les effets secondaires die Nebenwirkungen los efectos secundarios gli effetti collaterali	soluble soluble löslich soluble solubile	laxative le laxatif das Abführmittel el laxante il lassativo	sedative le sédatif das Beruhigungsmittel el calmante il sedativo
magnesium le magnésium das Magnesium el magnesio il magnesio	expiration date la date d'expiration das Verfallsdatum la fecha de caducidad la data di scadenza	dosage la posologie die Dosierung la dosis il dosaggio	diarrhea la diarrhée der Durchfall la diarrea la diarrea	sleeping pill le somnifère die Schlaftablette el somnífero il sonnifero
insulin l'insuline das Insulin la insulina l'insulina	travel-sickness pills les cachets antinaupathiques die Reisekrankheitstabletten las píldoras para el mareo le pasticche antinausea	medication la médication die Verordnung la medicación il medicamento	throat lozenge la pastille pour la gorge die Halspastille la pastilla para la garganta la pasticca per la gola	anti-inflammatory l'anti-inflammatoire der Entzündungshemmer el antiinflamatorio l'antinfiammatorio

florist • le fleuriste • das Blumengeschäft • la floristería • il fioraio

flowers
les fleurs
die Blumen
las flores
i fiori

gladiolus
le glaïeul
die Gladiole
el gladiolo
il gladiolo

lily
le lis
die Lilie
la azucena
il giglio

iris
l'iris
die Iris
el iris
l'iris

acacia
l'acacia
die Akazie
la acacia
l'acacia

daisy
la marguerite
die Margerite
la margarita
la margherita

carnation
l'œillet
die Nelke
el clavel
il garofano

chrysanthemum
le chrysanthème
die Chrysantheme
el crisantemo
il crisantemo

potted plant
la plante en pot
die Topfpflanze
la maceta
la pianta da vaso

gypsophila
la gypsophile
das Schleierkraut
la gypsofila
la gipsofila

stocks • la giroflée
• die Levkoje • el alhelí
• la violacciocca

gerbera • le gerbera
• die Gerbera • la
gerbera • la gerbera

foliage • le feuillage
• die Blätter • el follaje
• il fogliame

rose • la rose • die
Rose • la rosa • la rosa

freesia • le freesia
• die Freesie • la fresia
• la fresia

english • français • deutsch • español • italiano

vase • le vase • die Blumenvase • el jarrón • il vaso

orchid • l'orchidée • die Orchidee • la orquídea • l'orchidea

peony • la pivoine • die Pfingstrose • la peonía • la peonia

arrangements • les compositions florales • die Blumenarrangements • los arreglos • gli arrangiamenti

ribbon
le ruban
das Band
la cinta
il nastro

bouquet • le bouquet • der Blumenstrauß • el ramo • il mazzo di fiori

dried flowers • les fleurs séchées • die Trockenblumen • las flores secas • i fiori secchi

bunch
la botte
der Strauß
el ramo
il mazzetto

stem
la tige
der Stängel
el tallo
lo stelo

potpourri • le pot-pourri • das Potpourri • el popurrí • il pot-pourri

wreath • la couronne • der Kranz • la corona • la corona

daffodil • la jonquille • die Osterglocke • el narciso • il narciso

bud
le bourgeon
die Knospe
el capullo
il bocciolo

garland • la guirlande de fleurs • die Blumengirlande • la guirnalda • la ghirlanda

wrapping
l'emballage
das Einwickelpapier
el envoltorio
l'incarto

Can I have a bunch of... please? Je voudrais un bouquet de..., SVP? Ich möchte einen Strauß..., bitte? ¿Me da un ramo de... por favor? Mi dà un mazzo di... per favore?	How long will these last? Elles tiennent combien de temps? Wie lange halten sie? ¿Cuánto tiempo durarán éstos? Quanto dureranno?
Can I have them wrapped? Pouvez-vous les emballer? Können Sie die Blumen bitte einwickeln? ¿Me los puede envolver? Me li può incartare?	Are they fragrant? Est-ce qu'elles sentent bon? Duften sie? ¿Huelen? Sono profumati?
Can I attach a message? Je peux y attacher un message? Kann ich eine Nachricht mitschicken? ¿Puedo adjuntar un mensaje? Posso allegare un messaggio?	Can you send them to...? Pouvez-vous les envoyer à...? Können Sie die Blumen an...schicken? ¿Los puede enviar a...? Li può mandare a...?

tulip • la tulipe • die Tulpe • el tulipán • il tulipano

newsstand • le marchand de journaux • der Zeitungshändler • el vendedor de periódicos • l'edicola

cigarettes
les cigarettes
die Zigaretten
los cigarrillos
le sigarette

pack of cigarettes
le paquet de cigarettes
das Päckchen Zigaretten
el paquete de tabaco
il pacchetto di sigarette

stamps
les timbres
die Briefmarken
los sellos
i francobolli

postcard • la carte postale
• die Postkarte • la tarjeta
postal • la cartolina

comic book • la bande dessinée
• das Comicheft • el tebeo
• il giornalino a fumetti

magazine • le magazine
• die Zeitschrift • la revista
• la rivista

newspaper • le journal
• die Zeitung • el periódico
• il giornale

---

smoking • fumer • das Rauchen • fumar • fumare

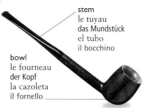

stem
le tuyau
das Mundstück
el tubo
il bocchino

bowl
le fourneau
der Kopf
la cazoleta
il fornello

tobacco • le tabac • der Tabak
• el tabaco • il tabacco

lighter • le briquet • das
Feuerzeug • el mechero
• l'accendino

pipe • la pipe • die Pfeife
• la pipa • la pipa

cigar • le cigare • die Zigarre
• el puro • il sigaro

candy store • le confiseur • der Süßwarenhändler • el vendedor de golosinas • il confettiere

box of chocolates
la boîte de chocolats
die Schachtel Pralinen
la caja de bombones
la scatola di cioccolatini

snack bar
la friandise
die Nascherei
la barrita
il dolciume

potato chips
les chips
die Chips
las patatas fritas
le patatine

milk chocolate
le chocolat au lait
die Milchschokolade
el chocolate con leche
il cioccolato al latte

caramel
le caramel
der Karamell
el caramelo
il caramello

dark chocolate
le chocolat noir
die Zartbitterschokolade
el chocolate negro
il cioccolato fondente

truffle
la truffe
der Trüffel
la trufa
il tartufo

white chocolate
le chocolat blanc
die weiße Schokolade
el chocolate blanco
il cioccolato bianco

cookie
le biscuit
der Keks
la galleta
il biscotto

pick and mix
les bonbons assortis
die bunte Mischung
las golosinas a granel
la caramelle assortite

candy store • la confiserie • das Süßwarengeschäft • la tienda de golosinas
• il negozio di dolciumi

---

confectionery • la confiserie • die Süßwaren • las golosinas • i dolciumi

chocolate • le chocolat
• die Praline • el bombón
• il cioccolatino

chocolate bar • la tablette de
chocolat • die Tafel Schokolade
• la tableta de chocolate
• la tavoletta di cioccolata

hard candy • les bonbons
• die Bonbons • los caramelos
• le caramelle

lollipop • la sucette
• der Lutscher • la piruleta
• il lecca lecca

toffee • le caramel • das Toffee
• el toffee • la caramella mou

nougat • le nougat • der
Nugat • el turrón • il torrone

marshmallow • la guimauve
• das Marshmallow • la nube
• la caramella gommosa

mint • le bonbon à la menthe
• das Pfefferminz • la pastilla
de menta • la mentina

chewing gum • le chewing-
gum • der Kaugummi
• el chicle • la gomma
da masticare

jellybean • la dragée à la
gelée • der Geleebonbon
• el caramelo blando
• la caramella di gelatina

gumdrop • le bonbon au
fruit • der Fruchtgummi
• la gominola • la caramella
alla frutta

licorice • le réglisse
• die Lakritze • el regaliz
• la liquirizia

other stores • les autres magasins • andere Geschäfte • las otras tiendas • gli altri negozi

bakery • la boulangerie
• die Bäckerei • la panadería
• il panificio

pastry shop • la pâtisserie
• die Konditorei • la confitería
• la pasticceria

butcher shop • la boucherie
• die Metzgerei • la carnicería
• la macelleria

fish counter • la poissonnerie
• die Fischgeschäft • la
pescadería • la pescheria

produce stand • le marchand
de légumes • der Gemüseladen
• la verdulería
• il fruttivendolo

grocery store • l'épicerie
• das Lebensmittelgeschäft
• la tienda de comestibles
• il negozio di alimentari

shoe store • le magasin de
chaussures • das Schuhgeschäft
• la zapatería • il negozio
di calzature

hardware store • la
quincaillerie • die Eisenwaren-
handlung • la ferretería
• il negozio di ferramenta

antique store • le magasin
d'antiquités • der
Antiquitätenladen • la tienda
de antigüedades • il negozio
di antiquariato

gift shop • la boutique de
cadeaux • der Geschenkartikelladen • la tienda de artículos
de regalo • il negozio di
articoli da regalo

travel agency • l'agence de
voyage • das Reisebüro
• la agencia de viajes
• l'agenzia di viaggi

jewelry store • la bijouterie
• das Juweliergeschäft • la
joyería • la gioielleria

bookstore • la librairie • der Buchladen • la librería • la libreria

record store • le magasin de disques • das Musikgeschäft • la tienda de discos • il negozio di dischi

liquor store • le magasin de vins et spiritueux • die Weinhandlung • la tienda de licores • l'enoteca

pet store • l'animalerie • die Tierhandlung • la pajarería • il negozio di animali

furniture store • le magasin de meubles • das Möbelgeschäft • la tienda de muebles • il negozio di mobili

boutique • la boutique • die Boutique • la boutique • la boutique

real estate office l'agent immobilier der Immobilienmakler la agencia inmobiliaria l'agenzia immobiliare	camera store le magasin d'appareils photos das Fotogeschäft la tienda de fotografía il negozio di articoli fotografici
garden centre la pépinière das Gartencenter el vivero il centro di giardinaggio	secondhand store le marchand d'occasion der Gebrauchtwarenhändler la tienda de artículos usados il negozio dell'usato
dry cleaner le pressing die Reinigung la tintorería il lavasecco	health food store le magasin de produits diététiques das Reformhaus la herboristería il negozio prodotti dietetici naturali
laundromat la laverie automatique der Waschsalon la lavandería la lavanderia	art supply store la boutique d'art die Kunsthandlung la tienda de arte il negozio di articoli per l'arte

tailor shop • le tailleur • die Schneiderei • la sastrería • la sartoria

salon • le salon de coiffure • der Frisiersalon • la peluquería • il parrucchiere

market • le marché • der Markt • el mercado • il mercato

food
la nourriture
die Nahrungsmittel
los alimentos
il cibo

meat • la viande • das Fleisch • la carne • la carne

lamb
l'agneau
das Lamm
el cordero
l'agnello

butcher
le boucher
der Metzger
el carnicero
il macellaio

meat hook
l'allonge
der Fleischerhaken
el gancho
il gancio

scale
la balance
die Waage
el peso
la bilancia

knife sharpener
le fusil
der Messerschärfer
el afilador
l'affilacoltelli

bacon • le bacon • der Speck • el bacon • la pancetta

sausages • les saucisses • die Würstchen • las salchichas • le salsicce

liver • le foie • die Leber • el hígado • il fegato

pork	venison	variety meat	free range	red meat
le porc	la venaison	les abats	de ferme	la viande rouge
das Schweinefleisch	das Wild	die Innereien	aus Freilandhaltung	das rote Fleisch
el cerdo	el venado	las asaduras	de granja	la carne roja
il maiale	il cervo	le frattaglie	ruspante	la carne rossa
beef	rabbit	cured	organic	lean meat
le bœuf	le lapin	salé	naturel	la viande maigre
das Rindfleisch	das Kaninchen	gepökelt	biologisch kontrolliert	das magere Fleisch
la vaca	el conejo	curado	biológico	la carne magra
il manzo	il coniglio	salmistrato	biologico	la carne magra
veal	tongue	smoked	white meat	cooked meat
le veau	la langue de bœuf	fumé	la viande blanche	la viande cuite
das Kalbfleisch	die Zunge	geräuchert	das weiße Fleisch	der Aufschnitt
la ternera	la lengua	ahumado	la carne blanca	el fiambre
il vitello	la lingua	affumicato	la carne bianca	la carne cotta

cuts • les morceaux de viande • die Fleischsorten • los cortes • i tagli

ham
le jambon
der Schinken
el jamón
il prosciutto

rind
la couenne
die Schwarte
la corteza
la cotenna

slice • la tranche • die Scheibe • la loncha • la fetta

bacon strip • la tranche de lard • die Speckscheibe • la loncha • la fetta

ground meat • la viande hachée • das Hackfleisch • la carne picada • la carne macinata

fillet • le filet • das Filet • el solomillo • il filetto

rump steak • le rumsteck • das Rumpsteak • el filete de cadera • la costata di manzo

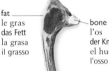

fat
le gras
das Fett
la grasa
il grasso

bone
l'os
der Knochen
el hueso
l'osso

kidney
le rognon
die Niere
el riñón
il rognone

heart • le cœur • das Herz • el corazón • il cuore

sirloin steak • le bifteck d'aloyau • das Lendensteak • el filete de lomo • la lombatina

rib • la côte de bœuf • das Rippenstück • la costilla • la costata

chop • la côtelette • das Kotelett • la chuleta • la costoletta

joint • le gigot • die Keule • el asado • il cosciotto

poultry • la volaille • das Geflügel • las aves • il pollo

skin
la peau
die Haut
la piel
la pelle

breast
le blanc
die Brust
la pechuga
il petto

game
le gibier
das Wildbret
la carne de caza
la cacciagione

leg
la cuisse
das Bein
la pata
la zampa

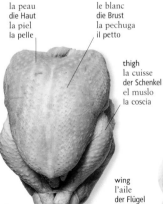

thigh
la cuisse
der Schenkel
el muslo
la coscia

dressed chicken
le poulet préparé
das bratfertige Huhn
el pollo preparado
il pollo preparato

pheasant • le faisan • der Fasan • el faisán • il fagiano

quail • la caille • die Wachtel • la codorniz • la quaglia

wing
l'aile
der Flügel
el ala
l'ala

turkey • la dinde • die Pute • el pavo • il tacchino

chicken • le poulet • das Hähnchen • el pollo • il pollo

duck • le canard • die Ente • el pato • l'anatra

goose • l'oie • die Gans • la oca • l'oca

fish • le poisson • der Fisch • el pescado • il pesce

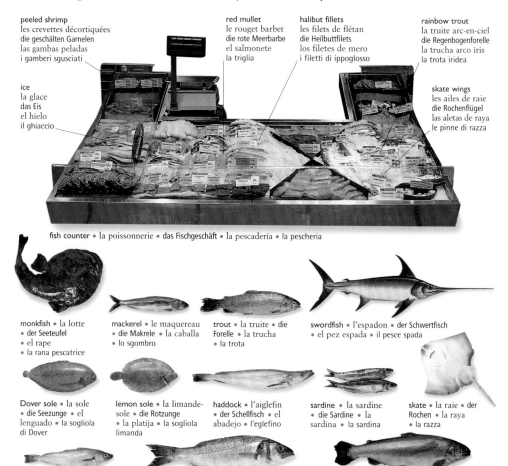

peeled shrimp
les crevettes décortiquées
die geschälten Garnelen
las gambas peladas
i gamberi sgusciati

ice
la glace
das Eis
el hielo
il ghiaccio

red mullet
le rouget barbet
die rote Meerbarbe
el salmonete
la triglia

halibut fillets
les filets de flétan
die Heilbuttfilets
los filetes de mero
i filetti di ippoglosso

rainbow trout
la truite arc-en-ciel
die Regenbogenforelle
la trucha arco iris
la trota iridea

skate wings
les ailes de raie
die Rochenflügel
las aletas de raya
le pinne di razza

fish counter • la poissonnerie • das Fischgeschäft • la pescadería • la pescheria

monkfish • la lotte
• der Seeteufel
• el rape
• la rana pescatrice

mackerel • le maquereau
• die Makrele • la caballa
• lo sgombro

trout • la truite • die
Forelle • la trucha
• la trota

swordfish • l'espadon • der Schwertfisch
• el pez espada • il pesce spada

Dover sole • la sole
• die Seezunge • el
lenguado • la sogliola
di Dover

lemon sole • la limande-
sole • die Rotzunge
• la platija • la sogliola
limanda

haddock • l'aiglefin
• der Schellfisch • el
abadejo • l'eglefino

sardine • la sardine
• die Sardine • la
sardina • la sardina

skate • la raie • der
Rochen • la raya
• la razza

whiting • le merlan
• der Merlan • la pescadilla
• il merlano

sea bass • le bar • der Seebarsch
• la lubina • la spigola

salmon • le saumon • der Lachs • el salmón
• il salmone

cod • la morue • der Kabeljau • el bacalao
• il merluzzo

sea bream • la daurade
• die Goldbrasse • el
besugo • l'orata

tuna • le thon • der Tunfisch • el atún • il tonno

seafood • les fruits de mer • die Meeresfrüchte • el marisco • i frutti di mare

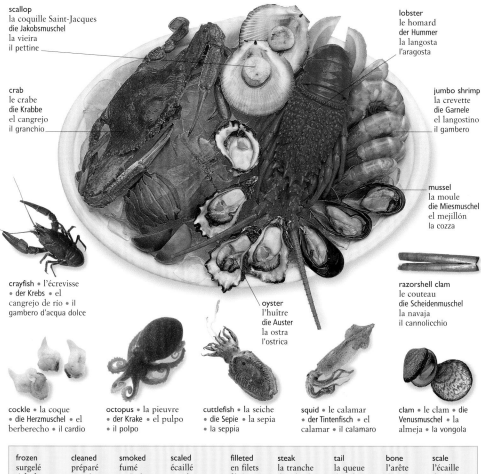

scallop
la coquille Saint-Jacques
die Jakobsmuschel
la vieira
il pettine

crab
le crabe
die Krabbe
el cangrejo
il granchio

lobster
le homard
der Hummer
la langosta
l'aragosta

jumbo shrimp
la crevette
die Garnele
el langostino
il gambero

mussel
la moule
die Miesmuschel
el mejillón
la cozza

crayfish • l'écrevisse
• der Krebs • el
cangrejo de río • il
gambero d'acqua dolce

razorshell clam
le couteau
die Scheidenmuschel
la navaja
il cannolicchio

oyster
l'huître
die Auster
la ostra
l'ostrica

cockle • la coque
• die Herzmuschel • el
berberecho • il cardio

octopus • la pieuvre
• der Krake • el pulpo
• il polpo

cuttlefish • la seiche
• die Sepie • la sepia
• la seppia

squid • le calamar
• der Tintenfisch • el
calamar • il calamaro

clam • le clam • die
Venusmuschel • la
almeja • la vongola

frozen	cleaned	smoked	scaled	filleted	steak	tail	bone	scale
surgelé	préparé	fumé	écaillé	en filets	la tranche	la queue	l'arête	l'écaille
tiefgefroren	gesaubert	geräuchert	entschuppt	filetiert	die Schneibe	der Schwanz	die Gräte	die Schuppe
congelado	limpio	ahumado	sin escamas	en filetes	la rodaja	la cola	la espina	la escama
congelato	pulito	affumicato	desquamato	a filetti	la trancia	la coda	la spina	la squama

fresh	salted	skinned	boned	fillet	loin	Will you clean it for me?
frais	salé	sans peau	sans arêtes	le filet	la longe	Pouvez-vous le préparer pour moi?
frisch	gesalzen	enthäutet	entgrätet	das Filet	das Loin	Können Sie ihn mir säubern?
fresco	salado	sin piel	sin espinas	el filete	el lomo	¿Me lo puede limpiar?
fresco	salato	spellato	spinato	il filetto	il lombo	Me lo pulisce?

vegetables 1 • les légumes 1 • das Gemüse 1 • las verduras 1 • la verdura 1

seed
la graine
der Samen
la semilla
il seme

fava bean • la fève
• die dicke Bohne
• la haba • la fava

runner bean
le haricot grimpant
die Stangenbohne
la judía verde
il fagiolino

green bean • le
haricot vert • die
grüne Bohne • la judía
verde • il fagiolino

pea • le petit pois • die
grüne Erbse • el guisante
• il pisello

pod
la gousse
die Schote
la vaina
il baccello

bean sprout • le
germe de soja • die
Sojabohnensprosse
• los brotes de soja
• il germoglio di soia

bamboo • le bambou
• der Bambus • el
bambú • il bambù

okra • l'okra • die
Okra • el quingombó
• l'okra

corn • le maïs
• der Mais • el maíz
dulce • il granturco

chicory • l'endive
• der Chicorée • la
endibia • la cicoria

fennel • le fenouil
• der Fenchel • el
hinojo • il finocchio

palm hearts • les cœurs
de palmier • die
Palmherzen • los palmitos
• i cuori di palma

celery • le céleri
• der Stangensellerie
• el apio • il sedano

leaf	floret	tip	organic	Do you sell organic vegetables?
la feuille	la fleurette	la pointe	biologique	Est-ce que vous vendez des légumes bios?
das Blatt	das Röschen	die Spitze	biologisch	Verkaufen Sie Biogemüse?
la hoja	la cabezuela	la punta	biológico	¿Vende verduras biológicas?
la foglia	il germoglio	la punta	biologico	Vendete verdure biologiche?
stalk	kernel	heart	plastic bag	Are these grown locally?
le trognon	le grain	le cœur	le sac en plastique	Est-ce qu'ils sont cultivés dans la région?
der Strunk	der Kern	das Herz	die Plastiktüte	Werden sie in dieser Gegend angebaut?
el tallo	la almendra	el centro	la bolsa de plástico	¿Son productos locales?
lo stelo	il nocciolo	il cuore	la busta di plastica	Queste sono della zona?

arugula • la roquette
• der Rucola • la rúcula
• la rucola

watercress • le cresson
• die Brunnenkresse
• el berro • il crescione

radicchio • le radicchio
• der Radicchio • el radicchio
• il radicchio

Brussels sprout • le chou
de Bruxelles • der Rosenkohl
• la col de bruselas
• il cavolino di Bruxelles

Swiss chard • la bette
• der Mangold • la acelga
• la bietola

kale • le chou frisé
• der Grünkohl • la col rizada
• il cavolo riccio

sorrel • l'oseille • der Garten-
Sauerampfer • la acedera
• l'acetosa

endive • la chicorée
• die Endivie • la escarola
• l'indivia

dandelion • le pissenlit
• der Löwenzahn • el diente
de León • il dente di leone

spinach • les épinards
• der Spinat • la espinaca
• gli spinaci

kohlrabi • le chou-rave
• der Kohlrabi • el colinabo
• il cavolo rapa

bok choy • le chou chinois
• der Pak-Choi • la acelga
china • la bieta

lettuce • la laitue • der Salat
• la lechuga • la lattuga

broccoli • le brocoli
• der Brokkoli • el brócoli
• il broccolo

cabbage • le chou • der Kohl
• la col de Milán• il cavolo

spring greens • le chou précoce
• der Frühkohl • la berza
• il cavolo primaticcio

vegetables 2 • les légumes 2 • das Gemüse 2 • las verduras 2 • la verdura 2

turnip
le navet
die Rübe
el nabo
la rapa

artichoke
l'artichaut
die Artischocke
la alcachofa
il carciofo

radish
le radis
das Radieschen
el rábano
il ravanello

cauliflower
le chou-fleur
der Blumenkohl
la coliflor
il cavolfiore

asparagus
l'asperge
der Spargel
el espárrago
l'asparago

potato
• la pomme
de terre
• die Kartoffel
• la patata
• la patata

onion
l'oignon
die Zwiebel
la cebolla
la cipolla

pepper
le poivron
die Paprika
el pimiento
il peperone

chilli pepper • le piment • die Peperoni • la guindilla • il peperoncino

sweetcorn
le maïs
der Mais
el maíz dulce
il mais

squash
la courge
der Gartenkürbis
el calabacín gigante
la zucca

---

cherry tomato
la tomate cerise
die Kirschtomate
el tomate cherry
il pomodoro ciliegino

carrot
la carotte
die Karotte
la zanahoria
la carota

breadfruit
le fruit de l'arbre à pain
die Brotfrucht
el fruto del pan
il frutto dell'albero del pane

new potato
la pomme de terre nouvelle
die neue Kartoffel
la patata nueva
la patata novella

celeriac
le céleri
der Sellerie
el apio-nabo
il sedano rapa

taro root
le taro
die Tarowurzel
la raíz del taro
la radice di taro

water chestnut
la châtaigne d'eau
die Wasserkastanie
la castaña de agua
la castagna d'acqua

cassava
le manioc
der Maniok
la mandioca
la cassava

frozen
surgelé
tiefgefroren
congelado
congelato

raw
cru
roh
crudo
crudo

hot (spicy)
épicé
scharf
picante
piccante

sweet
sucré
süß
dulce
dolce

bitter
amer
bitter
amargo
amaro

firm
ferme
fest
firme
sodo

flesh
la pulpe
das Fleisch
la pulpa
la polpa

root
la racine
die Wurzel
la raíz
la radice

May I have one kilo of potatoes, please?
Puis-je avoir un kilo de pommes de terre s'il vous plaît?
Könnte ich bitte ein Kilo Kartoffeln haben?
¿Me da un kilo de patatas, por favor?
Mi dà un chilo di patate per favore?

What's the price per kilo?
C'est combien le kilo?
Was kostet ein Kilo?
¿Cuánto vale el kilo?
Quanto costa al chilo?

What are those called?
Ils s'appellent comment?
Wie heißen diese?
¿Cómo se llaman ésos?
Quelli come si chiamano?

sweet potato
la patate douce
die Süßkartoffel
el boniato
la patata dolce

yam • l'igname • die Jamswurzel • el ñame • l'igname

beet • la betterave • die Rote Bete • la remolacha • la barbabietola

rutabaga • le rutabaga • die Kohlrübe • el nabo sueco • la rapa svedese

Jerusalem artichoke
le topinambour
der Topinambur
el topinambur
il topinambur

horseradish • le raifort • der Meerrettich • el rábano picante • il rafano

parsnip • le panais • die Pastinake • la chirivía • la pastinaca

ginger • le gingembre • der Ingwer • el jengibre • lo zenzero

eggplant • l'aubergine • die Aubergine • la berenjena • la melanzana

tomato • la tomate • die Tomate • el tomate • il pomodoro

clove
la gousse
die Zehe
el diente
lo spicchio

scallion • la ciboule • die Frühlingszwiebel • la cebolleta • la cipollina

leek • le poireau • der Lauch • el puerro • il porro

shallot • l'échalote • die Schalotte • el chalote • lo scalogno

garlic • l'ail • der Knoblauch • el ajo • l'aglio

truffle
la truffe
die Trüffel
la trufa
il tartufo

mushroom • le champignon • der Pilz • la seta • il fungo

cucumber
• le concombre
• die Gurke • el pepino • il cetriolo

zucchini • la courgette • die Zucchini • el calabacín • la zucchina

butternut squash
la courge musquée
der Butternusskürbis
la calabaza
la zucca Butternut

acorn squash • la courge gland • der Eichelkürbis • la calabaza bellota • la zucca a ghianda

pumpkin • la citrouille • der Kürbis • la calabaza • la zucca

fruit I • le fruit 1 • das Obst 1 • la fruta 1 • la frutta 1

citrus fruit • les agrumes • die Zitrusfrüchte
• los cítricos • gli agrumi

stone fruit • les fruits à noyau • das Steinobst
• la fruta con hueso • la frutta col nocciolo

orange • l'orange
• die Orange • la naranja
• l'arancia

clementine • la clémentine
• die Klementine • la mandarina
clementina • la clementina

pith
• la peau
blanche
• die weiße
Haut • la
médula
• la scorza
interna

ugli fruit • le tangelo • die
Tangelo • el ugli • il mapo

grapefruit • le pamplemousse
• die Grapefruit • el pomelo
• il pompelmo

tangerine • la mandarine
• die Mandarine • la mandarina
• il mandarino

segment
le quartier
der Schnitz
el gajo
lo spicchio

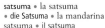

satsuma • la satsuma
• die Satsuma • la mandarina
satsuma • il satsuma

zest
le zeste
die Schale
la cáscara
la scorza

lime • le citron vert
• die Limone • la lima
• la limetta

lemon • le citron • die Zitrone
• el limón • il limone

kumquat • le kumquat
• die Kumquat • el kumquat
• l'arancino cinese

peach • la pêche • der Pfirsich
• el melocotón • la pesca

nectarine • la nectarine
• die Nektarine • la nectarina
• la pesca noce

apricot • l'abricot
• die Aprikose
• el albaricoque
• l'albicocca

plum • la prune
• die Pflaume
• la ciruela
• la prugna

cherry • la cerise
• die Kirsche • la
cereza • la ciliegia

pear • la poire • die Birne
• la pera • la pera

apple • la pomme • der Apfel
• la manzana • la mela

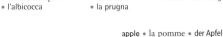

basket of fruit • la corbeille de fruits • der Obstkorb
• la cesta de fruta • il cestino di frutta

berries and melons • les fruits rouges et les melons • das Beerenobst und die Melonen • las bayas y los melones • i frutti di bosco e i meloni

strawberry • la fraise
• die Erdbeere • la fresa
• la fragola

raspberry • la framboise
• die Himbeere • la frambuesa
• il lampone

melon • le melon
• die Melone • el melón
• il melone

grapes • les raisins
• die Weintrauben • la uva
• l'uva

blackberry • la mûre
• die Brombeere • la mora
• la mora

red currant • la groseille
• die Johannisbeere • la
grosella • il ribes rosso

cranberry • la canneberge
• die Preiselbeere
• el arándano rojo
• il mirtillo rosso

black currant • le cassis
• die schwarze Johannisbeere
• la grosella negra
• il ribes nero

blueberry • la myrtille
• die Heidelbeere
• el arándano • il mirtillo

white currant • la groseille
blanche • die weiße
Johannisbeere • la grosella
blanca • il ribes bianco

rind
l'écorce
die Schale
la corteza
la buccia

seed
le pépin
der Kern
la pepita
il seme

flesh
la pulpe
das Fruchtfleisch
la pulpa
la polpa

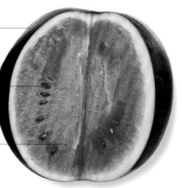

watermelon • la pastèque • die Wassermelone
• la sandía • l'anguria

loganberry • la loganberry
• die Loganbeere • la frambuesa
Logan • la mora-lampone

gooseberry • la groseille à
maquereau • die Stachelbeere
• la grosella espinosa
• l'uva spina

rhubarb	sour	crisp	seedless	Are they ripe?
la rhubarbe	aigre	croquant	sans pépins	Est-ce qu'ils sont mûrs?
der Rhabarber	sauer	knackig	kernlos	Sind sie reif?
el ruibarbo	amargo	fresco	sin pepitas	¿Están maduros?
il rabarbaro	agro	croccante	senza semi	Sono maturi?
fiber	fresh	rotten	juice	Can I try one?
le fibre	frais	pourri	le jus	Je peux goûter?
die Faser	frisch	faul	der Saft	Könnte ich eine probieren?
la fibra	fresco	podrido	el zumo	¿Puedo probar uno?
la fibra	fresco	marcio	il succo	Posso assaggiarne uno?
sweet	juicy	pulp	core	How long will they keep?
sucré	juteux	la pulpe	le trognon	Ils se gardent combien de temps?
süß	saftig	das Fruchtmark	das Kerngehäuse	Wie lange halten sie sich?
dulce	jugoso	la pulpa	el corazón	¿Hasta cuándo durarán?
dolce	sugoso	la polpa	il torsolo	Per quanto tempo si mantengono?

fruit 2 • les fruits 2 • das Obst 2 • la fruta 2 • la frutta 2

mango
la mangue
die Mango
el mango
il mango

pineapple
l'ananas
die Ananas
la piña
l'ananas

avocado
l'avocat
die Avocado
el aguacate
l'avocado

papaya
la papaye
die Papaya
la papaya
la papaia

peach
la pêche
der Pfirsich
el melocotón
la pesca

lychee
le litchi
die Litschi
el lichi
il litchi

seed
le pépin
der Kern
la semilla
il seme

kiwifruit
le kiwi
die Kiwi
el kiwi
il kiwi

Cape gooseberry
le physalis
die Kapstachelbeere
el alquequenje
l'alchechengi

peel
la peau
die Schale
la piel
la buccia

quince • le coing • die Quitte • el membrillo • la mela cotogna

passion fruit • le fruit de la passion • die Passionsfrucht • el maracuyá • il frutto della passione

banana • la banane • die Banane • el plátano • la banana

guava • la goyave • die Guave • la guayaba • la guaiava

pomegranate • la grenade • der Granatapfel • la granada • la melagrana

persimmon • le kaki • die Kaki • el caqui • il cachi

feijoa • le feijoa • die Feijoa • la feijoa • il feijoa

prickly pear • la figue de Barbarie • die Kaktusfeige • el higo chumbo • il fico d'india

starfruit • la carambole • die Sternfrucht • la carambola • la carambola

tamarillo • le tamarillo • die Tamarillo • el tamarillo • il tamarillo

nuts and dried fruit • les noix et les fruits secs • die Nüsse und das Dörrobst • los frutos secos • le noci e la frutta secca

pine nut • le pignon • die Piniennuss • el piñón • il pinolo

pistachio • la pistache • die Pistazie • el pistacho • il pistacchio

cashew • la noix de cajou • die Cashewnuss • el anacardo • l'anacardio

peanut • la cacahouète • die Erdnuss • el cacahuete • l'arachide

hazelnut • la noisette • die Haselnuss • la avellana • la nocciola

brazil nut • la noix du Brésil • die Paranuss • la nuez de Brasil • la mandorla brasiliana

pecan • la noix pacane • die Pecannuss • la pacana • la noce di pecan

almond • l'amande • die Mandel • la almendra • la mandorla

walnut • la noix • die Walnuss • la nuez • la noce

chestnut • le marron • die Esskastanie • la castaña • la castagna

macadamia le macadamia die Macadamianuss la macadamia la noce di macadamia

fig • la figue • die Feige • el higo • il fico

date • la datte • die Dattel • el dátil • il dattero

prune • le pruneau • die Backpflaume • la ciruela pasa • la prugna secca

shell
la coquille
die Schale
la cáscara
il guscio

sultana • le raisin de Smyrne • die Sultanine • la pasa sultana • l'uva sultanina

raisin • le raisin sec • die Rosine • la pasa • l'uvetta

currant • le raisin de Corinthe • die Korinthe • la pasa de Corinto • l'uva passa

flesh
la chair
das Fruchtfleisch
la pulpa
la polpa

coconut • la noix de coco • die Kokosnuss • el coco • la noce di cocco

green	hard	kernel	salted	roasted	tropical fruit	shelled
vert	dur	l'amande	salé	grillé	les fruits tropicaux	décortiqué
grün	hart	der Kern	gesalzen	geröstet	die Südfrüchte	geschält
verde	duro	la almendra	salado	tostado	las frutas tropicales	pelado
verde	duro	il nocciolo	salato	arrostito	la frutta tropicale	sgusciato
ripe	soft	dessicated	raw	seasonal	candied fruit	whole
mûr	mou	séché	cru	de saison	le fruit confit	complet
reif	weich	getrocknet	roh	saisonal	die kandierten Früchte	ganz
maduro	blando	desecado	crudo	de temporada	la fruta escarchada	entero
maturo	morbido	essiccato	crudo	stagionale	la frutta candita	intero

grains and legumes • les céréales et les légumes secs • die Getreidearten und die Hülsenfrüchte • los granos y las legumbres • le granaglie e i legumi secchi

grains • les céréales • das Getreide • los granos • le granaglie

wheat • le blé
• der Weizen • el
trigo • il grano

oats • l'avoine
• der Hafer • la avena
• l'avena

barley • l'orge
• die Gerste • la
cebada • l'orzo

millet • le millet
• die Hirse • el mijo
• il miglio

corn • le maïs
• der Mais • el maíz
• il mais

quinoa • le quinoa
• die Reismelde • la
quinoa • la quinoa

seed	fresh	quick cooking
la graine	frais	facile à cuisiner
der Samen	frisch	leicht zu kochen
la semilla	fresco	de fácil cocción
il seme	fresco	cottura facile
husk	fragranced	whole-grain
la balle	parfumé	complet
die Hülse	aromatisch	Vollkorn
la cáscara	perfumado	integral
la pula	profumato	integrale
kernel	cereal	long-grain
le grain	la céréale	à grains longs
der Kern	die Getreideflocken	Langkorn
el grano	los cereales	largo
il seme	il cereale	a chicco lungo
dry	soak (v)	short-grain
sec	laisser tremper	à grains ronds
trocken	einweichen	Rundkorn
seco	poner a remojo	corto
secco	mettere a bagno	a chicco corto

rice • le riz • der Reis • el arroz • il riso

white rice • le riz blanc
• der weiße Reis • el arroz
largo • il riso bianco

brown rice • le riz complet
• der Naturreis • el arroz
integral • il riso integrale

wild rice • le riz sauvage
• der Wildreis • el arroz
salvaje • il riso selvatico

arborio rice • le riz rond
• der Milchreis • el arroz
bomba • il riso da budino

processed grains • les céréales traitées • die verarbeiteten Getreidearten • los granos procesados • i cereali trattati

couscous • le couscous
• der Kuskus • el cuscús
• il cuscus

cracked wheat • le blé écrasé
• der Weizenschrot • el trigo
partido • il grano spezzato

semolina • la semoule
• der Grieß • la sémola
• la semola

bran • le son • die Kleie
• el salvado • la crusca

legumes • les légumineuses • die Hülsenfrüchte • las legumbres • i legumi

butter beans • les haricots blancs • die Mondbohnen • la alubia blanca • i fagioli bianchi

haricot beans • les haricots blancs • die weißen Bohnen • la alubia blanca pequeña • i fagioli cannellini

red kidney beans • les haricots rouges • die roten Bohnen • la alubia roja • i fagioli di Spagna

adzuki beans • les adzukis • die Adzuki bohnen • la alubia morada • i fagioli aduki

fava beans • les fèves • die Saubohnen • las habas • le fave

soybeans • les graines de soja • die Sojabohnen • la semilla de soja • i semi di soia

black-eyed peas • les haricots à œil noir • die Augenbohnen • la alubia de ojo negro • i fagioli dall'occhio nero

pinto beans • les haricots pinto • die Pintobohnen • la alubia pinta • i fagioli borlotti

mung beans • les haricots mung • die Mungbohnen • la alubia mung • i fagioli mung

flageolet beans • les flageolets • die französischen Bohnen • la alubia flageolet • i fagioli nani

brown lentils • les lentilles • die braunen Linsen • la lenteja castellana • le lenticchie marroni

red lentils • les lentilles rouges • die roten Linsen • la lenteja roja • le lenticchie rosse

green peas • les petits pois • die grünen Erbsen • los guisantes tiernos • i piselli

chickpeas • les pois chiches • die Kichererbsen • los garbanzos • i ceci

split peas • les pois cassés • die getrockneten Erbsen • los guisantes secos • i piselli spaccati

seeds • les graines • die Körner • las semillas • i semi

pumpkin seed • la graine de potiron • der Kürbiskern • la pipa de calabaza • il seme di zucca

mustard seed • le grain de moutarde • das Senfkorn • la mostaza en grano • il seme di mostarda

caraway • la graine de carvi • der Kümmel • el carvi • il seme di carvi

sesame seed • la graine de sésame • das Sesamkorn • la semilla de sésamo • il seme di sesamo

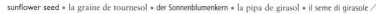

sunflower seed • la graine de tournesol • der Sonnenblumenkern • la pipa de girasol • il seme di girasole

herbs and spices • les herbes et les épices • die Kräuter und Gewürze • las hierbas y las especias • le erbe aromatiche e le spezie

spices • les épices • die Gewürze • las especias • le spezie

vanilla • la vanille
• die Vanille • la
vainilla • la vaniglia

nutmeg • la noix
de muscade • die
Muskatnuss • la nuez
moscada • la noce
moscata

mace • le macis • die
Muskatblüte • la macis
• il macis

turmeric • le curcuma
• die Gelbwurz • la
cúrcuma • la curcuma

cumin • le cumin
• der Kreuzkümmel • el
comino • il cumino

bouquet garni
• le bouquet garni
• die Kräutermischung
• el ramillete
aromático • il
mazzetto odoroso

allspice • le poivre
de la Jamaïque • der
Piment • la pimienta
de Jamaica • il pepe
della Giamaica

peppercorn • le grain
de poivre • das Pfeffer-
korn • la pimienta en
grano • il grano di pepe

fenugreek • le fenugrec
• der Bockshornklee
• el heno griego
• il fieno greco

chili powder • le
piment • der Chili
• la guindilla • il
peperoncino rosso

whole
en morceaux
ganz
entero
intero

crushed
écrasé
zerstoßen
machacado
tritato

saffron • le safran
• der Safran • el
azafrán • lo zafferano

cardamom
• la cardamome
• der Kardamom
• el cardamomo
• il cardamomo

curry powder • la
poudre de curry • das
Currypulver • el curry
en polvo • la polvere
di curry

ground
moulu
gemahlen
molido
macinato

paprika • le paprika
• der Paprika • el
pimentón • la paprica

flakes
en flocons
geraspelt
laminado
grattugiato

garlic • l'ail • der
Knoblauch • el ajo
• l'aglio

herbs • les herbes • die Kräuter • las hierbas • le erbe aromatiche

sticks
les bâtons
die Stangen
las ramas
i bastoncini

cinnamon • la cannelle
• der Zimt • la canela
• la cannella

lemon grass
• la citronnelle
• das Zitronengras • la
citronela • la citronella

cloves • le clou
de girofle • die
Gewürznelke • los clavos
• i chiodi di garofano

star anise • l'anis
étoilé • der Sternanis
• el anís estrellado
• l'anice stellato

ginger • le gingembre
• der Ingwer • el
jengibre • lo zenzero

fennel • le fenouil • der
Fenchel • el hinojo
• il finocchio

chives • la ciboulette
• der Schnittlauch • el
cebollino • l'erba cipollina

tarragon • l'estragon
• der Estragon • el
estragón • il
dragoncello

oregano • l'origan
• der Oregano • el
orégano • l'origano

fennel seeds
les graines de fenouil
die Fenchelsamen
las semillas de hinojo
i semi di finocchio

mint • la menthe
• die Minze • la menta
• la menta

marjoram • la
marjolaine • der
Majoran • la mejorana
• la maggiorana

cilantro • la coriandre
• der Koriander • el
cilantro • il coriandolo

bay leaf • la feuille de
laurier • das Lorbeerblatt
• el laurel • l'alloro

thyme • le thym • der
Thymian • el tomillo
• il timo

basil • le basilic • das
Basilikum • la albahaca
• il basilico

dill • l'aneth • der Dill
• el eneldo • l'aneto

parsley • le persil
• die Petersilie • el
perejil • il prezzemolo

sage • la sauge
• der Salbei • la salvia
• la salvia

rosemary • le romarin
• der Rosmarin • el
romero • il rosmarino

bottled foods • les aliments en bouteilles et bocaux • die Nahrungsmittel in Flaschen und Gläsern • los alimentos embotellados • i cibi imbottigliati

cork
le bouchon
der Korken
el corcho
il tappo

sunflower oil
• l'huile de
tournesol • das
Sonnenblumenöl
• el aceite de
girasol • l'olio di
semi di girasole

grapeseed oil • l'huile de pépins
de raisin • das Traubenkernöl
• el aceite de semillas de uva
• l'olio di semi d'uva

walnut oil • l'huile de noix
• das Walnussöl • el aceite
de nueces • l'olio di noce

almond oil • l'huile
d'amande • das
Mandelöl • el aceite
de almendras
• l'olio di mandorla

sesame seed oil
• l'huile de sésame
• das Sesamöl • el
aceite de sésamo
• l'olio di sesamo

hazelnut oil • l'huile
de noisette • das
Haselnussöl • el aceite
de avellanas • l'olio
di noccioline

olive oil • l'huile
d'olive • das Olivenöl
• el aceite de oliva
• l'olio d'oliva

herbs • les herbes
• die Kräuter
• las hierbas
• le erbe
aromatiche

flavored oil • l'huile
parfumée • das
aromatische Öl • el
aceite aromatizado
• l'olio aromatizzato

oils • les huiles • die Öle • los aceites • gli oli

---

sweet spreads • les produits à tartiner • der süße Aufstrich • las confituras • le confetture

honeycomb • le gâteau
de miel • der Wabenhonig
• el panal • il favo

set honey
le miel solide
der feste Honig
la miel compacta
il miele condensato

jar • le pot • das Glas
• el tarro • il barattolo

lemon curd • la pâte à
tartiner au citron
• der Zitronenaufstrich
• la crema de limón
• la crema al limone

raspberry jam • la
confiture de framboises
• die Himbeerkonfitüre • la
mermelada de frambuesa
• la marmellata di lamponi

marmalade • la confiture
d'oranges • die
Orangenmarmelade • la
mermelada de naranja
• la marmellata di agrumi

clear honey • le miel
liquide • der flüssige
Honig • la miel líquida
• il miele sciolto

maple syrup
• le sirop d'érable
• der Ahornsirup
• el jarabe de arce
• lo sciroppo d'acero

sauces and condiments • les sauces et les condiments • die Soßen und die Kondimente • las salsas y los condimentos • le salse e i condimenti

cider vinegar
le vinaigre de cidre
der Apfelweinessig
el vinagre de sidra
l'aceto di sidro

balsamic vinegar
le vinaigre balsamique
der Gewürzessig
el vinagre balsámico
l'aceto balsamico

bottle
la bouteille
die Flasche
la botella
la bottiglia

mayonnaise • la mayonnaise • die Majonäse • la mayonesa • la maionese

English mustard • la moutarde anglaise • der englische Senf • la mostaza inglesa • la senape

ketchup • le ketchup • der Ketchup • el ketchup • il ketchup

French mustard • la moutarde française • der französische Senf • la mostaza francesa • la mostarda

chutney • le chutney • das Chutney • el chutney • il chutney

malt vinegar
le vinaigre de malt
der Malzessig
el vinagre de malta
l'aceto di malto

wine vinegar
le vinaigre de vin
der Weinessig
el vinagre de vino
l'aceto di vino

sauce • la sauce • die Soße • la salsa • la salsa

whole-grain mustard • la moutarde en grains • der grobe Senf • la mostaza en grano • la mostarda con semi

vinegar • le vinaigre • der Essig • el vinagre • l'aceto

canning jar • le bocal scellé • das Einmachglas • el tarro hermético • il barattolo a chiusura ermetica

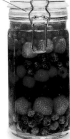

peanut butter • le beurre de cacahouètes • die Erdnussbutter • la mantequilla de cacahuetes • il burro di arachidi

chocolate spread • la pâte à tartiner au chocolat • der Schokoladenaufstrich • el chocolate para untar • la cioccolata spalmabile

preserved fruit • les fruits en bocaux • das eingemachte Obst • la fruta en conserva • la conserva di frutta

vegetable oil l'huile végétale das Pflanzenöl el aceite vegetal l'olio vegetale	**canola oil** l'huile de colza das Rapsöl el aceite de colza l'olio di colza
corn oil l'huile de maïs das Maiskeimöl el aceite de maíz l'olio di mais	**cold-pressed oil** l'huile pressée à froid das kaltgepresste Öl el aceite de presión en frío l'olio spremuto a freddo
peanut oil l'huile d'arachide das Erdnussöl el aceite de cacahuete l'olio di arachide	

dairy products • les produits laitiers • die Milchprodukte • los productos lácteos • i latticini

cheese • le fromage • der Käse • el queso • il formaggio

grated cheese
le fromage râpé
der geriebene Käse
el queso rallado
il formaggio grattugiato

rind
la croûte
die Rinde
la corteza
la crosta

semi-hard cheese
le fromage à pâte pressée non cuite
der mittelharte Käse
el queso semicurado
il formaggio semiduro

hard cheese • le fromage à pâte pressée cuite • der Hartkäse • el queso curado • il formaggio duro

semi-soft cheese • le fromage à pâte semi-molle • der halbfeste Käse • el queso cremoso semicurado • il formaggio semimorbido

cottage cheese • le cottage • der Hütten-käse • el requesón • il formaggio molle fresco

cream cheese • le fromage à la crème • der Rahmkäse • el queso cremoso • il formaggio cremoso

blue cheese • le bleu • der Blauschimmelkäse • el queso azul • il formaggio erborinato

soft cheese • le fromage à pâte molle • der Weichkäse • el queso cremoso • il formaggio morbido

fresh cheese • le fromage frais • der Frischkäse • el queso fresco • il formaggio fresco

milk • le lait • die Milch • la leche • il latte

whole milk
le lait entier
die Vollmilch
la leche entera
il latte intero

reduced-fat milk
le lait demi-écrémé
die Halbfettmilch
la leche semidesnatada
il latte parzialmente scremato

skim milk
le lait écrémé
die Magermilch
la leche desnatada
il latte scremato

milk carton
le carton de lait
die Milchtüte
el cartón de leche
il cartone di latte

goat's milk • le lait de chèvre • die Ziegenmilch • la leche de cabra • il latte di capra

condensed milk
le lait condensé
die Kondensmilch
la leche condensada
il latte condensato

cow's milk • le lait de vache • die Kuhmilch • la leche de vaca • il latte di mucca butter • le beurre • die Butter • la mantequilla • il burro

margarine • la margarine • die Margarine • la margarina • la margarina

cream • la crème • die Sahne • la nata • la panna

half-and-half • la crème allégée • die fettarme Sahne • la nata líquida • la panna liquida

heavy cream
la crème épaisse
die Schlagsahne
la nata para montar
la panna densa

whipped cream
la crème fouettée
die Schlagsahne
la nata montada
la panna montata

sour cream
la crème fraîche
die saure Sahne
la nata agria
la panna acida

yogurt
le yaourt
der Joghurt
el yogurt
lo yogurt

ice cream
la glace
das Eis
el helado
il gelato

eggs • les œufs • die Eier • los huevos • le uova

yolk
le jaune d'œuf
das Eigelb
la yema
il tuorlo

egg white
le blanc d'œuf
das Eiweiß
la clara
la chiara

shell
la coquille
die Eierschale
la cáscara
il guscio

hen's egg • l'œuf de poule • das Hühnerei • el huevo de gallina • l'uovo di gallina

duck egg • l'œuf de cane • das Entenei • el huevo de pato • l'uovo di anatra

eggcup
le coquetier
der Eierbecher
la huevera
il porta uovo

goose egg • l'œuf d'oie • das Gänseei • el huevo de oca • l'uovo d'oca

quail egg • l'œuf de caille • das Wachtelei • el huevo de codorniz • l'uovo di quaglia

soft-boiled egg • l'œuf à la coque • das gekochte Ei • el huevo pasado por agua • l'uovo alla coque

pasteurized	fat-free	salted	sheep's milk	lactose	milk shake
pasteurisé	sans matières grasses	salé	le lait de brebis	le lactose	le milk-shake
pasteurisiert	fettfrei	gesalzen	die Schafmilch	die Laktose	der Milchshake
pasteurizado	sin grasa	salado	la leche de oveja	la lactosa	el batido
pastorizzato	senza grassi	salato	il latte di pecora	il lattosio	il frullato
unpasteurized	powdered milk	unsalted	buttermilk	homogenized	frozen yogurt
non pasteurisé	le lait en poudre	non salé	le babeurre	homogénéisé	le yaourt surgelé
unpasteurisiert	das Milchpulver	ungesalzen	die Buttermilch	homogenisiert	der gefrorene Joghurt
sin pasteurizar	la leche en polvo	sin sal	el suero de la leche	homogeneizado	el yogurt helado
non pastorizzato	il latte in polvere	senza sale	il latte fermentato	omogeneizzato	lo yogurt gelato

breads and flours • les pains et la farine • das Brot und das Mehl • el pan y las harinas • il pane e le farine

sliced bread
le pain tranché
das Scheibenbrot
el pan de molde
il pane affettato

poppy seeds
les graines de pavot
der Mohn
las semillas de amapola
i semi di papavero

rye bread
le pain de seigle
das Roggenbrot
el pan de centeno
il pane di segale

baguette
la baguette
das Baguette
la baguette
il filone

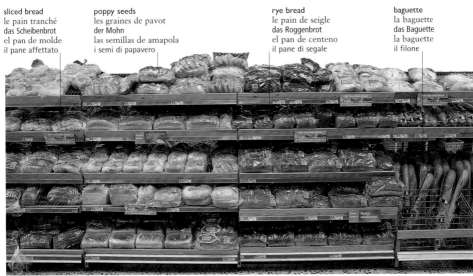

bakery • la boulangerie • die Bäckerei • la panadería • il panificio

making bread • faire du pain • Brot backen • hacer pan • fare il pane

white flour • la farine
blanche • das Weizenmehl
• la harina blanca • la farina
bianca

brown flour • la farine
complète • das Roggenmehl
• la harina morena • la
farina di segale

whole-wheat flour • la farine
brute • das Vollkornmehl
• la harina integral
• la farina integrale

yeast • la levure • die Hefe
• la levadura de panadería
• il lievito

dough
la pâte
der Teig
la masa
la pasta

sift (v) • tamiser • sieben
• cribar • setacciare

mix (v) • mélanger • verrühren
• mezclar • mescolare

knead (v) • pétrir • kneten
• amasar • impastare

bake (v) • faire cuir au four • backen
• hornear • cuocere al forno

 crust
la croûte
die Kruste
la corteza
la crosta

 loaf
le pain
der Laib
la hogaza
la pagnotta

 slice
la tranche
die Scheibe
la rebanada
la fetta

white bread • le pain blanc
• das Weißbrot • el pan
blanco • il pane bianco

brown bread • le pain bis
• das Graubrot • el pan
moreno • il pane nero

whole-wheat bread • le pain de
son • das Vollkornbrot • el pan
integral • il pane integrale

multigrain bread • le pain
complet • das Mehrkornbrot
• el pan con grano • il pane
di granaio

corn bread • le pain de maïs
• das Maisbrot • el pan de
maíz • il pane di mais

soda bread • le pain au
bicarbonate de soude
• das Sodabrot • el pan al
bicarbonato sódico • il pane
lievitato con bicarbonato di sodio

sourdough bread • le pain
au levain • das Sauerteigbrot
• el pan fermentado
• il pane di lievito naturale

flat bread • le pain plat
• das Fladenbrot • el pan sin
levadura • la schiacciata

bagel • le petit pain américain
• der Bagel • el bagel • il bagel

bun • le petit pain rond • das
weiche Brötchen • el bollo • la
pagnotella

roll • le petit pain • das
Brötchen • el panecillo
• il panino

fruit bread • le pain aux
raisins secs • das Rosinenbrot
• el plumcake • il pane
alla frutta

seeded bread • le pain aux
graines • das Körnerbrot • el pan
con semillas • il pane con semi

naan bread • le naan
• das Naanbrot • el naan
• il naan

pita bread • le pita
• das Pitabrot • el pan
de pita • la pita

crispbread • le biscuit
scandinave • das Knäckebrot
• el pan tostado • i crackers

self-rising flour la farine avec la levure das Mehl mit Backpulver la harina con levadura la farina autolievitante	all-purpose flour la farine sans levure das Mehl ohne Backpulver la harina blanca la farina semplice	prove (v) lever gehen lassen levar lievitare	breadcrumbs la chapelure das Paniermehl el pan rallado il pangrattato	slicer la machine à couper der Brotschneider el rebanador l'affettatrice
bread flour la farine traitée das angereicherte Mehl la harina para pan la farina per il pane	rise (v) se lever aufgehen subir lievitare	glaze (v) glacer glasieren glasear glassare	flute la flûte das Stangenweißbrot la barra il filoncino	baker le boulanger der Bäcker el panadero il panettiere

cakes and desserts • les gâteaux et les desserts • Kuchen und Nachspeisen • la repostería • i dolci e i dessert

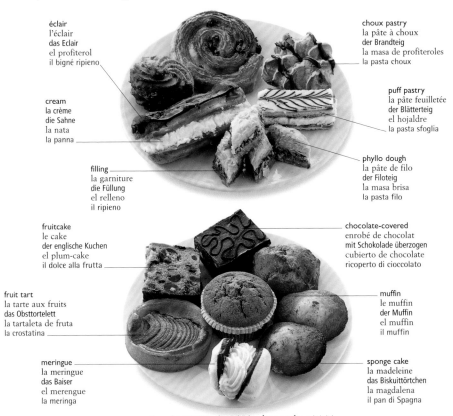

éclair
l'éclair
das Eclair
el profiterol
il bignè ripieno

cream
la crème
die Sahne
la nata
la panna

filling
la garniture
die Füllung
el relleno
il ripieno

choux pastry
la pâte à choux
der Brandteig
la masa de profiteroles
la pasta choux

puff pastry
la pâte feuilletée
der Blätterteig
el hojaldre
la pasta sfoglia

phyllo dough
la pâte de filo
der Filoteig
la masa brisa
la pasta filo

fruitcake
le cake
der englische Kuchen
el plum-cake
il dolce alla frutta

chocolate-covered
enrobé de chocolat
mit Schokolade überzogen
cubierto de chocolate
ricoperto di cioccolato

fruit tart
la tarte aux fruits
das Obsttortelett
la tartaleta de fruta
la crostatina

muffin
le muffin
der Muffin
el muffin
il muffin

meringue
la meringue
das Baiser
el merengue
la meringa

sponge cake
la madeleine
das Biskuittörtchen
la magdalena
il pan di Spagna

cakes • les gâteaux • das Gebäck • los pasteles • i dolci

crème pâtissière la crème pâtissière die Konditorcreme la crema pastelera la crema pasticcera	bun le petit gâteau das Teilchen el bollo la pastina	pastry la pâte der Teig la masa la pasta	rice pudding le riz au lait der Milchreis el arroz con leche il budino di riso	May I have a slice please? Est-ce que je peux avoir une tranche s'il vous plaît? Könnte ich bitte ein Stück haben? ¿Puedo tomar un trozo? Posso avere una fetta?
chocolate cake le gâteau au chocolat die Schokoladentorte el pastel de chocolate la torta al cioccolato	custard la crème anglaise der Vanillepudding las natillas la crema	slice la tranche das Stück el trozo la fetta	celebration la fête die Feier la celebración la festa	

english • français • deutsch • español • italiano

chocolate chip • les pépites de chocolat • das Schokoladenstückchen • el trocito de chocolate • il biscotto con scaglie di cioccolato

ladyfinger les boudoirs die Löffelbiskuits las soletillas i savoiardi

Florentine • le florentine • der Florentiner • la florentina • il biscotto alle noci

trifle • le diplomate • das Trifle • el postre de soletillas, gelatina de frutas y nata • la zuppa inglese

cookies • les biscuits • die Kekse • las galletas • i biscotti

mousse • la mousse • die Mousse • la mousse • la mousse

sherbet • le sorbet • das Sorbett • el sorbete • il sorbetto

cream pie • la tarte à la crème • die Sahnetorte • el pastel de nata • la torta alla crema

crème caramel • la crème caramel • der Karamellpudding • el flan • il crème caramel

celebration cakes • les gâteaux de fête • die festlichen Kuchen • las tartas para celebraciones • le torte per celebrazioni

top tier l'étage supérieur der obere Kuchenteil el piano superiore il piano superiore

bottom tier l'étage inférieur der untere Kuchenteil el primer piso il piano inferiore

marzipan la pâte d'amandes das Marzipan el mazapán il marzapane

ribbon le ruban das Band la cinta il nastro

frosting le glaçage der Zuckerguss la alcorza la glassa

decoration la décoration die Dekoration la decoración la decorazione

birthday candles les bougies d'anniversaire die Geburtstagskerzen las velas de cumpleaños le candeline

blow out (v) souffler ausblasen apagar soffiare

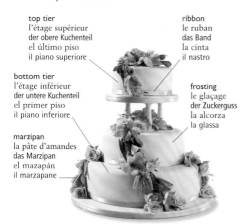

wedding cake • le gâteau de mariage • die Hochzeitstorte • la tarta nupcial • la torta nuziale

birthday cake • le gâteau d'anniversaire • der Geburtstagskuchen • la tarta de cumpleaños • la torta di compleanno

delicatessen • la charcuterie • die Feinkost • la charcutería • la salumeria

quiche • la quiche • die
Quiche • la quiche
• lo sformato

spicy sausage
le saucisson piquant
die pikante Wurst
el fiambre
la salsiccia piccante

vinegar
le vinaigre
der Essig
el vinagre
l'aceto

oil
l'huile
das Öl
el aceite
l'olio

uncooked meat
la viande non cuite
das frische Fleisch
la carne fresca
la carne cruda

counter
le comptoir
die Theke
el mostrador
il banco

salami • le salami
• die Salami • el salami
• il salame

pepperoni • le pepperoni
• die Pepperoniwurst
• el salchichón
• il salame piccante

pâté • le pâté • die Pastete
• el paté • il pâté

mozzarella • la mozzarella
• der Mozzarella • la
mozzarella • la mozzarella

Brie • le brie • der Brie
• el brie • il brie

goat cheese • le fromage de
chèvre • der Ziegenkäse • el
queso de cabra • il formaggio
di capra

cheddar • le cheddar
• der Cheddar • el cheddar
• il cheddar

rind
la croûte
die Rinde
la corteza
la scorza

Parmesan • le parmesan
• der Parmesan • el
parmesano • il parmigiano

Camembert • le camembert
• der Camembert • el
camembert • il camembert

Edam • l'édam • der
Edamer • el queso
de bola • l'edam

Manchego • le manchego
• der Manchego • el
manchego • il manchego

potpie • les pâtés en croûte • die Pasteten • los pasteles de carne • i pasticci di carne

black olive
l'olive noire
die schwarze Olive
la aceituna negra
l'oliva nera

chili pepper
le piment
die Peperoni
la guindilla
il peperoncino

sauce
la sauce
die Soße
la salsa
la salsa

bread roll
le petit pain
das Brötchen
el panecillo
il panino

cooked meat
la viande cuite
der Aufschnitt
el fiambre
la carne cotta

green olive
l'olive verte
die grüne Olive
la aceituna verde
l'oliva verde

sandwich counter • le comptoir sandwichs • die Sandwichtheke • el mostrador de bocadillos • la paninoteca

ham • le jambon • der Schinken • el jamón • il prosciutto

smoked fish • le poisson fumé • der Räucherfisch • el pescado ahumado • il pesce affumicato

capers • les câpres • die Kapern • las alcaparras • i capperi

in oil • à l'huile • in Öl • en aceite • sott'olio

in brine • en saumure • in Lake • en salmuera • in salamoia

marinated • mariné • mariniert • adobado • marinato

salted • salé • gepökelt • salado • salmistrato

smoked • fumé • geräuchert • ahumado • affumicato

cured • séché • getrocknet • curado • trattato

Take a number, please.
Prenez un numéro, s'il vous plaît.
Nehmen Sie bitte eine Nummer.
Coja un número, por favor.
Prenda un numero, per favore.

Can I try some of that please?
Est-ce que je peut goûter un peu de ça, s'il vous plaît?
Kann ich bitte etwas davon probieren?
¿Puedo probar un poco de eso?
Posso assaggiare un po' di quello, per favore?

May I have six slices of that, please?
Je voudrais six tranches, s'il vous plaît.
Ich hätte gerne sechs Scheiben davon, bitte.
¿Me pone seis lonchas de aquél?
Mi dà sei fette di quello, per favore?

chorizo • le chorizo • die Chorizo • el chorizo • il chorizo

prosciutto • le prosciutto • der Prosciutto • el jamón curado • il prosciutto crudo

stuffed olive • l'olive fourrée • die gefüllte Olive • la aceituna rellena • le olive ripiene

drinks • les boissons • die Getränke • las bebidas • le bevande

water • l' eau • das Wasser • el agua • l'acqua

bottled water
l'eau en bouteille
das Flaschenwasser
el agua embotellada
l'acqua in bottiglia

sparkling
gazeux
mit Kohlensäure
con gas
frizzante

tap water • l'eau du robinet
• das Leitungswasser • el agua
del grifo • l'acqua dal rubinetto

still
non gazeux
ohne Kohlensäure
sin gas
naturale

tonic water • le tonic
• das Tonicwater
la tónica • l'acqua
tonica

soda water • le soda
• das Sodawasser
la soda • la soda

mineral water • l'eau minérale • das Mineralwasser
• el agua mineral • l'acqua minerale

hot drinks • les boissons chaudes • die heißen Getränke • las bebidas calientes • le bevande calde

teabag • le sachet de thé
• der Teebeutel • la bolsita
de té • la bustina di tè

loose-leaf tea
• les feuilles de
thé • die Teeblätter
• el té en hoja
• il tè sciolto

tea • le thé • der Tee • el té • il tè

beans • les grains
• die Bohnen • los
granos • i chicchi

ground coffee
le café moulu
der gemahlene Kaffee
el café molido
il caffè macinato

coffee • le café • der Kaffee • el café • il caffè

hot chocolate • le
chocolat chaud • die
heiße Schokolade • el
chocolate caliente
• il cioccolato calda

malted drink • la
boisson maltée • das
Malzgetränk • la bebida
malteada • la bevanda
al malto

soft drinks • les boissons non alcoolisées • die alkoholfreien Getränke • los refrescos • le bibite

straw • la paille
• der Strohhalm • la
pajita • la cannuccia

tomato juice • le jus de
tomate • der Tomatensaft
• el zumo de tomate
• il succo di pomodoro

grape juice • le jus de
raisin • der Traubensaft
• el zumo de uva
• il succo d'uva

lemonade • la limonade
• die Limonade • la
limonada • la limonata

orangeade • l'orangeade
• die Orangenlimonade
• la naranjada
• l'aranciata

cola • le coca
• die Cola • la cola
• la coca

alcoholic drinks • les boissons alcoolisées • die alkoholischen Getränke • las bebidas alcohólicas • le bevande alcoliche

gin • le gin • der Gin
• la ginebra • il gin

can
la boîte
die Dose
la lata
la lattina

beer • la bière • das
Bier • la cerveza
• la birra

hard cider • le cidre
• der Apfelwein • la
• sidra • il sidro

bitter • la bière anglaise
• das halbdunkle Bier
• la cerveza amarga
• la birra amara

stout • la bière
brune • der Stout
• la cerveza negra
• la birra scura

vodka • la vodka
• der Wodka • el
vodka • la vodka

whiskey • le whisky
• der Whisky • el
whisky • il whisky

rum • le rhum
• der Rum • el
ron • il rum

brandy • le brandy
• der Weinbrand • el
coñac • il brandy

port • le porto • der
Portwein • el oporto
• il porto

dry • sec • trocken
• seco • secco

sherry • le sherry
• der Sherry • el vino
de jerez • lo sherry

Campari • le campari
• der Campari • el
campari • il Campari

rosé   white   red
rosé   blanc   rouge
rosé   weiß   rot
rosado   blanco   tinto
rosé   bianco   rosso

liqueur • la liqueur
• der Likör • el licor
• il liquore

tequila • la téquila
• der Tequila • el
tequila • la tequila

champagne • le cham-
pagne • der Champagner
• el champán
• lo champagne

wine • le vin • der
Wein • el vino
• il vino

eating out
sortir manger
auswärts essen
comer fuera
mangiare fuori

café • le café • das Café • la cafetería • il caffè

umbrella
le parasol
der Sonnenschirm
la sombrilla
l'ombrellone

awning
le store
die Markise
el toldo
la tenda

menu
le menu
die Speisekarte
la carta
il menù

patio café • la terrasse de café • das Terrassencafé
• la terraza • il bar con terrazza

server
le serveur
der Kellner
el camarero
il cameriere

coffee machine
le percolateur
die Kaffeemaschine
la máquina del café
la macchina del caffè

table
la table
der Tisch
la mesa
il tavolo

sidewalk café • la terrasse de café • das Straßencafé
• la cafetería con mesas fuera • il bar all'aperto

snack bar • le snack • die Snackbar • el bar • lo snack bar

---

coffee • le café • der Kaffee • el café • il caffè

coffee with milk
le crème
der Milchkaffee
el café con leche
il caffè macchiato

black coffee
le noir
der schwarze Kaffee
el café solo
il caffè nero

cocoa powder
le chocolat en poudre
das Kakaopulver
el cacao en polvo
la polvere di cacao

froth
la mousse
der Schaum
la espuma
la schiuma

filter coffee • le café filtre • der
Filterkaffee • el café de cafetera
eléctrica • il caffè filtrato

espresso • l'expresso
• der Espresso • el café
solo • l'espresso

cappuccino • le cappuccino
• der Cappuccino • el
cappuccino • il cappuccino

iced coffee • le café glacé
• der Eiskaffee • el café con
hielo • il caffè freddo

tea • le thé • der Tee • el té • il tè

herbal tea
la tisane
der Kräutertee
la infusión
il tè alle erbe

chamomile tea • la camomille • der Kamillentee • la manzanilla • la camomilla

green tea • le thé vert • der grüne Tee • el té verde • il tè verde

tea with milk • le thé au lait • der Tee mit Milch • el té con leche • il tè con latte

black tea • le thé nature • der schwarze Tee • el té negro • il tè nero

tea with lemon • le thé au citron • der Tee mit Zitrone • el té con limón • il tè al limone

mint tea • l'infusion de menthe • der Pfefferminztee • la menta poleo • il tè alla menta

iced tea • le thé glacé • der Eistee • el té con hielo • il tè freddo

juices and milkshakes • les jus et milk-shakes • die Säfte und Milchshakes • los zumos y los batidos • le spremute e i frappé

chocolate milkshake
le milk-shake au chocolat
der Schokoladenmilchshake
el batido de chocolate
il frappé al cioccolato

strawberry milkshake
le milk-shake à la fraise
der Erdbeermilchshake
el batido de fresa
il frappé alle fragole

orange juice • le jus d'orange • der Orangensaft • el zumo de naranja • il succo d'arancia

apple juice • le jus de pomme • der Apfelsaft • el zumo de manzana • il succo di mela

pineapple juice le jus d'ananas der Ananassaft el zumo de piña il succo d'ananas

tomato juice • le jus de tomate • der Tomatensaft • el zumo de tomate • il succo di pomodoro

coffee milkshake
le milk-shake au café
der Kaffeemilchshake
el batido de café
il frappé al caffè

food • la nourriture • das Essen • la comida • il cibo

whole-wheat bread
le pain bis
das Graubrot
el pan integral
il pane integrale

scoop
la boule
die Kugel
la bola
la pallina

toasted sandwich • le sandwich grillé • der getoastete Sandwich • el sandwich tostado • il tramezzino tostato

salad • la salade • der Salat • la ensalada • l'insalata

ice cream • la glace • das Eis • el helado • il gelato

pastry • la pâtisserie • das Gebäck • el pastel • le paste

bar • le bar • die Bar • el bar • il bar

glasses	dispenser	cash register	bartender	beer tap	coffee machine
les verres	la mesure	la caisse	le barman	la pompe à biere	le percolateur
die Gläser	das Maß	die Kasse	der Barkeeper	der Zapfhahn	die Kaffeemaschine
los vasos	el medidor óptico	la caja	el camarero	el grifo de cerveza	la máquina del café
i bicchieri	il misurino	la cassa	il barista	lo spillatore di birra	la macchina da caffè

ice bucket	bar stool	ashtray	coaster	bar counter
le seau à glace	le tabouret de bar	le cendrier	le dessous de verre	le comptoir
der Eiskübel	der Barhocker	der Aschbecher	der Untersetzer	die Theke
la champanera	el taburete	el cenicero	el posavasos	la barra
il portaghiaccio	lo sgabello	il posacenere	il sottobicchiere	il banco

bottle opener
l'ouvre-bouteille
der Flaschenöffner
el abrebotellas
l'apribottiglie

lever
le levier
der Hebel
la palanca
la leva

tongs
les pinces
die Eiszange
las pinzas
le pinze

stirrer
l'agitateur
der Cocktailrührer
el agitador
il miscelatore

measure
le verre gradué
der Messbecher
el medidor
il misurino

corkscrew • le tire-bouchon • der Korkenzieher
• el sacacorchos • il cavatappi

cocktail shaker • le shaker à cocktails • der Cocktailshaker
• la coctelera • lo shaker

english • français • deutsch • español • italiano

pitcher
le pichet
der Krug
la jarra
la brocca

ice cube
le glaçon
der Eiswürfel
el cubito de hielo
il cubetto di ghiaccio

gin and tonic • le gin tonic • der Gin Tonic • el gin tonic • il gin tonic

scotch and water • le scotch à l'eau • der Scotch mit Wasser • el whisky escocés con agua • il whisky con acqua

rum and cola • le rhum coca • der Rum mit Cola • el cuba libre / el ron cola • il cuba libre

screwdiver • la vodka à l'orange • der Wodka mit Orangensaft • el vodka con naranja • la vodka all'arancia

martini • le martini • der Martini • el martini • il martini

cocktail • le cocktail • der Cocktail • el cóctel • il cocktail

wine • le vin • der Wein • el vino • il vino

beer • la bière • das Bier • la cerveza • la birra

single
simple
einfach
sencillo
singolo

double
double
doppelt
doble
doppio

ice and lemon
citron et glaçons
Eis und Zitrone
con hielo y limón
ghiaccio e limone

shot • un coup • ein Schnaps • un chupito • una acquavite

measure • la mesure • das Maß • la medida • la misura

without ice • sans glaçons • ohne Eis • sin hielo • liscio

with ice • avec des glaçons • mit Eis • con hielo • con ghiaccio

bar snacks • les amuse-gueule • die Knabbereien • los aperitivos • gli stuzzichini

almonds
les amandes
die Mandeln
las almendras
le mandorle

cashews
les noix de cajou
die Cashewnüsse
los anacardos
gli anacardi

peanuts
les cacahouètes
die Erdnüsse
los cacahuetes
le noccioline americane

potato chips • les chips • die Kartoffelchips • las patatas fritas • le patatine

nuts • les noix • die Nüsse • los frutos secos • le noccioline

olives • les olives • die Oliven • las aceitunas • le olive

restaurant • le restaurant • das Restaurant • el restaurante • il ristorante

table setting
le couvert
das Gedeck
el cubierto
il coperto

sous chef
le commis
der Hilfskoch
el ayudante del chef
l'aiuto cuoco

glass
le verre
das Glas
la copa
il bicchiere

tray
le plateau
das Tablett
la bandeja
il vassoio

chef
le chef de cuisine
der Küchenchef
el chef
il cuoco

kitchen • la cuisine • die Küche • la cocina • la cucina

server • le garçon • der Kellner • el camarero • il cameriere

lunch menu	specials	price	tip	buffet	salt
le menu du déjeuner	les spécialités	le prix	le pourboire	le buffet	le sel
das Mittagsmenü	die Spezialitäten	der Preis	das Trinkgeld	das Buffet	das Salz
el menú de la comida	los platos del día	el precio	la propina	el bufet	la sal
il menù del pranzo	la specialità	il prezzo	la mancia	il buffet	il sale
dinner menu	à la carte	check	service charge included	bar	pepper
le menu du soir	à la carte	l'addition	service compris	le bar	le poivre
das Abendmenü	à la carte	die Rechnung	Bedienung inbegriffen	die Bar	der Pfeffer
el menú de la cena	a la carta	la cuenta	servicio incluido	el bar	la pimienta
il menù della cena	à la carte	il conto	servizio compreso	il bar	il pepe
wine list	dessert cart	receipt	service charge not included	customer	
la carte des vins	le plateau à desserts	le reçu	service non compris	le client	
die Weinkarte	der Dessertwagen	die Quittung	ohne Bedienung	der Kunde	
la lista de vinos	el carrito de los postres	el recibo	servicio no incluido	el cliente	
la lista dei vini	il carrello dei dolci	la ricevuta	servizio non compreso	il cliente	

english • français • deutsch • español • italiano

menu • la carte • die Speisekarte • la carta • il menù

child's meal • le menu d'enfant • die Kinderportion • el menú para niños • il menù per bambini

order (v) • commander • bestellen • pedir • ordinare

pay (v) • payer • bezahlen • pagar • pagare

courses • les plats • die Gänge • los platos • le portate

apéritif • l'apéritif • der Aperitif • el aperitivo • l'aperitivo

appetizer • l'entrée • die Vorspeise • el entrante • l'antipasto

soup • la soupe • die Suppe • la sopa • la minestra

entrée • le plat principal • das Hauptgericht • el plato principal • il piatto principale

side order • l'accompagnement • die Beilage • el acompañamiento • il contorno

dessert • le dessert • der Nachtisch • el postre • il dessert

coffee • le café • der Kaffee • el café • il caffè

A table for two, please.
Une table pour deux, s'il vous plaît.
Einen Tisch für zwei Personen, bitte.
Una mesa para dos, por favor.
Un tavolo per due, per favore.

Can I see the menu/winelist please?
La carte/la carte des vins, s'il vous plaît.
Könnte ich bitte die Speisekarte/Weinkarte sehen?
¿Podría ver la carta/lista de vinos, por favor?
Posso vedere il menù\la lista dei vini, per favore?

Is there a fixed-price menu?
Avez-vous un menu à prix fixe?
Gibt es ein Festpreismenü?
¿Hay menú del día?
C'è un menù a prezzo fisso?

Do you have any vegetarian dishes?
Avez vous des plats végétariens?
Haben Sie vegetarische Gerichte?
¿Tiene platos vegetarianos?
Avete dei piatti vegetariani?

Could I have the check/a receipt, please?
L'addition/un reçu, s'il vous plaît.
Könnte ich bitte die Rechnung/Quittung haben?
¿Me podría traer la cuenta/un recibo?
Posso avere il conto\una ricevuta per favore?

Can we pay separately?
Pouvons-nous payer chacun notre part?
Können wir getrennt zahlen?
¿Podemos pagar por separado?
Possiamo pagare separatamente?

Where is the restroom, please?
Où sont les toilettes, s'il vous plaît?
Wo sind die Toiletten, bitte?
¿Dónde están los servicios, por favor?
Dove sono i bagni per favore?

fast food • la restauration rapide • der Schnellimbiss • la comida rápida • il fast food

straw
la paille
der Strohhalm
la pajita
la cannuccia

burger
le hamburger
der Hamburger
la hamburguesa
l'hamburger

soft drink
la boisson non-alcoolisée
das alkoholfreie Getränk
el refresco
la bibita

French fries
les frites
die Pommes frites
las patatas fritas
le patate fritte

paper napkin
la serviette en papier
die Papierserviette
la servilleta de papel
il tovagliolo di carta

tray
le plateau
das Tablett
la bandeja
il vassoio

burger meal • le hamburger avec des frites • der Hamburger mit Pommes frites • la hamburguesa con patatas fritas • l'hamburger con patatine fritte

pizza • la pizza • die Pizza • la pizza • la pizza

price list • le tarif • die Preisliste • la lista de precios • il listino

canned drink
la boisson en boîte
das Dosengetränk
la lata de bebida
la bibita in lattina

home delivery • la livraison à domicile • die Lieferung ins Haus • la entrega a domicilio • la consegna a domicilio

street vendor • le marchand de hot-dogs • der Imbissstand • el puesto callejero • il venditore ambulante

pizzeria
la pizzeria
die Pizzeria
la pizzeria
la pizzeria

burger bar
le restaurant rapide
die Imbissstube
la hamburguesería
il fastfood

menu
la carte
die Speisekarte
el menú
il menù

eat-in
manger sur place
hier essen
para comer en el local
mangiare sul posto

to go
à emporter
zum Mitnehmen
para llevar
da asporto

reheat (v)
réchauffer
aufwärmen
recalentar
riscaldare

ketchup
le ketchup
der Tomatenketchup
el ketchup
il ketchup

Can I have that to go please?
À emporter, s'il vous plaît.
Ich möchte das mitnehmen.
¿Me lo pone para llevar?
Me lo dà da asporto?

Do you deliver?
Est-ce que vous livrez à domicile?
Liefern Sie ins Haus?
¿Entregan a domicilio?
Consegnate a domicilio?

bun
le petit pan
das Brötchen
el bollo
il panino

mustard
la moutarde
der Senf
la mostaza
la senape

sausage
la saucisse
die Wurst
la salchicha
il wurstel

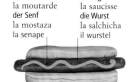

hamburger • le hamburger • der Hamburger • la hamburguesa • l'hamburger

chicken burger • le hamburger au poulet • der Chickenburger • la hamburguesa de pollo • l'hamburger di pollo

veggie burger • le hamburger végétarien • der vegetarische Hamburger • la hamburguesa vegetariana • l'hamburger vegetariano

hot dog • le hot-dog • das Hot Dog • el perrito caliente • l'hot dog

filling
la garniture
die Füllung
el relleno
il ripieno

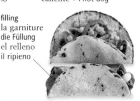

sandwich • le sandwich • das Sandwich • el bocadillo • il tramezzino

club sandwich • le sandwich mixte • das klubsandwich • el club sandwich • il tramezzino a strati

open-faced sandwich • le canapé • das belegte Brot • el sandwich abierto • il tramezzino aperto

wrap • le taco • das gefüllte Fladenbrot • el taco • la piadina

sauce
la sauce
die Soße
la salsa
la salsa

savory
salé
salzig
salado
salato

sweet
sucré
süß
dulce
dolce

topping
la garniture
der Pizzabelag
los ingredientes
il condimento

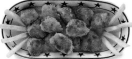

kebab • la viande à la broche • der Fleischspieß • el pincho moruno • il spiedino

chicken nuggets • les beignets de poulet • die Hähnchenstückchen • las porciones de pollo • i bocconcini di pollo

crepes • les crêpes • die Crêpes • las crepes • la crêpes

fish and chips • le poisson avec des frites • der Bratfisch mit Pommes frites • el pescado y las patatas fritas • il pesce con patatine

ribs • les côtes • die Rippen • las costillas • le costolette

fried chicken • le poulet frit • das gebratene Hähnchen • el pollo frito • il pollo fritto

pizza • la pizza • die Pizza • la pizza • la pizza

breakfast • le petit déjeuner • das Frühstück • el desayuno • la colazione

milk	cereal	jam	dried fruit	ham	cheese	crispbread
le lait	les céréales	la confiture	les fruit secs	le jambon	le fromage	le biscuit scandinave
die Milch	die Getreideflocken	die Konfitüre	das Dörrobst	der Schinken	der Käse	das Knäckebrot
la leche	los cereales	la mermelada	la fruta desecada	el jamón	el queso	la galleta de centeno
il latte	i cereali	la marmellata	la frutta secca	il prosciutto	il formaggio	il pane biscottato

breakfast buffet • le buffet du petit déjeuner • das Frühstücks-buffet • el buffet de desayuno • il buffet della colazione

marmalade	pâté	butter
la confiture d'oranges	le pâté	le beurre
die Orangenmarmelade	die Pastete	die Butter
la mermelada de naranja	el paté	la mantequilla
la marmellata di agrumi	il pâté	il burro

fruit juice	coffee
le jus de fruit	le café
der Obstsaft	der Kaffee
el zumo de frutas	el café
il succo di frutta	il caffè

croissant	hot chocolate
le croissant	le chocolat chaud
das Croissant	die Schokolade
el croissant	el cacao
il cornetto	la cioccolata calda

tea
le thé
der Tee
el té
il tè

breakfast table • la table du petit déjeuner • der Frühstückstisch • la mesa del desayuno • il tavolo della colazione

drinks • les boissons • die Getränke • las bebidas • le bevande

tomato
la tomate
die Tomate
el tomate
il pomodoro

black pudding
le boudin
die Blutwurst
la morcilla
il sanguinaccio

toast
le toast
der Toast
el pan tostada
il pane tostato

sausage
la saucisse
das Würstchen
la salchicha
la salsiccia

fried egg
l'œuf sur le plat
das Spiegelei
el huevo frito
l'uovo fritto

bacon
le bacon
der Frühstücksspeck
el bacon
la pancetta

brioche • la brioche • die Brioche • el brioche • la brioche

bread • le pain • das Brot • el pan • il pane

English breakfast • le petit déjeuner anglais • das englische Frühstück • el desayuno inglés • la colazione all'inglese

yolk
le jaune d'œuf
das Eigelb
la yema
il tuorlo

kippers • les kippers • die Räucherheringe • los arenques ahumados • le aringhe affumicate

French toast • le pain perdu • die Armen Ritter • la torrija • il pane fritto all'uovo

soft-boiled egg • l'œuf à la coque • das gekochte Ei • el huevo pasado por agua • l'uovo alla coque

scrambled eggs • les œufs brouillés • das Rührei • los huevos revueltos • le uova strapazzate

whipped cream
la crème
die Sahne
la nata
la panna

fruit yogurt
le yaourt aux fruits
der Früchtejoghurt
el yogurt de frutas
lo yogurt alla frutta

crepes • les crêpes • die Pfannkuchen • los crepes • le crêpes

waffles • les gaufres • die Waffeln • los gofres • i waffle

oatmeal • le porridge • der Haferbrei • las gachas de avena • la pappa d'avena

fresh fruit • les fruits • das Obst • la fruta fresca • la frutta fresca

dinner • le repas • die Hauptmahlzeit • la comida principal • la cena

soup • le potage • die Suppe • la sopa • la minestra

broth • le bouillon • die Brühe • el caldo • il brodo

stew • le ragoût • der Eintopf • el guiso • lo stufato

curry • le curry • das Curry • el curry • il curry

roast • le rôti • der Braten • el asado • l'arrosto

potpie • la tourte • die Pastete • el pastel • il pasticcio

soufflé • le soufflé • das Soufflé • el soufflé • il soufflé

kebab • le chiche-kébab • der Schaschlik • el pincho • lo spiedino

noodles • les nouilles • die Nudeln • los fideos • i taglierini

meatballs • les boulettes de viande • die Fleischklöße • las albóndigas • le polpette

omelet • l'omelette • das Omelett • la tortilla • la frittata

stir-fry • le sauté • das Pfannengericht • la fritura • la frittura

pasta • les pâtes • die Nudeln • la pasta • la pasta

rice • le riz • der Reis • el arroz • il riso

tossed salad • la salade composée • der gemischte Salat • la ensalada mixta • l'insalata mista

green salad • la salade verte • der grüne Salat • la ensalada verde • l'insalata verde

dressing • la vinaigrette • die Salatsoße • el aliño • il condimento

techniques • la préparation • die Zubereitung • las técnicas • i metodi

stuffed • farci • gefüllt
• relleno • ripieno

in sauce • en sauce • in Soße
• en salsa • al sugo

grilled • grillé • gegrillt
• a la plancha • alla griglia

marinated • mariné • mariniert
• adobado • marinato

poached • poché • pochiert
• escalfado • affogato

mashed • en purée • püriert
• hecho puré • schiacciato

baked • cuit • gebacken
• cocido en el horno
• cotto al forno

pan fried • sauté • kurzgebraten
• frito con poco aceite
• fritto in padella

fried • frit • gebraten
• frito • fritto

pickled • macéré • eingelegt
• en vinagre • sottaceto

smoked • fumé • geräuchert
• ahumado • affumicato

deep-fried • frit • frittiert • frito
con mucho aceite • fritto in
olio abbondante

in syrup • au sirop • in Saft
• en almíbar • allo sciroppo

dressed • assaisonné
• angemacht • aliñado
• condito

steamed • cuit à la vapeur
• gedämpft • al vapor
• al vapore

cured • séché • getrocknet
• curado • stagionato

study
l'étude
das Lernen
el estudio
lo studio

school • l'école • die Schule • el colegio • la scuola

whiteboard
le tableau blanc
die Weißwandtafel
la pizarra blanca
la lavagna bianca

teacher
l'institutrice
die Lehrerin
la profesora
l'insegnante

schoolbag
le cartable
die Schultasche
la cartera
la cartella

student
l'élève
der Schüler
el alumno
l'alluno

desk
le pupitre
das Pult
el pupitre
il banco

classroom • la salle de classe • das Klassenzimmer • el aula • l'aula

schoolgirl • l'écolière • das Schulmädchen • la colegiala • la scolara

schoolboy • l'écolier • der Schuljunge • el colegial • lo scolaro

history	art	physics
l'histoire	l'art	la physique
die Geschichte	die Kunst	die Physik
la historia	el arte	la física
la storia	l'arte	la fisica
geography	music	chemistry
la géographie	la musique	la chimie
die Erdkunde	die Musik	die Chemie
la geografía	la música	la química
la geografia	la musica	la chimica
literature	math	biology
la littérature	les mathématiques	la biologie
die Literatur	die Mathematik	die Biologie
la literatura	las matemáticas	la biología
la letteratura	la matematica	la biologia
languages	science	physical education
les langues	les sciences	l'éducation physique
die Sprachen	die Naturwissenschaft	der Sport
los idiomas	las ciencias	la educación física
le lingue	le scienze naturali	l'educazione fisica

activities • les activités • die Aktivitäten • las actividades • le attività

read (v) • lire • lesen • leer • leggere

write (v) • écrire • schreiben • escribir • scrivere

spell (v) • épeler • buchstabieren • deletrear • scandire

draw (v) • dessiner • zeichnen • dibujar • disegnare

nib
la plume
die Feder
la punta
la punta

colored pencil
le crayon de couleur
der Buntstift
el lápiz de colores
la matita colorata

pencil sharpener
le taille-crayon
der Anspitzer
el sacapuntas
il temperamatite

digital projector • le projecteur
numérique • der Digitalprojektor
• el proyector digital
• il proiettore digitale

pen • le stylo
• der Füller
• la pluma
• la penna

pencil • le crayon • der
Bleistift • el lápiz • la matita

notebook • le cahier • das Heft
• el cuaderno • il quaderno

eraser • la gomme
• der Radiergummi
• la goma • la gomma

textbook • le livre • das Schulbuch • el libro de texto
• il libro di testo

pencil case • la trousse
• das Federmäppchen
• el estuche • l'astuccio

ruler • la règle
• das Lineal • la regla
• il righello

question (v) • questionner
• fragen • preguntar
• domandare

answer (v) • répondre
• antworten • contestar
• rispondere

discuss (v) • discuter
• diskutieren • discutir
• discutere

learn (v) • apprendre • lernen
• aprender • imparare

principal	answer	grade
le directeur	la réponse	la note
der Schulleiter	die Antwort	die Note
el director	la respuesta	la nota
il preside	la risposta	il voto
lesson	homework	year
la leçon	les devoirs	la classe
die Stunde	die Hausaufgabe	die Klasse
la lección	los deberes	el curso
la lezione	i compiti	la classe
take notes (v)	essay	dictionary
prendre des notes	la rédaction	le dictionnaire
Notizen machen	der Aufsatz	das Wörterbuch
tomar apuntes	la redacción	el diccionario
prendere appunti	il tema	il dizionario
question	test	encyclopedia
la question	l'examen	l'encyclopédie
die Frage	die Prüfung	das Lexikon
la pregunta	el examen	la enciclopedia
la domanda	l'esame	l'enciclopedia

math • les mathématiques • die Mathematik • las matemáticas • la matematica

shapes • les formes • die Formen • las formas • le forme

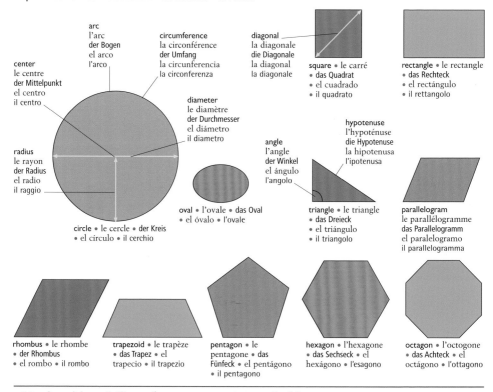

arc
l'arc
der Bogen
el arco
l'arco

center
le centre
der Mittelpunkt
el centro
il centro

circumference
la circonférence
der Umfang
la circunferencia
la circonferenza

diameter
le diamètre
der Durchmesser
el diámetro
il diametro

diagonal
la diagonale
die Diagonale
la diagonal
la diagonale

square • le carré
• das Quadrat
• el cuadrado
• il quadrato

rectangle • le rectangle
• das Rechteck
• el rectángulo
• il rettangolo

radius
le rayon
der Radius
el radio
il raggio

angle
l'angle
der Winkel
el ángulo
l'angolo

hypotenuse
l'hypoténuse
die Hypotenuse
la hipotenusa
l'ipotenusa

oval • l'ovale • das Oval
• el óvalo • l'ovale

circle • le cercle • der Kreis
• el círculo • il cerchio

triangle • le triangle
• das Dreieck
• el triángulo
• il triangolo

parallelogram
le parallélogramme
das Parallelogramm
el paralelogramo
il parallelogramma

rhombus • le rhombe
• der Rhombus
• el rombo • il rombo

trapezoid • le trapèze
• das Trapez • el
trapecio • il trapezio

pentagon • le
pentagone • das
Fünfeck • el pentágono
• il pentagono

hexagon • l'hexagone
• das Sechseck • el
hexágono • l'esagono

octagon • l'octogone
• das Achteck • el
octágono • l'ottagono

---

solids • les solides • die Körper • los cuerpos geométricos • i solidi

base
la base
die Grundfläche
la base
la base

side
le côté
die Seite
el lado
il lato

apex
le sommet
die Spitze
el ápice
l'apice

cone • le cône
• der Kegel • el
cono • il cono

cylinder • le cylindre
• der Zylinder • el
cilindro • il cilindro

cube • le cube
• der Würfel • el
cubo • il cubo

pyramid • la pyramide
• die Pyramide • la
pirámide • la piramide

sphere • la sphère
• die Kugel • la esfera
• la sfera

---

lines • les lignes • die Linien • las líneas • le linee

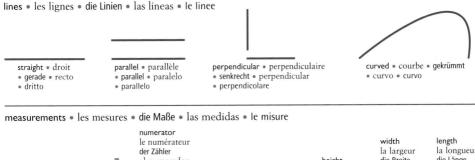

straight • droit • gerade • recto • dritto

parallel • parallèle • parallel • paralelo • parallelo

perpendicular • perpendiculaire • senkrecht • perpendicular • perpendicolare

curved • courbe • gekrümmt • curvo • curvo

measurements • les mesures • die Maße • las medidas • le misure

numerator
le numérateur
der Zähler
el numerador
il numeratore

denominator
le dénominateur
der Nenner
el denominador
il denominatore

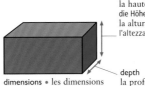

height
la hauteur
die Höhe
la altura
l'altezza

depth
la profondeur
die Tiefe
la profundidad
la profondità

width
la largeur
die Breite
la anchura
la larghezza

length
la longueur
die Länge
la longitud
la lunghezza

volume • le volume • das Volumen • el volumen • il volume

fraction • la fraction • der Bruch • el quebrado • la frazione

dimensions • les dimensions • die Abmessungen • las dimensiones • le dimensioni

area • l'aire • die Fläche • el área • la superficie

equipment • l'équipement • die Ausrüstung • los materiales • l'attrezzatura

triangle • l'équerre • das Zeichendreieck • la escuadra • la squadra

protractor • le rapporteur • der Winkelmesser • el transportador • il goniometro

ruler • la règle • das Lineal • la regla • il righello

compass • le compas • der Zirkel • el compás • il compasso

calculator
la calculatrice
der Taschenrechner
la calculadora
la calcolatrice

geometry	plus	times	equals	add (v)	multiply (v)	equation
la géométrie	plus	fois	égale(nt)	additionner	multiplier	l'équation
die Geometrie	plus	mal	gleich	addieren	multiplizieren	die Gleichung
la geometría	más	multiplicado por	igual a	sumar	multiplicar	la ecuación
la geometria	più	moltiplicato per	uguale	sommare	moltiplicare	l'equazione
arithmetic	minus	divided by	count (v)	subtract (v)	divide (v)	percentage
l'arithmétique	moins	divisé par	compter	soustraire	diviser	le pourcentage
die Arithmetik	minus	geteilt durch	zählen	subtrahieren	dividieren	der Prozentsatz
la aritmética	menos	dividido por	contar	restar	dividir	el porcentaje
l'aritmetica	meno	diviso per	contare	sottrarre	dividere	la percentuale

science • la science • die Naturwissenschaft • las ciencias • le scienze naturale

laboratory • le laboratoire • das Labor • el laboratorio • il laboratorio

scale • la balance • die Laborwaage • la báscula • la bilancia

weight
le poids
das Gewicht
la pesa
il peso

spring balance • la balance à ressort • die Federwaage • la balanza de muelle • la bilancia a molla

crucible • le creuset • der Tiegel • el crisol • il crogiolo

bunsen burner
le bec Bunsen
der Bunsenbrenner
el mechero Bunsen
il becco Bunsen

tripod • le trépied • der Dreifuß • el trípode • il treppiede

test tube
l'éprouvette
das Reagenzglas
el tubo de ensayo
la provetta

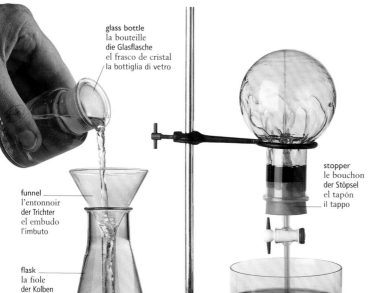

glass bottle
la bouteille
die Glasflasche
el frasco de cristal
la bottiglia di vetro

rack • le support • das Gestell • el soporte • la rastrelliera

stopper
le bouchon
der Stöpsel
el tapón
il tappo

funnel
l'entonnoir
der Trichter
el embudo
l'imbuto

flask
la fiole
der Kolben
el matraz
l'alambicco

timer • le chronomètre • der Zeitmesser • el cronómetro • il cronometro

petri dish • la boîte de Pétri • die Petrischale • la cápsula de Petri • la capsula di Petri

experiment • l'expérience • der Versuch • el experimento • l'esperimento

thermometer • le thermomètre • das Thermometer • el termómetro • il termometro

syringe • la seringue • die Spritze • la jeringuilla • la siringa

tweezers • la pince fine • die Pinzette • las pinzas • le pinzette

scalpel • le scalpel • das Skalpell • el bisturí • il bisturi

dropper • le compte-gouttes • der Tropfer • el cuentagotas • il contagocce

forceps • le forceps • die Zange • el fórceps • il forcipe

tongs • la pince • die Greifzange • las tenazas • le pinze

spatula • la spatule • der Spatel • la espátula • la spatola

pestle • le pilon • der Stößel • la mano de mortero • il pestello

eyepiece • l'oculaire das Okular • el ocular l'oculare

focusing knob • le bouton de mise au point • der Einstell-knopf • el botón de ajuste • la manopola di messa a fuoco

mortar • le mortier • der Mörser • el mortero • il mortaio

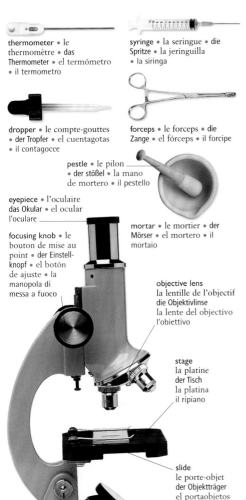

objective lens la lentille de l'objectif die Objektivlinse la lente del objectivo l'obiettivo

stage la platine der Tisch la platina il ripiano

slide le porte-objet der Objektträger el portaobjetos la lastrina

mirror le miroir der Spiegel el espejo lo specchio

filter paper • le papier filtre • das Filterpapier • el filtro de papel • il filtro di carta

safety goggles • les lunettes de protection • die Schutzbrille • las gafas protectoras • gli occhiali protettivi

glass stirring rod la tige de verre das Glasstäbchen la varilla de cristal la bacchetta di vetro

pipette • la pipette • die Pipette • la pipeta • la pipetta

beaker • le bécher • das Becherglas • el vaso de precipitados • il becher

magnet • l'aimant • der Magnet • el imán • la calamita

alligator clip • la pince crocodile • die Krokodilklemme • la pinza • il morsetto a coccodrillo

negative electrode • l'électrode négative • der minuspol • el electrodo negativo • l'elettrodo negativo

positive electrode • l'électrode positive • die Pluspol • el electrodo positivo • l'elettrodo positivo

microscope • le microscope • das Mikroskop • el microscopio • il microscopio

battery • la pile • die Batterie • la pila • la batteria

college • l'enseignement supérieur • die Hochschule • la enseñanza superior • l'università

admissions office
le secrétariat
das Sekretariat
la secretaría
l'ufficio iscrizioni

cafeteria
• le restaurant
universitaire
• die Mensa
• el refectorio
• il refettorio

health center
• le service de
santé • die
Gesundheitsfürsorge
• el centro de
salud • l'ambulatorio

playing field
• le terrain
de sport
• der Sportplatz
• el campo de
deportes • il
campo sportivo

residence hall
• la résidence
universitaire
• das Studentenwohnheim
• el colegio mayor
• la casa dello
studente

librarian
la bibliothécaire
die Bibliothekarin
la bibliotecaria
la bibliotecaria

campus • le campus • der Campus • el campus • il campus

library card	help desk	loan
la carte de lecteur	les renseignements	le prêt
der Leserausweis	die Auskunft	die Ausleihe
la tarjeta de la biblioteca	la información	el préstamo
il tesserino	il banco informazioni	il prestito
reading room	borrow (v)	book
la salle de lecture	emprunter	le livre
der Lesesaal	ausleihen	das Buch
la sala de lecturas	coger prestado	el libro
la sala di lettura	prendere in prestito	il libro
reading list	reserve (v)	title
les ouvrages recommandés	réserver	le titre
die Literaturliste	vorbestellen	der Titel
la lista de lecturas	reservar	el título
la lista dei libri	prenotare	il titolo
due date	renew (v)	aisle
la date de retour	renouveler	le couloir
das Rückgabedatum	verlängern	der Gang
la fecha de devolución	renovar	el pasillo
la data di restituzione	rinnovare	la corsia

circulation desk • le
service de prêt • die
Ausleihe • el mostrador
de préstamos • il
banco prestiti

bookshelf
l'étagère à
livres
das Bücherregal
la estantería
lo scaffale

periodical
le périodique
das Periodikum
el periódico
il periodico

journal
la revue
die Zeitschrift
la revista
la rivista

library • la bibliothèque • die Bibliothek
• la biblioteca • la biblioteca

undergraduate • l'étudiant
• der Student • el estudiante
• lo studente universitario

professor • le maître de
conférence • der Dozent
• el profesor • il docente

graduate • la licenciée
• die Graduierte • la
licenciada • la laureata

gown • la robe • die
Robe • la toga • la toga

lecture hall • la salle de cours • der Hörsaal • el anfiteatro
• l'aula

graduation ceremony • la cérémonie de la remise des diplômes
• die Graduierungsfeier • la ceremonia de graduación
• la consegna delle lauree

schools • les écoles • die Fachhochschulen • las escuelas universitarias • le scuole

model
le modèle
das Model
la modelo
la modella

art school • l'école des beaux arts
• die Kunsthochschule • la escuela de
Bellas Artes • la scuola d'arte

music school • le Conservatoire
• die Musikhochschule • el conservatorio
• il conservatorio

dance school • l'école de danse
• die Tanzakademie • la academia
de danza • l'accademia di danza

scholarship la bourse das Stipendium la beca la borsa di studio	research la recherche die Forschung la investigación la ricerca	dissertation la dissertation die Examensarbeit la tesina la dissertazione	medicine la médecine die Medizin la medicina la medicina	economics les sciences économiques die Wirtschaftswissenschaft las ciencias económicas l'economia
diploma le diplôme das Diplom el diploma il diploma	master's la maîtrise der Magister el máster il master	department l'U.F.R. der Fachbereich el departamento il dipartimento	zoology la zoologie die Zoologie la zoología la zoologia	political science les sciences politiques die Politologie la sciencas políticas la politica
degree la licence der akademische Grad la carrera la laurea	doctorate le doctorat die Promotion el doctorado il dottorato	law le droit die Rechtswissenschaft el derecho il diritto	physics la physique die Physik la fisica la fisica	literature la littérature die Literaturwissenschaft la literatura la letteratura
postgraduate de troisième cycle postgraduiert posgrado di perfezionamento	thesis la thèse die Dissertation la tesis la tesi	engineering les études d'ingénieur der Maschinenbau la ingeniería l'ingegneria	philosophy la philosophie die Philosophie la filosofia la filosofia	art history l'histoire d'art die Kunstgeschichte la historia del arte la storia dell'arte

work
le travail
die Arbeit
el trabajo
il lavoro

office 1 • le bureau 1 • das Büro 1 • la oficina 1 • l'ufficio 1

in-tray
la corbeille arrivée
die Ablage für Eingänge
la bandeja de entrada
il vassoio in arrivo

monitor
le moniteur
der Bildschirm
la pantalla
il monitor

desktop organizer
le porte-crayons
der Stifthalter
el portabolígrafos
il portapenne

laptop
le portable
der Laptop
el ordenador portátil
il laptop

notebook
le carnet
das Notizbuch
el cuaderno
il blocco

out-tray
la corbeille départ
die Ablage für Ausgänge
la bandeja de salida
il vassoio in partenza

drawer
le tiroir
die Schublade
el cajón
il cassetto

desk
le bureau
der Schreibtisch
el escritorio
la scrivania

swivel chair
le chaise tournante
der Drehstuhl
la silla giratoria
la sedia girevole

wastebasket
la corbeille à papier
der Papierkorb
la papelera
il cestino

filing cabinet
le meuble-classeur
der Aktenschrank
el archivador
lo schedario

---

office equipment • l'équipement de bureau • die Büroausstattung • el equipo de oficina • l'apparecchiature da ufficio

paper tray • le magasin à papier • der Papierbehälter • la bandeja para el papel • il vassoio per la carta

printer • l'imprimante • der Drucker • la impresora • la stampante

shredder • le destructeur de documents • der Aktenvernichter • la destructora de papel • il distruggidocumenti

print (v)	**enlarge** (v)
imprimer	agrandir
drucken	vergrößern
imprimir	ampliar
stampare	ingrandire
copy (v)	**reduce** (v)
photocopier	réduire
kopieren	verkleinern
fotocopiar	reducir
copiare	ridurre

I need to make some copies.
J'ai besoin de faire des photocopies.
Ich möchte fotokopieren.
Necesito hacer unas fotocopias.
Devo fare delle copie.

office supplies • les fournitures de bureau • der Bürobedarf • los materiales de oficina • gli articoli di cancelleria

compliments slip
• la fiche compliments
• der Empfehlungszettel
• la nota con saludos
• il biglietto di accompagnamento

box file
le dossier-classeur
der Aktenordner
la caja archivador
la scatola d'archivio

letterhead • le papier à lettres • das Briefpapier • el membrete • la carta intestata

envelope • l'enveloppe • der Briefumschlag • el sobre • la busta

divider
la fiche intercalaire
el divisor
il divisore

tab • l'étiquette • der Kartenreiter • el rótulo • l'etichetta

clipboard • le clipboard • das Klemmbrett • la tablilla con sujetapapeles • il portablocco con fermaglio

notepad • le bloc-notes • der Notizblock • el bloc de apuntes • il blocco per appunti

hanging file • le dossier suspendu • der Hängeordner • el archivador suspendido • la cartella sospesa

expanding file • le porte-dossiers • der Fächerordner • la carpeta de acordeón • il portacarte a fisarmonica

binder • le classeur à levier • der Ringordner • la carpeta de anillas • il raccoglitore a leva

staples
les agrafes
die Klammern
las grapas
i punti

tape • le scotch
• der Tesafilm • el papel celo • il nastro adesivo

ink pad
le tampon encreur
das Stempelkissen
la almohadilla de la tinta
il tampone di inchiostro

personal organizer
• l'agenda • der Terminkalender • la agenda • l'agenda

stapler • l'agrafeuse • der Hefter • la grapadora • la cucitrice

tape dispenser • le dévidoir de scotch • der Tesafilmhalter • el soporte del papel celo • il dispenser

hole punch • le perforateur • der Locher • la perforadora • il perforatore

rubber stamp • le cachet • der Stempel • el sello • il timbro di gomma

thumbtack
la punaise
der Reißnagel
la chincheta
la puntina

rubber band
• l'élastique • das Gummiband • la goma elástica • l'elastico

bulldog clip • la pince à dessin • die Papierklammer • el clip • il fermafogli

paper clip • le trombone • die Büro-klammer • el sujeta-papeles • la graffetta

bulletin board • le panneau d'affichage • die Pinnwand • el tablón de anuncios • la bacheca

office 2 • le bureau 2 • das Büro 2 • la oficina 2 • l'ufficio 2

flip chart
à feuilles mobiles
• das Flipchart • el
rotafolio • la
lavagna a fogli

minutes
le compte rendu
das Protokoll
el acta
il verbale

easel
le chevalet
das Gestell
el caballete
il cavalletto

report
le rapport
der Bericht
el informe
la relazione

manager
le directeur
der Manager
el gerente
il direttore

proposal
la proposition
la propuesta
la propuesta
la proposta

executive
le cadre
der leitende Angestellte
el ejecutivo
il dirigente

meeting • le réunion • die Sitzung • la reunión • la riunione

meeting room la salle de conférence der Sitzungsraum la sala de reuniones la sala da riunione	**attend** *(v)* assister à teilnehmen asistir partecipare
agenda l'ordre du jour die Tagesordnung el orden del día l'ordine del giorno	**chair** *(v)* présider den Vorsitz führen presidir presiedere

What time is the meeting?
La conférence est à quelle heure?
Um wie viel Uhr ist die Sitzung?
¿A qué hora es la reunión?
A che ora è la riunione?

What are your office hours?
Quelles sont vos heures de bureau?
Was sind Ihre Geschäftszeiten?
¿Cuál es su horario de oficina?
Qual è il vostro orario di lavoro?

speaker
la conférencière
die Sprecherin
la oradora
l'oratrice

presentation • la présentation • die Präsentation
• la presentación • la presentazione

business • les affaires • das Geschäft • los negocios • gli affari

businessman
l'homme d'affaires
der Geschäftsmann
el hombre de negocios
l'uomo d'affari

businesswoman
la femme d'affaires
die Geschäftsfrau
la mujer de negocios
la donna d'affari

business lunch • le déjeuner d'affaires • das Arbeitsessen • la comida de negocios • il pranzo di lavoro

business trip • le voyage d'affaires • die Geschäftsreise • el viaje de negocios • il viaggio d'affari

appointment
le rendez-vous
der Termin
la cita
l'appuntamento

CEO
• le directeur général
• der Geschäftsführer
• el director general
• l'amministratore delegato

client • la cliente • die Kundin • la clienta • la cliente

day planner • l'agenda • der Terminkalender • la agenda • l'agenda

business deal • le contrat • das Geschäftsabkommen • el trato • l'accordo di affari

company	staff	accounting department	legal department
la société	le personnel	la comptabilité	le service du contentieux
die Firma	das Personal	die Buchhaltung	die Rechtsabteilung
la empresa	el personal	el departamento de contabilidad	el departamento legal
la ditta	il personale	l'ufficio contabilità	l'ufficio legale
head office	payroll	marketing department	customer service department
le siège social	le livre de paie	le service marketing	le service après-vente
die Zentrale	die Lohnliste	die Marketingabteilung	die Kundendienstabteilung
la oficina central	la nómina	el departamento de márketing	el departamento de atención al cliente
la sede centrale	il libro paga	l'ufficio mark22eting	l'ufficio di assistenza clienti
regional office	salary	sales department	human resources department
la succursale	le salaire	le service des ventes	le service de ressources humaines
die Zweigstelle	das Gehalt	die Verkaufsabteilung	die Personalabteilung
la sucursal	el sueldo	el departamento de ventas	el departamento de recursos humanos
la succursale	lo stipendio	l'ufficio vendite	l'ufficio del personale

computer • l'ordinateur • der Computer • el ordenador • il computer

printer
l'imprimante
der Drucker
la impresora
la stampante

screen
l'écran
der Bildschirm
la pantalla
lo schermo

scanner
le scanneur
der Scanner
el escáner
lo scanner

laptop • le portable
• der Laptop • el
ordenador portátil
• il computer portatile

speaker • le
haut-parleur • der
Lautsprecher • el
altavoz • l'altoparlante

key
la touche
die Taste
la tecla
il tasto

keyboard • le
clavier • die Tastatur
• el teclado
• la tastiera

mouse • la souris
• die Maus • el ratón
• il mouse

hardware • le matériel • die Hardware • el hardware • l'hardware

memory la mémoire der Speicher la memoria la memoria	software le logiciel die Software el software il software	server le serveur der Server el servidor il server
RAM la RAM das RAM la RAM la RAM	application l'application die Anwendung la aplicación l'applicazione	port le port der Port el puerto la porta
bytes les bytes die Bytes los bytes i byte	program le programme das Programm el programa il programma	power cord le câble électrique das Stromkabel el cable de alimentación il cavo di alimentazione
system le système das System el sistema il sistema	network le réseau das Netzwerk la red la rete	processor le processeur der Prozessor el procesador il processore

memory stick • la clé
USB • der Memorystick
• la llave de memoria
• la chiavetta USB

external hard drive
le disque dur externe
die Externe Festplatte
el disco duro externo
il disco rigido esterno

tablet • la tablette
• das Tablet • la tablet
• il tablet

smartphone • le smartphone
• das Smartphone • el teléfono
inteligente • lo smartphone

desktop • le bureau • das Desktop • el escritorio • il desktop

font • la police de charactères
• die Schriftart • la fuente
• il carattere

icon • l'icône
• das Symbol • el
icono • l'icona

menubar
la barre de menus
die menüleiste
la barra del menú
la barra del menu

file • le fichier • die
Datei • el fichero
• il file

toolbar • la barre
d'outils • die
Werkzeugleiste • la
barra de acceso
• la barra degli
strumenti

scrollbar • la barre
de défilement
• der Scrollbalken
• la barra de
desplazamiento
• la barra di
scorrimento

folder • le dossier
• der Ordner • la
carpeta • la cartella

window • la fenêtre
• das Fenster
• la ventana
• la finestra

wallpaper
• le papier peint
• der Bildschirmhintergrund
• el fondo • lo sfondo

trash • la poubelle • der
Papierkorb • la papelera
• il cestino

internet • l'internet • das Internet • el internet • Internet

email • l'e-mail • die E-Mail • el correo electrónico • l'e-mail

browser
le navigateur
der Browser
el navegador
il browser

email address • l'adresse e-mail • die E-Mail-Adresse
• la dirección electrónica • l'indirizzo e-mail

inbox • la boîte
de réception
• der Posteingang
• la bandeja de
entrada • la
posta in arrivo

website
le site web
die Webseite
el sitio web
il sito web

browse (v) • naviguer • browsen • navegar • navigare

connect (v)	service provider	log on (v)	download (v)	send (v)	save (v)
connecter	le fournisseur d'accès	entrer	télécharger	envoyer	sauvegarder
verbinden	der Serviceprovider	einloggen	herunterladen	senden	sichern
conectar	el proveedor de servicios	entrar en el sistema	bajar	enviar	guardar
collegare	il fornitore di servizi	collegarsi	scaricare	spedire	salvare
install (v)	email account	online	attachment	receive (v)	search (v)
installer	le compte e-mail	en ligne	la pièce jointe	recevoir	chercher
installieren	das E-Mail-Konto	online	der Anhang	erhalten	suchen
instalar	la cuenta de correo	en línea	el documento adjunto	recibir	buscar
installare	l'account di posta elettronica	in rete	l'allegato	ricevere	cercare

media • les médias • die Medien • los medios de comunicación • i mass media

television studio • le studio de télévision • das Fernsehstudio • el estudio de televisión • lo studio televisivo

set
le plateau
die Studioeinrichtung
el plató
il set

host
le présentateur
der Moderator
el presentador
il presentatore

light
l'éclairage
die Beleuchtung
el foco
la lampada

camera
la caméra
die Kamera
la cámara
la telecamera

camera crane
la grue de caméra
der Kamerakran
la grúa de la cámara
il carrello della telecamera

cameraman
le cameraman
der Kameramann
el cámara
il cameraman

channel	documentary	press	soap opera	cartoon	live
la chaîne	le documentaire	la presse	le feuilleton	le dessin animé	en direct
der Kanal	der Dokumentarfilm	die Presse	die Seifenoper	der Zeichentrickfilm	live
el canal	el documental	la prensa	la telenovela	los dibujos animados	en directo
il canale	il documentario	la stampa	la telenovela	il cartone animato	in diretta
programming	news	television series	game show	prerecorded	broadcast (v)
la programmation	les nouvelles	la série télévisée	le jeu télévisé	en différé	émettre
die Programmgestaltung	die Nachrichten	die Fernsehserie	die Spielshow	vorher aufgezeichnet	senden
la programación	las noticias	la serie televisiva	el concurso	en diferido	emitir
la programmazione	il telegiornale	le serie televisiva	il gioco a premi	in differita	trasmettere

english • français • deutsch • español • italiano

interviewer • l'interviewer
• der Interviewer
• el entrevistador
• l'intervistatore

reporter • la reporter
• die Reporterin • la reportera
• la cronista

teleprompter • le
télésouffleur • der Teleprompter
• el autocue • il gobbo

anchor • la présentatrice
• die Nachrichtensprecherin
• la presentadora de las
noticias • l'annunciatrice

actors • les acteurs • die
Schauspieler • los actores
• gli attori

sound boom • la perche
• der Mikrofongalgen
• la jirafa • la giraffa

clapper board • la claquette
• die Klappe • la claqueta
• il ciac

movie set • le décor de
cinéma • das Set • el plató
de rodaje • il set

radio • la radio • das Radio • la radio • la radio

sound technician	mixing desk	microphone
l'ingénieur du son	le pupitre de mixage	le microphone
der Tonmeister	das Mischpult	das Mikrofon
el técnico de sonido	la mesa de mezclas	el micrófono
il tecnico del suono	il piano di mixaggio	il microfono

recording studio • le studio d'enregistrement • das Tonstudio
• el estudio de grabación • lo studio di registrazione

DJ
le D.J.
der DJ
el pinchadiscos
il DJ

broadcast
l'émission
die Sendung
la emisión
la trasmissione

wavelength
la longueur
   d'ondes
die Wellenlänge
la longitud de onda
la lunghezza d'onda

radio station
la station de radio
die Rundfunkstation
la estación de radio
il canale radiofonico

frequency
la fréquence
die Frequenz
la frecuencia
la frequenza

short wave
les ondes
courtes
die Kurzwelle
la onda corta
l'onda corta

analog
analogique
analog
analógico
analogico

digital
numérique
digital
digital
digitale

volume
le volume
die Lautstärke
el volumen
il volume

tune (v)
régler
einstellen
sintonizar
sintonizzaree

medium wave
les ondes
moyennes
die Mittelwelle
la onda media
l'onda media

long wave
les grandes
ondes
die Langwelle
la onda larga
l'onda lunga

law • le droit • das Recht • el derecho • la legge

bailiff
l'huissier de tribunal
der Gerichtsdiener
el alguacil
la guardia

lawyer
l'avocat
der Rechtsanwalt
el abogado
l'avvocato

jury
le jury
die Geschworenen
el jurado
la giuria

jury box
le banc des jurés
die Geschworenenbank
la tribuna del jurado
il banco della giuria

witness
le témoin
der Zeuge
el testigo
il testimone

judge • le juge • der Richter
• el juez • il giudice

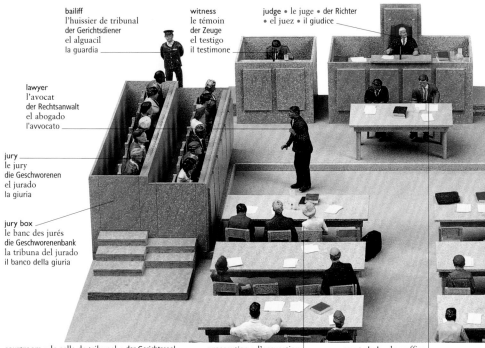

courtroom • la salle de tribunal • der Gerichtssaal
• la sala del tribunal • l'aula del tribunale

prosecution • l'accusation
• die Staatsanwaltschaft • la
acusación • il pubblico ministero

court clerk • le greffier
• der Protokollführer • el
auditor • il cancelliere

lawyer's office le cabinet das Anwaltsbüro el bufete lo studio dell'avvocato	**summons** l'assignation die Vorladung la citación la citazione	**writ** l'acte judiciaire die Verfügung la orden judicial l'ordine	**court case** la cause das Gerichtsverfahren el juicio il procedimento
legal advice le conseil juridique die Rechtsberatung la asesoría jurídica la consulenza legale	**statement** la déposition die Aussage la declaración la dichiarazione	**court date** la date du procès der Gerichtstermin la fecha del juicio la data di comparizione	**charge** l'accusation die Anklage el cargo l'imputazione
client le client der Klient el cliente il cliente	**warrant** le mandat der Haftbefehl la orden judicial il mandato	**plea** le plaidoyer das Plädoyer el alegato l'arringa	**accused** l'accusé der Angeklagte el acusado l'accusato

english • français • deutsch • español • italiano

stenographer
le sténographe
der Gerichtsstenograf
la taquígrafa
lo stenografo

suspect
le suspect
der Verdächtige
el sospechoso
la persona sospetta

criminal
le criminel
der Straftäter
el criminal
il criminale

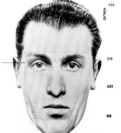

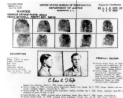

defendant • l'accusé
• der Angeklagte • el
acusado • l'imputato

defense • la défense • die
Verteidigung • la defensa
• la difesa

composite sketch • le portrait-
robot • das Phantombild • el
retrato robot • il fotofit

criminal record • le casier
judiciare • das Strafregister • los
antecedentes • la fedina penale

prison guard • le gardien de prison
• der Gefängniswärter • el funcionario
de prisiones • la guardia carceraria

cell • la cellule • die
Gefängniszelle • la celda
• la cella

prison • la prison • das Gefängnis
• la cárcel • il carcere

evidence	guilty	bail	I want to see a lawyer.
la preuve	coupable	la caution	Je voudrais voir un avocat.
das Beweismittel	schuldig	die Kaution	Ich möchte mit einem Anwalt sprechen.
la prueba	culpable	la fianza	Quiero ver a un abogado.
la prova	colpevole	la cauzione	Voglio vedere un avvocato.
verdict	acquitted	appeal	Where is the courthouse?
le verdict	acquitté	l'appel	Où est le palais de justice?
das Urteil	freigesprochen	die Berufung	Wo ist das Gericht?
el veredicto	absuelto	la apelación	¿Dónde está el juzgado?
il verdetto	assolto	il ricorso	Dov'è il palazzo di giustizia?
innocent	sentence	parole	Can I post bail?
innocent	la condamnation	la liberté conditionnelle	Est-ce que je peux verser la caution?
unschuldig	das Strafmaß	die Haftentlassung auf Bewährung	Kann ich die Kaution leisten?
inocente	la sentencia	la libertad condicional	¿Puedo pagar la fianza?
innocente	la sentenza	la libertà condizionale	Posso versare una cauzione?

farm 1 • la ferme 1 • der Bauernhof 1 • la granja 1 • la fattoria 1

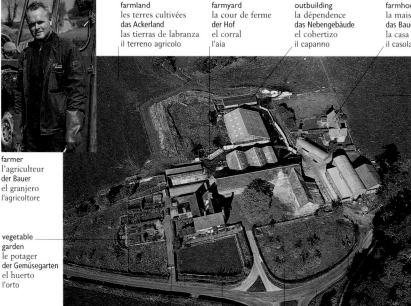

farmland
les terres cultivées
das Ackerland
las tierras de labranza
il terreno agricolo

farmyard
la cour de ferme
der Hof
el corral
l'aia

outbuilding
la dépendance
das Nebengebäude
el cobertizo
il capanno

farmhouse
la maison d'habitation
das Bauernhaus
la casa de labranza
il casolare

field
le champ
das Feld
el campo
il campo

farmer
l'agriculteur
der Bauer
el granjero
l'agricoltore

barn
la grange
die Scheune
el granero
il granaio

vegetable garden
le potager
der Gemüsegarten
el huerto
l'orto

hedge
la haie
die Hecke
el seto
la siepe

gate
la barrière
das Tor
la puerta
il cancello

fence
la clôture
der Zaun
la cerca
il recinto

pasture
le pré
die Weide
el pasto
il pascolo

livestock
le bétail
das Vieh
el ganado
il bestiame

cultivator
le cultivateur
der Kultivator
el cultivador
l'aratro

tractor • le tracteur • der Traktor • el tractor • il trattore

combine • la moissonneuse-batteuse • der Mähdrescher • la cosechadora • la mietitrebbiatrice

english • français • deutsch • español • italiano

types of farms • les exploitations agricoles • die landwirtschaftlichen Betriebe • los tipos de granja • i tipi di fattoria

crop • la culture • die Feldfrucht • la cosecha • il prodotto dei campi

flock • le troupeau • die Herde • el rebaño • il gregge

crop farm • la ferme de culture • der Ackerbaubetrieb • la granja de tierras cultivables • l'azienda agricola

dairy farm • la ferme laitière • der Betrieb für Milchproduktion • la vaquería • il caseificio

sheep farm • la ferme d'élevage de moutons • die Schaffarm • la granja de ganado ovino • l'allevamento di pecore

poultry farm • la ferme d'aviculture • die Hühnerfarm • la granja avícola • l'azienda avicola

vine • la vigne • der Weinstock • la vid • la vigna

pig farm • la ferme d'élevage porcin • die Schweinefarm • la granja de ganado porcino • l'allevamento di maiali

fish farm • le centre de pisciculture • die Fischzucht • la piscifactoría • la piscicoltura

fruit farm • l'exploitation fruitière • der Obstanbau • la granja de frutales • la frutticoltura

vineyard • la vigne • der Weinberg • el viñedo • il vigneto

actions • les activités • die Tätigkeiten • las actividades • le attività

furrow le sillon die Furche el surco il solco

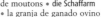

plow (v) • labourer • pflügen • arar • arare

sow (v) • semer • säen • sembrar • seminare

milk (v) • traire • melken • ordeñar • mungere

feed (v) • donner à manger • füttern • dar de comer • dar da mangiare

water (v) • arroser • bewässern • regar • irrigare

harvest (v) • récolter • ernten • cosechar • raccogliere

herbicide	herd	trough
l'herbicide	le troupeau	l'auge
das Herbizid	die Herde	der Trog
el herbicida	la manada	el comedero
l'erbicida	la mandria	la mangiatoia
pesticide	silo	plant (v)
le pesticide	le silo	planter
das Pestizid	der Silo	pflanzen
el pesticida	el silo	plantar
il pesticida	il silos	piantare

farm 2 • la ferme 2 • der Bauernhof 2 • la granja 2 • la fattoria 2

crops • les cultures • die Feldfrüchte • las cosechas • le colture

wheat • le blé • der Weizen • el trigo • il grano

corn • le maïs • der Mais • el maíz • il granturco

barley • l'orge • die Gerste • la cebada • l'orzo

rapeseed • le colza • der Raps • la colza • la colza

sunflower • le tournesol • die Sonnenblume • el girasol • il girasole

bale • la balle • der Ballen • la bala • la balla

hay • le foin • das Heu • el heno • il fieno

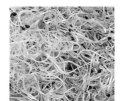

alfalfa • la luzerne • die Luzerne • la alfalfa • l'alfalfa

tobacco • le tabac • der Tabak • el tabaco • il tabacco

rice • le riz • der Reis • el arroz • il riso

tea • le thé • der Tee • el té • il tè

coffee • le café • der Kaffee • el café • il caffè

scarecrow • l'épouvantail • die Vogelscheuche • el espantapájaros • lo spaventapasseri

flax • le lin • der Flachs • el lino • il lino

sugarcane • la canne à sucre • das Zuckerrohr • la caña de azúcar • la canna da zucchero

cotton • le coton • die Baumwolle • el algodón • il cotone

livestock • le bétail • das Vieh • el ganado • il bestiame

piglet • le porcelet
• das Ferkel • el lechón
• il maialino

pig • le cochon • das Schwein
• el cerdo • il maiale

calf
le veau
das Kalb
el ternero
il vitello

cow • la vache • die Kuh
• la vaca • la mucca

bull • le taureau • der Stier
• el toro • il toro

sheep • le mouton • das
Schaf • la oveja • la pecora

kid
le chevreau
das Zicklein
el cabrito
il capretto

lamb • l'agneau • das
Lamm • el cordero • l'agnello

goat • la chèvre • die
Ziege • la cabra • la capra

foal
le poulain
das Fohlen
el potro
il puledro

horse • le cheval • das
Pferd • el caballo • il cavallo

donkey • l'âne • der Esel
• el burro • l'asino

chick • le poussin
• das Küken
• el polluelo
• il pulcino

duckling
le caneton
das Entenküken
el patito
l'anatroccolo

chicken • la poule • das Huhn
• la gallina • la gallina

rooster • le coq • der Hahn
• el gallo • il gallo

turkey • le dindon
• der Truthahn • el pavo
• il tacchino

duck • le canard • die Ente
• el pato • l'anatra

stable • l'écurie • der Stall
• el establo • la stalla

pen • l'enclos • der Pferch
• el redil • il recinto

chicken coop • le poulailler
• der Hühnerstall • el gallinero
• il pollaio

pigsty • la porcherie
• der Schweinestall • la pocilga
• il porcile

construction • la construction • der Bau • la construcción • l'edilizia

scaffolding • l'échafaudage
das Gerüst • el andamio
• l'impalcatura

pallet
la palette
die Palette
el palet
il pallet

ladder
l'échelle
die Leiter
la escalera
la scala

window
la fenêtre
das Fenster
la ventana
la finestra

rafter • le chevron
• der Dachsparren • la viga
del tejado • la trave del
tetto

construction site • le chantier • die Baustelle • la obra • il cantiere

forklift
le chariot de levage
der Gabelstapler
la carretilla elevadora
il carrello elevatore

toolbelt • la ceinture à outils
• der Werkzeuggürtel • el cinturón
de las herramientas • la cintura
porta attrezzi

beam
la poutre
der Balken
la viga de madera
la trave

lintel
le linteau
der Sturz
el dintel
l'architrave

wall
le mur
die Mauer
la pared
il muro

girder
la poutre
der Träger
la viga de acero
la trave

hard hat • le casque de
sécurité • der Schutzhelm
• el casco • il casco

cement
le ciment
der Zement
el cemento
il cemento

build (v) • construire • bauen • construir
• costruire

construction worker • le maçon
• der Bauarbeiter • el albañil
• il muratore

cement mixer • la bétonnière • die
Betonmischmaschine • la hormigonera
• la betoniera

materials • les matériaux • das Material • los materiales • i materiali

brick • la brique • der Ziegelstein • el ladrillo • il mattone

lumber • le bois • das Bauholz • la madera • il legno

roof tile • la tuile • der Dachziegel • la teja • la tegola

cinder block • le parpaing • der Baustein • el bloque de hormigón • il mattone di cemento

tools • les outils • die Werkzeuge • las herramientas • gli attrezzi

mortar • le mortier • der Mörtel • la argamasa • la malta

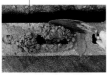

trowel • la truelle • die Kelle • la paleta • la cazzuola

level • le niveau à bulle • die Wasserwaage • el nivel • la livella

handle
le manche
der Stiel
el mango
il manico

sledgehammer • le marteau de forgeron • der Vorschlaghammer • el mazo • la mazza

pickax • la pioche • die Spitzhacke • el pico • il piccone

shovel • la pelle • die Schaufel • la pala • la pala

machinery • les machines • die Maschinen • la maquinaria • i macchinari

road roller • le rouleau compresseur • die Walze • la apisonadora • il rullo compressore

dump truck • le tombereau • der Kipper • el camión volquete • il camion con cassone ribaltabile

support • le support • die Stütze • el soporte • il supporto

hook
le crochet
der Haken
el gancho
il gancio

crane • la grue • der Kran • la grúa • la gru

roadwork • les travaux • die Straßenarbeiten • las obras • i lavori stradali

asphalt
le macadam goudronné
der Asphalt
el asfalto
l'asfalto

cone
le cône
der Leitkegel
el cono
il birillo

jackhammer • le marteau-piqueur • der Pressluftbohrer • el martillo neumático • il martello pneumatico

resurfacing
le revêtement
der Neubelag
el revestimiento
la riasfaltatura

excavator • la pelle mécanique • der Bagger • la excavadora mecánica • l'escavatrice meccanica

occupations 1 • les professions 1 • die Berufe 1 • las profesiones 1 • i mestieri 1

carpenter • le menuisier • der Schreiner • el carpintero • il falegname

electrician • l'électricien • der Elektriker • el electricista • l'elettricista

plumber • le plombier • der Klempner • el fontanero • l'idraulico

construction worker • le maçon • der Maurer • el albañil • il muratore

vacuum cleaner
l'aspirateur
der Staubsauger
la aspiradora
l'aspirapolvere

gardener • le jardinier • der Gärtner • el jardinero • il giardiniere

cleaner • le nettoyeur • der Gebäudereiniger • el empleado de la limpieza • l'addetto alle pulizie

mechanic • le mécanicien • der Mechaniker • el mecánico • il meccanico

butcher • le boucher • der Metzger • el carnicero • il macellaio

fish seller • la marchande de poissons • die Fischhändlerin • la pescadera • la pescivendola

produce seller • le marchand de légumes • der Gemüsehändler • el frutero • il fruttivendolo

florist • la fleuriste • die Floristin • la florista • la fioraia

hairdresser • le coiffeur • der Friseur • el peluquero • il parrucchiere

barber • le coiffeur • der Herrenfriseur • el barbero • il barbiere

jeweler • le bijoutier • der Juwelier • el joyero • il gioielliere

salesperson • l'employée de magasin • die Verkäuferin • la dependienta • la commessa

realtor • l'agent immobilier • die Immobilienmaklerin • la agente immobiliaria • l'agente immobiliare

optometrist • l'opticien • der Optiker • el óptico • l'ottico

mask
la masque
der mundschutz
la mascarilla
la mascherina

dentist • la dentiste • die Zahnärztin • la dentista • la dentista

doctor • le docteur • der Arzt • el médico • il medico

pharmacist • la pharmacienne • die Apothekerin • la farmacéutica • la farmacista

nurse • l'infirmière • die Krankenschwester • la enfermera • l'infermiera

veterinarian • la vétérinaire • die Tierärztin • la veterinaria • la veterinaria

farmer • le fermier • der Landwirt • el agricultor • l'agricoltore

fisherman • le pêcheur • der Fischer • el pescador • il pescatore

machine gun
la mitrailleuse
das Maschinen gewehr
la metralleta
la mitragliatrice

badge
• le badge
• das Abzeichen
• la placa de identificación
• il distintivo

security guard • le garde • der Wächter • el guardia de seguridad • la guardia di sicurezza

uniform
l'uniforme
die Uniform
el uniforme
la divisa

sailor • le marin • der Seemann • el marino • il marinaio

soldier • le soldat • der Soldat • el soldado • il soldato

police officer • le policier • der Polizist • el policía • il poliziotto

firefighter • le pompier • der Feuerwehrmann • el bombero • il vigile del fuoco

occupations 2 • les professions 2 • die Berufe 2 • las profesiones 2 • i mestieri 2

lawyer • l'avocate • der Rechtsanwältin • la abogada • l'avvocatessa

accountant • le comptable • der Wirtschaftsprüfer • el contable • il commercialista

model
la maquette
das Modell
la maqueta
il modello

architect • l'architecte • der Architekt • el arquitecto • l'architetto

scientist • la scientifique • die Wissenschaftlerin • la científica • la scienziata

teacher • l'institutrice • die Lehrerin • la profesora • l'insegnante

librarian • le bibliothécaire • der Bibliothekar • el bibliotecario • il bibliotecario

receptionist • la réceptionniste • die Empfangsdame • la recepcionista • l'addetta alla ricezione

mailbag
le sac postal
die Posttasche
la cartera
la borsa

mail carrier • le facteur • der Briefträger • el cartero • il postino

bus driver • le conducteur de bus • der Busfahrer • el conductor de autobús • l'autista

truck driver • le camionneur • der Lastwagenfahrer • el camionero • il camionista

taxi driver • le chauffeur de taxi • der Taxifahrer • el taxista • il tassista

pilot • le pilote • der Pilot • el piloto • il pilota

flight attendant • l'hôtesse de l'air • die Flugbegleiterin • la azafata • l'assistente di volo

travel agent • l'agent de voyages • die Reisebürokauffrau • la agente de viajes • l'agente di viaggio

chef's hat
• la toque
• die Kochmütze
• el gorro de cocinero
• il cappello

chef • le chef • der Koch • el cocinero • il cuoco

tutu
le tutu
das Ballettröckchen
el tutú
il tutù

musician • le musicien
• der Musiker • el músico
• il musicista

dancer • la danseuse
• die Tänzerin • la
bailarina • la ballerina

actress • l'atrice • der
Schauspielerin • la actriz
• l 'attrice

singer • la chanteuse
• die Sängerin • la
cantante • la cantante

waitress • la serveuse
• die Kellnerin • la
camarera • la cameriera

bartender • le barman
• der Barkeeper • el
camarero • il barista

sportsman • le sportif
• der Sportler • el
deportista • l'atleta

sculptor • le sculpteur
• der Bildhauer • el
escultor • lo scultore

notes
les notes
die Notizen
las notas
gli appunti

painter • la peintre
• die Malerin • la pintora
• la pittrice

photographer • le
photographe • der Fotograf
• el fotógrafo • il fotografo

anchor • la présentatrice
• die Nachrichtensprecherin • la
presentadora • l'annunciatrice

journalist • le journaliste
• der Journalist • el periodista
• il giornalista

editor • la rédactrice
• die Redakteurin • la
redactora • la redattrice

designer • la dessinateur
• der Designer • el diseñador
• il disegnatore

seamstress • la couturière
• die Damenschneiderin
• la modista • la costumista

tailor • le couturier
• der Schneider • el
sastre • il sarto

transportation
le transport
der Verkehr
el transporte
i trasporti

roads • les routes • die Straßen • las carreteras • le strade

freeway
l'autoroute
die Autobahn
la autopista
l'autostrada

toll booth
le poste de péage
die Mautstelle
la caseta de peaje
il casello

road markings
les signalisations
die Straßenmarkierungen
las señales horizontales
la segnaletica orizzontale

on-ramp
la bretelle d'accès
die Zufahrtsstraße
la vía de acceso
la rampa di accesso

one-way street
la rue à sens unique
die Einbahnstraße
la calle de sentido único
la strada a senso unico

divider
l'îlot directionnel
die Trennlinie
la línea divisoria
la linea divisoria

interchange
le carrefour
die Kreuzung
el cruce
l'incrocio

traffic light
les feux
die Verkehrsampel
el semáforo
il semaforo

right lane • la file de
droite • die rechte
Spur • el carril para
el tráfico lento
• la corsia interna

middle lane
la voie centrale
die mittlere Spur
el carril central
la corsia centrale

left lane
• la voie de
dépassement
• die Überholspur
• el carril de
adelantamiento
• la corsia di sorpasso

off-ramp
la bretelle de sortie
die Ausfahrts
la vía de salida
la rampa di uscita

traffic
la circulation
der Verkehr
el tráfico
il traffico

overpass
l'autopont
die Überführung
el paso elevado
il cavalcavia

shoulder
l'accotement stabilisé
der Seitenstreifen
el arcén
la corsia d'emergenza

underpass
le passage inférieur
die Unterführung
el paso subterráneo
il sottopassaggio

truck
le camion
der Lastwagen
el camión
il camion

median strip
le terre-plein
der Mittelstreifen
la mediana
lo spartitraffico

emergency phone • le téléphone de secours • die Notrufsäule • el teléfono de emergencia • il telefono per emergenze

disabled parking • le parking réservé aux personnes handicapées • der Behindertenparkplatz • el aparcamiento para minusválidos • il parcheggio per disabili

traffic jam • l'embouteillage • der Verkehrsstau • el atasco de tráfico • l'ingorgo

crosswalk
le passage clouté
der Fußgängerüberweg
el paso de peatones
il passaggio pedonale

satnav • le GPS • das Navi • el navegador por satélite • il navigatore satellitare

parking meter
le parc-mètre
die Parkuhr
el parquímetro
il parchimetro

traffic policeman • l'agent de la circulation • der Verkehrspolizist • el policía de tráfico • il vigile urbano

roundabout le rond-point der Kreisverkehr la glorieta la rotatoria	reverse (v) faire marche arrière rückwärts fahren dar marcha atrás fare marcia indietro	tow away (v) remorquer abschleppen remolcar rimorchiare
detour la déviation die Umleitung el desvío la deviazione	drive (v) conduire fahren conducir guidare	divided highway la route à quatre voies die Schnellstraße la autovía la carreggiata doppia
park (v) garer parken aparcar parcheggiare	roadwork les travaux die Straßenbaustelle las obras i lavori stradali	Is this the road to...? C'est la route pour...? Ist dies die Straße nach...? ¿Es ésta la carretera hacia...? È questa la strada per ...?
pass (v) doubler überholen adelantar sorpassare	guardrail la glissière de sécurité die Leitplanke la barrera de seguridad il guardrail	Where can I park? Où peut-on se garer? Wo kann ich parken? ¿Dónde se puede aparcar? Dove posso parcheggiare?

road signs • les panneaux routiers • die Verkehrsschilder • las señales de tráfico • i cartelli stradali

do not enter
sens interdit
keine Einfahrt
prohibido el paso
ingresso vietato

speed limit
la limitation de vitesse
die Geschwindig- keitsbegrenzung
el límite de velocidad
il limite di velocità

hazard
danger
Gefahr
peligro
pericolo

no stopping
arrêt interdit
halten verboten
prohibido parar
sosta vietata

no right turn
interdit de tourner à droite
rechts abbiegen verboten
no torcer a la derecha
svolta a destra vietata

bus • le bus • der Bus • el autobús • l'autobus

driver's seat
le siège du conducteur
der Fahrersitz
el asiento del conductor
il sedile dell'autista

handrail
la poignée
der Haltegriff
la barandilla
la maniglia

automatic door
la porte automatique
die Automatiktür
la puerta automática
la porta a soffietto

front wheel
la roue avant
das Vorderrad
la rueda delantera
la ruota anteriore

luggage hold
le compartiment à bagages
das Gepäckfach
el portaequipajes
il bagagliaio

door • la porte • die Tür • la puerta • la porta

long-distance bus • le car • der Reisebus • el autocar • il pullman

---

types of buses • les types de bus • die Bustypen • los tipos de autobuses • i tipi di autobus

route number
le numéro de bus
die Liniennummer
el número de ruta
il numero del percorso

driver
le conducteur
der Fahrer
el conductor
l'autista

double-decker bus • le bus à deux étages • der Doppeldecker • el autobús de dos pisos • l'autobus a due piani

tram • le tramway • die Straßenbahn • el tranvía • il tram

streetcar • le trolleybus • der Obus/der Trolleybus • el trolebús • il filobus

school bus • le bus scolaire • der Schulbus • el autobús escolar • lo scuolabus

stop button • le bouton
d'arrêt • der Halteknopf
• el botón de parada
• il pulsante di chiamata

rear wheel
la roue arrière
das Hinterrad
la rueda trasera
la ruota posteriore

window
la fenêtre
das Fenster
la ventana
il finestrino

bus ticket • le ticket
• der Fahrschein
• el billete de autobús
• il biglietto

bell • la sonnette
• die Klingel
• el timbre
• il campanello

bus station • la gare routière
• der Busbahnhof • la estación de autobuses
• l'autostazione

bus stop • l'arrêt de
bus • die Bushaltestelle
• la parada de autobús
• la fermata dell'autobus

fare	wheelchair access
le prix du ticket	l'accès aux handicapés
der Fahrpreis	der Rollstuhlzugang
la tarifa	la rampa para sillas de ruedas
la tariffa	l'accesso per sedie a rotelle
schedule	bus shelter
l'horaire	l'abribus
der Fahrplan	das Wartehäuschen
el horario	la marquesina
l'orario	la pensilina
Do you stop at…?	Which bus goes to…?
Vous arrêtez à…?	C'est quel bus pour aller à…?
Halten Sie am…?	Welcher Bus fährt nach…?
¿Para usted en…?	¿Qué autobús va a…?
Ferma a…?	Qual è l'autobus per…?

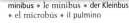

minibus • le minibus • der Kleinbus
• el microbús • il pulmino

tour bus • le bus de touristes • der Touristenbus
• el autobús turístico • il pullman turistico

shuttle bus • la navette • der Zubringer
• el autobús de enlace • la navetta

car 1 • la voiture 1 • das Auto 1 • el coche 1 • l'automobile 1

exterior • l'extérieur • das Äußere • el exterior • l'esterno

side mirror
le rétroviseur
der Seitenspiegel
el retrovisor exterior
lo specchietto laterale

windshield
le pare-brise
die Windschutzscheibe
el parabrisas
il parabrezza

rearview mirror
le rétroviseur
der Rückspiegel
el espejo retrovisor
lo specchietto retrovisore

windshield wiper
l'essuie-glace
der Scheibenwischer
el limpiaparabrisas
il tergicristallo

door
la porte
die Autotür
la puerta
lo sportello

hood
le capot
die Motorhaube
el capó
il cofano

trunk
le coffre
der Kofferraum
el maletero
il bagagliaio

turn signal
le clignotant
der Blinker
el intermitente
la freccia

license plate
la plaque d'immatriculation
das Nummernschild
la matrícula
la targa

bumper
le pare-chocs
die Stoßstange
el parachoques
il paraurti

headlight
le phare
der Scheinwerfer
el faro
il faro

wheel
la roue
das Rad
la rueda
la ruota

tire
le pneu
der Reifen
el neumático
il pneumatico

luggage
les bagages
das Gepäck
el equipaje
i bagagli

roof rack • la galerie • der Dachgepäckträger • la baca • il portabagagli

tailgate • le hayon • die Hecktür • la puerta del maletero • il portellone

seat belt • la ceinture de sécurité • der Sicherheitsgurt • el cinturón de seguridad • la cintura di sicurezza

car seat • le siège d'enfant • der Kindersitz • la silla para niños • il seggiolino per bambino

types • les modèles • die Wagentypen • los modelos • i tipi

electric car • la voiture électrique • das Elektroauto • el coche eléctrico • l'automobile elettrica

hatchback • la berline à hayon • die Fließhecklimousine • el coche de cinco puertas • l'auto a cinque porte

sedan • la berline • die Limousine • el turismo • la berlina

station wagon • le break • der Kombiwagen • el coche ranchera • l'auto familiare

convertible • la décapotable • das Cabrio • el coche descapotable • l'auto decappottabile

sports car • la voiture de sport • der Sportwagen • el coche deportivo • l'auto sportiva

minivan • la voiture à six places • die Großraumlimousine • el monovolumen • la monovolume

four-wheel drive • la quatre-quatre • der Geländewagen • el todoterreno • il fuoristrada

vintage • la voiture d'époque • der Oldtimer • el coche de época • l'auto d'epoca

limousine • la limousine • die Strechlimousine • la limusina • la limousine

---

gas station • la station-service • die Tankstelle • la gasolinera • la stazione di servizio

gas pump
la pompe
die Zapfsäule
el surtidor
il distributore di benzin

price
le tarif
der Benzinpreis
el precio
il prezzo

forecourt
l'aire de stationnement
der Tankstellenplatz
la zona de abastecimiento
l'area di stazionamento

oil	leaded	car wash
l'huile	avec plomb	le lave-auto
das Öl	verbleit	die Autowaschanlage
el aceite	con plomo	el lavadero de coches
l'olio	piombata	l'autolavaggio
gasoline	diesel	antifreeze
l'essence	le diesel	l'antigel
das Benzin	der Diesel	das Frostschutzmittel
la gasolina	el diesel	el anticongelante
la benzina	il diesel	l'antigelo
unleaded	garage	windshield washer fluid
sans plomb	le garage	le lave-glace
bleifrei	die Werkstatt	die Scheibenwaschanlage
sin plomo	el taller	el líquido limpiaparabrisas
senza piombo	il garage	il detergente per vetri

Fill it up, please.
Le plein, s'il vous plaît.
Voll tanken, bitte.
Lleno por favor.
Il pieno per favore.

car 2 • la voiture 2 • das Auto 2 • el coche 2 • l'automobile 2

interior • l'intérieur • die Innenausstattung • el interior • l'interno

backseat	armrest	headrest	door lock	handle
le siège arrière	l'accoudoir	le repose-tête	le verrouillage	la poignée
der Rücksitz	die Armstütze	die Kopfstütze	die Türverriegelung	der Türgriff
el asiento trasero	el reposabrazos	el reposacabezas	el pestillo	el tirador
il sedile posteriore	il bracciolo	il poggiatesta	la sicura	la maniglia

two-door	four-door	automatic	brake	accelerator
à deux portes	à quatre portes	automatique	le frein	l'accélérateur
zweitürig	viertürig	mit Automatik	die Bremse	das Gaspedal
de los puertas	de cuatro puertas	automático	el freno	el acelerador
a due porte	a quattro porte	automatico	il freno	l'acceleratore

hatchback	manual	ignition	clutch	air-conditioning
à trois portes	manuel	l'allumage	l'embrayage	la climatisation
dreitürig	mit Handschaltung	die Zündung	die Kupplung	die Klimaanlage
de tres puertas	manual	el encendido	el embrague	el aire acondicionado
a tre porte	manuale	l'accensione	la frizione	l'aria condizionata

Can you tell me the way to…?	Where is the parking lot?	Can I park here?
Pouvez-vous m'indiquer la route pour…?	Où est le parking?	On peut se garer ici?
Wie komme ich nach…?	Wo ist hier ein Parkplatz?	Kann ich hier parken?
¿Me puede decir cómo se va a…?	¿Dónde hay un parking?	¿Se puede aparcar aquí?
Può indicarmi la strada per…?	Dov'è il parcheggio?	Posso parcheggiare qui?

english • français • deutsch • español • italiano

controls • les commandes • die Armaturen • los controles • i comandi

steering wheel	horn	dashboard	hazard lights	satellite navigation
le volant	le klaxon	le tableau de bord	les feux de détresse	le navigateur par satellite
das Lenkrad	die Hupe	das Armaturenbrett	die Warnlichter	das GPS-System
el volante	la bocina	el salpicadero	las luces de emergencia	la navegación por satélite
il volante	il clacson	il cruscotto	le luci intermittenti	la navigazione via satellite

left-hand drive • la conduite à gauche • die Linkssteuerung • el volante a la izquierda • la guida a sinistra

temperature gauge	tachometer	speedometer	fuel gauge
le thermomètre	le compte-tours	le compteur	la jauge d'essence
die Temperaturanzeige	der Drehzahlmesser	der Tachometer	die Kraftstoffanzeige
el indicador de temperatura	el cuentarrevoluciones	el indicador de velocidad	el indicador de la gasolina
la spia della temperatura	il contagiri	il tachimetro	la spia del carburante

car stereo
la stéréo
die Autostereoanlage
la radio del coche
l'autoradio

heater controls
la manette de chauffage
der Heizungsregler
los mandos de la calefacción
i comandi per il riscaldamento

gearshift
le levier de vitesses
der Schalthebel
la palanca de cambios
la leva del cambio

light switch
l'interrupteur feux
der Lichtschalter
el conmutador de luces
l'interruttore per le luci

odometer
l'odomètre
der Kilometerzähler
el cuentakilómetros
il contachilometri

air bag
l'airbag
der Airbag
el airbag
l'airbag

right-hand drive • la conduite à droite • die Rechtssteuerung
• el volante a la derecha • la guida a destra

car 3 • la voiture 3 • das Auto 3 • el coche 3 • l'automobile 3

mechanics • la mécanique • die Mechanik • la mecánica • la meccanica

washer fluid reservoir
le réservoir de lave-glace
der Scheibenputzmittelbehälter
el depósito del limpiaparabrisas
il serbatoio del liquido lavavetri

dipstick
la jauge d'huile
der Ölmessstab
la varilla del nivel del aceite
l'indicatore di livello dell'olio

air filter
le filtre à air
der Luftfilter
el filtro del aire
il filtro dell'aria

brake fluid reservoir
le réservoir de liquide de frein
der Bremsflüssigkeitsbehälter
el depósito del líquido de frenos
il serbatoio del liquido per i freni

battery
la batterie
die Batterie
la batería
la batteria

bodywork
la carrosserie
die Karosserie
la chapa
la carrozzeria

sunroof
le toit ouvrant
das Schiebedach
el techo solar
il tettuccio

coolant reservoir • le réservoir de
liquide de refroidissement • der
Kühlmittelbehälter • el depósito del
liquido refrigerante • il serbatoio
per il liquido refrigerante

cylinder head
la culasse
der Zylinderkopf
la culata
la testa del cilindro

pipe
le tuyau
das Rohr
el tubo
il tubo

engine
le moteur
der Motor
el motor
il motore

radiator
le radiateur
der Kühler
el radiador
il radiatore

fan
le ventilateur
der Ventilator
el ventilador
il ventilatore

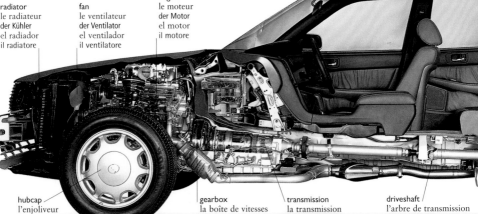

hubcap
l'enjoliveur
die Radkappe
el tapacubos
il coprimozzo

gearbox
la boîte de vitesses
das Getriebe
la caja de cambios
il cambio

transmission
la transmission
die Transmission
la transmisión
la trasmissione

driveshaft
l'arbre de transmission
die Kardanwelle
el eje de la transmisión
l'albero di trasmissione

flat tire • la crevaison • die Reifenpanne • el pinchazo • la foratura

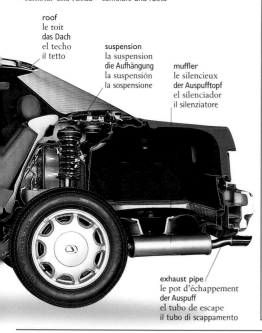

spare tire
la roue de secours
das Ersatzrad
la rueda de repuesto
la ruota di scorta

tire iron
la manivelle
der Radschlüssel
la llave
la chiave

lug nuts
les écrous de roue
die Radmuttern
las tuercas de la rueda
i bulloni della ruota

jack
le cric
der Wagenheber
el gato
il cric

change a tire (v) • changer une roue • ein Rad wechseln
• cambiar una rueda • cambiare una ruota

roof
le toit
das Dach
el techo
il tetto

suspension
la suspension
die Aufhängung
la suspensión
la sospensione

muffler
le silencieux
der Auspufftopf
el silenciador
il silenziatore

exhaust pipe
le pot d'échappement
der Auspuff
el tubo de escape
il tubo di scappamento

car accident
l'accident de voiture
der Autounfall
el accidente de coche
l'incidente stradale

breakdown
la panne
die Panne
la avería
il guasto

insurance
l'assurance
die Versicherung
el seguro
l'assicurazione

tow truck
la dépanneuse
der Abschleppwagen
la grúa
il carro attrezzi

mechanic
le mécanicien
der Mechaniker
el mecánico
il meccanico

tire pressure
la pression des pneus
der Reifendruck
la presión del neumático
la pressione dei pneumatici

fuse box
le porte-fusibles
der Sicherungskasten
la caja de fusibles
la scatola dei fusibili

spark plug
la bougie
die Zündkerze
la bujía
la candela

fan belt
la courroie de ventilateur
der Keilriemen
la correa del ventilador
la cinghia della ventola

gas tank
le réservoir d'essence
der Benzintank
el tanque de la gasolina
il serbatoio della benzina

cam belt
la courroie de cames
der Nockenriemen
la correa del disco
la cinghia della camma

turbocharger
le turbocompresseur
der Turbolader
el turbo
il tubocompressore

distributor
le distributeur
der Verteiler
el distribuidor
il distributore

timing
le réglage de l'allumage
die Einstellung
el ralentí
la messa in fase

chassis
le châssis
das Chassis
el chasis
il telaio

parking brake
le frein à main
die Handbremse
el freno de mano
il freno a mano

alternator
l'alternateur
die Lichtmaschine
el alternador
l'alternatore

My car has broken down.
Ma voiture est en panne.
Ich habe eine Panne.
Mi coche se ha averiado.
Sono in panne.

My car won't start.
Ma voiture ne démarre pas.
Mein Auto springt nicht an.
Mi coche no arranca.
La mia macchina non parte.

motorcycle • la moto • das Motorrad • la motocicleta • la motocicletta

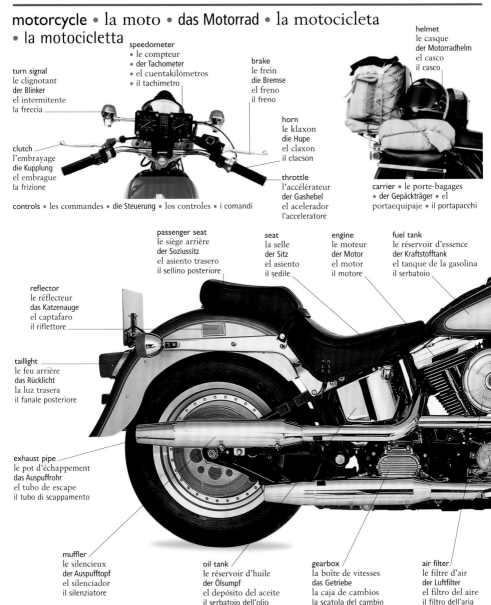

helmet
le casque
der Motorradhelm
el casco
il casco

speedometer
• le compteur
• der Tachometer
• el cuentakilómetros
• il tachimetro

turn signal
le clignotant
der Blinker
el intermitente
la freccia

brake
le frein
die Bremse
el freno
il freno

horn
le klaxon
die Hupe
el claxon
il clacson

clutch
l'embrayage
die Kupplung
el embrague
la frizione

throttle
l'accélérateur
der Gashebel
el acelerador
l'acceleratore

carrier • le porte-bagages
• der Gepäckträger • el
portaequipaje • il portapacchi

controls • les commandes • die Steuerung • los controles • i comandi

passenger seat
le siège arrière
der Soziussitz
el asiento trasero
il sellino posteriore

seat
la selle
der Sitz
el asiento
il sedile

engine
le moteur
der Motor
el motor
il motore

fuel tank
le réservoir d'essence
der Kraftstofftank
el tanque de la gasolina
il serbatoio

reflector
le réflecteur
das Katzenauge
el captafaro
il riflettore

taillight
le feu arrière
das Rücklicht
la luz trasera
il fanale posteriore

exhaust pipe
le pot d'échappement
das Auspuffrohr
el tubo de escape
il tubo di scappamento

muffler
le silencieux
der Auspufftopf
el silenciador
il silenziatore

oil tank
le réservoir d'huile
der Ölsumpf
el depósito del aceite
il serbatoio dell'olio

gearbox
la boîte de vitesses
das Getriebe
la caja de cambios
la scatola del cambio

air filter
le filtre d'air
der Luftfilter
el filtro del aire
il filtro dell'aria

english • français • deutsch • español • italiano

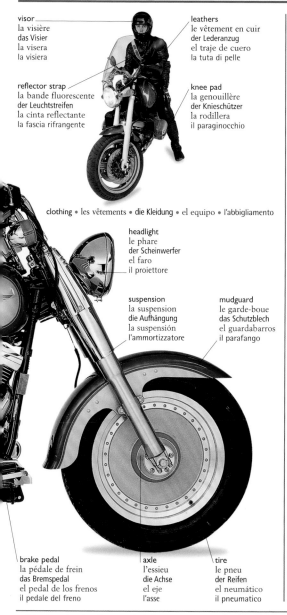

visor
la visière
das Visier
la visera
la visiera

leathers
le vêtement en cuir
der Lederanzug
el traje de cuero
la tuta di pelle

reflector strap
la bande fluorescente
der Leuchtstreifen
la cinta reflectante
la fascia rifrangente

knee pad
la genouillère
der Knieschützer
la rodillera
il paraginocchio

clothing • les vêtements • die Kleidung • el equipo • l'abbigliamento

headlight
le phare
der Scheinwerfer
el faro
il proiettore

suspension
la suspension
die Aufhängung
la suspensión
l'ammortizzatore

mudguard
le garde-boue
das Schutzblech
el guardabarros
il parafango

brake pedal
la pédale de frein
das Bremspedal
el pedal de los frenos
il pedale del freno

axle
l'essieu
die Achse
el eje
l'asse

tire
le pneu
der Reifen
el neumático
il pneumatico

types • les types • die Typen • los tipos
• i tipi

racing bike • la moto de course • die Rennmaschine
• la moto de carreras • la moto da corsa

windshield • le pare-brise
• die Windschutzscheibe • el
parabrisas • il parabrezza

tourer • la moto routière • der Tourer • la moto
de carretera • la moto da turismo

dirt bike • la moto tout-terrain • das Geländemotorrad
• la moto de cross • la moto da cross

stand • la béquille • der
Motorradständer • el soporte
• il cavalletto

scooter • le scooter • der Roller • la vespa • il
motorino

bicycle • la bicyclette • das Fahrrad • la bicicleta • la bicicletta

tandem • le tandem • das Tandem • el tándem • il tandem

racing bike • le vélo de course • das Rennrad • la bicicleta de carreras • la bicicletta da corsa

mountain bike • le vélo tout-terrain • das Mountainbike • la bicicleta de montaña • la mountain bike

touring bike • le vélo de randonnée • das Tourenfahrrad • la bicicleta de paseo • la bicicletta da turismo

road bike • le vélo de ville • das Straßenrad • la bicicleta de carretera • la bicicletta da strada

saddle
la selle
der Sattel
el sillín
il sellino

seat post
le tube porte-selle
die Sattelstütze
el soporte del sillín
il tubo reggisella

water bottle
la bouteille d'eau
die Wasserflasche
la botella del agua
la borraccia

frame
le cadre
der Rahmen
el cuadro
il telaio

brake
le frein
die Felgenbremse
el freno
il freno

hub
le moyeu
die Nabe
el eje
il mozzo

gears
les vitesses
die Gänge
las marchas
le marce

rim
la jante
die Felge
la llanta
il cerchione

tire
le pneu
der Reifen
la cubierta
il pneumatico

chain
la chaîne
die Fahrradkette
la cadena
la catena

cog
la roue dentée
das Zahnrad
el diente de la rueda
la ruota dentata

pedal
la pédale
das Pedal
el pedal
il pedale

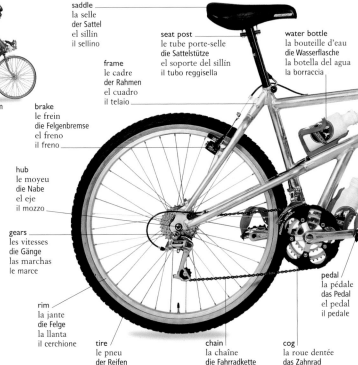

helmet
le casque
der Fahrradhelm
el casco
il casco

bike lane • la piste cyclable • der Fahrradweg • el carril de bicicletas • la pista ciclabile

english • français • deutsch • español • italiano

crossbar • la barre • die Stange • el tubo superior • la canna

handlebar le guidon die Lenkstange el manillar il manubrio

gear lever le levier de vitesse der Schalthebel la palanca de cambio la leva del cambio

brake lever le levier de frein der Bremsgriff los frenos la leva del freno

fork la fourche die Gabel la horquilla la forcella

spoke le rayon die Speiche el radio il raggio

wheel la roue das Rad la rueda la ruota

valve la valve das Ventil la válvula la valvola

tread la bande de roulement das Reifenprofil la banda de rodadura il battistrada

tire lever • le démonte-pneu • der Reifenschlüssel • la palanca de la llanta • la leva per il pneumatico

patch la rustine der Flicken el parche la toppa

repair kit • la boîte d'outils • der Reparaturkasten • el kit de reparaciones • il kit per riparazioni

key la clef der Schlüssel la llave la chiave

pump • la pompe • die Luftpumpe • la bomba • la pompa

lock • l'antivol • das Fahrradschloss • el candado • il lucchetto

inner tube • la chambre à air • der Schlauch • la cámara • la camera d'aria

child seat • le siège d'enfant • der Kindersitz • la silla de niños • il seggiolino per bambino

headlight	kickstand	brake block	basket	toe clip	change gears (v)
le phare	la béquille	le patin de frein	le panier	le cale-pied	changer de vitesse
die Fahrradlampe	der Fahrradständer	die Bremsbacke	der Korb	der Rennbügel	schalten
el faro	la patilla de apoyo	el taco del freno	la cesta	el calzapié	cambiar de marcha
il fanale	il cavalletto	il blocca freni	il cestello	il fermapiedi	cambiare marcia
rear light	traning wheels	cable	dynamo	toe strap	brake (v)
le feu arrière	les roues d'entraînement	le câble	la dynamo	la lanière	freiner
das Rücklicht	die Stützräder	das Kabel	der Dynamo	der Riemen	bremsen
el faro trasero	las ruedas de apoyo	el cable	la dinamo	la correa del calzapié	frenar
il fanale posteriore	le rotelle	il cavo	la dinamo	il cinghietto	frenare
reflector	bike rack	sprocket	flat tire	pedal (v)	cycle (v)
le cataphote	la galerie à vélo	le pignon	la crevaison	pédaler	faire du vélo
der Rückstrahler	der Fahrradständer	das Kettenzahnrad	die Reifenpanne	treten	Rad fahren
el captafaro	el aparcamiento para bicicletas	el piñón	el pinchazo	pedalear	ir en bicicleta
il catarifrangente	il posteggio per bici	il dente	la foratura	pedalare	andare in bici

train • le train • der Zug • el tren • il treno

railcar
la voiture
der Wagen
el vagón
il vagone

platform
le quai
der Bahnsteig
el andén
il binario

cart
le caddie
der Kofferkuli
el carrito
il carrello

platform number
le numéro de voie
die Gleisnummer
el número de andén
il numero del binario

commuter
le voyageur
der Pendler
el viajero
de cercanías
il pendolare

train station • la gare • der Bahnhof • la estación de tren • la stazione ferroviaria

types of train • les types de trains • die Zugtypen • los tipos de tren • i tipi di treno

engine
la locomotive
die Lokomotive
la locomotora
la locomotiva

engineer's cab
la cabine du conducteur
der Führerstand
la cabina del conductor
la cabina del conducente

rail
le rail
die Schiene
el rail
la rotaia

steam train • le train à vapeur
• die Dampflokomotive • el tren de vapor
• il treno a vapore

diesel train • le train diesel • die Diesellokomotive • el tren diesel • il treno diesel

electric train • le train électrique
• die Elektrolokomotive • el tren eléctrico
• il treno elettrico

high-speed train • le train à grande vitesse
• der Hochgeschwindigkeitszug • el tren de
alta velocidad • il treno ad alta velocità

monorail • le monorail • die
Einschienenbahn • el monorrail
• la monorotaia

subway • le métro • die U-Bahn •
el metro • la metropolitana

tram • le tram • die Straßenbahn
• el tranvía • il tram

freight train • le train de marchandises
• der Güterzug • el tren de mercancías
• il treno merci

english • français • deutsch • español • italiano

luggage rack • le porte-bagages • die Gepäckablage • el portaequipajes • il portabagagli

window	track
la fenêtre	la voie ferrée
das Zugfenster	das Gleis
la ventanilla	la vía
il finestrino	il binario

door	seat
la porte	le siège
die Tür	der Sitz
la puerta	el asiento
la porta	il sedile

compartment • le compartiment • das Abteil • el vagón • lo scompartimento

public address system	schedule
le haut-parleur	l'horaire
der Lautsprecher	der Fahrplan
el sistema de megafonía	el horario
l'altoparlante	l'orario

ticket gates • le portillon • die Eingangssperre • la barrera • la barriera

ticket • le billet • die Fahrkarte • el billete • il biglietto

dining car • la voiture-restaurant • der Speisewagen • el vagón restaurante • il vagone ristorante

concourse • le hall de gare • die Bahnhofshalle • el vestíbulo • l'atrio

sleeping compartment • le compartiment-couchettes • das Schlafabteil • el cochecama • lo scompartimento a cuccette

railroad network	subway map	ticket office	live rail
le réseau ferroviaire	le plan de métro	le guichet	le rail conducteur
das Bahnnetz	der U-Bahnplan	der Fahrkartenschalter	die stromführende Schiene
la red ferroviaria	el plano del metro	la taquilla	el raíl electrificado
la rete ferroviaria	la mappa della metropolitana	la biglietteria	il binario elettrificato
express train	delay	ticket inspector	signal
le rapide	le retard	le contrôleur	le signal
der Intercity	die Verspätung	der Schaffner	das Signal
el tren intercity	el retraso	el revisor	la señal
il treno intercity	il ritardo	il controllore	il segnale
rush hour	fare	transfer (v)	emergency lever
l'heure de pointe	le prix	changer	la manette de secours
die Stoßzeit	der Fahrpreis	umsteigen	die Notbremse
la hora punta	el precio	cambiar	el freno de emergencia
l'ora di punta	la tariffa	cambiare	la leva di emergenza

aircraft • l'avion • das Flugzeug • el avión • l'aeroplano

airliner • l'avion de ligne • das Verkehrsflugzeug • el avión de pasajeros • l'aereo di linea

nose	cockpit	engine	fuselage	wing	tail
le nez	le cockpit	le réacteur	le fuselage	l'aile	la queue
der Bug	das Cockpit	das Triebwerk	der Rumpf	die Tragfläche	das Heck
el morro	la cabina de pilotaje	el motor	el fuselaje	el ala	la cola
il muso	la cabina di pilotaggio	il motore	la fusoliera	l'ala	la coda

rudder
la gouverne
das Seitenruder
el timón
il timone

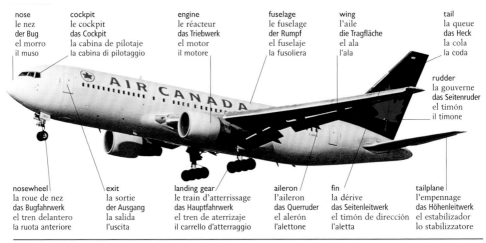

nosewheel	exit	landing gear	aileron	fin	tailplane
la roue de nez	la sortie	le train d'atterrissage	l'aileron	la dérive	l'empennage
das Bugfahrwerk	der Ausgang	das Hauptfahrwerk	das Querruder	das Seitenleitwerk	das Höhenleitwerk
el tren delantero	la salida	el tren de aterrizaje	el alerón	el timón de dirección	el estabilizador
la ruota anteriore	l'uscita	il carrello d'atterraggio	l'alettone	l'aletta	lo stabilizzatore

cabin • la cabine • die Kabine • la cabina • la cabina

emergency exit	flight attendant	overhead bin
la sortie de secours	l'hôtesse de l'air	le casier à bagages
der Notausgang	die Flugbegleiterin	das Gepäckfach
la salida de emergencia	la azafata de vuelo	el compartimento portaequipajes
l'uscita di emergenza	l'assistente di volo	il compartimento portabagagli

air vent
le ventilateur
die Luftdüse
el ventilador
la ventola per l'aria

window
le hublot
das Fenster
la ventanilla
il finestrino

reading light
la liseuse
die Leselampe
la luz de lectura
la luce di lettura

seat
le siège
der Sitz
el asiento
il sedile

row
la rangée
die Reihe
la fila
la fila

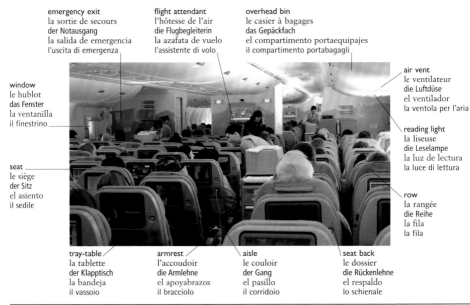

tray-table	armrest	aisle	seat back
la tablette	l'accoudoir	le couloir	le dossier
der Klapptisch	die Armlehne	der Gang	die Rückenlehne
la bandeja	el apoyabrazos	el pasillo	el respaldo
il vassoio	il bracciolo	il corridoio	lo schienale

ultralight • l'U.L.M. • das Ultraleichtflugzeug • el ultraligero • l'aereo biposto

glider • le planeur • das Segelflugzeug • el planeador • l'aliante

biplane • le biplan • der Doppeldecker • el biplano • il biplano

propeller
l'hélice
der Propeller
la hélice
l'elica

hot-air balloon • la montgolfière • der Heißluftballon • el globo aerostático • la mongolfiera

light aircraft • l'avion léger • das Leichtflugzeug • la avioneta • l'aereo da diporto

seaplane • l'hydravion • das Wasserflugzeug • el hidroavión • l'idrovolante

missile
le missile
die Rakete
el misil
il missile

private jet • le jet privé • der Privatjet • el jet privado • l'aereo privato

fighter plane • le chasseur • das Jagdflugzeug • el caza • l'aereo da caccia

rotor blade
la pale de rotor
das Rotorblatt
el aspa
la lama rotante

helicopter • l'hélicoptère • der Hubschrauber • el helicóptero • l'elicottero

bomber • le bombardier • das Bombenflugzeug • el avión de bombardeo • il bombardiere

pilot	take off (v)	land (v)	economy class	carry-on luggage
le pilote	décoller	atterrir	la classe économique	les bagages à main
der Pilot	starten	landen	die Economyclass	das Handgepäck
el piloto	despegar	aterrizar	la clase turista	el equipaje de mano
il pilota	decollare	atterrare	la classe economica	il bagaglio a mano
copilot	fly (v)	altitude	business class	seat belt
le copilote	voler	l'altitude	la classe affaires	la ceinture de sécurité
der Kopilot	fliegen	die Höhe	die Businessclass	der Sicherheitsgurt
el copiloto	volar	la altitud	la clase preferente	el cinturón de seguridad
il copilota	volare	la quota	la business class	la cintura di sicurezza

airport • l'aéroport • der Flughafen • el aeropuerto • l'aeroporto

apron
l'aire de stationnement
das Vorfeld
la pista de estacionamiento
l'area di stazionamento

baggage trailer
le porte-bagages
der Gepäckanhänger
el remolque del equipaje
il carrello portabagagli

terminal
le terminal
der Terminal
la terminal
il terminal

service vehicle
le véhicule de service
das Versorgungsfahrzeug
el vehículo de servicio
il veicolo di servizio

jetway
la passerelle
die Fluggastbrücke
la pasarela
il passaggio pedonale

airliner • l'avion de ligne • das Verkehrsflugzeug • el avión de línea • l'aereo di linea

runway la piste die Start- und Landebahn la pista la pista	flight number le numéro de vol die Flugnummer el número de vuelo il numero del volo	baggage carousel le tapis roulant das Gepäckband la cinta de equipajes il nastro trasportatore	vacation les vacances der Urlaub las vacaciones la vacanza
international flight le vol international der Auslandsflug el vuelo internacional il volo internazionale	immigration l'immigration die Einwanderung inmigración l'immigrazione	security la sécurité die Sicherheitsvorkehrungen la seguridad la sicurezza	book a flight (v) faire une réservation de vol einen Flug buchen reservar un vuelo prenotare un volo
domestic flight le vol domestique der Inlandsflug el vuelo nacional il volo nazionale	customs la douane der Zoll la aduana la dogana	x-ray machine la machine de rayons x die Gepäckröntgenmaschine la máquina de rayos x l'apparecchio a raggi x	check in (v) enregistrer einchecken facturar fare il check-in
connection la correspondance die Flugverbindung la conexión la coincidenza	excess baggage l'excédent de bagages das Übergepäck el exceso de equipaje il bagaglio in eccedenza	travel brochure la brochure de vacances der Urlaubsprospekt el folleto de viajes l'opuscolo vacanze	control tower la tour de contrôle der Kontrollturm la torre de control la torre di controllo

visa
le visa
das Visum
el visado
il visto

passport • le passeport • der Pass • el pasaporte • il passaporto

carry-on luggage
les bagages à main
das Handgepäck
el equipaje de mano
il bagaglio a mano

luggage
les bagages
das Gepäck
el equipaje
il bagaglio

cart
le chariot
der Kofferkuli
el carro
il carrello

boarding pass
la carte d'embarquement
die Bordkarte
la tarjeta de embarque
la carta d'imbarco

check-in desk • l'enregistrement des bagages • der Abfertigungsschalter • el mostrador de facturación • il banco accettazione

passport control • le contrôle de passeports • die Passkontrolle • el control de pasaportes • il controllo passaporti

ticket • le billet • das Flugticket • el billete • il biglietto

gate number • le numéro de la porte d'embarquement • die Gatenummer • el número de puerta de embarque • il numero dell'uscita

departures
les départs
der Abflug
las salidas
le partenze

destination
la destination
das Reiseziel
el destino
la destinazione

arrivals
les arrivées
die Ankunft
las llegadas
gli arrivi

departure lounge • la salle de départ • die Abflughalle • la sala de embarque • la sala delle partenze

information screen • l'écran d'information • die Fluginformationsanzeige • la pantalla de información • il pannello degli orari

duty-free shop
la boutique hors taxes
der Duty-free-Shop
la tienda libre de impuestos
il negozio duty free

baggage claim
le retrait des bagages
die Gepäckausgabe
la recogida de equipajes
il ricupero bagagli

taxi stand
la station de taxis
der Taxistand
la parada de taxis
il posteggio dei taxi

car rental
la location de voitures
der Autoverleih
el alquiler de coches
l'autonoleggio

ship • le navire • das Schiff • el barco • la nave

radar
le radar
der Radar
el radar
il radar

radio antenna
l'antenne radio
die Funkantenne
la antena de radio
l'antenna della radio

deck
le pont
das Deck
la cubierta
il ponte

funnel
la cheminée
der Schornstein
la chimenea
il fumaiolo

quarterdeck
le pont arrière
das Achterdeck
el alcázar
il casseretto

prow
la proue
der Bug
la proa
la prua

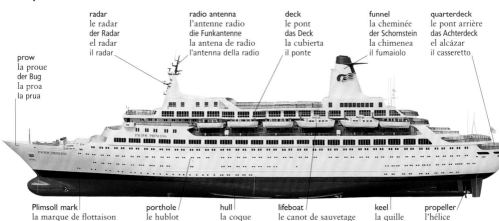

Plimsoll mark
la marque de flottaison
die Höchsttlademarke
la línea de flotación
la marca di bordo libero

porthole
le hublot
das Bullauge
el ojo de buey
l'oblò

hull
la coque
der Rumpf
el casco
lo scafo

lifeboat
le canot de sauvetage
das Rettungsboot
el bote salvavidas
la lancia di salvataggio

keel
la quille
der Kiel
la quilla
la chiglia

propeller
l'hélice
die Schiffsschraube
la hélice
l'elica

ocean liner • le paquebot • der Ozeandampfer • el transatlántico • la nave da crociera

bridge • la passerelle de commandement • die Kommandobrücke • el puente • il ponte di comando

engine room • la salle des moteurs • der Maschinenraum • la sala de máquinas • la sala macchine

cabin • la cabine • die Kabine • el camarote • la cabina

galley • la cuisine • die Kombüse • la cocina • la cucina di bordo

dock
le dock
das Dock
el muelle
il bacino

windlass
le guindeau
die Ankerwinde
el cabrestante
il mulinello

port
le port
der Hafen
el puerto
il porto

captain
le capitaine
der Kapitän
el capitán
il capitano

gangway
la passerelle
die Landungsbrücke
la pasarela
la passerella

speedboat
le runabout
das Rennboot
la lancha motora
il motoscafo

anchor
l'ancre
der Anker
el ancla
l'ancora

rowboat
la barque
das Ruderboot
la barca de remos
la barca a remi

bollard
le bollard
der Poller
el noray
la colonna d'ormeggio

canoe
le canoë
das Kanu
la piragua
la canoa

other ships • autres bateaux • andere Schiffe • otras embarcaciones • altre imbarcazioni

outboard motor
le hors-bord
der Außenbordmotor
el motor fueraborda
il motore fuoribordo

ferry • le ferry • die Fähre • el ferry • il traghetto

inflatable dinghy • le dinghy pneumatique • das Schlauchboot • la zodiac • il gommone

hydrofoil • l'hydroptère • das Tragflügelboot • el hidrodeslizador • l'aliscafo

yacht • le yacht • die Jacht • el yate • lo yacht

catamaran • le catamaran • der Katamaran • el catamarán • il catamarano

tugboat • le remorqueur • der Schleppdampfer • el remolcador • il rimorchiatore

hovercraft • l'aéroglisseur • das Luftkissenboot • el aerodeslizador • l'hovercraft

rigging
le gréement
die Takelung
las jarcias
il sartiame

hold
la cale
der Frachtraum
la bodega
la stiva

container ship • le navire porte-conteneurs • das Containerschiff • el buque portacontenedores • la nave porta container

sailboat • le voilier • das Segelboot • el barco de vela • la barca a vela

freighter • le cargo • das Frachtschiff • el buque de carga • la nave da trasporto

conning tower
le kiosque
der Kommandoturm
la falsa torre
la torretta di comando

oil tanker • le pétrolier • der Öltanker • el petrolero • la petroliera

aircraft carrier • le porte-avions • der Flugzeugträger • el portaaviones • la portaerei

battleship • le navire de guerre • das Kriegsschiff • el barco de guerra • la nave da guerra

submarine • le sous-marin • das U-Boot • el submarino • il sottomarino

port • le port • der Hafen • el puerto • il porto

warehouse	crane	forklift	access road	customs house
l'entrepôt	la grue	le chariot élévateur	la route d'accès	le bureau des douanes
das Warenlager	der Kran	der Gabelstapler	die Zufahrtstraße	das Zollamt
el almacén	la grúa	la carretilla elevadora	la vía de acceso	las aduanas del puerto
il magazzino	la gru	il carrello elevatore	la strada di accesso	l'ufficio della dogana

container	dock	quay	cargo	ferry terminal	ferry
le conteneur	le dock	le quai	la cargaison	le terminal de ferrys	le ferry
der Container	das Dock	der Kai	die Fracht	der Fährterminal	die Fähre
el contenedor	la dársena	el muelle	la carga	la terminal del ferry	el ferry
il container	il bacino	la banchina	il carico	il terminale dei traghetti	il traghetto

ticket office
le guichet
der Fahrkartenschalter
la ventanilla de pasajes
la biglietteria

passenger
le passager
der Passagier
el pasajero
il passeggero

container port • le port de conteneurs • der Containerhafen • el muelle comercial • il porto per container

passenger port • le port de passagers • der Passagierhafen • el muelle de pasajeros • il porto per passeggeri

net
le filet
das Netz
la red
la rete

fishing boat
le bateau de pêche
das Fischerboot
el barco de pesca
la barca da pesca

mooring
les amarres
die Verankerung
el punto de amarre
l'ormeggio

marina • la marina • der Jachthafen • el puerto deportivo • il porto turistico

fishing port • le port de pêche • der Fischereihafen • el puerto de pesca • il porto da pesca

harbor • le port • der Hafen • el puerto • il porto

pier • l'embarcadère • der Pier • el embarcadero • il pontile

jetty • la jetée • der Landungssteg • el espigón • il molo

shipyard • le chantier naval • die Werft • el astillero • il cantiere navale

lamp
le feu
die Laterne
la lámpara
la luce

lighthouse • le phare • der Leuchtturm • el faro • il faro

buoy • la bouée • die Boje • la boya • la boa

coast guard	dry dock	board (v)
le garde-côte	la cale sèche	embarquer
die Küstenwache	das Trockendock	an Bord gehen
el guardacostas	el dique seco	embarcar
il guardacoste	il bacino di carenaggio	imbarcare
harbor master	moor (v)	disembark (v)
le capitaine de port	mouiller	débarquer
der Hafenmeister	festmachen	von Bord gehen
el capitán del puerto	amarrar	desembarcar
il capitano di porto	ormeggiare	sbarcare
drop anchor (v)	dock (v)	set sail (v)
jeter l'ancre	se mettre à quai	prendre la mer
den Anker werfen	anlegen	auslaufen
fondear	atracar	zarpar
mollare l'ancora	approdare	salpare

sports
les sports
der Sport
los deportes
gli sport

football • le football américain • der Football • el fútbol americano • il football americano

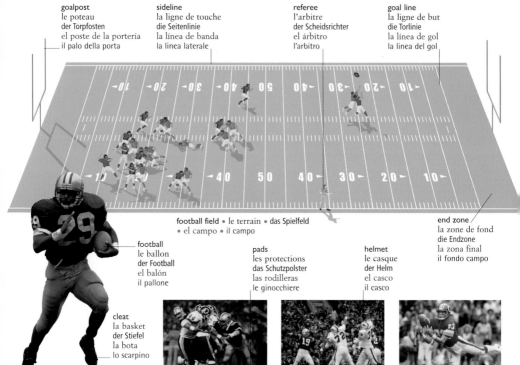

goalpost
le poteau
der Torpfosten
el poste de la portería
il palo della porta

sideline
la ligne de touche
die Seitenlinie
la línea de banda
la linea laterale

referee
l'arbitre
der Scheidsrichter
el árbitro
l'arbitro

goal line
la ligne de but
die Torlinie
la línea de gol
la linea del gol

football field • le terrain • das Spielfeld • el campo • il campo

end zone
la zone de fond
die Endzone
la zona final
il fondo campo

football
le ballon
der Football
el balón
il pallone

pads
les protections
das Schutzpolster
las rodilleras
le ginocchiere

helmet
le casque
der Helm
el casco
il casco

cleat
la basket
der Stiefel
la bota
lo scarpino

football player • le joueur de football • der Footballspieler • el jugador • il giocatore

tackle (v) • tacler • angreifen • placar • placcare

pass (v) • faire une passe • den Ball abgeben • pasar • passare

catch (v) • attraper • fangen • coger • prendere

time out le temps mort die Auszeit el tiempo muerto il time-out	team l'équipe die Mannschaft el equipo la squadra	defense la défense die Verteidigung la defensa la difesa	cheerleader la majorette der Cheerleader la animadora la cheerleader	What is the score? Où en est le match? Wie ist der Stand? ¿Cómo van? A quanto stanno?
fumble la prise de ballon maladroite das unsichere Fangen des Balls el mal pase de balón il fumble	attack l'attaque der Angriff el ataque l'attacco	score le score der Spielstand la puntuación il punteggio	touchdown le but der Touchdown el ensayo il touch-down	Who is winning? Qui est-ce qui gagne? Wer gewinnt? ¿Quién va ganando? Chi vince?

rugby • le rugby • das Rugby • el rugby • il rugby

goal
le but
das Tor
la portería
la porta

in-goal area
la surface de but
der Torraum
la zona de marca
l'area della porta

touch line
la ligne de touche
die Seitenlinie
la línea de banda
la linea di touch

flag
le drapeau
die Fahne
la bandera
la bandierina

dead ball line
la ligne de ballon mort
die Feldauslinie
la línea de fondo
la linea di palla morta

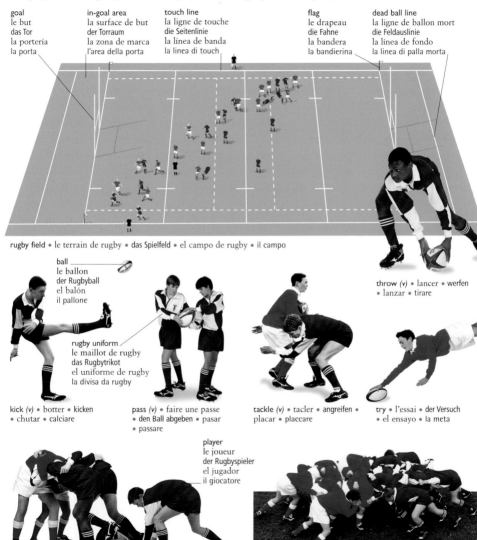

rugby field • le terrain de rugby • das Spielfeld • el campo de rugby • il campo

ball
le ballon
der Rugbyball
el balón
il pallone

rugby uniform
le maillot de rugby
das Rugbytrikot
el uniforme de rugby
la divisa da rugby

throw (v) • lancer • werfen
• lanzar • tirare

kick (v) • botter • kicken
• chutar • calciare

pass (v) • faire une passe
• den Ball abgeben • pasar
• passare

tackle (v) • tacler • angreifen
placar • placcare

try • l'essai • der Versuch
• el ensayo • la meta

player
le joueur
der Rugbyspieler
el jugador
il giocatore

ruck • la mêlée ouverte • das offene Gedränge • la abierta • il ruck

scrum • la mêlée • das Gedränge • la melée • la mischia

soccer • le football • der Fußball • el fútbol • il calcio

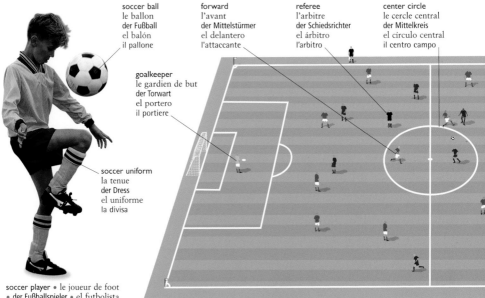

soccer ball
le ballon
der Fußball
el balón
il pallone

goalkeeper
le gardien de but
der Torwart
el portero
il portiere

soccer uniform
la tenue
der Dress
el uniforme
la divisa

forward
l'avant
der Mittelstürmer
el delantero
l'attaccante

referee
l'arbitre
der Schiedsrichter
el árbitro
l'arbitro

center circle
le cercle central
der Mittelkreis
el círculo central
il centro campo

soccer player • le joueur de foot
• der Fußballspieler • el futbolista
• il calciatore

soccer field • le terrain • das Fußballfeld • el campo de fútbol • il campo di calcio

goalpost
le poteau
der Torpfosten
el poste
il palo

net
le filet
das Tornetz
la red
la rete

crossbar
la barre transversale
die Querlatte
el larguero
la traversa

dribble (v) • dribbler • dribbeln
• regatear • dribblare

head (v) • faire une tête
• köpfen • tirar de cabeza
• colpire di testa

wall
le mur
die Mauer
la barrera
il muro

goal • le but • das Tor • el gol • il gol

free kick • le coup franc • der Freistoß
• tirar una falta • il calcio di punizione

english • français • deutsch • español • italiano

penalty area
la surface de réparation
der Strafraum
el área de penalti
l'area di rigore

goal line
la ligne de but
die Torlinie
la línea de meta
la linea di fondo

goal area
la surface de but
der Torraum
el área de meta
l'area di porta

goal
le but
das Tor
la portería
la porta

defender
le défenseur
der Verteidiger
el defensa
il difensore

linesman
le juge de ligne
der Linienrichter
el juez de línea
il guardialinee

corner flag
le drapeau de coin
die Eckfahne
la bandera de esquina
la bandierina

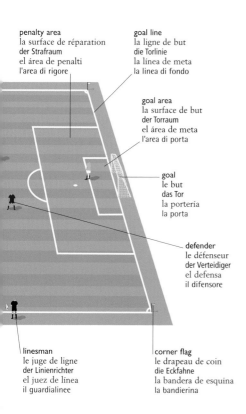

throw-in • la rentrée en touche • der Einwurf • el saque de banda • la rimessa in gioco

kick (v) • botter • kicken • chutar • calciare

cleat
la chaussure
der Fußballschuh
la bota
lo scarpino

pass (v) • faire une passe • den Ball abgeben • hacer un pase • passare

shoot (v) • shooter • schießen • tirar • tirare

save (v) • sauver • halten • hacer una parada • parare

tackle (v) • tacler • angreifen • hacer una entrada • contrastare

stadium	foul	yellow card	league	extra time
le stade	la faute	le carton jaune	le championnat	la prolongation
das Stadion	das Foul	die gelbe Karte	die Liga	die Verlängerung
el estadio	la falta	la tarjeta amarilla	la liga	la prórroga
lo stadio	il fallo	il cartellino giallo	il campionato	il tempo supplementare
score a goal (v)	corner	offside	tie	substitute
marquer un but	le corner	l'hors-jeu	le match nul	le remplaçant
ein Tor schießen	der Eckball	das Abseits	das Unentschieden	der Ersatzspieler
marcar un gol	el córner	el fuera de juego	el empate	el reserva
segnare	il calcio d'angolo	il fuorigioco	il pareggio	il sostituto
penalty	red card	send off	halftime	substitution
le penalty	le carton rouge	l'expulsion	la mi-temps	le remplacement
der Elfmeter	die rote Karte	der Platzverweis	die Halbzeit	die Auswechslung
el penalti	la tarjeta roja	la expulsión	el descanso	la sustitución
il rigore	il cartellino rosso	l'espulsione	l'intervallo	la sostituzione

hockey • le hockey • das Hockey • el hockey • l'hockey

ice hockey • le hockey sur glace • das Eishockey • el hockey sobre hielo • l'hockey su ghiaccio

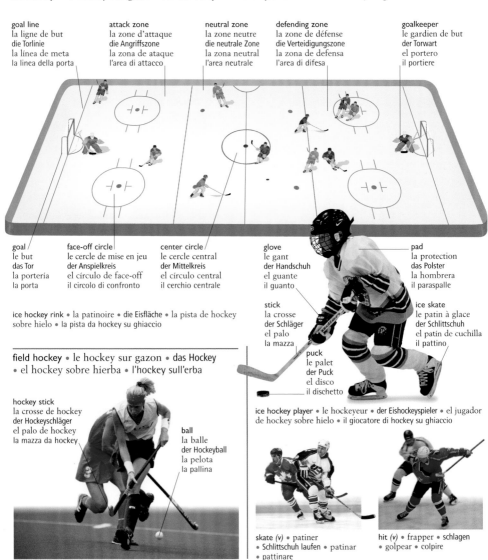

goal line
la ligne de but
die Torlinie
la línea de meta
la linea della porta

attack zone
la zone d'attaque
die Angriffszone
la zona de ataque
l'area di attacco

neutral zone
la zone neutre
die neutrale Zone
la zona neutral
l'area neutrale

defending zone
la zone de défense
die Verteidigungszone
la zona de defensa
l'area di difesa

goalkeeper
le gardien de but
der Torwart
el portero
il portiere

goal
le but
das Tor
la portería
la porta

face-off circle
le cercle de mise en jeu
der Anspielkreis
el círculo de face-off
il circolo di confronto

center circle
le cercle central
der Mittelkreis
el círculo central
il cerchio centrale

glove
le gant
der Handschuh
el guante
il guanto

pad
la protection
das Polster
la hombrera
il paraspalle

stick
la crosse
der Schläger
el palo
la mazza

ice skate
le patin à glace
der Schlittschuh
el patín de cuchilla
il pattino

puck
le palet
der Puck
el disco
il dischetto

ice hockey rink • la patinoire • die Eisfläche • la pista de hockey sobre hielo • la pista da hockey su ghiaccio

ice hockey player • le hockeyeur • der Eishockeyspieler • el jugador de hockey sobre hielo • il giocatore di hockey su ghiaccio

field hockey • le hockey sur gazon • das Hockey • el hockey sobre hierba • l'hockey sull'erba

hockey stick
la crosse de hockey
der Hockeyschläger
el palo de hockey
la mazza da hockey

ball
la balle
der Hockeyball
la pelota
la pallina

skate (v) • patiner • Schlittschuh laufen • patinar • pattinare

hit (v) • frapper • schlagen • golpear • colpire

cricket • le cricket • das Kricket • el críquet • il cricket

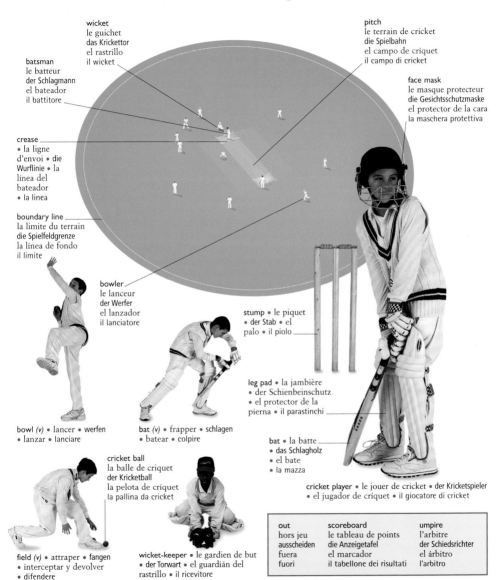

wicket
le guichet
das Krickettor
el rastrillo
il wicket

pitch
le terrain de cricket
die Spielbahn
el campo de críquet
il campo di cricket

batsman
le batteur
der Schlagmann
el bateador
il battitore

face mask
le masque protecteur
die Gesichtsschutzmaske
el protector de la cara
la maschera protettiva

crease
• la ligne
d'envoi • die
Wurflinie • la
línea del
bateador
• la linea

boundary line
la limite du terrain
die Spielfeldgrenze
la línea de fondo
il limite

bowler
le lanceur
der Werfer
el lanzador
il lanciatore

stump • le piquet
• der Stab • el
palo • il piolo

leg pad • la jambière
• der Schienbeinschutz
• el protector de la
pierna • il parastinchi

bowl (v) • lancer • werfen
• lanzar • lanciare

bat (v) • frapper • schlagen
• batear • colpire

bat • la batte
• das Schlagholz
• el bate
• la mazza

cricket ball
la balle de criquet
der Kricketball
la pelota de críquet
la pallina da cricket

cricket player • le jouer de cricket • der Kricketspieler
• el jugador de críquet • il giocatore di cricket

field (v) • attraper • fangen
• interceptar y devolver
• difendere

wicket-keeper • le gardien de but
• der Torwart • el guardián del
rastrillo • il ricevitore

out	scoreboard	umpire
hors jeu	le tableau de points	l'arbitre
ausscheiden	die Anzeigetafel	der Schiedsrichter
fuera	el marcador	el árbitro
fuori	il tabellone dei risultati	l'arbitro

english • français • deutsch • español • italiano

basketball • le basket • der Basketball • el baloncesto • la pallacanestro

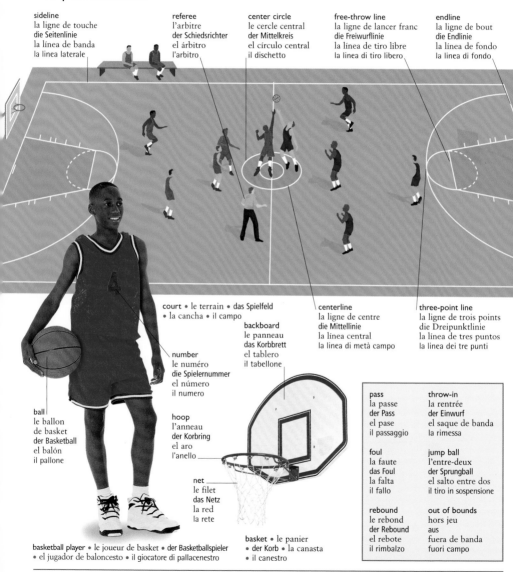

sideline
la ligne de touche
die Seitenlinie
la línea de banda
la linea laterale

referee
l'arbitre
der Schiedsrichter
el árbitro
l'arbitro

center circle
le cercle central
der Mittelkreis
el círculo central
il dischetto

free-throw line
la ligne de lancer franc
die Freiwurflinie
la línea de tiro libre
la linea di tiro libero

endline
la ligne de bout
die Endlinie
la línea de fondo
la linea di fondo

court • le terrain • das Spielfeld
• la cancha • il campo

backboard
le panneau
das Korbbrett
el tablero
il tabellone

centerline
la ligne de centre
die Mittellinie
la línea central
la linea di metà campo

three-point line
la ligne de trois points
die Dreipunktlinie
la línea de tres puntos
la linea dei tre punti

number
le numéro
die Spielernummer
el número
il numero

hoop
l'anneau
der Korbring
el aro
l'anello

ball
le ballon
de basket
der Basketball
el balón
il pallone

net
le filet
das Netz
la red
la rete

pass
la passe
der Pass
el pase
il passaggio

throw-in
la rentrée
der Einwurf
el saque de banda
la rimessa

foul
la faute
das Foul
la falta
il fallo

jump ball
l'entre-deux
der Sprungball
el salto entre dos
il tiro in sospensione

rebound
le rebond
der Rebound
el rebote
il rimbalzo

out of bounds
hors jeu
aus
fuera de banda
fuori campo

basketball player • le joueur de basket • der Basketballspieler
• el jugador de baloncesto • il giocatore di pallacanestro

basket • le panier
• der Korb • la canasta
• il canestro

226

actions • les actions • die Aktionen • las acciones • le azioni

throw (v) • lancer
• werfen • lanzar • tirare

catch (v) • attraper
• fangen • coger
• acchiappare

shoot (v) • tirer
• zielen • tirar
• tirare

jump (v) • sauter
• springen • saltar
• saltare

mark (v) • marquer • decken
• marcar • marcare

block (v) • bloquer • blocken
• bloquear • bloccare

dribble (v) • dribbler
• aufspringen lassen
• botar • rimbalzare

dunk (v) • faire un dunk
• einen Dunk spielen
• hacer un mate • segnare

volleyball • le volley • der Volleyball • el voleibol • la pallavolo

block (v)
bloquer
blocken
bloquear
contrastare

net
le filet
das Netz
la red
la rete

dig (v)
• faire une
manchette
• baggern
• recibir
• difendere

referee
l'arbitre
der Schiedsrichter
el árbitro
l'arbitro

knee support
la genouillère
der Knieschützer
la rodillera
la ginocchiera

court • le terrain • das Spielfeld • la cancha • il campo

baseball • le baseball • der Baseball • el béisbol • il baseball

field • le terrain • das Spielfeld • el campo • il campo

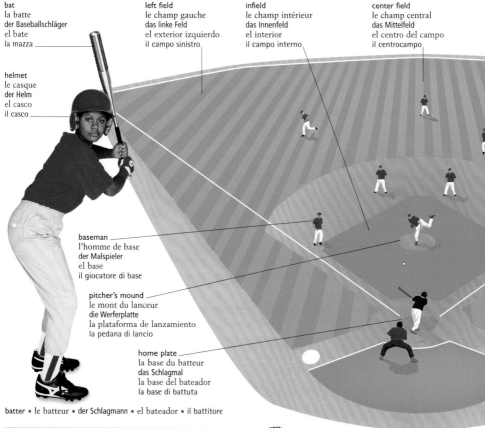

bat
la batte
der Baseballschläger
el bate
la mazza

left field
le champ gauche
das linke Feld
el exterior izquierdo
il campo sinistro

infield
le champ intérieur
das Innenfeld
el interior
il campo interno

center field
le champ central
das Mittelfeld
el centro del campo
il centrocampo

helmet
le casque
der Helm
el casco
il casco

baseman
l'homme de base
der Malspieler
el base
il giocatore di base

pitcher's mound
le mont du lanceur
die Werferplatte
la plataforma de lanzamiento
la pedana di lancio

home plate
la base du batteur
das Schlagmal
la base del bateador
la base di battuta

batter • le batteur • der Schlagmann • el bateador • il battitore

inning	safe	strike
le tour de batte	sauf	le coup manqué
das Inning	in Sicherheit	der Schlagfehler
el turno	a salvo	el strike
il turno di battuta	salvo	lo strike
run	out	foul ball
le point	hors jeu	la fausse balle
der Lauf	aus	der ungültige Schlag
la carrera	fuera	el fallo
il giro	fuori	il fallo

ball
la balle
der Baseball
la pelota
la palla

glove • le gant • der Handschuh
• el guante • il guantone

mask • le masque • die
Schutzmaske • la máscara
• la maschera

actions • les actions • die Aktionen • las acciones • le azioni

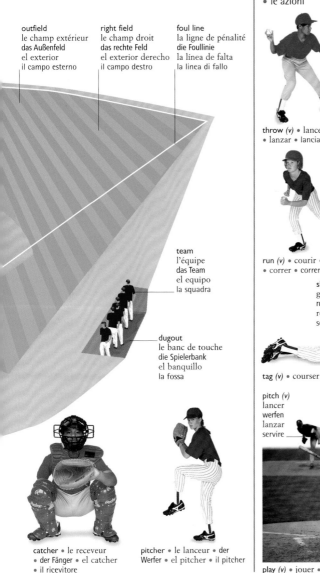

outfield
le champ extérieur
das Außenfeld
el exterior
il campo esterno

right field
le champ droit
das rechte Feld
el exterior derecho
il campo destro

foul line
la ligne de pénalité
die Foullinie
la línea de falta
la linea di fallo

team
l'équipe
das Team
el equipo
la squadra

dugout
le banc de touche
die Spielerbank
el banquillo
la fossa

catcher • le receveur
• der Fänger • el catcher
• il ricevitore

pitcher • le lanceur • der
Werfer • el pitcher • il pitcher

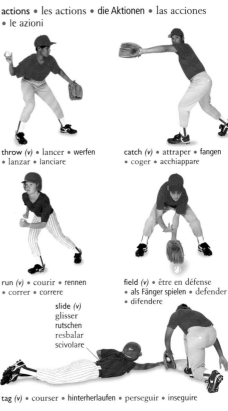

throw (v) • lancer • werfen
• lanzar • lanciare

catch (v) • attraper • fangen
• coger • acchiappare

run (v) • courir • rennen
• correr • correre

field (v) • être en défense
• als Fänger spielen • defender
• difendere

slide (v)
glisser
rutschen
resbalar
scivolare

tag (v) • courser • hinterherlaufen • perseguir • inseguire

pitch (v)
lancer
werfen
lanzar
servire

bat (v)
batter
schlagen
batear
battere

umpire
l'arbitre
der Schiedsrichter
el árbitro
l'arbitro

play (v) • jouer • spielen • jugar • giocare

tennis • le tennis • das Tennis • el tenis • il tennis

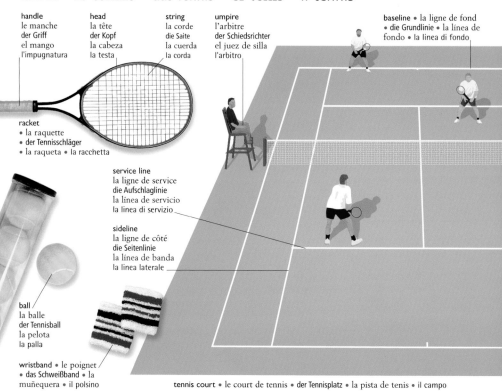

handle
le manche
der Griff
el mango
l'impugnatura

head
la tête
der Kopf
la cabeza
la testa

string
la corde
die Saite
la cuerda
la corda

umpire
l'arbitre
der Schiedsrichter
el juez de silla
l'arbitro

baseline • la ligne de fond
• die Grundlinie • la linea de
fondo • la linea di fondo

racket
• la raquette
• der Tennisschläger
• la raqueta • la racchetta

service line
la ligne de service
die Aufschlaglinie
la línea de servicio
la linea di servizio

sideline
la ligne de côté
die Seitenlinie
la línea de banda
la linea laterale

ball
la balle
der Tennisball
la pelota
la palla

wristband • le poignet
• das Schweißband • la
muñequera • il polsino

tennis court • le court de tennis • der Tennisplatz • la pista de tenis • il campo

singles	set	deuce	fault	slice	spin
le simple	le set	l'égalité	la faute	le slice	l'effet
das Einzel	der Satz	der Einstand	der Fehler	der Slice	der Spin
el individual	el set	cuarenta iguales	la falta	el tiro con efecto	el efecto
il singolare	il set	il deuce	il fallo	il taglio	l'avvitamento
doubles	match	advantage	ace	rally	linesman
le double	le match	l'avantage	l'as	l'échange	le juge de ligne
das Doppel	das Match	der Vorteil	das Ass	der Ballwechsel	der Linienrichter
los dobles	el partido	la ventaja	el ace	el peloteo	el juez de línea
il doppio	la partita	il vantaggio	l'asso	il palleggio	il giudice di linea
game	tiebreaker	love	dropshot	let!	championship
le jeu	le tiebreak	zéro	l'amorti	net!	le championnat
das Spiel	der Tiebreak	null	der Stoppball	Netz!	die Meisterschaft
el juego	el tiebreak	nada	la dejada	¡red!	el campeonato
il gioco	il tiebreak	a zero	la smorzata	colpo nullo!	il campionato

net
le filet
das Netz
la red
la rete

smash
le smash
der Schmetterball
el mate
la schiacciata

ball boy
le ramasseur de balles
der Balljunge
el recogepelotas
il raccattapalle

serve (v)
servir
aufschlagen
sacar
battere il servizio

tennis shoes
• les tennis
• die Tennisschuhe
• los tenis • le
scarpe da tennis

player • le joueur • der Tennisspieler • el jugador • il tennista

strokes • les coups • die Schläge • los golpes • i colpi

serve • le service • der
Aufschlag • el servicio
• il servizio

volley • la volée • der Volley
• la volea • la volée

return • le retour • der Return
• el resto • il ritorno

lob • le lob • der Lob
• el globo • il pallonetto

forehand • le coup droit
• die Vorhand • el derecho
• il dritto

backhand • le revers
• die Rückhand • el revés
• il rovescio

racket games • les jeux de raquette • die Schlägerspiele • los juegos de raqueta • i giochi con la racchetta

shuttlecock
le volant
der Federball
el volante
il volano

paddle • la raquette
• der Tischtennisschläger
• la pala • la racchetta

badminton • le badminton
• das Badminton • el
bádminton • il badminton

table tennis • le tennis de
table • das Tischtennis • el
ping-pong • il ping pong

squash • le squash
• das Squash • el squash
• lo squash

racquetball • le racquetball
• das Racquetball • el
racketball • il racquetball

golf • le golf • das Golf • el golf • il golf

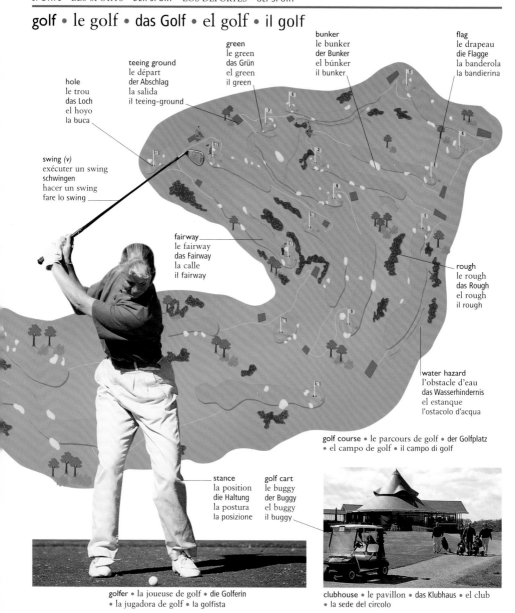

hole
le trou
das Loch
el hoyo
la buca

teeing ground
le départ
der Abschlag
la salida
il teeing-ground

green
le green
das Grün
el green
il green

bunker
le bunker
der Bunker
el búnker
il bunker

flag
le drapeau
die Flagge
la banderola
la bandierina

swing *(v)*
exécuter un swing
schwingen
hacer un swing
fare lo swing

fairway
le fairway
das Fairway
la calle
il fairway

rough
le rough
das Rough
el rough
il rough

water hazard
l'obstacle d'eau
das Wasserhindernis
el estanque
l'ostacolo d'acqua

golf course • le parcours de golf • der Golfplatz
• el campo de golf • il campo di golf

stance
la position
die Haltung
la postura
la posizione

golf cart
le buggy
der Buggy
el buggy
il buggy

golfer • la joueuse de golf • die Golferin
• la jugadora de golf • la golfista

clubhouse • le pavillon • das Klubhaus • el club
• la sede del circolo

equipment • l'équipement • die Ausrüstung • el equipo • le attrezzature

golf ball
la balle de golf
der Golfball
la pelota de golf
la pallina da golf

golf bag
le sac de golf
die Golftasche
la bolsa de golf
la sacca da golf

tee • le tee • das Tee
• el tee • il tee

spikes
les pointes
die Spikes
los clavos
i chiodi

golf clubs • les clubs de golf • die Golf-schläger • los palos de golf • le mazze da golf

wood • le bois • das Holz
• el palo de madera
• la mazza di legno

glove • le gant • der Handschuh • el guante • il guanto

bag cart • le caddie • der Caddie • el carrito de golf • il carrellino

golf shoe • la chaussure de golf • der Golfschuh • el zapato de golf • la scarpa da golf

putter • le putter
• der Putter • el putter
• il putter

actions • les actions • die Aktionen • las acciones • le azioni

tee-off (v) • partir du tee • vom Abschlag spielen • salir • cominciare la partita

drive (v) • driver • driven • hacer un drive • colpire a distanza

putt (v) • putter • einlochen • tirar al hoyo con un putter • colpire leggermente

chip (v) • cocher • chippen • hacer un chip • colpire da vicino

iron • le fer • das Eisen
• el palo de hierro
• la mazza di ferro

wedge • la cale
• das Wedge • el wedge
• la mazza ricurva

par	over par	handicap	caddy	stroke	backswing
le par	le over par	le handicap	le caddie	le coup	le swing en arrière
das Par	über par	das Handicap	der Trolley	der Schlag	der Durchschwung
el par	el sobre par	el handicap	el caddy	el golpe	el backswing
il par	l'overpar	l'handicap	il caddy	il colpo	il back-swing
under par	hole in one	tournament	spectators	practice swing	line of play
le under par	le trou en un	le tournoi	les spectateurs	le swing d'essai	la ligne de jeu
unter par	das Hole-in-One	das Golfturnier	die Zuschauer	der Übungsschwung	die Spielbahn
el bajo par	el hoyo en uno	el torneo	los espectadores	el swing de práctica	la línea de juego
l'underpar	la buca in uno	il torneo	gli spettatori	lo swing di pratica	la linea di gioco

track and field • l'athlétisme • die Leichtathletik • el atletismo • l'atletica leggera

lane
le couloir
die Bahn
la calle
la corsia

track • a piste • die
Rennbahn • la pista
• la pista

finish line
la ligne d'arrivée
die Ziellinie
la línea de meta
il traguardo

starting line
la ligne de départ
die Startlinie
la línea de salida
la linea di partenza

field • le terrain • der Sportplatz • el campo • il campo

athlete
l'athlète
die Leichtathletin
la atleta
l'atleta

starting blocks
le bloc de départ
der Startblock
el bloque de salida
la pedana di partenza

sprinter • le sprinter
• der Sprinter • el esprinter
• il velocista

discus • le discobole
• das Diskuswerfen
• el lanzamiento de
disco • il lancio del disco

shotput • le lancement du
poids • das Kugelstoßen
• el lanzamiento de peso
• il lancio del peso

javelin • le javelot • das
Speerwerfen • el lanzamiento
de jabalina • il lancio del
giavellotto

race	record	photo finish	pole vault
la course	le record	le photo-finish	le saut à la perche
das Rennen	der Rekord	das Fotofinish	der Stabhochsprung
la carrera	el récord	la fotofinish	el salto con pértiga
la gara	il primato	il fotofinish	il salto con l'asta
time	break a record (v)	marathon	personal best
le temps	battre un record	le marathon	le record personnel
die Zeit	einen Rekord brechen	der Marathon	die persönliche Bestleistung
el tiempo	batir un récord	la maratón	la marca personal
il tempo	battere un primato	la maratona	il primato personale

stopwatch • le chronomètre
• die Stoppuhr • el
cronómetro • il cronometro

english • français • deutsch • español • italiano

baton • le bâton • der Stab • el testigo • il testimone

crossbar • la barre • die Latte • el listón • la sbarra

relay race • le relais • der Staffellauf • la carrera de relevos • la staffetta

high jump • le saut en hauteur • der Hochsprung • el salto de altura • il salto in alto

long jump • le saut en longueur • der Weitsprung • el salto de longitud • il salto in lungo

hurdles • les haies • der Hürdenlauf • la carrera de vallas • la corsa a ostacoli

gymnastics • la gymnastique • das Turnen • la gimnasia • la ginnastica

springboard
le tremplin
das Sprungbrett
el trampolín
la pedana elastica

gymnast
la gymnaste
die Turnerin
la gimnasta
la ginnasta

horse
le cheval
das Pferd
el caballo
il cavallo

somersault • le salto • der Salto • el salto mortal • la capriola

beam • la poutre • der Schwebebalken • la barra de equilibrio • la trave

ribbon • le ruban • das Gymnastikband • la cinta • il nastro

mat • le tapis • die Matte • la colchoneta • la pedana

vault • le saut • der Sprung • el salto • il volteggio

floor exercises • les exercises au sol • das Bodenturnen • los ejercicios de suelo • la ginnastica a terra

cartwheel • la roue • das Rad • la voltereta • la ruota

rhythmic gymnastics • la gymnastique rythmique • die rhythmische Gymnastik • la gimnasia rítmica • la ginnastica ritmica

horizontal bar la barre fixe das Reck la barra fija la sbarra	asymmetric bars les barres asymétriques der Stufenbarren las paralelas asimétricas le sbarre asimmetriche	rings les anneaux die Ringe las anillas gli anelli	medals les médailles die Medaillen las medallas le medaglie	silver l'argent das Silber la plata l'argento
parallel bars les barres parallèles der Barren las paralelas le parallele	pommel horse le cheval d'arçons das Seitpferd el caballo con arcos il cavallo	podium le podium das Siegerpodium el podio il podio	gold l'or das Gold el oro l'oro	bronze le bronze die Bronze el bronce il bronzo

combat sports • les sports de combat • der Kampfsport • los deportes de combate • gli sport da combattimento

opponent
l'adversaire
der Gegner
el adversario
l'avversario

guard
le protège-tête
der Kopfschutz
el protector
il casco

glove
le gant
der Handschuh
el guante
il guanto

belt
la ceinture
der Gürtel
el cinturón
la cintura

karate • le karaté • das Karate • el karate • il karate

tae kwon do • le taekwondo • das Taekwondo • el taekwondo • il tae kwondo

judo • le judo • das Judo • el judo • il judo

mask
le masque
die Maske
la careta
la maschera

sword
le sabre
der Säbel
la espada
la sciabola

aikido • l'aïkido • das Aikido • el aikido • l'aikido

kendo • le kendo • das Kendo • el kendo • il kendo

kung fu • le kung-fu • das Kung-Fu • el kung fu • il kung fu

kickboxing • la boxe thaïlandaise • das Kickboxen • el full contact • il kickboxing

wrestling • la lutte • das Ringen • la lucha libre • la lotta greco-romana

boxing • la boxe • das Boxen • el boxeo • il pugilato

actions • les actions • die Techniken • los movimientos • le mosse

fall • la chute • das Fallen • la caída • la scivolata

hold • la prise • der Griff • el agarre • la presa

throw • la projection • der Wurf • el derribo • la proiezione

pin • l'immobilisation • das Fesseln • la inmovilización • la caduta

kick • le coup de pied • der Seitfußstoß • la patada • il calcio

punch • le coup de poing • der Stoß • el puñetazo • il pugno

strike • le coup • der Angriff • el golpe • il colpo

jump • le saut • der Sprung • el salto • il salto

block • le blocage • der Block • la parada • la parata

chop • le coup • der Hieb • el golpe • il colpo di taglio

boxing ring le ring der Boxring el ring il ring	round le round die Runde el asalto il round	fist le poing die Faust el puño il pugno	black belt la ceinture noire der schwarze Gürtel el cinturón negro la cintura nera	capoeira la capoeira die Capoeira la capoeira la capoeira
boxing gloves les gants de boxe die Boxhandschuhe los guantes de boxeo i guantoni	bout le combat der Kampf el combate l'incontro	knockout le knock-out der Knock-out el K.O. il k.o	self-defense l'autodéfense die Selbstverteidigung la defensa personal l'autodifesa	sumo wrestling le sumo das Sumo el sumo il sumo
mouth guard le protège-dents der Mundschutz el protegedientes il paradenti	sparring l'entraînement das Sparren el entrenamiento l'allenamento	punching bag le punching-ball der Sandsack el saco de arena il sacco	martial arts les arts martiaux die Kampfsportarten las artes marciales le arti marziali	Tai Chi le taï chi das Thai-Chi el tai-chi il tai-chi

swimming • la natation • der Schwimmsport • la natación • il nuoto

equipment • l'équipement • die Ausrüstung • el equipo • l'attrezzatura

nose clip
la pince pour le nez
die Nasenklemme
la pinza para la nariz
la molletta per il naso

water wings • la brassière
• der Schwimmflügel
• el manguito
• il bracciolo

goggles • les lunettes protectrices
• die Schwimmbrille • las gafas de
natación • gli occhialetti

kickboard • la planche
• das Schwimmfloß • el
flotador • la tavoletta

swimsuit • le maillot de bain
• der Badeanzug • el traje de
baño • il costume da bagno

swimming cap • le
bonnet de natation
• die Badekappe
• el gorro de
baño • la cuffia

lane
le couloir
die Bahn
la calle
la corsia

water
l'eau
das Wasser
el agua
l'acqua

starting block
le plot de départ
der Startblock
el bloque de salida
il podio di partenza

trunks
• le slip de bain
• die Badehose
• el bañador
• il costume da
bagno

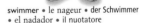

swimming pool • la piscine • das Schwimmbecken • la piscina • la piscina

diving board
le tremplin
das Sprungbrett
el trampolín
il trampolino

diver
le plongeur
der Springer
el saltador
il tuffatore

swimmer • le nageur • der Schwimmer
• el nadador • il nuotatore

dive (v) • plonger • springen
• tirarse de cabeza • tuffarsi

swim (v) • nager • schwimmen
• nadar • nuotare

turn • le virage-culbute • die Wende
• el giro • la giravolta

styles • les styles • die Schwimmstile • los estilos • gli stili

front crawl • le crawl • das Kraulen • el crol • lo stile libero

breaststroke • la brasse • das Brustschwimmen • la braza • la rana

stroke
la nage
der Zug
la brazada
la bracciata

kick
le coup de pied
der Stoß
la patada
la gambata

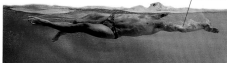

backstroke • le dos crawlé • das Rückenschwimmen • la espalda • il dorso

butterfly • le papillon • der Schmetterling • la mariposa • la farfalla

---

scuba diving • la plongée • das Tauchen • el buceo • il nuoto subacqueo

air cylinder
la bouteille d'air
die Druckluftflasche
la botella de aire
la bombola

wetsuit
• la combinaison de plongée • der Taucheranzug • el traje de buzo • la tuta subacquea

mask • le masque
• die Tauchermaske
• las gafas de bucear
• la maschera

fin
la palme
die Schwimmflosse
la aleta
la pinna

regulator
le régulateur
der Lungenautomat
el regulador
il regolatore

weight belt
la ceinture de plomb
der Bleigürtel
el cinturón de pesas
la cintura dei pesi

snorkel • le tuba
• der Schnorchel • el tubo • il boccaglio

dive	racing dive	lockers	water polo	shallow end	cramp
le plongeon	le départ plongé	les casiers	le water-polo	le petit bassin	la crampe
der Sprung	der Startsprung	die Schließfächer	der Wasserball	das flache Ende	der Krampf
el salto	el salto de salida	las taquillas	el waterpolo	la zona poco profunda	el calambre
il tuffo	il tuffo di rincorsa	gli armadietti	la pallanuoto	la parte bassa	il crampo
high dive	tread water (v)	lifeguard	deep end	synchronized swimming	drown (v)
le plongeon de haut vol	nager sur place	le maître nageur	le grand bassin	la nage synchronisée	se noyer
der Turmsprung	Wasser treten	der Bademeister	das tiefe Ende	das Synchronschwimmen	ertrinken
el salto alto	hacer agua	el socorrista	la zona profunda	la natación sincronizada	ahogarse
il tuffo alto	tenersi a galla	il bagnino	la parte profonda	il nuoto sincronizzato	annegare

sailing • la voile • der Segelsport • la vela • la vela

compass • le compas • der Kompass • la brújula • la bussola

anchor • l'ancre • der Anker • el ancla • l'ancora

mast
le mât
der Mast
el mástil
l'albero

rigging
le gréement
die Takelung
las jarcias
il sartiame

mainsail
la grand-voile
das Großsegel
la vela mayor
la vela di maestra

headsail
la voile d'avant
die Fock
el foque
la vela di prua

cleat
le taquet
die Klampe
la escotera
la galloccia

sidedeck
le pont de côté
das Seitendeck
la cubierta
il ponte laterale

boom
la bôme
der Baum
la botavara
il boma

stern
l'arrière
das Heck
la popa
la poppa

bow
l'avant
der Bug
la proa
la prua

tiller
• la barre
• die Pinne
• la caña
  del timón
• la barra

hull
la coque
der Rumpf
el casco
lo scafo

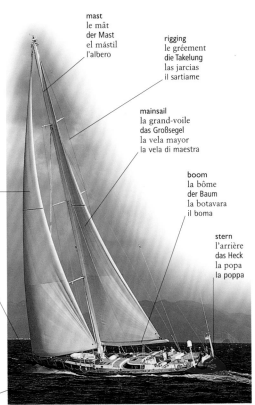

navigate (v) • naviguer • navigieren • navegar • navigare

yacht • le yacht • die Segeljacht • el yate de vela • lo yacht

---

safety • la sécurité • die Sicherheit • la seguridad • la sicurezza

flare • la fusée éclairante • die Leuchtrakete • la bengala • il razzo illuminante

life buoy • la bouée de sauvetage • der Rettungsring • el salvavidas • il salvagente

life jacket • le gilet de sauvetage • die Schwimmweste • el chaleco salvavidas • il giubbotto di salvataggio

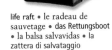

life raft • le radeau de sauvetage • das Rettungsboot • la balsa salvavidas • la zattera di salvataggio

watersports • les sports aquatiques • **der Wassersport** • los deportes acuáticos • gli sport acquatici

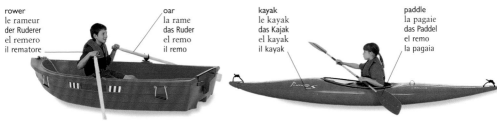

rower
le rameur
der Ruderer
el remero
il rematore

oar
la rame
das Ruder
el remo
il remo

kayak
le kayak
das Kajak
el kayak
il kayak

paddle
la pagaie
das Paddel
el remo
la pagaia

row (v) • ramer • rudern • remar • remare

kayaking • faire du kayak • Kajakfahren • hacer kayak • fare kayak

sail
la voile
das Segel
la vela
la vela

surfboard • la planche
de surf • das Surfbrett
• la tabla de surf
• il surf

ski • le ski • der Wasserski
• el esquí • lo sci

windsurfer
le planchiste
der Windsurfer
el windsurfista
il windsurfista

surfing • le surf • das
Wellenreiten • el surfing
• il surfing

waterskiing • le ski nautique
• das Wasserski • el esquí
acuático • lo sci d'acqua

speedboating • le moto-
nautisme • der Motorbootsport
• la carrera de motoras
• la corsa in motoscafo

board
la planche
das Surfbrett
la tabla
la tavola

footstrap
la bride
die Fußschlaufe
la cinta para el pie
la presa per il piede

rafting • le rafting • das
Rafting • el rafting • rafting

jet skiing • le jet-ski
• das Jetskifahren • la moto
acuática • l'acquascooter

windsurfing • la planche à voile • das Windsurfing • el windsurf
• il windsurfing

waterskier	crew	wind	surf	sheet	centerboard
le skieur nautique	l'équipage	le vent	l'écume	l'écoute	la dérive
der Wasserskifahrer	die Crew	der Wind	die Brandung	die Schot	das Schwert
el esquiador acuático	la tripulación	el viento	la rompiente	la escota	la orza
lo sciatore d'acqua	l'equipaggio	il vento	la cresta dell'onda	la scotta	il centro della tavola
surfer	tack (v)	wave	rapids	rudder	capsize (v)
le surfeur	louvoyer	la vague	les rapides	le gouvernail	chavirer
der Surfer	kreuzen	die Welle	das Wildwasser	das Ruder	kentern
el surfista	virar	la ola	los rápidos	el timón	volcar
il surfista	bordeggiare	l'onda	il torrente	il timone	capovolgersi

horseback riding • l'équitation • der Reitsport • la equitación • l'equitazione

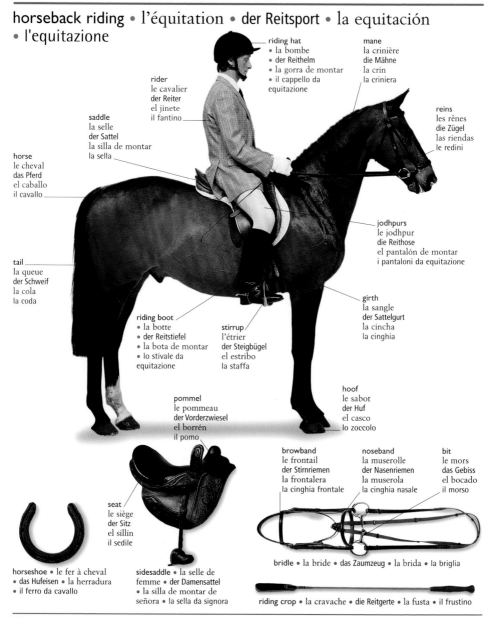

riding hat
• la bombe
• der Reithelm
• la gorra de montar
• il cappello da equitazione

mane
la crinière
die Mähne
la crin
la criniera

rider
le cavalier
der Reiter
el jinete
il fantino

reins
les rênes
die Zügel
las riendas
le redini

saddle
la selle
der Sattel
la silla de montar
la sella

horse
le cheval
das Pferd
el caballo
il cavallo

jodhpurs
le jodhpur
die Reithose
el pantalón de montar
i pantaloni da equitazione

tail
la queue
der Schweif
la cola
la coda

girth
la sangle
der Sattelgurt
la cincha
la cinghia

riding boot
• la botte
• der Reitstiefel
• la bota de montar
• lo stivale da equitazione

stirrup
l'étrier
der Steigbügel
el estribo
la staffa

hoof
le sabot
der Huf
el casco
lo zoccolo

pommel
le pommeau
der Vorderzwiesel
el borrén
il pomo

browband
le frontail
der Stirnriemen
la frontalera
la cinghia frontale

noseband
la muserolle
der Nasenriemen
la muserola
la cinghia nasale

bit
le mors
das Gebiss
el bocado
il morso

seat
le siège
der Sitz
el sillín
il sedile

bridle • la bride • das Zaumzeug • la brida • la briglia

horseshoe • le fer à cheval • das Hufeisen • la herradura • il ferro da cavallo

sidesaddle • la selle de femme • der Damensattel • la silla de montar de señora • la sella da signora

riding crop • la cravache • die Reitgerte • la fusta • il frustino

english • français • deutsch • español • italiano

events • les courses • die Veranstaltungen • las modalidades • le corse

racehorse • le cheval de course • das Rennpferd • el caballo de carreras • il cavallo da corsa

fence • l'obstacle • das Hindernis • la valla • l'ostacolo

horse race • la course de chevaux • das Pferderennen • la carrera de caballos • la corsa di cavalli

steeplechase • le steeple • das Jagdrennen • la carrera de obstáculos • la corsa a ostacoli

harness race • la course de trot • das Trabrennen • la carrera al trote • la corsa al trotto

rodeo • le rodéo • das Rodeo • el rodeo • il rodeo

showjumping • le jumping • das Springreiten • el concurso de saltos • il concorso di salto a ostacoli

carriage race • la course attelée • das Zweispännerrennen • la carrera de carrozas • la corsa di carrozze

trail riding • la randonnée • das Wanderreiten • el paseo • l'escursione a cavallo

dressage • le dressage • das Dressurreiten • la doma y monta • il dressage

polo • le polo • das Polo • el polo • il polo

walk	canter	jump	halter	paddock	flat race
le pas	le petit galop	le saut	le licou	l'enclos	la course de plat
der Schritt	der Kanter	der Sprung	das Halfter	die Koppel	das Flachrennen
el paso	el medio galope	el salto	el cabestro	el cercado	la carrera sin obstáculos
il passo	il piccolo galoppo	il salto	la cavezza	il recinto	la corsa in piano
trot	gallop	groom	stable	arena	racecourse
le trot	le galop	le valet d'écurie	l'écurie	l'arène	le champs de courses
der Trab	der Galopp	der Stallbursche	der Pferdestall	der Turnierplatz	die Rennbahn
el trote	el galope	el mozo de cuadra	la cuadra	el ruedo	el hipódromo
il trotto	il galoppo	lo stalliere	la stalla	l'arena	l'ippodromo

fishing • la pêche • der Angelsport • la pesca • la pesca

sinker • le plomb • das Gewicht • el plomo • il peso

barb
le barbillon
der Widerhaken
la lengüeta
l'uncino

eye
l'œillet
das Öhr
el ojo
l'occhiello

fishhook • l'hameçon • der Angelhaken • el anzuelo • l'amo

bait • l'amorce • der Köder • el cebo • l'esca

float • le flotteur • die Pose • el flotador • il galleggiante

fly • la mouche • die Fliege • la mosca • la mosca

landing net • l'épuisette • der Kescher • la red para recoger • la retina

lure • l'appât • der Köderhaken • el señuelo • l'esca

keep net • la bourriche • der Setzkescher • la red para las capturas • la rete da pesca

tackle box • la boîte d'équipement • der Spinnerkasten • la caja de aparejos • la scatola portaesche

line
la ligne
die Schnur
el sedal
la lenza

fishing rod
la canne à pêche
die Angelrute
la caña de pescar
la canna da pesca

reel
le moulinet
die Rolle
el carrete
il mulinello

waders
les bottes de pêche
die Watstiefel
las botas altas de goma
gli stivaloni di gomma

angler • le pêcheur • der Angler • el pescador de caña • il pescatore

types of fishing • les genres de pêche • die Fischfangarten • los tipos de pesca • i tipi di pesca

freshwater fishing • la pêche en eau douce • das Süßwasserangeln • la pesca en agua dulce • la pesca in acqua dolce

fly fishing • la pêche à la mouche • das Fliegenangeln • la pesca con mosca • la pesca con la mosca

sport fishing • la pêche sportive • das Sportangeln • la pesca deportiva • la pesca sportiva

deep sea fishing • la pêche hauturière • die Hochseefischerei • la pesca de altura • la pesca il alto mare

surfcasting • la pêche au lancer en mer • das Brandungsangeln • la pesca en la orilla • la pesca dalla riva

activities • les activités • die Aktivitäten • las acciones • le attività

cast (v) • lancer • auswerfen • lanzar • lanciare

catch (v) • attraper • fangen • coger • prendere

reel in (v) • ramener • einholen • recoger • tirare con il mulinello

net (v) • prendre au filet • mit dem Netz fangen • coger con la red • pescare con la rete

release (v) • lâcher • loslassen • soltar • rilasciare

bait (v)	tackle	rain gear	fishing license	creel
amorcer	le matériel de pêche	l'imperméable	le permis de pêche	le panier de pêche
ködern	die Angelgeräte	die Regenhaut	der Angelschein	der Fischkorb
cebar	los aparejos	la ropa impermeable	la licencia de pesca	la nasa
fornire di esca	l'attrezzatura	l'impermeabile	la licenza di pesca	la nassa
bite (v)	spool	pole	marine fishing	spearfishing
mordre	le tambour	la perche	la pêche maritime	la pêche sous-marine
anbeißen	die Rolle	die Stake	die Seefischerei	das Speerfischen
picar	el carrete	la pértiga	la pesca en alta mar	la pesca con arpón
abboccare	la bobina	la canna da pesca	la pesca in mare	la pesca con la fiocina

skiing • le ski • der Skisport • el esquí • lo sci

ski slope • la pente de ski
• der Skihang • la pista
• la pista da sci

chairlift
le télésiège
der Sessellift
la telesilla
la seggiovia

cable car
la télécabine
der Kabinenlift
el teleférico
la funivia

glove
le gant
der Handschuh
el guante
il guanto

ski pole
le bâton de ski
der Skistock
el bastón
il bastone da sci

ski run • la piste de ski
• die Skipiste • la pista
de esquí • la pista da sci

edge • la carre
• die Kante
• el canto
• la lama

tip • la pointe
• die Spitze • la
punta • la punta

ski jacket
la veste de ski
die Skijacke
el chaqueta de esquí
la giacca da sci

safety barrier
la barrière de sécurité
die Sicherheitssperre
la barrera de seguridad
la transenna di sicurezza

ski • le ski • der Ski
• el esquí • lo sci

skier • la skieuse
• die Skiläuferin • la
esquiadora • la sciatrice

ski boot • la chaussure
de ski • der Skistiefel
• la bota de esquí
• lo scarpone da sci

english • français • deutsch • español • italiano

events • les épreuves • die Disziplinen • las modalidades • le gare

gate • la porte
• das Tor • el poste
• la porta

downhill skiing • la descente
• der Abfahrtslauf
• el descenso • la discesa

slalom • le slalom
• der Slalom • el slalom
• lo slalom

ski jump • le saut
• der Skisprung • el salto
• il salto

cross-country skiing • le ski de
randonnée • der Langlauf • el
esquí de fondo • lo sci di fondo

winter sports • les sports d'hiver • der Wintersport
• los deportes de invierno • gli sport invernali

skate
le patin à glace
der Schlittschuh
el patin
il pattino

goggles • les lunettes
de ski • die Skibrille
• las gafas de
ventisca
• gli occhiali

ice climbing • l'escalade en
glace • das Eisklettern
• la escalada en hielo
• l'arrampicata su ghiaccio

ice-skating • le patinage
• das Eislaufen • el patinaje
sobre hielo • il pattinaggio
su ghiaccio

figure skating • le patinage
artistique • der Eiskunstlauf
• el patinaje artístico
• il pattinaggio artistico

snowboarding
• le surf des neiges
• das Snowboarding • el
snowboarding • lo snowboard

bobsled • le bobsleigh
• der Bobsport • el bobsleigh
• il bob

luge • la luge • das Rennrodeln
• el luge • lo slittino

alpine skiing le ski alpin die alpine Kombination el esquí alpino lo sci alpino	dogsledding le traîneau à chiens das Hundeschlittenfahren el trineo con perros la corsa su slitta trainata da cani
giant slalom le slalom géant der Riesenslalom el slálom gigante lo slalom gigante	speed skating le patinage de vitesse das Eisschnelllauf el patinaje de velocidad il pattinaggio di velocità
off-piste hors piste abseits der Piste fuera de pista fuoripista	biathlon le biathlon das Biathlon el biatlón il biathlon
curling le curling das Curling el curling il curling	avalanche l'avalanche die Lawine la avalancha la valanga

snowmobile • la motoneige
• das Schneemobil • la moto
de nieve • la motoslitta

sledding • la luge • das
Schlittenfahren • tirarse en
trineo • la corsa su slitta

other sports • les autres sports • die anderen Sportarten • los otros deportes • gli altri sport

glider
le planeur
das Segelflugzeug
el planeador
l'aliante

gliding • le vol plané • das Segelfliegen
• el vuelo sin motor • il volo a vela

hang-glider
le deltaplane
der Drachen
el ala delta
il deltaplano

hang-gliding • le deltaplane • das
Drachenfliegen • el vuelo con ala delta
• il volo in deltaplano

parachute
le parachute
der Fallschirm
el paracaídas
il paracadute

rope
la corde
das Seil
la cuerda
la corda

rock climbing • l'escalade • das Klettern
• la escalada • l'alpinismo in parete

parachuting • le parachutisme • das
Fallschirmspringen • el paracaidismo
• il paracadutismo

paragliding • le parapente
• das Gleitschirmfliegen • el parapente
• il parapendio

skydiving • le saut en chute libre • das
Fallschirmspringen • el paracaidismo en
caída libre • il paracadutismo libero

rappelling • le rappel • das Abseilen
• el rappel • la cordata

bungee jumping • le saut à l'élastique
• das Bungeejumping • el puenting
• il bungee jumping

rally driving • le rallye • das Rallyefahren • el rally • il rally

race-car driver
le coureur automobile
der Rennfahrer
el piloto de carreras
il pilota da corsa

auto racing • la course automobile • der Rennsport • el automovilismo • l'automobilismo

motocross • le motocross • das Motocross • el motocross • il motocross

motorcycle racing • la course de moto • das Motorradrennen • el motociclismo • il motociclismo

skateboard
la planche à roulettes
das Skateboard
el monopatín
la tavola da skateboard

skateboarding • la planche à roulettes • das Skateboard-fahren • montar en monopatín • lo skate board

inline skating • le patin en ligne • das Inlineskaten • el patinaje en línea • il pattinaggio in linea

stick
la crosse
der Lacrosseschläger
el palo
la mazza

lacrosse • le lacrosse • das Lacrosse • el lacrosse • il lacrosse

mask	foil
le masque	le fleuret
die Maske	das Florett
la máscara	el florete
la maschera	il fioretto

fencing • l'escrime • das Fechten • el esgrima • la scherma

pin • la quille • der Kegel • el bolo • il birillo

bowling • le bowling • das Bowling • los bolos • il bowling

arrow
la flèche
der Pfeil
la flecha
la freccia

quiver
le carquois
der Köcher
el carcaj
la faretra

bowling ball
• la boule de bowling • die Bowlingkugel
• la bola de bowling
• la palla da bowling

bow • l'arc • der Bogen • el arco • l'arco

archery • le tir à l'arc • das Bogenschießen • el tiro con arco • il tiro con l'arco

pool • le billard américain • das Poolbillard • el billar americano • il biliardo

target • la cible • die Zielscheibe • la diana • il bersaglio

target shooting • le tir à cible • das Scheibenschießen • el tiro • il tiro al bersaglio

snooker • le billard • das Snooker • el billar • lo snooker

fitness • la form physique • die Fitness • la forma física • il fitness

gym machine • l'appareil de gym • das Fitnessgerät • la máquina de ejercicios • la macchina per esercizi

bench • le banc • die Bank • el banco • la panca

exercise bike
le vélo d'entraînement
das Trainingsrad
la bicicleta fija
la cyclette

free weights
les poids
die Gewichte
las pesas
i manubri

bar
la barre
die Stange
la barra
la sbarra

gym • le gymnase • das Fitnesscenter • el gimnasio • la palestra

rowing machine • la machine à ramer • die Rudermaschine • la máquina de remos • il vogatore

treadmill • la tapis roulant • das Laufband • la banda de paseo • il tapis roulant

elliptical trainer • la machine de randonnée • die Langlauf-maschine • la máquina de cross • il cross trainer

personal trainer • l'entraîneuse individuelle • die private Fitness-trainerin • la entrenadora personal • l'istruttore individuale

stair machine • l'escalier d'entraînement • die Tretmaschine • la máquina de step • la macchina per step

swimming pool • la piscine • das Schwimmbecken • la piscina • la piscina

sauna • le sauna • die Sauna • la sauna • la sauna

exercises • les exercices • die Übungen • los ejercicios • gli esercizi

tights
le collant
die Gymnastikhose
los leotardos
il collant

stretch • l'étirement • das Strecken • el estiramiento • lo stretching

lunge • la fente en avant • der Ausfallschritt • la flexión con estiramiento • lo stiramento

push-up • la traction • der Liegestütz • la flexión • le flessioni

dumbbell
l'haltère
die Hantel
la pesa
il manubrio

squat • la flexion de jambes • die Kniebeuge • ponerse en cuclillas • il piegamento delle ginocchia

sit-up • le redressement assis • das Rumpfheben • el abdominal • gli addominali

bicep curl • l'exercice pour les biceps • die Bizepsübung • el ejercicio de bíceps • le alzate con il manubrio

leg press • la traction pour les jambes • der Beinstütz • los ejercicios de piernas • la pressa per le gambe

sneakers
les baskets
Die Sportschuhe
las zapatillas
gli scarponcini

weight bar
la barre à poids
die Gewichthantel
la barra de pesas
il bilanciere

chest press • l'exercice pour la poitrine • die Brustübung • los ejercicios pectorales • la pressa per pettorali

weight training • l'entraînement poids et haltères • das Kraft-training • el levantamiento de pesas • l'addestramento ai pesi

jogging • le jogging • das Jogging • el footing • il footing

Pilates • le pilates • das pilates • el pilates • il pilates

train (v)	jog in place (v)	extend (v)	boxercise	jumping rope
s'entraîner	jogger sur place	étendre	l'aéroboxe	le saut à la corde
trainieren	auf der Stelle joggen	ausstrecken	die Boxgymnastik	das Seilspringen
entrenar	correr en parada	estirar	la gimnasia prepugilística	saltar a la comba
allenarsi	correre sul posto	stendere	la ginnastica prepugilistica	saltare con la corda
warm up (v)	flex (v)	pull up (v)	circuit training	
s'échauffer	fléchir	tirer	l'entraîne en circuit	
sich aufwärmen	beugen	hochziehen	das Zirkeltraining	
calentar	flexionar	levantar	el entrenamiento en circuito	
riscaldarsi	flettere	sollevare	l'allenamento in circuito	

leisure
le temps libre
die Freizeit
el ocio
il tempo libero

theater • le théâtre • das Theater • el teatro • il teatro

curtain
le rideau
der Vorhang
el telón
il sipario

wings
les coulisses
die Kulisse
los bastidores
la quinta

set
le décor
das Bühnenbild
el decorado
la scenografia

audience
le public
das Publikum
el público
il pubblico

orchestra
l'orchestre
das Orchester
la orquesta
l'orchestra

stage • la scène • die Bühne • el escenario • il palcoscenico

seat
le fauteuil
der Sitzplatz
la butaca
la poltrona

balcony seats
la deuxième galerie
der zweite Rang
la platea alta
la seconda galleria

row
la rangée
die Reihe
la fila
la fila

box
la loge
die Loge
el palco
il palco

mezzanine
la corbeille
der erste Rang
la platea
la galleria

balcony
le balcon
der Balkon
la galería
la balconata

aisle
l'allée
der Gang
el pasillo
il corridoio

orchestra
seats
• l'orchestre
• das Parkett
• el patio
de butacas
• la platea

seating • les places • die Bestuhlung
• las butacas • le poltrone

play	director	opening night
la pièce de théâtre	le metteur en scène	la première
das Theaterstück	der Regisseur	die Premiere
la obra de teatro	el director	el estreno
l'opera teatrale	il regista	la prima
cast	producer	intermission
la distribution	le producteur	l'entracte
die Besetzung	der produzent	die Pause
el reparto	el productor	el descanso
il cast	il produttore	l'intervallo
actor	script	program
l'acteur	le texte	le programme
der Schauspieler	das Rollenheft	das Programm
el actor	el guión	el programa
l'attore	il copione	il programma
actress	backdrop	orchestra pit
l'actrice	la toile de fond	la fosse d'orchestre
die Schauspielerin	der Prospekt	der Orchestergraben
la actriz	el telón de fondo	el foso de la orquesta
l'attrice	il fondale	il golfo mistico

english • français • deutsch • español • italiano

concert • le concert • das Konzert
• el concierto • il concerto

musical • la comédie musicale
• das Musical • el musical • il musical

costume
le costume
das Theaterkostüm
el traje
il costume

usher	soundtrack	I'd like two tickets for tonight's performance.
le placeur	la bande sonore	Je voudrais deux billets pour la
der Platzanweiser	der Soundtrack	représentation de ce soir.
el acomodador	la banda sonora	Ich möchte zwei Karten für die Aufführung heute
la maschera	la colonna sonora	Abend.
		Quisiera dos entradas para la sesión de esta
classical music	applaud (v)	noche.
la musique classique	applaudir	Vorrei due biglietti per lo spettacolo di stasera.
die klassische Musik	applaudieren	
la música clásica	aplaudir	What time does it start?
la musica classica	applaudire	Ça commence à quelle heure?
		Um wie viel Uhr beginnt die Aufführung?
musical score	encore	¿A qué hora empieza?
la partition	le bis	A che ora inizia?
die Noten	die Zugabe	
la partitura	el bis	
la partitura musicale	il bis	

ballet • le ballet
• das Ballett • el ballet
• il balletto

opera • l'opéra
• die Oper • la ópera
• l'opera

---

movies • le cinéma • das Kino • el cine • il cinema

popcorn
le pop-corn
das Popcorn
las palomitas
il popcorn

box office
la caisse
die Kasse
la taquilla
la biglietteria

lobby
le foyer
das Foyer
el vestíbulo
l'atrio

poster
l'affiche
das Plakat
el póster
il poster

movie theater • la salle de
cinéma • der Kinosaal
• el cine • il cinema

screen • l'écran • die Leinwand
• la pantalla • lo schermo

comedy	romance
la comédie	la comédie romantique
die Komödie	der Liebesfilm
la comedia	la película romántica
la commedia	il film d'amore
thriller	science fiction movie
le thriller	le film de science-fiction
der Thriller	der Science-Fiction-Film
la película de suspense	la película de ciencia ficción
il thriller	il film di fantascienza
horror movie	adventure movie
le film d'horreur	le film d'aventures
der Horrorfilm	der Abenteuerfilm
la película de terror	la película de aventuras
il film di orrore	il film di avventura
western	animated movie
le western	le film d'animation
der Western	der Zeichentrickfilm
la película del oeste	la película de dibujos animados
il western	il film di animazione

---

orchestra • l'orchestre • das Orchester • la orquesta • l'orchestra

strings • les cordes • die Saiteninstrumente • la cuerda • gli strumenti a corda

harp
la harpe
die Harfe
el arpa
l'arpa

conductor
le chef d'orchestre
der Dirigent
el director de orquesta
il direttore di orchestra

double bass
le contrebasse
der Kontrabass
el contrabajo
il contrabbasso

violin
le violon
die Geige
el violín
il violino

podium
le podium
das Podium
el podio
il podio

viola
l'alto
die Bratsche
la viola
la viola

cello
le violoncelle
das Cello
el violoncelo
il violoncello

score
la partition
die Noten
la partitura
lo spartito

treble clef
la clé de sol
der Violinschlüssel
la clave de sol
la chiave di sol

note
la note
die Note
la nota
la nota

staff
la portée
das Liniensystem
el pentagrama
il pentagramma

bass clef
la clé de fa
der Bassschlüssel
la clave de fa
la chiave di basso

notation • la notation • die Notation • la notación
• l'annotazione

piano • le piano • das Klavier • el piano • il pianoforte

overture	sonata	rest	sharp	natural	scale
l'ouverture	la sonate	le silence	la dièse	le bécarre	la gamme
die Ouvertüre	die Sonate	das Pausenzeichen	das Kreuz	das Auflösungszeichen	die Tonleiter
la obertura	la sonata	la pausa	sostenido	el becuadro	la escala
l'ouverture	la sonata	la pausa	il diesis	naturale	la scala
symphony	instruments	pitch	flat	bar	baton
la symphonie	les instruments	le ton	le bémol	la barre de mesure	la baguette
die Symphonie	die Musikinstrumente	die Tonhöhe	das B	der Taktstrich	der Taktstock
la sinfonía	los instrumentos	el tono	bemol	el compás	la batuta
la sinfonia	gli strumenti	il tono	il bemolle	la battuta	la bacchetta

english • français • deutsch • español • italiano

woodwind • les bois • die Holzblasinstrumente • el viento-madera • gli strumenti a fiato

piccolo • le piccolo • die Pikkoloflöte • el flautín • il piffero

flute • la flûte traversière • die Querflöte • la flauta travesera • il flauto

oboe • le hautbois • die Oboe • el oboe • l'oboe

English horn • le cor anglais • das Englischhorn • el corno inglés • il corno inglese

clarinet • la clarinette • die Klarinette • el clarinete • il clarinetto

bass clarinet • la clarinette basse • die Bassklarinette • el clarinete bajo • il clarinetto basso

bassoon • le basson • das Fagott • el fagot • il fagotto

double bassoon • le contrebasson • das Kontrafagott • el contra-fagot • il controfagotto

saxophone • le saxophone • das Saxofon • el saxofón • il sassofono

percussion • les percussions • die Schlaginstrumente • la percusión • la percussione

vibraphone • le vibraphone • das Vibrafon • el vibráfono • il vibrafono

bongos • les bongos • die Bongos • los bongos • i bongo

snare drum • la caisse claire • die kleine Trommel • el tambor pequeño • il tamburo militare

kettledrum • la timbale • die Kesselpauke • el timbal • il timpano

gong • le gong • der Gong • el gong • il gong

cymbals • les cymbales • das Becken • los platillos • i cembali

tambourine le tambour das Tamburin la pandereta il tamburino

foot pedal • la pédale • das Fußpedal • el pedal • il pedale

triangle le triangle der Triangel el triángulo il triangolo

maracas les maracas die Maracas las maracas i maracas

brass • les cuivres • die Blechblasinstrumente • el viento-metal • gli ottoni

trumpet • la trompette • die Trompete • la trompeta • la tromba

trombone • le trombone • die Posaune • el trombón de varas • il trombone

French horn • le cor • das Horn • el corno de caza • il corno

tuba • le tuba • die Tuba • la tuba • la tuba

concert • le concert • das Konzert • el concierto • il concerto

fans
les fans
die Fans
los fans
i fans

speaker
le haut-parleur
der Lautsprecher
el altavoz
l'altoparlante

lead singer
le chanteur
der Leadsänger
el cantante
il cantante

guitarist
le guitariste
der Gitarrist
el guitarrista
il chitarrista

microphone
le microphone
das Mikrofon
el micrófono
il microfono

drummer
le batteur
der Schlagzeuger
el batería
il batterista

rock concert • le concert de rock • das Rockkonzert • el concierto de rock • il concerto rock

instruments • les instruments • die Instrumente • los instrumentos • gli strumenti

pickup
le pick-up
der Tonabnehmer
la pastilla
il riproduttore acustico

neck
le manche
der Hals
el mástil
il manico

fret
le sillet
der Bund
el traste
il tasto

tuning peg
la cheville
der Wirbel
la clavija
la meccanica

bridge
le chevalet
der Steg
el puente
il ponte

string
la corde
die Saite
la cuerda
la corda

drum
le tambour
die Trommel
el tambor
il tamburo

bass guitar • la basse • die Bassgitarre
• el bajo • il basso

keyboard • le piano électronique • das
Keyboard • el teclado • la tastiera

electric guitar • la guitare électrique
• die elektrische Gitarre • la guitarra
eléctrica • la chitarra elettrica

drum kit • la batterie
• das Schlagzeug • la
batería • la batteria

english • français • deutsch • español • italiano

musical styles • les styles de musique • **die Musikstile** • los estilos musicales • gli stili musicali

jazz • le jazz • der Jazz • el jazz • il jazz

blues • le blues • der Blues • el blues • il blues

punk • la musique punk • der Punk • el punk • il punk

folk music • la musique folk • der Folk • la música folk • la musica folk

pop • la pop • die Popmusik • el pop • il pop

dance • la danse • die Tanzmusik • la música de baile • la musica da ballo

rap • le rap • der Rap • el rap • il rap

heavy metal • la heavy métal • das Heavy Metal • el heavy metal • l'heavy metal

classical music • la musique classique • die klassische Musik • la música clásica • la musica classica

song	lyrics	melody	beat	reggae	country	spotlight
la chanson	les paroles	la mélodie	le beat	le reggae	la country	le projecteur
das Lied	der Text	die Melodie	der Beat	der Reggae	die Countrymusik	der Scheinwerfer
la canción	la letra	la melodía	el ritmo	el reggae	la música country	el foco
la canzone	il testo	la melodia	il ritmo	il reggae	il country	il proiettore

sightseeing • le tourisme • die Besichtigungstour • el turismo • il giro turistico

tourist
le touriste
der Tourist
el turista
il turista

itinerary
l'itinéraire
die Route
el itinerario
l'itinerario

open-top
à impériale
mit offenem Oberdeck
descubierto
scoperto

tour guide
le guide
die Fremdenführerin
el guío turístico
la guida turistica

tour bus • le bus touristique • der Stadtrundfahrtbus • el autobús turístico • il pullman turistico

figurine • la statuette • die Figur • la estatuilla • la statuina

guided tour • la visite guidée • die Führung • la visita guiada • la visita guidata

souvenirs • les souvenirs • die Andenken • los recuerdos • i ricordi

tourist attraction • l'attraction touristique • die Touristenattraktion • la atracción turística • il luogo d'interesse turistico

open	guide book	camcorder	left	Where is…?	I'm lost.
ouvert	le guide	le caméscope	à gauche	Où est…?	Je me suis perdu.
geöffnet	der Reiseführer	der Camcorder	links	Wo ist…?	Ich habe mich verlaufen.
abierto	la guía del viajero	la cámara de vídeo	la izquierda	¿Dónde está…?	Me he perdido.
aperto	la guida	la videocamera	a sinistra	Dov'è…?	Mi sono perso.
closed	film	camera	right	Can you tell me the way to….?	
fermé	la pellicule	l'appareil photo	à droite	Pour aller à…, s'il vous plaît?	
geschlossen	der Film	die Kamera	rechts	Können Sie mir sagen, wie ich nach…	
cerrado	el carrete	la máquina fotográfica	la derecha	komme?	
chiuso	la pellicola	la macchina fotografica	a destra	¿Podría decirme cómo se va a…?	
				Mi può dire come si arriva a…?	
entrance fee	batteries	directions	straight ahead		
le prix d'entrée	les piles	les directions	tout droit		
das Eintrittsgeld	die Batterien	die Richtungsangaben	geradeaus		
el precio de entrada	las pilas	las indicaciones	recto		
la tariffa d'ingresso	le batterie	le indicazioni	dritto		

attractions • les attractions • die Sehenswürdigkeiten • los lugares de interés • i luoghi d'interesse

painting
le tableau
das Gemälde
el cuadro
il quadro

exhibit
l'objet exposé
das Ausstellungsstück
la muestra
l'oggetto

exhibition • l'exposition
• die Ausstellung • la exposición
• l'esposizione

famous ruin
la ruine célèbre
die berühmte Ruine
la ruina famosa
la rovina famosa

art gallery • le musée d'art
• die Kunstgalerie • la galería
de arte • la galleria d'arte

monument • le monument
• das Monument • el
monumento • il monumento

museum • le musée
• das Museum • el museo
• il museo

historic building • le
monument historique • das
historische Gebäude • el edificio
histórico • l'edificio storico

casino • le casino • das Kasino
• el casino • il casinò

gardens • le parc • der Park
• los jardines • i giardini

national park • le parc national • der Nationalpark • el parque
nacional • il parco nazionale

information • l'information • die Information • la información • l'informazione

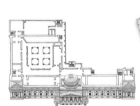

floor plan • le plan
• der Grundriss • el plano
de la planta • la pianta
del piano

map • le plan • der
Stadtplan • el plano
• la mappa

times
les heures
die Zeiten
las horas
gli orari

schedule • l'horaire
• der Fahrplan • el horario
• l'orario

tourist information
l'information touristique
die Touristeninformation
la oficina de información
l'ufficio informazioni turistiche

outdoor activities • les activités de plein air • die Aktivitäten im Freien • las actividades al aire libre • le attività all'aria aperta

footpath
le sentier
der Fußweg
el sendero
il sentiero

sundial
le cadran solaire
die Sonnenuhr
el reloj de sol
la meridiana

café
le café
das Café
la cafetería
il caffè

park • le parc • der Park • el parque • il parco

grass
la pelouse
das Gras
la hierba
il prato

bench
le banc
die Bank
el banco
la panchina

formal gardens
les jardins à la française
die Gartenanlagen
los jardines clásicos
il giardino all'italiana

roller coaster
les montagnes russes
die Berg-und-Talbahn
la montaña rusa
le montagne russe

fairground • la foire
• der Jahrmarkt • la feria
• il luna park

theme park • le parc
d'attractions • der
Vergnügungspark • el parque de
atracciones • il parco a tema

safari park • la réserve
• der Safaripark • el safari
park • lo zoosafari

zoo • le zoo • der Zoo
• el zoo • lo zoo

english • français • deutsch • español • italiano

activites • les activités • die Aktivitäten • las actividades • le attività

cycling • le vélo • das Radfahren • el ciclismo • il ciclismo

jogging • le jogging • das Jogging • el footing • il footing

skateboarding • la planche à roulette • das Skateboardfahren • montar en patinete • lo skateboard

rollerblading • le roller • das Inlinerfahren • el patinaje • il pattinaggio

bridle path • la piste cavalière • der Reitweg • el sendero para caballos • il sentiero per cavalli

hamper • le panier à pique-nique • der Picknickkorb • la cesta • la cesta

bird-watching • l'observation des oiseaux • das Vogelbeobachten • la ornitología • l'ornitologia

horseback riding • l'équitation • das Reiten • la equitación • l'equitazione

hiking • la randonnée • das Wandern • el senderismo • l'escursionismo

picnic • le pique-nique • das Picknick • el picnic • il picnic

---

playground • le terrain de jeux • der Spielplatz • el área de juegos • il parco giochi

sandbox • le bac à sable • der Sandkasten • el cajón de arena • la fossa di sabbia

wading pool • la pataugeoire • das Planschbecken • la piscina de plástico • la piscina gonfiabile

swing • la balançoire • die Schaukel • los columpios • l'altalena

seesaw • la bascule • die Wippe • el subibaja • il bilanciere

slide • le toboggan • die Rutsche • el tobogán • lo scivolo

climbing frame • la cage à poules • das Klettergerüst • la estructura para escalar • la struttura per arrampicarsi

beach • la plage • der Strand • la playa • la spiaggia

hotel	beach umbrella	beach hut	sand	wave	sea
l'hôtel	le parasol	la cabine de plage	le sable	la vague	la mer
das Hotel	der Sonnenschirm	das Strandhäuschen	der Sand	die Welle	das Meer
el hotel	la sombrilla	la caseta	la arena	la ola	el mar
l'albergo	l'ombrellone	la cabina	la sabbia	l'onda	il mare

beach bag
le sac de plage
die Strandtasche
la bolsa de playa
la borsa da spiaggia

bikini • le bikini
• der Bikini • el
bikini• il bikini

sunbathe *(v)* • prendre un bain de soleil • sonnenbaden • tomar el sol • prendere il sole

english • français • deutsch • español • italiano

lifeguard
le maître nageur
der Rettungsschwimmer
el socorrista
il bagnino

lifeguard tower • la tour
de surveillance • der
Rettungsturm • la torre de
vigilancia • la torre di
sorveglianza

windbreak • le pare-vent
• der Windschutz • la barrera
contra el viento • il
paravento

boardwalk • la promenade
• die Promenade • el paseo
marítimo • il lungomare

deck chair • le transat
• der Liegestuhl • la hamaca
• la sedia a sdraio

sunglasses • les lunettes de
soleil • die Sonnenbrille • las
gafas de sol • gli occhiali
da sole

sun hat • le chapeau de plage
• der Sonnenhut • el sombrero
para el sol • il cappello
da spiaggia

suntan lotion • la créme
solaire • die Sonnenmilch
• la crema bronceadora
• la crema abbronzante

sunblock • l'écran total
• der Sonnenblock • la crema
protectora • la crema
protettiva

swimsuit
le maillot de bain
der Badeanzug
el bañador
il costume da bagno

shovel
la pelle
die Schaufel
la pala
la paletta

pail
le seau
der Eimer
el cubo
il secchiello

beach ball • le ballon de
plage • der Wasserball • la
pelota de playa • il pallone
da spiaggia

inflatable ring • la bouée • der
Schwimmreifen • el flotador
• la ciambella

sandcastle
le château de sable
die Sandburg
el castillo de arena
il castello di sabbia

shell
le coquillage
die Muschel
la concha
la conchiglia

beach towel • la serviette
de plage • das Strandtuch
• la toalla de playa
• l'asciugamano da spiaggia

camping • le camping • das Camping • el camping • il campeggio

restrooms
les toilettes
die Toiletten
los aseos
i bagni

waste disposal
les poubelles
die Mülleimer
el contenedor de la basura
i rifuti

shower block
les douches
die Duschen
las duchas
le docce

electric hookup
le branchement électrique
der Stromanschluss
el punto eléctrico
la presa di corrente

flysheet
le double toit
das Überdach
il telo protettivo

tent peg
le piquet
der Hering
la clavija
il piolo

guy rope
la corde
die Zeltspannleine
la cuerda
la corda tirante

camper
la caravane
der Wohnwagen
la roulotte
la roulotte

campground • le terrain de camping • der Campingplatz • el camping • il campeggio

camp (v)
camper
zelten
acampar
campeggiare

site manager's office
le bureau du chef
die Campingplatzverwaltung
la oficina del director
l'ufficio del direttore

sites available
les emplacements libres
Zeltplätze frei
hay plazas libres
le piazzole disponibili

full
complet
voll
completo
completo

site
l'emplacement
der Zeltplatz
la plaza
il posteggio

pitch a tent (v)
monter une tente
ein Zelt aufschlagen
montar una tienda
piantare una tenda

tent pole
le mât
die Zeltstange
el palo de la tienda
il palo

camp bed
le lit de camp
das Faltbett
el catre de campaña
il lettino da campeggio

picnic bench
le banc à pique-nique
die Picknickbank
la mesa de picnic
la tavola da picnic

hammock
le hamac
die Hängematte
la hamaca
l'amaca

camper van
le camping-car
das Wohnmobil
la autocaravana
il camper

trailer
la remorque
der Anhänger
el remolque
il rimorchio

charcoal
le charbon de bois
die Holzkohle
el carbón vegetal
la carbonella

firelighter
l'allume-feu
der Feueranzünder
la pastilla para hogueras
l'accendifuoco

light a fire (v)
allumer un feu
ein Feuer machen
encender una hoguera
accendere un fuoco

campfire
le feu de camp
das Lagerfeuer
la hoguera
il fuoco

frame
le cadre
das Gestänge
la estructura
la struttura

ground sheet
le tapis de sol
der Zeltboden
el suelo aislante
il telo isolante

backpack
le sac à dos
der Rucksack
la mochila
lo zaino

vacuum flask
le thermos
die Thermosflasche
el termo
il thermos

water bottle
la bouteille d'eau
die Wasserflasche
la cantimplora
la borraccia

tent • la tente • das Zelt • la tienda de campaña • la tenda

insect repellent • le spray contre les insectes • der Insektenspray • el repelente (contra insectos) • l'insettifugo

flashlight • la lampe torche • die Taschenlampe • la linterna • la torcia

mosquito net
la moustiquaire
das Moskitonetz
la mosquitera
la zanzariera

thermal underwear
les sous-vêtements thermiques
die Thermowäsche
la ropa termoaislante
gli indumenti termici

hiking boots • les chaussures de marche • die Wanderschuhe • las botas de trekking • le scarpe da escursionismo

rain gear • l'imperméable • die Regenhaut • la ropa impermeable • gli indumenti impermeabili

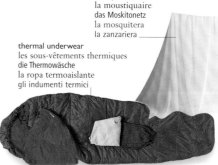

sleeping bag • le sac de couchage • der Schlafsack • el saco de dormir • il sacco a pelo

sleeping mat
le tapis de sol
die Schlafmatte
la esterilla
il materassino

camping stove • le réchaud • der Gasbrenner • el hornillo • il fornelletto da campeggio

barbecue grill • le barbecue • der Grill • la barbacoa • la griglia per barbecue

air mattress • le matelat pneumatique • die Luftmatratze • la colchoneta • il materassino gonfiabile

home entertainment • les loisirs électroniques • die Unterhaltungselektronik • la electrónica de consumo • l'elettronica d'intrattenimento

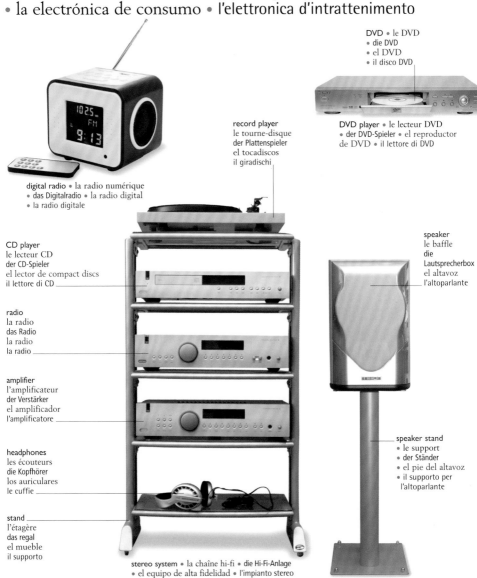

DVD • le DVD
• die DVD
• el DVD
• il disco DVD

record player
le tourne-disque
der Plattenspieler
el tocadiscos
il giradischi

DVD player • le lecteur DVD
• der DVD-Spieler • el reproductor
de DVD • il lettore di DVD

digital radio • la radio numérique
• das Digitalradio • la radio digital
• la radio digitale

speaker
le baffle
die Lautsprecherbox
el altavoz
l'altoparlante

CD player
le lecteur CD
der CD-Spieler
el lector de compact discs
il lettore di CD

radio
la radio
das Radio
la radio
la radio

amplifier
l'amplificateur
der Verstärker
el amplificador
l'amplificatore

speaker stand
• le support
• der Ständer
• el pie del altavoz
• il supporto per
l'altoparlante

headphones
les écouteurs
die Kopfhörer
los auriculares
le cuffie

stand
l'étagère
das regal
el mueble
il supporto

stereo system • la chaîne hi-fi • die Hi-Fi-Anlage
• el equipo de alta fidelidad • l'impianto stereo

screen
l'écran
der Bildschirm
la pantalla
lo schermo

eyecup
l'œilleton
die Okular
el borde del ocular
l'oculare

DTV converter box • le box • die Digitale box
• el sintonizador digital • il decoder

camcorder • le caméscope
• der Camcorder • la cámara
de vídeo • la videocamera

satellite dish • l'antenne parabolique
• die Satellitenschüssel • la antena
parabólica • l'antenna parabolica

flatscreen TV • la télévision à
écran plat • der Flachbildfernseher
• el televisor de pantalla plana
• il televisore a schermo piatto

console
la console
die Spielkonsole
la consola
la console

fast-forward • l'avance
rapide • der Vorlauf
• el avance rápido
• l'avanzamento veloce

pause
la pause
die Pause
la pausa
la pausa

record
• l'enregistrement
• die Aufnahme
• el botón para
grabar • la
registrazione

volume
le volume
die Lautstärke
el volumen
il volume

controller
la commande
der Controller
los controles
il comando

rewind
le retour rapide
der Rücklauf
el botón para rebobinar
il riavvolgimento

play
la lecture
das Abspielen
el play
il play

stop
l'arrêt
der Stop
el stop
lo stop

video game • le jeu vidéo • das Videospiel • el videojuego • il videogioco

remote control • la télécommande • die Fernbedienung
• el mando a distancia • il telecomando

CD le CD die CD el compact disc il compact disc	Wi-Fi le wifi WLAN la Wi-Fi Wifi	advertisement la publicité die Werbung el anuncio la pubblicità	pay-per-view channel la chaîne à péage der Pay-Kanal el canal de pay per view il canale a pagamento	streaming le streaming das Streaming la transmisión por secuencias lo streaming	turn off the television (v) éteindre la télévision den Fernseher abschalten apagar la televisión spegnere la televisione
cassette tape la cassette die Kassette la casete l'audiocassetta	high definition haute définition hochauflösend alta definición alta definizione (HD)	digital numérique digital digital digitale	program le programme das Programm el programa il programma	turn on the television (v) allumer la télévision den Fernseher einschalten encender la televisión accendere la televisione	tune the radio (v) régler la radio das Radio einstellen sintonizar la radio sintonizzare la radio
cassette player le lecteur cassettes der Kassettenrekorder el magnetófono il mangianastri	feature film le film der Spielfilm el largometraje il lungometraggio	cable television la télévision par câble das Kabelfernsehen la televisión por cable la televisione via cavo	change channel (v) changer de chaîne den Kanal wechseln cambiar de canal cambiare canale	watch television (v) regarder la télévision fernsehen ver la televisión guardare la televisione	stereo stéréo stereo estéreo stereo

photography • la photographie • die Fotografie • la fotografía • la fotografia

shutter release
le déclencheur
der Auslöser
el disparador
il pulsante di scatto

aperture dial
le réglage de l'ouverture
der Blendenregler
la rueda del diafragma
il regolatore di espossizione

lens
l'objectif
die Linse
el objetivo
l'obiettivo

filter • le filtre • der Filter
• el filtro • il filtro

lens cap • le bouchon
d'objectif • die Schutzkappe
• la tapa del objetivo
• il copriobiettivo

SLR camera • l'appareil réflex mono-
objectif • die Spiegelreflexkamera • la
cámara réflex • la macchina fotografica SLR

flash gun • le flash compact
• der Elektronenblitz • el flash
electrónico • il flash

lightmeter • le posemètre
• der Belichtungsmesser
• el fotómetro • l'esposimetro

zoom lens • le zoom
• das Wechselobjektiv • el
teleobjetivo • lo zoom

tripod • le trépied • das Stativ
• el trípode • il treppiede

---

types of camera • les types d'appareils photo • die Fotoapparattypen • los tipos de cámara
• i tipi di macchina fotorafica

flash
le flash
der Blitz
el flash
il flash

polaroid camera • le Polaroid®
• die Polaroidkamera • la
cámara Polaroid • la
macchina fotografica Polaroid

digital camera • l'appareil
numérique • die Digitalkamera
• la cámara digital • la
macchina fotografica digitale

camera phone • le photophone
• das Kamerahandy • el teléfono
con cámara • il telefono con
macchina fotografica

disposable camera • l'appareil
jetable • die Einwegkamera
• la cámara desechable • la
macchina fotografica usa e getta

photograph (v) • photographier • fotografieren • fotografiar • fotografare

film roll
le rouleau de pellicule
die Filmspule
el carrete
il rullino

film • la pellicule • der Film
• la película • la pellicola

focus (v) • mettre au point
• einstellen • enfocar
• mettere a fuoco

develop (v) • développer
• entwickeln • revelar
• sviluppare

negative • le négatif • das
Negativ • el negativo • il
negativo

landscape • paysage
• quer • apaisado
• orrizontale

portrait • portrait
• hoch • en formato
vertical • verticale

photograph • la photo • das Foto • la fotografía • la fotografia

photo album • l'album de photos
• das Fotoalbum • el álbum de
fotos • l'album fotografico

picture frame • le cadre de
photo • der Fotorahmen • el
portarretratos • la cornice

problems • les problèmes • die Probleme • los problemas • i difetti

underexposed • sous-exposé
• unterbelichtet • subexpuesto
• sottoesposto

overexposed • surexposé
• überbelichtet • sobreexpuesto
• sovraesposto

out of focus • flou • unscharf
• desenfocado • sfocato

red eye • les yeux rouges
• die roten augen • los ojos
rojos • l'occhio rosso

viewfinder	print
le viseur	l'épreuve
der Bildsucher	der Abzug
el visor	la copia
il mirino	la fotografia (sviluppata)
camera case	matte
le sac d'appareil photo	mat
die Kameratasche	matt
la funda de la cámara	mate
la custodia	opaco
exposure	gloss
la pose	brilliant
die Belichtung	hochglanz
la exposición	con brillo
l'esposizione	lucido
darkroom	enlargement
la chambre noire	l'agrandissement
die Dunkelkammer	die Vergrößerung
el cuarto oscuro	la ampliación
la camera oscura	l'ingrandimento

I'd like this film processed.
Pourriez-vous faire développer cette pellicule?
Könnten Sie diesen Film entwickeln lassen?
Me gustaría revelar este carrete.
Vorrei far sviluppare questo rollino.

games • les jeux • die Spiele • los juegos • i giochi

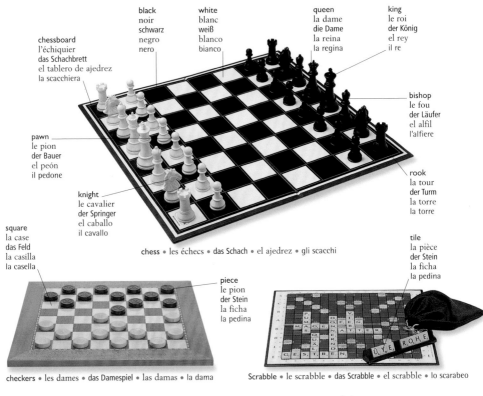

black
noir
schwarz
negro
nero

white
blanc
weiß
blanco
bianco

queen
la dame
die Dame
la reina
la regina

king
le roi
der König
el rey
il re

chessboard
l'échiquier
das Schachbrett
el tablero de ajedrez
la scacchiera

bishop
le fou
der Läufer
el alfil
l'alfiere

pawn
le pion
der Bauer
el peón
il pedone

rook
la tour
der Turm
la torre
la torre

knight
le cavalier
der Springer
el caballo
il cavallo

square
la case
das Feld
la casilla
la casella

chess • les échecs • das Schach • el ajedrez • gli scacchi

tile
la pièce
der Stein
la ficha
la pedina

piece
le pion
der Stein
la ficha
la pedina

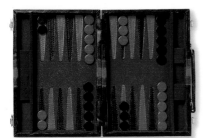

checkers • les dames • das Damespiel • las damas • la dama

Scrabble • le scrabble • das Scrabble • el scrabble • lo scarabeo

counter • le jeton
• die Spielmarke
• la ficha • la pedina

dice
le dé
der Würfel
el dado
il dado

Monopoly
le monopoly
das Monopoly
el monopoly
il monopoly

backgammon • le jaquet • das Backgammon
• el backgammon • il backgammon

board games • les jeux de société • die Brettspiele
• los juegos de mesa • i giochi da tavolo

english • français • deutsch • español • italiano

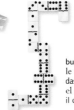

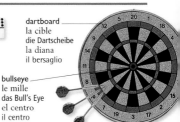

dartboard
la cible
die Dartscheibe
la diana
il bersaglio

bullseye
le mille
das Bull's Eye
el centro
il centro

stamp collecting • la philatélie
• das Briefmarkensammeln
• la filatelia • la filatelia

jigsaw puzzle • le puzzle
• das Puzzle • el puzzle
• il puzzle

dominoes • les dominos
• das Domino • el dominó
• il domino

darts • les fléchettes
• das Darts • los dardos
• le freccette

joker
le joker
der Joker
el comodín
il jolly

jack
le valet
der Bube
la jota
il fante

queen
la dame
die Dame
la reina
la regina

king
le roi
der König
el rey
il re

ace • l'as
• das Ass • el as
• l'asso

diamond
le carreau
das Karo
el rombo
il quadro

spade
le pique
das Pik
la pica
la picca

heart
le cœur
das Herz
el corazón
il cuore

club
le trèfle
das Kreuz
el trébol
il fiore

shuffle (v) • battre • mischen
• barajar • mescolare

deal (v) • donner • geben
• dar • distribuire

cards • les cartes • die Karten • las cartas
• le carte

move	win (v)	loser	point	bridge	Whose turn is it?
le coup	gagner	le perdant	le point	le bridge	C'est à qui de jouer?
der Zug	gewinnen	der Verlierer	der Punkt	das Bridge	Wer ist dran?
el turno	ganar	el perdedor	el punto	el bridge	¿A quién le toca?
la mossa	vincere	il perdente	il punto	il bridge	A chi tocca?
play (v)	winner	game	score	deck of cards	It's your move.
jouer	le gagnant	le jeu	la marque	le jeu de cartes	C'est à toi de jouer.
spielen	der Gewinner	das Spiel	das Spielergebnis	das Kartenspiel	Du bist dran.
jugar	el ganador	la partida	la puntuación	la baraja	Te toca a ti.
giocare	il vincitore	il gioco	il punteggio	il mazzo di carte	Tocca a te.
player	lose (v)	bet	poker	suit	Roll the dice.
le joueur	perdre	le pari	le poker	la couleur	Jette le dé.
der Spieler	verlieren	die Wette	das Poker	die Farbe	Würfle.
el jugador	perder	la apuesta	el póquer	el palo	Tira los dados.
il giocatore	perdere	la scommessa	il poker	il colore	Tira i dadi.

arts and crafts 1 • les arts et métiers 1 • das Kunsthandwerk 1 • las manualidades 1 • arte e artigianato 1

paints • les couleurs • die Farben • las pinturas • la vernice

artist
l'artiste peintre
die Künstlerin
la pintora
l'artista

painting
le tableau
das Gemälde
el cuadro
il quadro

easel
le chevalet
die Staffelei
el caballete
il cavalletto

canvas
la toile
die Leinwand
el lienzo
la tela

brush
le pinceau
der Pinsel
el pincel
il pennello

palette
la palette
die Palette
la paleta
la tavolozza

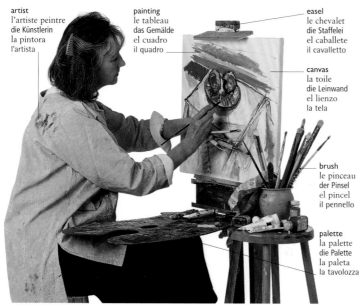

oil paint • les couleurs à l'huile • die Ölfarben • las pinturas al óleo • i colori ad olio

watercolor paint • l'aquarelle à l'eau • die Aquarellfarbe • las acuarelas • gli acquarelli

pastels • les pastels • die Pastellstifte • los pasteles • i pastelli

acrylic paint • l'acrylique • die Acrylfarbe • la pintura acrílica • i colori acrilici

painting • la peinture • die Malerei • la pintura • la pittura

colors • les couleurs • die Farben • los colores • i colori

red • rouge • rot • rojo • rosso

blue • bleu • blau • azul • blu

yellow • jaune • gelb • amarillo • giallo

green • vert • grün • verde • verde

orange • orange • orange • naranja • arancione

purple • violet • lila • morado • viola

white • blanc • weiß • blanco • bianco

black • noir • schwarz • negro • nero

gray • gris • grau • gris • grigio

pink • rose • rosa • rosa • rosa

brown • marron • braun • marrón • marrone

indigo • indigo • indigoblau • azul añil • indaco

poster paint • la gouache • die Plakatfarbe • la témpera • la tempera

english • français • deutsch • español • italiano

other crafts • les autres arts • andere Kunstfertigkeiten • las otras manualidades • altri lavori artigianali

sketch pad
le carnet à croquis
der Skizzenblock
el bloc de dibujo
il blocco per schizzi

sketch
le croquis
die Skizze
el boceto
lo schizzo

ink
l'encre
die Druckfarbe
la tinta
l'inchiostro

pencil
le crayon
der Bleistift
el lápiz
la matita

charcoal
le fusain
der Kohlestift
el carboncillo
il carboncino

drawing • le dessin • das Zeichnen • el dibujo • il disegno

printing • l'imprimerie • das Drucken • la impresión • la stampa

engraving • la gravure • das Gravieren • el grabado • l'incisione

stone
la pierre
der Stein
la piedra
la pietra

mallet
le maillet
der Schlegel
el mazo
il martello

chisel
le burin
der Stechbeitel
el cincel
lo scalpello

wood
le bois
das Holz
la madera
il legno

modeling tool • la spatule • das Modellierholz • la herramienta para modelar • l'attrezzo per modellare

potter's wheel
le tour de potier
die Töpferscheibe
el torno de alfarero
il tornio da vasaio

clay
l'argile
der Ton
la arcilla
l'argilla

sculpting • la sculpture • die Bildhauerei • la escultura • la scultura

woodworking • la sculpture sur bois • die Holzarbeit • la talla en madera • la falegnameria

glue
la colle
der Klebstoff
la cola
la colla

cardboard
le carton
die Pappe
la cartulina
il cartone

collage • le collage • die Collage • el collage • il collage

pottery • la poterie • die Töpferei • la alfarería • la ceramica

jewelery-making • la joaillerie • die Juwelierarbeit • la orfebrería • l'oreficeria

papier-mâché • le papier mâché • das Pappmaschee • el papel maché • la cartapesta

origami • l'origami • das Origami • la papiroflexia • l'origami

model-making • le modélisme • der Modellbau • el modelismo • il modellismo

arts and crafts 2 • les arts et métiers 2 • das Kunsthandwerk 2 • las manualidades 2 • arte e artigianato 2

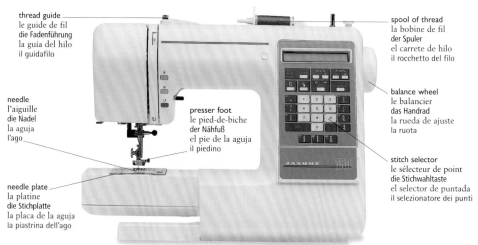

thread guide
le guide de fil
die Fadenführung
la guía del hilo
il guidafilo

spool of thread
la bobine de fil
der Spuler
el carrete de hilo
il rocchetto del filo

needle
l'aiguille
die Nadel
la aguja
l'ago

presser foot
le pied-de-biche
der Nähfuß
el pie de la aguja
il piedino

balance wheel
le balancier
das Handrad
la rueda de ajuste
la ruota

stitch selector
le sélecteur de point
die Stichwahltaste
el selector de puntada
il selezionatore dei punti

needle plate
la platine
die Stichplatte
la placa de la aguja
la piastrina dell'ago

sewing machine • la machine à coudre • die Nähmaschine • la máquina de coser • la macchina da cucire

scissors • les ciseaux • die Schere • las tijeras • le forbici

pattern • le patron • das Schnittmuster • el patrón • il modello

pincushion
la pelote à épingles
das Nadelkissen
el alfiletero
il puntaspilli

tape measure • le centimètre • das Zentimetermaß • la cinta métrica • il metro

material • le tissu • der Stoff • la tela • la stoffa

pin
l'épingle
die Stecknadel
el alfiler
lo spillo

sewing basket • la corbeille à couture • der Nähkorb • el costurero • la cesta del cucito

bobbin • la bobine • die Spule • la bobina • la bobina

thread
le fil
das Garn
el hilo
il filo

hook • l'agrafe • der Haken • el corchete • il gancio

eye
l'œillet
die Öse
el ojo
l'occhiello

thimble • le dé à coudre • der Fingerhut • el dedal • il ditale

tailor's chalk • la craie de tailleur • die Schneiderkreide • el jaboncillo • il gesso

tailor's dummy • le mannequin • die Schneiderpuppe • el maniquí • il manichino

thread (v) • enfiler • einfädeln • enhebrar • infilare

stitch
le point
der Stich
la puntada
il punto

sew (v) • coudre • nähen • coser • cucire

darn (v) • repriser • stopfen • zurcir • rammendare

tack (v) • bâtir • heften • hilvanar • imbastire

cut (v) • couper • schneiden • cortar • tagliare

needlepoint • la tapisserie • die Tapisserie • el bordado en cañamazo • il mezzopunto

embroidery • la broderie • die Stickerei • el bordado • il ricamo

crochet hook
le crochet
der Häkelhaken
la aguja de ganchillo
l'uncinetto

crochet • le crochet • das Häkeln • el ganchillo • il lavoro all'uncinetto

macramé • le macramé • das Makramee • el macramé • il macramè

patchwork • le patchwork • das Patchwork • la labor de retales • il patchwork

quilting • le ouatage • das Wattieren • el acolchado • il trapunto

lace bobbin • le fuseau • der Klöppel • el bolillo • la spoletta

lace-making • la dentelle • die Spitzenklöppelei • la labor de encaje • la fabbricazione dei merletti

loom • le métier à tisser • der Webstuhl • el telar • il telaio

weaving • le tissage • die Weberei • tejer • la tessitura

unpick (v)	nylon
défaire	le nylon
auftrennen	das Nylon
descoser	el nailon
scucire	il nailon
fabric	silk
le tissu	la soie
der Stoff	die Seide
la tela	la seda
il tessuto	la seta
cotton	designer
le coton	le styliste
die Baumwolle	der Modedesigner
el algodón	el diseñador
il cotone	lo stilista
linen	fashion
le lin	la mode
das Leinen	die Mode
el lino	la moda
il lino	la moda
polyester	zipper
le polyester	la fermeture éclair
das Polyester	der Reißverschluss
el poliéster	la cremallera
il poliestere	la chiusura lampo

knitting • le tricot • das Stricken • la labor de punto • il lavoro a maglia

knitting needle
l'aiguille à tricoter
die Stricknadel
la aguja de tejer
il ferro da calza

skein • l'écheveau • der Strang • la madeja • la matassa

yarn
la laine
die Wolle
la lana
la lana

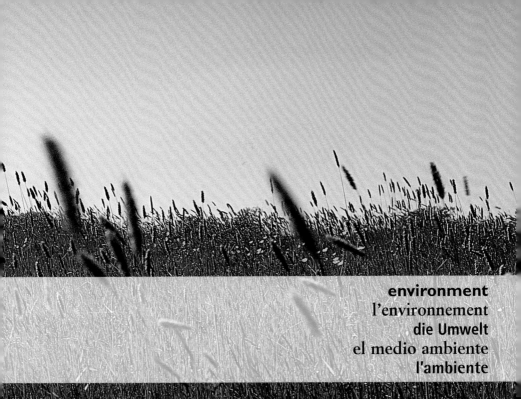

environment
l'environnement
die Umwelt
el medio ambiente
l'ambiente

space • l'espace • der Weltraum • el espacio • lo spazio

Mercury
Mercure
der Merkur
Mercurio
Mercurio

Earth
la Terre
die Erde
Tierra
la Terra

Mars
Mars
der Mars
Marte
Marte

Jupiter
Jupiter
der Jupiter
Júpiter
Giove

Uranus
Uranus
der Uranus
Urano
Uranio

Neptune
Neptune
der Neptun
Neptuno
Nettuno

Pluto
Pluton
der Pluto
Plutón
Plutone

Venus
Vénus
die Venus
Venus
Venere

Sun
le soleil
die Sonne
el sol
il sole

Moon
la lune
der Mond
la luna
la luna

Saturn
Saturne
der Saturn
Saturno
Saturno

tail
la queue
der Schweif
la cola
la coda

star
l'étoile
der Stern
la estrella
la stella

solar system • le sytème solaire • das Sonnensystem • el sistema solar • il sistema solare

galaxy • la galaxie
• die Galaxie • la galaxia
• la galassia

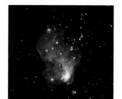

nebula • la nébuleuse
• der Nebelfleck • la nebulosa
• la nebulosa

asteroid • l'astéroïde
• der Asteroid • el asteroide
• l'asteroide

comet • la comète
• der Komet • el cometa
• la cometa

universe l'univers das Universum el universo l'universo	black hole le trou noir das schwarze Loch el agujero negro il buco nero	full moon la pleine lune der Vollmond la luna llena la luna piena
orbit l'orbite die Umlaufbahn la órbita l'orbita	planet la planète der Planet el planeta il pianeta	new moon la nouvelle lune der Neumond la luna nueva la luna nuova
gravity la pesanteur die Schwerkraft la gravedad la gravità	meteor le météore der Meteor el meteorito la meteora	crescent moon le croissant de lune die Mondsichel la media luna la mezzaluna

eclipse • l'éclipse • die Finsternis • el eclipse • l'eclisse

space exploration • l'exploration spatiale • die Raumforschung • la exploración espacial • l'esplorazione dello spazio

radar
le radar
der Radar
el radar
il radar

space shuttle
• la navette spatiale
• die Raumfähre
• el trasbordador
espacial • lo shuttle

space suit
le scaphandre spatial
der Raumanzug
el traje espacial
la tuta spaziale

thruster
la fusée d'orientation
die Steuerrakete
el propulsor
il reattore

crew hatch • le
sas d'équipage
• die Besatzungs-
luke • la escotilla
• lo sportello
dell'equipaggio

booster
l'accélérateur
der Beschleuniger
el lanzacohetes
il lanciarazzi

astronaut • l'astronaute
• der Astronaut • el
astronauta • l'astronauta

lunar module • le module lunaire • die Mondfähre • el módulo
lunar • il modulo lunare

launch pad • la rampe
de lancement
• die Abschussrampe
• la rampa de
lanzamiento
• la rampa
di lancio

launch • le lancement • der
Abschuss • el lanzamiento
• il lancio

satellite • le satellite • der
Satellit • el satélite • il satellite

space station • la station spatiale • die Raumstation • la estación
espacial • la stazione spaziale

---

astronomy • l'astronomie • die Astronomie • la astronomía • l'astronomia

telescope
le télescope
das Teleskop
el telescopio
il telescopio

tripod
le trépied
das Stativ
el trípode
il treppiede

constellation • la constellation
• das Sternbild • la constelación
• la costellazione

binoculars • les jumelles
• das Fernglas • los prismáticos
• il binocolo

Earth • la terre • die Erde • la Tierra • la Terra

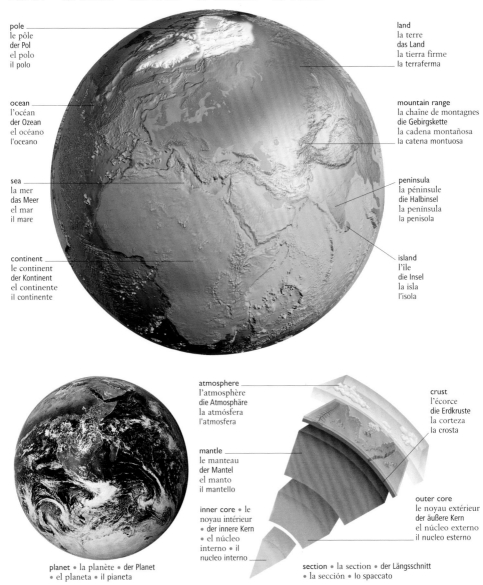

pole
le pôle
der Pol
el polo
il polo

land
la terre
das Land
la tierra firme
la terraferma

ocean
l'océan
der Ozean
el océano
l'oceano

mountain range
la chaîne de montagnes
die Gebirgskette
la cadena montañosa
la catena montuosa

sea
la mer
das Meer
el mar
il mare

peninsula
la péninsule
die Halbinsel
la península
la penisola

continent
le continent
der Kontinent
el continente
il continente

island
l'île
die Insel
la isla
l'isola

atmosphere
l'atmosphère
die Atmosphäre
la atmósfera
l'atmosfera

crust
l'écorce
die Erdkruste
la corteza
la crosta

mantle
le manteau
der Mantel
el manto
il mantello

inner core • le
noyau intérieur
• der innere Kern
• el núcleo
interno • il
nucleo interno

outer core
le noyau extérieur
der äußere Kern
el núcleo externo
il nucleo esterno

planet • la planète • der Planet
• el planeta • il pianeta

section • la section • der Längsschnitt
• la sección • lo spaccato

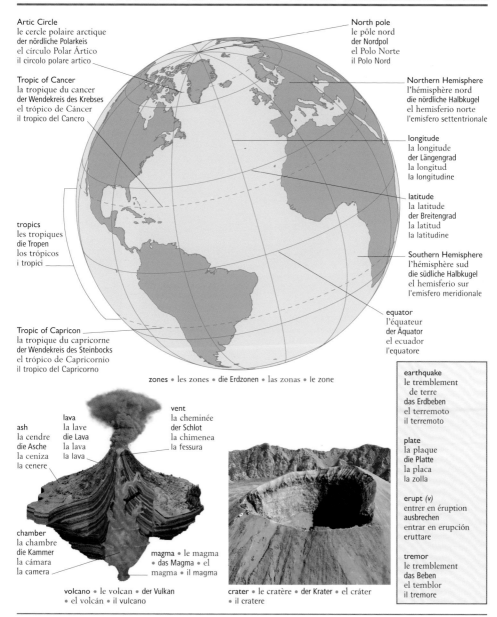

Artic Circle
le cercle polaire arctique
der nördliche Polarkeis
el círculo Polar Ártico
il circolo polare artico

Tropic of Cancer
la tropique du cancer
der Wendekreis des Krebses
el trópico de Cáncer
il tropico del Cancro

tropics
les tropiques
die Tropen
los trópicos
i tropici

Tropic of Capricon
la tropique du capricorne
der Wendekreis des Steinbocks
el trópico de Capricornio
il tropico del Capricorno

North pole
le pôle nord
der Nordpol
el Polo Norte
il Polo Nord

Northern Hemisphere
l'hémisphère nord
die nördliche Halbkugel
el hemisferio norte
l'emisfero settentrionale

longitude
la longitude
der Längengrad
la longitud
la longitudine

latitude
la latitude
der Breitengrad
la latitud
la latitudine

Southern Hemisphere
l'hémisphère sud
die südliche Halbkugel
el hemisferio sur
l'emisfero meridionale

equator
l'équateur
der Äquator
el ecuador
l'equatore

zones • les zones • die Erdzonen • las zonas • le zone

ash
la cendre
die Asche
la ceniza
la cenere

lava
la lave
die Lava
la lava
la lava

vent
la cheminée
der Schlot
la chimenea
la fessura

chamber
la chambre
die Kammer
la cámara
la camera

magma • le magma
• das Magma • el
magma • il magma

volcano • le volcan • der Vulkan
• el volcán • il vulcano

crater • le cratère • der Krater • el cráter
• il cratere

earthquake
le tremblement
  de terre
das Erdbeben
el terremoto
il terremoto

plate
la plaque
die Platte
la placa
la zolla

erupt (v)
entrer en éruption
ausbrechen
entrar en erupción
eruttare

tremor
le tremblement
das Beben
el temblor
il tremore

landscape • le paysage • die Landschaft • el paisaje • il paesaggio

mountain
la montagne
der Berg
la montaña
la montagna

slope
la pente
der Hang
la ladera
la pendice

bank
la rive
das Ufer
la orilla
la riva

river
la rivière
der Fluss
el río
il fiume

rapids
les rapides
die Stromschnellen
los rápidos
le rapide

rocks
les rochers
die Felsen
las rocas
le rocce

glacier • le glacier
• der Gletscher • el glaciar
• il ghiacciaio

valley • la vallée • das Tal
• el valle • la valle

hill • la colline • der Hügel
• la colina • la collina

plateau • le plateau
• das Plateau • la meseta
• l'altipiano

gorge • la gorge • die Schlucht
• el desfiladero • la gola

cave • la caverne • die Höhle
• la cueva • la caverna

plain • la plaine • die Ebene • la llanura • la pianura

desert • le désert • die Wüste • el desierto • il deserto

forest • la forêt • der Wald • el bosque • la foresta

woods • le bois • der Wald • el bosque • il bosco

rain forest • la forêt tropicale • der Regenwald • la selva tropical • la foresta pluviale

swamp • le marais • der Sumpf • el pantano • la palude

meadow • le pré • die Wiese label • el prado • il pascolo

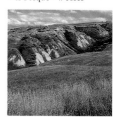

grassland • la prairie • das Grasland • la pradera • la prateria

waterfall • la cascade • der Wasserfall • la cascada • la cascata

stream • le ruisseau • der Bach • el arroyo • il torrente

lake • le lac • der See • el lago • il lago

geyser • le geyser • der Geysir • el géiser • il geyser

coast • la côte • die Küste • la costa • la costa

cliff • la falaise • die Klippe • el acantilado • la scogliera

coral reef • le récif de corail • das Korallenriff • el arrecife de coral • la barriera corallina

estuary • l'estuaire • die Flussmündung • el estuario • l'estuario

weather • le temps • das Wetter • el tiempo • il tempo

exosphere
l'exosphère
die Exosphäre
la exosfera
l'esosfera

aurora
l'aurore
das Polarlicht
la aurora
l'aurora

thermosphere
la thermosphère
die Thermosphäre
la termoesfera
la termosfera

ionosphere
l'ionosphère
die Ionosphäre
la ionosfera
la ionosfera

mesosphere
la mésosphère
die Mesosphäre
la mesoesfera
la mesosfera

ultraviolet rays
les rayons ultraviolets
die Ultraviolettstrahlen
los rayos ultravioleta
i raggi ultravioletti

stratosphere
la stratosphère
die Stratosphäre
la estratosfera
la stratosfera

ozone layer
la couche d'ozone
die Ozonschicht
la capa de ozono
lo strato di ozono

troposphere
la troposphère
die Troposphäre
la troposfera
la troposfera

atmosphere • l'atmosphère • die
Atmosphäre • la atmósfera • l'atmosfera

sunshine • le soleil • der Sonnenschein
• el sol • la luce del sole

wind • le vent • der Wind • el viento
• il vento

sleet	shower	hot	dry	windy	I'm hot/cold.
la neige fondue	l'averse	(très) chaud	sec	venteux	J'ai chaud/froid.
der Schneeregen	der Schauer	heiß	trocken	windig	Mir ist heiß/kalt.
el aguanieve	el chubasco	caluroso	seco	ventoso	Tengo calor/frío.
il nevischio	il rovescio	caldo	secco	ventoso	Ho caldo/freddo.
hail	sunny	cold	wet	gale	It's raining.
la grêle	ensoleillé	froid	mouillé	la tempête	Il pleut.
der Hagel	sonnig	kalt	nass	der Sturm	Es regnet.
el granizo	soleado	frío	lluvioso	el temporal	Está lloviendo.
la grandine	soleggiato	freddo	piovoso	la bufera	Sta piovendo.
thunder	cloudy	warm	humid	temperature	It's ... degrees.
le tonnerre	nuageux	chaud	moite	la température	Il fait ... degrés.
der Donner	bewölkt	warm	feucht	die Temperatur	Es sind ... Grad.
el trueno	nublado	cálido	húmedo	la temperatura	Estamos a ... grados.
il tuono	nuvoloso	tiepido	umido	la temperatura	Fa ... gradi.

cloud • le nuage • die Wolke • la nube • la nuvola

rain • la pluie • der Regen • la lluvia • la pioggia

lightning • l'éclair • der Blitz • el relámpago • il fulmine

storm • l'orage • das Gewitter • la tormenta • la tempesta

mist • la brume • der feine Nebel • la neblina • la foschia

fog • le brouillard • der dichte Nebel • la niebla • la nebbia

rainbow • l'arc-en-ciel • der Regenbogen • el arcoiris • l'arcobaleno

snow • la neige • der Schnee • la nieve • la neve

frost • le givre • der Raureif • la escarcha • il gelo

ice • la glace • das Eis • el hielo • il ghiaccio

icicle • le glaçon • der Eiszapfen • el carámbano • il ghiacciolo

freeze • le gel • der Frost • la helada • la gelata

hurricane • l'ouragan • der Hurrikan • el huracán • l'uragano

tornado • la tornade • der Tornado • el tornado • il tornado

monsoon • la mousson • der Monsun • el monzón • il monsone

flood • l'inondation • die Überschwemmung • la inundación • l'inondazione

rocks • les roches • das Gestein • las rocas • le rocce

igneous • igné • **eruptiv** • ígneo • igneo

granite • le granit • der Granit • el granito • il granito

obsidian • l'obsidienne • der Obsidian • la obsidiana • l'ossidiana

basalt • le basalte • der Basalt • el basalto • il basalto

pumice • la pierre ponce • der Bimsstein • la piedra pómez • la pomice

sedimentary • sédimentaire • **sedimentär** • sedimentario • sedimentario

sandstone • le grès • der Sandstein • la piedra arenisca • l'arenaria

limestone • le calcaire • der Kalkstein • la piedra caliza • il calcare

chalk • la craie • die Kreide • la tiza • il gesso

flint • le silex • der Feuerstein • el pedernal • la selce

conglomerate le conglomérat das Konglomerat el conglomerado il conglomerato

coal • le charbon • die Kohle • el carbón • il carbone

---

metamorphic • métamorphique • **metamorph** • metamórfico • metamorfico

slate • l'ardoise • der Schiefer • la pizarra • l'ardesia

schist • le schiste • der Glimmerschiefer • el esquisto • lo scisto

gneiss • le gneiss • der Gneis • el gneis • lo gneiss

marble • le marbre • der Marmor • el mármol • il marmo

---

gems • les gemmes • **die Schmucksteine** • las gemas • le gemme

ruby
le rubis
der Rubin
el rubí
il rubino

aquamarine
l'aigue-marine
der Aquamarin
la aguamarina
l'acquamarina

amethyst
l'améthyste
der Amethyst
la amatista
l'ametista

diamond
le diamant
der Diamant
el diamante
il diamante

jade
le jade
der Jade
el jade
la giada

jet
le jais
der Gagat
el azabache
il giaietto

emerald
l'émeraude
der Smaragd
la esmeralda
lo smeraldo

opal
l'opale
der Opal
el ópalo
l'opale

sapphire
le saphir
der Saphir
el zafiro
lo zaffiro

moonstone
la pierre de lune
der Mondstein
la piedra lunar
la lunaria

garnet
le grenat
der Granat
el granate
il granato

topaz
le topaze
der Topas
el topacio
il topazio

tourmaline
la toumaline
der Turmalin
la turmalina
la tormalina

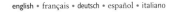

minerals • les minéraux • die Mineralien • los minerales • i minerali

quartz • le quartz • der Quarz • el cuarzo • il quarzo

mica • le mica • der Glimmer • la mica • la mica

sulfur • le soufre • der Schwefel • el azufre • lo zolfo

hematite • l'hématite • der Hämatit • el hematites • l'ematite

calcite • la calcite • der Kalzit • la calcita • la calcite

malachite la malachite der Malachit la malaquita la malachite

turquoise • la turquoise • der Türkis • la turquesa • il turchese

onyx • l'onyx • der Onyx • el ónice • l'onice

agate • l'agate • der Achat • el ágata • l'agata

graphite • le graphite • der Graphit • el grafito • la grafite

---

metals • les métaux • die Metalle • los metales • i metalli

gold • l'or • das Gold • el oro • l'oro

silver • l'argent • das Silber • la plata • l'argento

platinum • le platine • das Platin • el platino • il platino

nickel • le nickel • das Nickel • el níquel • il nichel

iron • le fer • das Eisen • el hierro • il ferro

copper • le cuivre • das Kupfer • el cobre • il rame

tin • l'étain • das Zinn • el estaño • lo stagno

aluminium • l'aluminium • das Aluminium • el aluminio • l'alluminio

mercury • le mercure • das Quecksilber • el mercurio • il mercurio

zinc • le zinc • das Zink • el zinc • lo zinco

animals 1 • les animaux 1 • die Tiere 1 • los animales 1 • gli animali 1

mammals • les mammifères • die Säugetiere • los mamíferos • i mammiferi

whiskers
les poils
die Schnurrhaare
los bigotes
i baffi

tail
la queue
der Schwanz
la cola
la coda

rabbit • le lapin
• das Kaninchen
• el conejo • il coniglio

hamster • le hamster
• der Hamster • el
hámster • il criceto

mouse • la souris
• die Maus • el ratón
• il topo

rat • le rat • die Ratte
• la rata • il ratto

hedgehog
• le hérisson • der Igel
• el erizo • il riccio

squirrel • l'écureuil
• das Eichhörnchen •
la ardilla • lo scoiattolo

bat • la chauve-souris
• die Fledermaus • el
murciélago
• il pipistrello

raccoon • le raton laveur
• der Waschbär • el
mapache • il procione

fox • le renard
• der Fuchs • el zorro
• la volpe

wolf • le loup
• der Wolf • el lobo
• il lupo

puppy
le chiot
der Welpe
el cachorro
il cucciolo

kitten
le chaton
das Kätzchen
el gatito
il gattino

pup
le bébé-phoque
das Junge
la cría
il cucciolo

dog • le chien • der Hund
• el perro • il cane

cat • le chat • die Katze
• el gato • il gatto

otter • la loutre • der Otter
• la nutria • la lontra

seal • le phoque • die Robbe
• la foca • la foca

blowhole
l'évent
das Atemloch
el orificio nasal
lo sfiatatoio

flipper
la nageoire
die Flosse
la aleta
la pinna

sea lion • l'otarie
• der Seelöwe • el león
marino • il leone marino

walrus • le morse
• das Walross • la
morsa • il tricheco

whale • la baleine • der Wal
• la ballena • la balena

dolphin
• le dauphin
• der Delfin
• el delfín • il delfino

antler
la ramure
das Geweih
la cornamenta
le corna

deer • le cerf • der Hirsch
• el ciervo • il cervo

mane
la crinière
die Mähne
la crin
la criniera

zebra • le zèbre
• das Zebra • la cebra
• la zebra

hoof
le sabot
der Huf
la pezuña
lo zoccolo

giraffe • la girafe
• die Giraffe • la jirafa
• la giraffa

hump • la bosse
• der Höcker • la
giba • la gobba

camel • le chameau
• das Kamel • el camello
• il cammello

trunk • la trompe • der Rüssel
• la trompa • la proboscide

tusk
la défense
der Stoßzahn
el colmillo
la zanna

hippopotamus • le
hippopotame • das Nilpferd
• el hipopótamo
• l'ippopotamo

elephant • l'éléphant
• der Elefant • el elefante
• l'elefante

horn • la corne
• das Horn • el
cuerno • il corno

rhinoceros • le rhinocéros
• das Nashorn • el rinoceronte
• il rinoceronte

tiger • le tigre • der Tiger
• el tigre • la tigre

mane
la crinière
die Mähne
la melena
la criniera

lion • le lion • der Löwe
• el león • il leone

monkey • le singe
• der Affe • el mono
• la scimmia

gorilla • le gorille
• der Gorilla • el gorila
• il gorilla

koala • le koala • der Koalabär
• el koala • il koala

pouch
la poche
der Beutel
la bolsa
il marsupio

kangaroo • le kangourou
• das Känguru • el canguro
• il canguro

bear • l'ours
• der Bär • el oso
• l'orso

claw
la griffe
die Klaue
la zarpa
l'artiglio

polar bear • l'ours blanc
• der Eisbär • el oso polar
• l'orso polare

panda • le panda
• der Pandabär
• el oso panda
• il panda

animals 2 • les animaux 2 • die Tiere 2 • los animales 2 • gli animali 2

birds • les oiseaux • die Vögel • las aves • gli uccelli

tail
la queue
der Schwanz
la cola
la coda

canary • le canari • der Kanarienvogel • el canario • il canarino

sparrow • le moineau • der Spatz • el gorrión • il passero

hummingbird • le colibri • der Kolibri • el colibrí • il colibri

swallow • l'hirondelle • die Schwalbe • la golondrina • la rondine

crow • le corbeau • die Krähe • la corneja • la cornacchia

pigeon • le pigeon • die Taube • la paloma • il piccione

woodpecker • le pic • der Specht • el pájaro carpintero • il picchio

falcon • le faucon • der Falke • el halcón • il falco

owl • la chouette • die Eule • la lechuza • il gufo

gull • la mouette • die Möwe • la gaviota • il gabbiano

eagle • l'aigle • der Adler • el águila • l'aquila

pelican • le pélican • der Pelikan • el pelícano • il pellicano

flamingo • le flamant • der Flamingo • el flamenco • il fenicottero

stork • la cigogne • der Storch • la cigüeña • la cicogna

crane • la grue • der Kranich • la grulla • la gru

penguin • le pingouin • der Pinguin • el pingüino • il pinguino

ostrich • l'autruche • der Strauß • el avestruz • lo struzzo

goose • l'oie • die Gans
• la oca • l'oca

swan • le cygne • der Schwan
• el cisne • il cigno

reptiles • les reptiles • die Reptilien • los reptiles
• i rettili

scales • les écailles
• die Schuppen • las
escamas • le scaglie

alligator • l'alligator • der Alligator • el caimán
• l'alligatore

peacock • le paon • der Pfau
• el pavo real • il pavone

pheasant • le faisan
• der Fasan • el
faisán • il fagiano

lizard • le lézard • die Eidechse
• el lagarto • la lucertola

iguana • l'iguane
• der Leguan • la iguana
• l'iguana

shell
la carapace
der Panzer
el caparazón
il guscio

beak
le bec
der Schnabel
el pico
il becco

turkey • le dindon
• der Truthahn • el pavo
• il tacchino

turtle • la tortue marine
• die Wasserschildkröte • el
galápago • la testuggine

tortoise • la tortue
• die Schildkröte • la tortuga
• la tartaruga

feather
la plume
die Feder
la pluma
la piuma

snake • le serpent
• die Schlange
• la serpiente
• il serpente

wing
l'aile
der Flügel
el ala
l'ala

claw
la griffe
die Kralle
la garra
l'artiglio

snout
le museau
die Schnauze
el hocico
il muso

cockatoo
le cacatoès
der Kakadu
la cacatúa
il cacatua

parrot • le perroquet
• der Papagei • el loro
• il pappagallo

crocodile • le crocodile
• das Krokodil • el
cocodrilo • il coccodrillo

animals 3 • les animaux 3 • die Tiere 3 • los animales 3 • gli animali 3

amphibians • les amphibiens • die Amphibien • los anfibios • gli anfibi

frog • la grenouille • der Frosch • la rana • la rana

toad • le crapaud • die Kröte • el sapo • il rospo

tadpole • le têtard • die Kaulquappe • el renacuajo • il girino

salamander • la salamandre • der Salamander • la salamandra • la salamandra

fish • les poissons • die Fische • los peces • i pesci

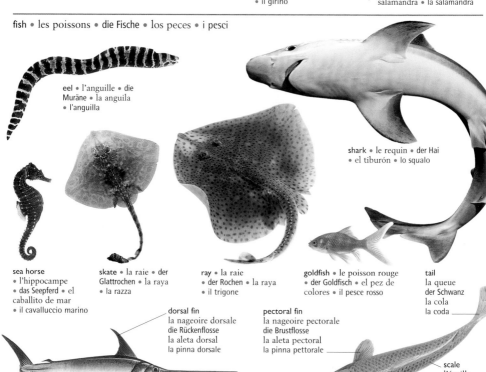

eel • l'anguille • die Muräne • la anguila • l'anguilla

shark • le requin • der Hai • el tiburón • lo squalo

sea horse • l'hippocampe • das Seepferd • el caballito de mar • il cavalluccio marino

skate • la raie • der Glattrochen • la raya • la razza

ray • la raie • der Rochen • la raya • il trigone

goldfish • le poisson rouge • der Goldfisch • el pez de colores • il pesce rosso

tail
la queue
der Schwanz
la cola
la coda

dorsal fin
la nageoire dorsale
die Rückenflosse
la aleta dorsal
la pinna dorsale

pectoral fin
la nageoire pectorale
die Brustflosse
la aleta pectoral
la pinna pettorale

scale
l'écaille
die Schuppe
la escama
la scaglia

gill
l'ouïe
die Kieme
la agalla
la branchia

swordfish • l'espadon • der Schwertfisch • el pez espada • il pesce spada

koi carp • la carpe koi • der Koikarpfen • la carpa koi • la carpa koi

invertebrates • les invertébrés • die Wirbellosen • los invertebrados • gli invertebrati

ant • la fourmi • die Ameise • la hormiga • la formica

termite • la termite • die Termite • la termita • la termite

bee • l'abeille • die Biene • la abeja • l'ape

wasp • la guêpe • die Wespe • la avispa • la vespa

beetle • le scarabée • der Käfer • el escarabajo • lo scarafaggio

antenna
l'antenne
der Fühler
la antena
l'antenna

cockroach • le cafard • der Kakerlak • la cucaracha • la blatta

moth • le papillon de nuit • der Nachtfalter • la polilla • la falena

butterfly • le papillon • der Schmetterling • la mariposa • la farfalla

cocoon • le cocon • der Kokon • el capullo • il bozzolo

caterpillar • la chenille • die Raupe • la oruga • il bruco

sting
le dard
der Stachel
el aquijón
il pungiglione

cricket • le grillon • die Grille • el grillo • il grillo

grasshopper • la sauterelle • die Heuschrecke • el saltamontes • la cavalletta

praying mantis • la mante religieuse • die Gottesanbeterin • la mantis religiosa • la mantide religiosa

scorpion • le scorpion • der Skorpion • el escorpión • lo scorpione

centipede • le mille-pattes • der Tausendfüßer • el ciempiés • il millepiedi

dragonfly • la libellule • die Libelle • la libélula • la libellula

fly • la mouche • die Fliege • la mosca • la mosca

mosquito • le moustique • die Stechmücke • el mosquito • la zanzara

ladybug • la coccinelle • der Marienkäfer • la mariquita • la coccinella

spider • l'araignée • die Spinne • la araña • il ragno

slug • la limace • die Nacktschnecke • la babosa • la lumaca

snail • l'escargot • die Schnecke • el caracol • la chiocciola

worm • le ver • der Wurm • el gusano • il verme

starfish • l'étoile de mer • der Seestern • la estrella de mar • la stella di mare

mussel • la moule • die Muschel • el mejillón • la cozza

crab • le crabe • der Krebs • el cangrejo • il granchio

lobster • le homard • der Hummer • la langosta • l'aragosta

octopus • la pieuvre • der Krake • el pulpo • la piovra

squid • le calmar • der Tintenfisch • el calamar • il calamaro

jellyfish • la méduse • die Qualle • la medusa • la medusa

plants • les plantes • die Pflanzen • las plantas • le piante

tree • l'arbre • der Baum • el árbol • l'albero

leaf
la feuille
das Blatt
la hoja
la foglia

twig
la brindille
der Zweig
la ramita
il ramoscello

willow • le saule
• die Weide • el sauce
• il salice

branch
la branche
der Ast
la rama
il ramo

bark
l'écorce
die Rinde
la corteza
la corteccia

root
la racine
die Wurzel
la raíz
la radice

trunk
le tronc
der Stamm
el tronco
il tronco

oak • le chêne • die Eiche • el roble • la quercia

poplar • le peuplier
• die Pappel • el álamo
• il pioppo

eucalyptus
• l'eucalyptus • der
Eukalyptus • el
eucalipto • l'eucalipto

larch • le mélèze
• die Lärche • el alerce
• il larice

beech • le hêtre
• die Buche • la haya
• il faggio

birch • le bouleau
• die Birke • el abedul
• la betulla

pine • le pin • die
Kiefer • el pino
• il pino

cedar • le cèdre
• die Zeder • el cedro
• il cedro

maple • l'érable
• der Ahorn • el arce
• l'acero

elm • l'orme • die
Ulme • el olmo
• l'olmo

lime • le tilleul
• die Linde • el tilo
• il tiglio

berry
la baie
die Beere
la baya
la bacca

holly • le houx
• die Stechpalme • el
acebo • l'agrifoglio

palm • le palmier
• die Palme • la
palmera • la palma

flowering plant • la plante à fleurs • die blühende Pflanze • la planta de flor • la pianta da fiori

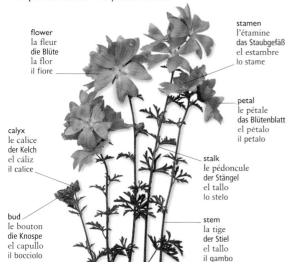

flower
la fleur
die Blüte
la flor
il fiore

stamen
l'étamine
das Staubgefäß
el estambre
lo stame

petal
le pétale
das Blütenblatt
el pétalo
il petalo

calyx
le calice
der Kelch
el cáliz
il calice

stalk
le pédoncule
der Stängel
el tallo
lo stelo

bud
le bouton
die Knospe
el capullo
il bocciolo

stem
la tige
der Stiel
el tallo
il gambo

buttercup • la renoncule
• der Hahnenfuß
• el ranúnculo
• il ranuncolo

daisy • la pâquerette
• das Gänseblümchen
• la margarita
• la margheritina

thistle • le chardon
• die Distel • el cardo
• il cardo

dandelion • le pissenlit
• der Löwenzahn
• el diente de león
• il dente di leone

heather • la bruyère
• das Heidekraut • el
brezo • l'erica

poppy • le coquelicot
• der Klatschmohn • la
amapola • il papavero

foxglove • la digitale
• der Fingerhut
• la dedalera
• la digitale

honeysuckle • le
chèvrefeuille • das
Geißblatt • la madreselva
• il caprifoglio

sunflower • le
tournesol • die
Sonnenblume • el
girasol • il girasole

clover • le trèfle
• der Klee • el trébol
• il trifoglio

bluebells • les jacinthes des
bois • die Sternhyazinthen
• los narcisos silvestres
• i giacinti di bosco

primrose • la
primevère • die
Schlüsselblume • la
prímula • la primula

lupines • les lupins
• die Lupinen • los
lupinos • i lupini

nettle • l'ortie
• die Nessel • la ortiga
• l'ortica

city • la ville • die Innenstadt • la ciudad • la città

street
la rue
die Straße
la calle
la strada

curb
le bord du trottoir
die Bordsteinkante
el bordillo
il ciglio

street corner
le coin de la rue
die Straßenecke
la esquina
l'angolo della strada

store
le magasin
der Laden
la tienda
il negozio

intersection
le carrefour
die Kreuzung
el cruce
il crocevia

one-way system
• la voie à sens
unique • die
Einbahnstraße
• la calle de
sentido único
• il senso unico

sidewalk
le trottoir
der Bürgersteig
la acera
il marciapiede

office building
• l'immeuble de
bureaux • das
Bürogebäude
• el edificio
de oficinas
• il complesso
di uffici

apartment building
• l'immeuble
• der Wohnblock
• el edificio de
pisos • il
caseggiato

alley
la ruelle
die Gasse
el callejón
il vicolo

parking lot
le parking
der Parkplatz
el aparcamiento
il parcheggio

street sign
le panneau de signalisation
das Straßenschild
la señal de tráfico
il segnale stradale

barrier
la borne
der Poller
la baliza
la colonnina

streetlight
le lampadaire
die Straßenlaterne
la farola
il lampione

buildings • les bâtiments • die Gebäude • los edificios • gli edifici

town hall • la mairie • das Rathaus • el ayuntamiento • il municipio

library • la bibliothèque • die Bibliothek • la biblioteca • la biblioteca

movie theater • le cinéma • das Kino • el cine • il cinema

theater • le théâtre • das Theater • el teatro • il teatro

university • l'université • die Universität • la universidad • l'università

skyscraper • le gratte-ciel • der Wolkenkratzer • el rascacielos • il grattacielo

school • l'école • die Schule • el colegio • la scuola

areas • les environs • die Gebiete • las zonas • le zone

industrial park • la zone industrielle • das Industriegebiet • la zona industrial • la zona industriale

city • la ville • die Innenstadt • la ciudad • la città

suburb • la banlieue • die Vorstadt • la periferia • la periferia

village • le village • das Dorf • el pueblo • il villaggio

pedestrian zone la zone piétonnière die Fußgängerzone la zona peatonal la zona pedonale	side street la rue transversale die Seitenstraße la calle lateral la via laterale	manhole la bouche d'égout der Kanalschacht la boca de alcantarilla il tombino	gutter le caniveau der Rinnstein la alcantarilla la cunetta	church l'église die Kirche la iglesia la chiesa
avenue l'avenue die Allee la avenida il viale	square la place der Platz la plaza la piazza	bus stop l'arrêt de bus die Bushaltestelle la parada de autobús la fermata dell'autobus	factory l'usine die Fabrik la fábrica la fabbrica	drain l'égout der Kanal el sumidero il canale di scolo

architecture • l'architecture • die Architektur • la arquitectura • l'architettura

buildings and structures • les bâtiments et structures • die Gebäude und Strukturen • los edificios y las estructuras • edifici e strutture

turret
la tourelle
der Mauerturm
el torreón
la torre

spire
la flèche
die Turmspitze
la aguja
la cima
della torre

finial
le fleuron
die Kreuzblume
el florón
il pinnacolo

moat
la douve
der Burggraben
el foso
il fossato

skyscraper • le gratte-ciel
• der Wolkenkratzer • el
rascacielos • il grattacielo

castle • le château • die Burg
• el castillo • il castello

gable
le pignon
der Giebel
el frontón
il frontone

dome
le dôme
die Kuppel
la cúpula
la cupola

tower
la tour
der Turm
la torre
la torretta

church • l'église • die Kirche
• la iglesia • la chiesa

mosque • la mosquée
• die Moschee • la mezquita
• la moschea

vault
la voûte
das Gewölbe
la bóveda
la volta

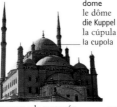

temple • le temple
• der Tempel • el templo
• il tempio

synagogue • la synagogue
• die Synagoge • la sinagoga
• la sinagoga

cornice
la corniche
das Gesims
la cornisa
il cornicione

dam • le barrage • der
Staudamm • el embalse
• la diga

bridge • le pont • die Brücke
• el puente • il ponte

pillar
la colonne
der Pfeiler
el pilar
la colonna

cathedral • la cathédrale • die Kathedrale
• la catedral • la cattedrale

styles • les styles • die Baustile • los estilos • gli stili

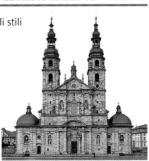

architrave
l'architrave
der Architrav
el arquitrabe
l'architrave

Baroque • baroque • barock • barroco
• barocco

Gothic • gothique • gotisch
• gótico • gotico

Renaissance • Renaissance
• Renaissance • Renacimiento
• rinascimentale

arch
l'arc
der Bogen
el arco
l'arco

frieze
la frise
der Fries
el friso
il fregio

choir
le chœur
der Chor
el coro
il coro

Rococo • rococo • Rokoko • rococó
• rococò

pediment
le fronton
das Giebeldreieck
el frontón
il frontone

buttress
le contrefort
der Strebepfeiler
el contrafuerte
il contrafforte

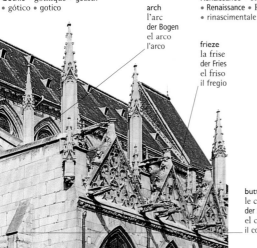

Neoclassical • néoclassique • klassizistisch
• neoclásico • neoclassico

Art Nouveau • art nouveau
• der Jugendstil • el estilo
modernista • l'art nouveau

Art Deco • art déco
• Art-déco- • art decó
• art déco

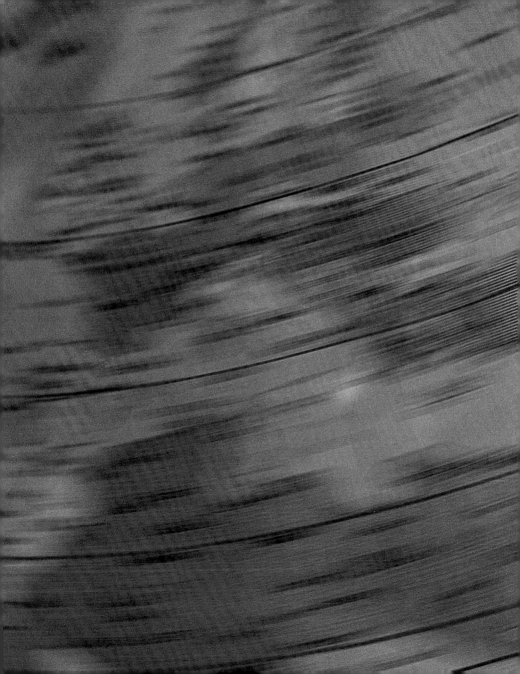

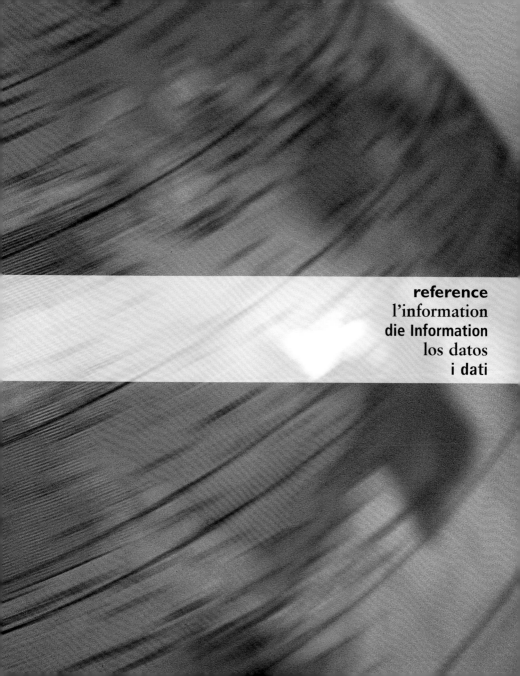

reference
l'information
die Information
los datos
i dati

time • l'heure • die Uhrzeit • el tiempo • l'ora

minute hand
la grande aiguille
der Minutenzeiger
el minutero
la lancetta dei minuti

hour hand
la petite aiguille
der Stundenzeiger
la aguja de la hora
la lancetta delle ore

clock • l'horloge • die Uhr • el reloj • l'orologio

second la seconde die Sekunde el segundo il secondo	now maintenant jetzt ahora adesso	a quarter of an hour un quart d'heure eine Viertelstunde un cuarto de hora un quarto d'ora
minute la minute die Minute el minuto il minuto	later plus tard später más tarde più tardi	twenty minutes vingt minutes zwanzig Minuten veinte minutos venti minuti
hour l'heure die Stunde la hora l'ora	half an hour une demi-heure eine halbe Stunde media hora una mezzora	forty minutes quarante minutes vierzig Minuten cuarenta minutos quaranta minuti

What time is it?   It's three o'clock.
Quelle heure est-il?   Il est trois heures.
Wie spät ist es?   Es ist drei Uhr.
¿Qué hora es?   Son las tres en punto.
Che ore sono?   Sono le tre.

five past one • une heure
cinq • fünf nach eins • la una
y cinco • l'una e cinque

ten past one • une heure dix
• zehn nach eins • la una y
diez • l'una e dieci

quarter past one • une heure
et quart • Viertel nach eins
• la una y cuarto • l'una
e un quarto

twenty past one • une heure
vingt • zwanzig nach eins
• la una y veinte • l'una
e venti

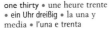

second hand • la
trotteuse • der
Sekundenzeiger
• el segundero
• la lancetta dei
secondi

twenty-five past one • une
heure vingt-cinq • fünf vor halb
zwei • la una y veinticinco
• l'una e venticinque

one thirty • une heure trente
• ein Uhr dreißig • la una y
media • l'una e trenta

twenty-five to two • deux
heures moins vingt-cinq • fünf
nach halb zwei • las dos menos
veinticinco • le due meno
venticinque

twenty to two • deux heures
moins vingt • zwanzig vor
zwei • las dos menos veinte
• le due meno venti

quarter to two • deux heures
moins le quart • Viertel vor
zwei • las dos menos cuarto
• le due meno un quarto

ten to two • deux heures
moins dix • zehn vor zwei
• las dos menos diez
• le due meno dieci

five to two • deux heures
moins cinq • fünf vor zwei
• las dos menos cinco
• le due meno cinque

two o'clock • deux heures
• zwei Uhr • las dos en punto
• le due

english • français • deutsch • español • italiano

night and day • la nuit et le jour • die Nacht und der Tag • la noche y el día • la notte e il giorno

midnight • le minuit • die Mitternacht • la medianoche • la mezzanotte

sunrise • le lever du soleil • der Sonnenaufgang • el amanecer • il sorgere del sole

dawn • l'aube • die Morgendämmerung • el alba • l'alba

morning • le matin • der Morgen • la mañana • il mattino

sunset • le coucher du soleil • der Sonnenuntergang • la puesta de sol • il tramonto

noon • le midi • der Mittag • el mediodía • il mezzogiorno

dusk • le crépuscule • die Abenddämmerung • el anochecer • l'imbrunire

evening • le soir • der Abend • la noche • la sera

afternoon • l'après-midi • der Nachmittag • la tarde • il pomeriggio

early	You're early.	Please be on time.	What time does it end?
tôt	Tu es en avance.	Sois à l'heure, s'il te plaît.	Ça finit à quelle heure?
früh	Du bist früh.	Sei bitte pünklich.	Wann ist es zu Ende?
temprano	Llegas temprano.	Por favor, sé puntual.	¿A qué hora termina?
presto	Sei in anticipo.	Per favore, vieni in orario.	A che ora finisce?
on time	You're late.	I'll see you later.	How long will it last?
à l'heure	Tu es en retard.	À tout à l'heure.	Ça dure combien de temps?
pünktlich	Du hast dich verspätet.	Bis später.	Wie lange dauert es?
puntual	Llegas tarde.	Hasta luego.	¿Cuánto dura?
in orario	Sei in ritardo.	A più tardi.	Quanto durerà?
late	I'll be there soon.	What time does it start?	It's getting late.
tard	J'y arriverai bientôt.	Ça commence à quelle heure?	Il se fait tard.
spät	Ich werde bald dort sein.	Wann fängt es an?	Es ist schon spät.
tarde	Llegaré dentro de poco.	¿A qué hora comienza?	Se está haciendo tarde.
tardi	Arrivo subito.	A che ora inizia?	Si sta facendo tardi.

calendar • le calendrier • der Kalender • el calendario • il calendario

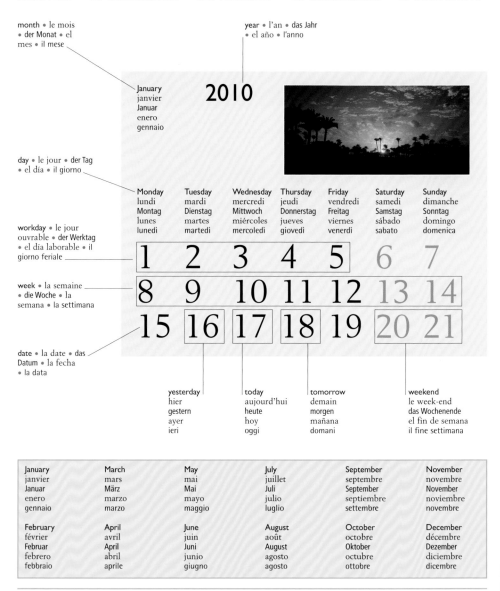

month • le mois • der Monat • el mes • il mese

year • l'an • das Jahr • el año • l'anno

January
janvier
Januar
enero
gennaio

2010

day • le jour • der Tag • el día • il giorno

Monday	Tuesday	Wednesday	Thursday	Friday	Saturday	Sunday
lundi	mardi	mercredi	jeudi	vendredi	samedi	dimanche
Montag	Dienstag	Mittwoch	Donnerstag	Freitag	Samstag	Sonntag
lunes	martes	miércoles	jueves	viernes	sábado	domingo
lunedi	martedi	mercoledi	giovedi	venerdi	sabato	domenica

workday • le jour ouvrable • der Werktag • el día laborable • il giorno feriale

| 1 | 2 | 3 | 4 | 5 | 6 | 7 |

week • la semaine • die Woche • la semana • la settimana

| 8 | 9 | 10 | 11 | 12 | 13 | 14 |

| 15 | 16 | 17 | 18 | 19 | 20 | 21 |

date • la date • das Datum • la fecha • la data

yesterday
hier
gestern
ayer
ieri

today
aujourd'hui
heute
hoy
oggi

tomorrow
demain
morgen
mañana
domani

weekend
le week-end
das Wochenende
el fin de semana
il fine settimana

January	March	May	July	September	November
janvier	mars	mai	juillet	septembre	novembre
Januar	März	Mai	Juli	September	November
enero	marzo	mayo	julio	septiembre	noviembre
gennaio	marzo	maggio	luglio	settembre	novembre
February	April	June	August	October	December
février	avril	juin	août	octobre	décembre
Februar	April	Juni	August	Oktober	Dezember
febrero	abril	junio	agosto	octubre	diciembre
febbraio	aprile	giugno	agosto	ottobre	dicembre

years • les ans • die Jahre • los años • gli anni

1900 nineteen hundred • mille neuf cents • neunzehnhundert • mil novecientos • millenovecento

1901 nineteen hundred and one • mille neuf cent un • neunzehnhunderteins • mil novecientos uno • millenovecentouno

1910 nineteen ten • mille neuf cent dix • neunzehnhundertzehn • mil novecientos diez • millenovecentodieci

2000 two thousand • deux mille • zweitausend • dos mil • duemila

2001 two thousand and one • deux mille un • zweitausendeins • dos mil uno • duemilauno

---

seasons • les saisons • die Jahreszeiten • las estaciones • le stagioni

spring • le printemps • der Frühling • la primavera • la primavera

summer • l'été • der Sommer • el verano • l'estate

fall • l'automne • der Herbst • el otoño • l'autunno

winter • l'hiver • der Winter • el invierno • l'inverno

---

century • le siècle • das Jahrhundert • el siglo • il secolo

decade • la décennie • das Jahrzehnt • la década • la decade

millennium • le millénaire • das Jahrtausend • el milenio • il millennio

two weeks • quinze jours • vierzehn Tage • quince días • quindici giorni

this week • cette semaine • diese Woche • esta semana • questa settimana

last week • la semaine dernière • letzte Woche • la semana pasada • la settimana scorsa

next week • la semaine prochaine • nächste Woche • la semana que viene • la settimana prossima

the day before yesterday • avant-hier • vorgestern • antes de ayer • l'altroieri

the day after tomorrow • après-demain • übermorgen • pasado mañana • il dopodomani

weekly • hebdomadaire • wöchentlich • semanalmente • settimanale

monthly • mensuel • monatlich • mensual • mensile

annual • annuel • jährlich • anual • annuo

What's the date today?
Quelle est la date aujourd'hui?
Welches Datum haben wir heute?
¿Qué día es hoy?
Oggi che giorno è?

It's February seventh, two thousand and twenty.
Nous sommes le sept février deux mille vingt.
Heute ist der siebte Februar zweitausendzwanzig.
Siete de febrero de dos mil veinte.
E' il sette settembre duemilaventi.

---

numbers • les nombres • die Zahlen • los números • i numeri

0 — zero • zéro • null • cero • zero

1 — one • un • eins • uno • uno

2 — two • deux • zwei • dos • due

3 — three • trois • drei • tres • tre

4 — four • quatre • vier • cuatro • quattro

5 — five • cinq • fünf • cinco • cinque

6 — six • six • sechs • seis • sei

7 — seven • sept • sieben • siete • sette

8 — eight • huit • acht • ocho • otto

9 — nine • neuf • neun • nueve • nove

10 — ten • dix • zehn • diez • dieci

11 — eleven • onze • elf • once • undici

12 — twelve • douze • zwölf • doce • dodici

13 — thirteen • treize • dreizehn • trece • tredici

14 — fourteen • quatorze • vierzehn • catorce • quattordici

15 — fifteen • quinze • fünfzehn • quince • quindici

16 — sixteen • seize • sechzehn • dieciséis • sedici

17 — seventeen • dix-sept • siebzehn • diecisiete • diciassette

18 — eighteen • dix-huit • achtzehn • dieciocho • diciotto

19 — nineteen • dix-neuf • neunzehn • diecinueve • diciannove

20 — twenty • vingt • zwanzig • veinte • venti

21 — twenty-one • vingt et un • einundzwanzig • veintiuno • ventuno

22 — twenty-two • vingt-deux • zweiundzwanzig • veintidós • ventidue

30 — thirty • trente • dreißig • treinta • trenta

40 — forty • quarante • vierzig • cuarenta • quaranta

50 — fifty • cinquante • fünfzig • cincuenta • cinquanta

60 — sixty • soixante • sechzig • sesenta • sessanta

70 — seventy • soixante-dix • siebzig • setenta • settanta

80 — eighty • quatre-vingt • achtzig • ochenta • ottanta

90 — ninety • quatre-vingt-dix • neunzig • noventa • novanta

100 — one hundred • cent • hundert • cien • cento

110 — one hundred and ten • cent dix • hundertzehn • ciento diez • centodieci

200 — two hundred • deux cents • zweihundert • doscientos • duecento

300 — three hundred • trois cents • dreihundert • trescientos • trecento

400 — four hundred • quatre cents • vierhundert • cuatrocientos • quattrocento

500 — five hundred • cinq cents • fünfhundert • quinientos • cinquecento

600 — six hundred • six cents • sechshundert • seiscientos • seicento

700 — seven hundred • sept cents • siebenhundert • setecientos • settecento

800 — eight hundred • huit cents • achthundert • ochocientos • ottocento

900 — nine hundred • neuf cents • neunhundert • novecientos • novecento

1000 one thousand • mille • tausend • mil • mille

10,000 ten thousand • dix mille • zehntausend • diez mil • diecimila

20,000 twenty thousand • vingt mille • zwanzigtausend • veinte mil • ventimila

50,000 fifty thousand • cinquante mille • fünfzigtausend • cincuenta mil • cinquantamila

55,500 fifty-five thousand five hundred • cinqante-cinq mille cinq cents • fünfundfünfzigtausend-fünfhundert • cincuenta y cinco mil quinientos • cinquantacinquemilacinquecento

100,000 one hundred thousand • cent mille • hunderttausend • cien mil • centomila

1,000,000 one million • un million • eine Million • un millón • un milione

1,000,000,000 one billion • un milliard • eine Milliarde • mil millones • un miliardo

first	second	third
premier	deuxième	troisième
erster	zweiter	dritter
primero	segundo	tercero
primo	secondo	terzo

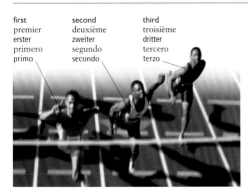

fourth • quatrième • vierter
• cuarto • quarto

fifth • cinquième • fünfter
• quinto • quinto

sixth • sixième • sechster
• sexto • sesto

seventh • septième • siebter
• séptimo • settimo

eighth • huitième • achter
• octavo • ottavo

ninth • neuvième • neunter
• noveno • nono

tenth • dixième • zehnter
• décimo • decimo

eleventh • onzième • elfter
• undécimo • undicesimo

twelfth • douzième
• zwölfter • duodécimo
• dodicesimo

thirteenth • treizième
• dreizehnter • decimotercero
• tredicesimo

fourteenth • quatorzième
• vierzehnter • decimocuarto
• quattordicesimo

fifteenth • quinzième
• fünfzehnter
• decimoquinto
• quindicesimo

sixteenth • seizième
• sechzehnter • decimosexto
• sedicesimo

seventeenth • dix-septième
• siebzehnter
• decimoséptimo
• diciassettesimo

eighteenth • dix-huitième
• achtzehnter • décimo
octavo • diciottesimo

nineteenth • dix-neuvième
• neunzehnter • décimo
noveno • diciannovesimo

twentieth • vingtième
• zwanzigster • vigésimo
• ventesimo

twenty-first • vingt et unième
• einundzwanzigster
• vigésimo primero
• ventunesimo

twenty-second
vingt-deuxième
zweiundzwanzigster
vigésimo segundo
ventiduesimo

twenty-third • vingt-troisième
• dreiundzwanzigster
• vigésimo tercero
• ventitreesimo

thirtieth • trentième
• dreißigster • trigésimo
• trentesimo

fortieth • quarantième
• vierzigster • cuadragésimo
• quarantesimo

fiftieth • cinquantième
• fünfzigster • quincuagésimo
• cinquantesimo

sixtieth • soixantième
• sechzigster • sexagésimo
• sessantesimo

seventieth • soixante-dixième
• siebzigster • septuagésimo
• settantesimo

eightieth • quatre-vingtième
• achtzigster • octogésimo
• ottantesimo

ninetieth • quatre-vingt-
dixième • neunzigster
• nonagésimo • novantesimo

(one) hundredth • centième
• hundertster • centésimo
• centesimo

weights and measures • les poids et mesures • die Maße und Gewichte • los pesos y las medidas • i pesi e le misure

pan • le plateau • die Waagschale • la bandeja • il piatto

area • la superficie • die Fläche • el área • la superficie

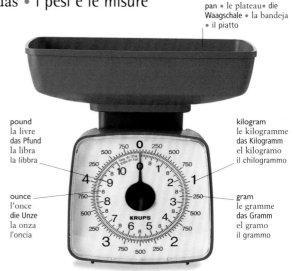

square foot
le pied carré
der Quadratfuß
el pie cuadrado
il piede quadro

square meter
le mètre carré
der Quadratmeter
el metro cuadrado
il metro quadro

pound
la livre
das Pfund
la libra
la libbra

kilogram
le kilogramme
das Kilogramm
el kilogramo
il chilogrammo

ounce
l'once
die Unze
la onza
l'oncia

gram
le gramme
das Gramm
el gramo
il grammo

KRUPS

scale • la balance • die Waage • la balanza • la bilancia

distance • la distance • die Entfernung • la distancia • la distanza

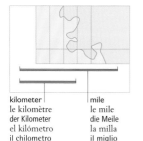

kilometer
le kilomètre
der Kilometer
el kilómetro
il chilometro

mile
le mile
die Meile
la milla
il miglio

yard	ton	measure (v)
le yard	la tonne	mesurer
das Yard	die Tonne	messen
la yarda	la tonelada	medir
la iarda	la tonnellata	misurare
meter	milligram	weigh (v)
le mètre	le milligramme	peser
der Meter	das Milligramm	wiegen
el metro	el miligramo	pesar
il metro	il milligrammo	pesare

length • la longueur • die Länge • la longitud • la lunghezza

foot • le pied • der Fuß • el pie • il piede

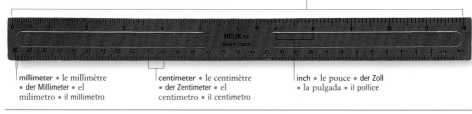

millimeter • le millimètre • der Millimeter • el milímetro • il millimetro

centimeter • le centimètre • der Zentimeter • el centímetro • il centimetro

inch • le pouce • der Zoll • la pulgada • il pollice

english • français • deutsch • español • italiano

capacity • la capacité • das Fassungsvermögen • la capacidad • la capacità

half-liter • le
demi-litre • der
halbe Liter • el
medio litro
• il mezzo
litro

pint • la pinte
• das Pint • la
pinta • la pinta

volume • le volume
• das Volumen • el
volumen • il volume

milliliter •
le millilitre
der Milliliter
el mililitro
il millilitro

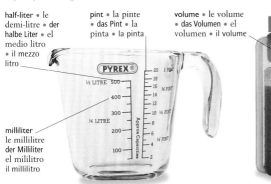

gallon
le gallon
die Gallone
el galón
il gallone

quart
deux pintes
das Quart
el cuarto de galón
il quarto di gallone

liter
le litre
der Liter
el litro
il litro

measuring cup • le verre mesureur • der Messbecher
• la jarra graduada • la brocca graduata

liquid measure • la mesure pour les
liquides • das Flüssigkeitsmaß • la medida
de capacidad • la misura di liquido

container • le récipient • der Behälter • el recipiente • il contenitore

bag • le sac
• der Beutel
• la bolsa
• il sacchetto

carton • la brique • die Tüte
• el tetrabrik • il cartone

packet • le paquet
• das Päckchen • el
paquete • il pacchetto

bottle • la bouteille
• die Flasche • la botella
• la bottiglia

can • la boîte
• die Dose • la
lata • la lattina

tub • le pot • die Dose
• la tarrina • la vaschetta

jar • le pot • das Glas
• el tarro • il barattolo

tin • la boîte • die Dose
• la lata • la scatoletta

spray bottle • le pulvérisateur •
der Sprühbehälter • el pulverizador
• il nebulizzatore

bar
le pain
das Stück
la pastilla
il pezzo

tube • le tube • die Tube
• el tubo • il tubetto

roll • le rouleau • die Rolle
• el rollo • il rotolo

pack • le paquet • das
Päckchen • el paquete
• il pacchetto

spray can • la bombe aérosol
• die Sprühdose • el spray • la
bomboletta spray

world map • la carte du monde • die Weltkarte • el mapamundi • il mappamondo

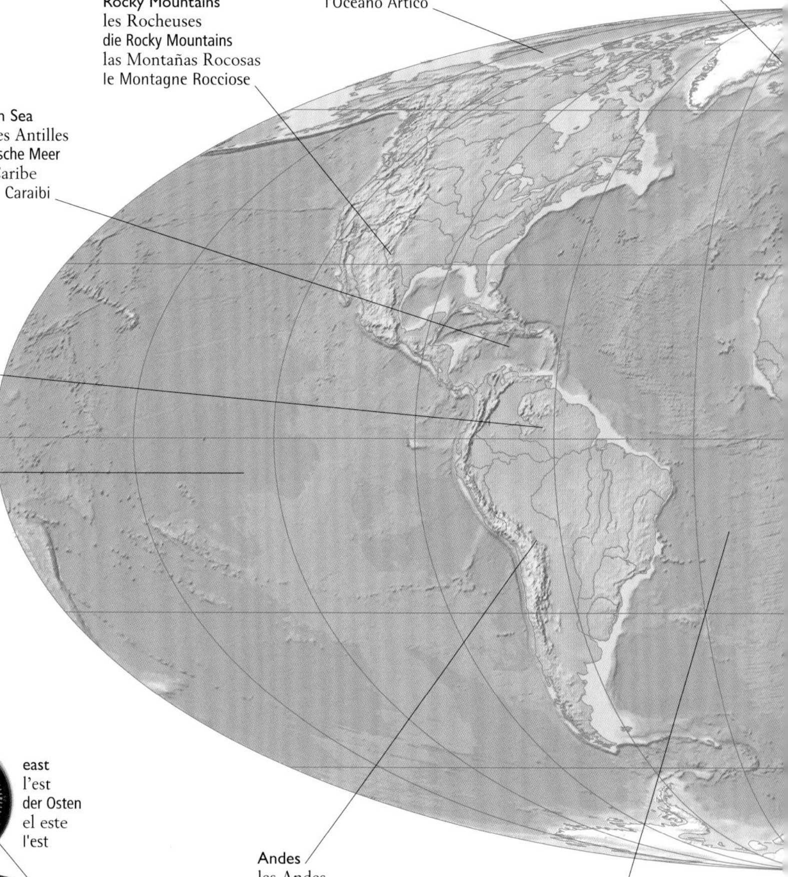

North Sea
la mer du Nord
die Nordsee
el Mar del Norte
il Mare del Nord

Arctic Ocean
l'océan Arctique
das Nordpolarmeer
el Océano Ártico
l'Oceano Artico

Rocky Mountains
les Rocheuses
die Rocky Mountains
las Montañas Rocosas
le Montagne Rocciose

Caribbean Sea
la mer des Antilles
das Karibische Meer
el Mar Caribe
il Mar dei Caraibi

Amazonia
l'Amazonie
Amazonien
el Amazonas
l'Amazzonia

Pacific Ocean
l'océan Pacifique
der Pazifische Ozean
el Océano Pacifico
l'Oceano Pacifico

north
le nord
der Norden
el norte
il nord

west
l'ouest
der Westen
el oeste
l'ovest

east
l'est
der Osten
el este
l'est

Andes
les Andes
die Anden
los Andes
le Ande

Atlantic Ocean
l'océan Atlantique
der Atlantische Ozean
el Océano Atlántico
l'Oceano Atlantico

compass
la boussole
der Kompass
la brújula
la bussola

south
le sud
der Süden
el sur
il sud

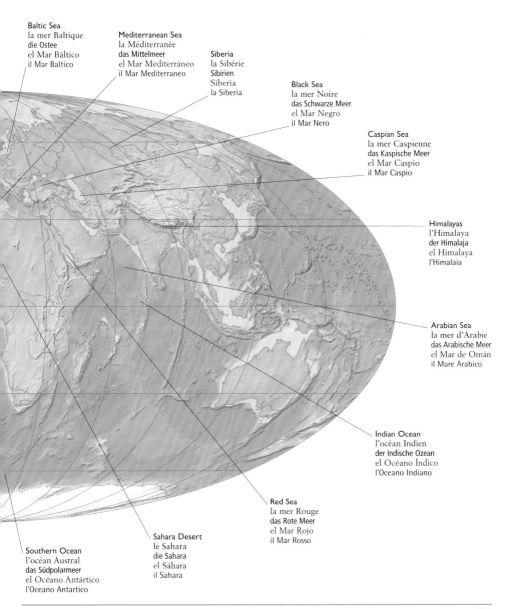

Baltic Sea
la mer Baltique
die Ostee
el Mar Báltico
il Mar Baltico

Mediterranean Sea
la Méditerranée
das Mittelmeer
el Mar Mediterráneo
il Mar Mediterraneo

Siberia
la Sibérie
Sibirien
Siberia
la Siberia

Black Sea
la mer Noire
das Schwarze Meer
el Mar Negro
il Mar Nero

Caspian Sea
la mer Caspienne
das Kaspische Meer
el Mar Caspio
il Mar Caspio

Himalayas
l'Himalaya
der Himalaja
el Himalaya
l'Himalaia

Arabian Sea
la mer d'Arabie
das Arabische Meer
el Mar de Omán
il Mare Arabico

Indian Ocean
l'océan Indien
der Indische Ozean
el Océano Índico
l'Oceano Indiano

Southern Ocean
l'océan Austral
das Südpolarmeer
el Océano Antártico
l'Oceano Antartico

Sahara Desert
le Sahara
die Sahara
el Sáhara
il Sahara

Red Sea
la mer Rouge
das Rote Meer
el Mar Rojo
il Mar Rosso

North and Central America • l'Amérique du Nord et centrale • Nord- und Mittelamerika • América del Norte y Central • l'America del Nord e Centrale

Barbados

Canada

Costa Rica

Cuba

Jamaica

Mexico

Panama

Trinidad and Tobago

United States of America

Antigua and Barbuda • Antigua-et-Barbuda • Antigua und
  Barbuda • Antigua y Barbuda • Antigua e Barbuda
Bahamas • les Bahamas • die Bahamas • Bahamas • le Bahamas
Barbados • la Barbade • Barbados • Barbados • Barbados
Belize • le Bélize • Belize • Belice • il Belize
Canada • le Canada • Kanada • Canadá • il Canada
Costa Rica • le Costa Rica • Costa Rica • Costa Rica
  • il Costa Rica
Cuba • Cuba • Kuba • Cuba • Cuba
Dominica • la Dominique • Dominica • Dominica • Dominica
Dominican Republic • la République dominicaine
  • die Dominikanische Republik • República Dominicana
  • la Repubblica Dominicana
El Salvador • Le Salvador • El Salvador • El Salvador
  • l'El Salvador
Greenland • le Groenland • Grönland• Groenlandia
  • la Groenlandia
Grenada • la Grenade • Grenada • Granada • Grenada
Guatemala • le Guatemala • Guatemala • Guatemala
  • il Guatemala
Haiti • Haïti • Haiti • Haití • Haiti

Honduras • le Honduras • Honduras • Honduras • l'Honduras
Jamaica • la Jamaïque • Jamaika • Jamaica • la Giamaica
Mexico • le Mexique • Mexiko • México • il Messico
Nicaragua • le Nicaragua • Nicaragua • Nicaragua
  • il Nicaragua
Panama • le Panama • Panama • Panamá • il Panama
Puerto Rico • la Porto Rico • Puerto Rico • Puerto Rico
  • Puerto Rico
St. Kitts and Nevis • Saint-Kitts-et-Nevis • Saint Kitts und Nevis
  • Saint Kitts y Nevis • Saint Kitts-Nevis
St. Lucia • Sainte-Lucie • Saint Lucia • Santa Lucía • Saint Lucia
St. Vincent and The Grenadines
  • Saint-Vincent-et-les-Grenadines
  • Saint Vinzent und die Grenadinen
  • San Vicente y las Granadinas • Saint Vincent e Grenadine
Trinidad and Tobago • la Trinité-et-Tobago
  • Trinidad und Tobago • Trinidad y Tobago
  • Trinidad e Tobago
United States of America • les États-Unis d'Amérique
  • die Vereinigten Staten von Amerika
  • Estados Unidos de América • gli Stati Uniti d'America

South America • l'Amérique du Sud • Südamerika • América del Sur • l'America del Sud

Argentina

Bolivia

Brazil

Chile

Colombia

Ecuador

Peru

Uruguay

Venezuela

Argentina • l'Argentine • **Argentinien** • Argentina • l'Argentina
Bolivia • la Bolivie • **Bolivien** • Bolivia • la Bolivia
Brazil • le Brésil • **Brasilien** • Brasil • il Brasile
Chile • le Chili • **Chile** • Chile • il Cile
Colombia • la Colombie • **Kolumbien** • Colombia • la Colombia
Ecuador • l'Équateur • **Ecuador** • Ecuador • l'Ecuador
Falkland Islands • les îles Malouines • **die Falklandinseln**
　　• las Malvinas • le Isole Falkland
French Guiana • la Guyane française • **Französisch-Guayana**
　　• la Guayana Francesa • la Guyana Francese
Galápagos Islands • les îles Galapagos • **die Galapagosinseln**
　　• las Islas Galápagos • le Isola Galapagos
Guyana • la Guyane • **Guyana** • Guyana • la Guyana
Paraguay • le Paraguay • **Paraguay** • Paraguay • il Paraguay
Peru • le Pérou • **Peru** • Perú • il Perù
Suriname • le Surinam • **Suriname** • Suriname • il Suriname
Uruguay • l'Uruguay • **Uruguay** • Uruguay • l'Uruguay
Venezuela • le Venezuela • **Venezuela** • Venezuela • il Venezuela

continent	province	zone
le continent	la province	la zone
der Kontinent	die Provinz	die Zone
el continente	la provincia	la zona
il continente	la provincia	la zona
country	territory	district
le pays	le territoire	le district
das Land	das Territorium	der Bezirk
el país	el territorio	el distrito
il paese	il territorio	il distretto
nation	principality	region
la nation	la principauté	la région
die Nation	das Fürstentum	die Region
la nación	el principado	la región
la nazione	il principato	la regione
state	colony	capital
l'État	la colonie	la capitale
der Staat	die Kolonie	die Hauptstadt
el estado	la colonia	la capital
lo stato	la colonia	la capitale

Europe • l'Europe • Europa • Europa • l'Europa

Albania • l'Albanie • Albanien
• Albania • l'Albania
Andorra • l'Andorre • Andorra
• Andorra • Andorra
Austria • l'Autriche • Österreich
• Austria • l'Austria
Balearic Islands • les Baléares
• die Balearen • las Islas Baleares
• le Isole Baleari
Belarus • la Bélarus • Weißrussland
• Belarús • la Bielorussia
Belgium • la Belgique • Belgien
• Bélgica • il Belgio
Bosnia and Herzegovina
• la Bosnie-Herzégovine
• Bosnien und Herzegowina • Bosnia y
Herzegovina • la Bosnia ed Erzegovina
Bulgaria • la Bulgarie • Bulgarien
• Bulgaria • la Bulgaria
Corsica • la Corse • Korsika
• Córcega • la Corsica
Croatia • la Croatie • Kroatien • Croacia
• la Croazia
Czech Republic • la République tchèque
• die Tschechische Republik
• República Checa
• la Repubblica Ceca
Denmark • le Danemark • Dänemark
• Dinamarca • la Danimarca
Estonia • l'Estonie • Estland
• Estonia • l'Estonia
Finland • la Finlande • Finnland
• Finlandia • la Finlandia
France • la France • Frankreich
• Francia • la Francia
Germany • l'Allemagne • Deutschland
• Alemania • la Germania
Greece • la Grèce • Griechenland
• Grecia • la Grecia
Hungary • la Hongrie • Ungarn
• Hungría • l'Ungheria
Iceland • l'Islande • Island • Islandia
• l'Islanda
Ireland • l'Irlande • Irland • Irlanda
• l'Irlanda
Italy • l'Italie • Italien • Italia • l'Italia
Kaliningrad • Kaliningrad • Kaliningrad
• Kaliningrado • Kaliningrad
Kosovo • le Kosovo • Kosovo • Kosovo
• il Kosovo
Latvia • la Lettonie • Lettland • Letonia
• la Lettonia

France

Spain

Liechtenstein • le Liechtenstein
• Liechtenstein • Liechtenstein
• il Liechtenstein
Lithuania • la Lituanie • Litauen
• Lituania • la Lituania
Luxembourg • le Luxembourg
• Luxemburg • Luxemburgo
• il Lussemburgo
Macedonia • la Macédonie • Mazedonien
• Macedonia • la Macedonia
Malta • Malte • Malta • Malta • Malta
Moldova • la Moldavie • Moldawien
• Moldavia • la Moldavia
Monaco • Monaco • Monaco
• Mónaco • Monaco
Montenegro • le Montenegro • Montenegro
• Montenegro • Montenegro
Netherlands • les Pays-Bas
• die Niederlande • los Países Bajos
• i Paesi Bassi
Norway • la Norvège • Norwegen
• Noruega • la Norvegia
Poland • la Pologne • Polen • Polonia
• la Polonia
Portugal • le Portugal • Portugal
• Portugal • il Portogallo
Romania • la Roumanie • Rumänien
• Rumanía • la Romania
Russian Federation
• la Fédération de Russie
• die Russische Föderation
• Federación Rusa
• la Federazione Russa

Italy

Germany

San Marino • le Saint-Marin • San Marino
• San Marino • San Marino
Sardinia • la Sardaigne • Sardinien
• Cerdeña • la Sardegna
Serbia • la Serbie • Serbien • Serbia
• la Serbia
Sicily • la Sicile • Sizilien • Sicilia
• la Sicilia
Slovakia • la Slovaquie • die Slowakei
• Eslovaquia • la Slovacchia
Slovenia • la Slovénie • Slowenien
• Eslovenia • la Slovenia
Spain • l'Espagne • Spanien • España
• la Spagna
Sweden • la Suède • Schweden
• Suecia • la Svezia
Switzerland • la Suisse • die Schweiz
• Suiza • la Svizzera
Ukraine • l'Ukraine • die Ukraine
• Ucrania • l'Ucraina
United Kingdom • le Royaume-Uni
• das Vereinigte Königreich
• Reino Unido • il Regno Unito
Vatican City • la Cité du Vatican
• die Vatikanstadt
• la Ciudad del Vaticano
• la Città del Vaticano

Africa • l'Afrique • Afrika • África • l'Africa

Egypt

Nigeria

Kenya

South Africa

Algeria • l'Algérie • Algerien • Argelia • l'Algeria

Angola • l'Angola • Angola • Angola • l'Angola

Benin • le Bénin • Benin • Benin • il Benin

Botswana • le Botswana • Botsuana • Botswana • il Botswana

Burkina Faso • le Burkina • Burkina Faso • Burquina Faso • il Burkina Faso

Burundi • le Burundi • Burundi • Burundi • il Burundi

Cabinda (Angola) • Cabinda • Kabinda • Cabinda • Cabinda

Cameroon • le Cameroun • Kamerun • Camerún • il Camerun

Central African Republic • la République centrafricaine • die Zentralafrikanische Republik • República Centroafricana • la Repubblica Centrafricana

Chad • le Tchad • Tschad • Chad • il Ciad

Comoros • les Comores • die Komoren • Comoros • le Comore

Congo • le Congo • Kongo • Congo • il Congo

Democratic Republic of the Congo • la République démocratique du Congo • die Demokratische Republik Kongo • República Democrática del Congo • la Repubblica Democratica del Congo

Djibouti • Djibouti • Dschibuti • Djibouti • Gibuti

Egypt • l'Égypte • Ägypten • Egipto • l'Egitto

Equatorial Guinea • la Guinée equatoriale • Äquatorialguinea • Guinea Ecuatorial • la Guinea Equatoriale

Eritrea • l'Érythrée • Eritrea • Eritrea • l'Eritrea

Ethiopia • l'Éthiopie • Äthiopien • Etiopía • l'Etiopia

Gabon • le Gabon • Gabun • Gabón • il Gabon

Gambia • la Gambie • Gambia • Gambia • il Gambia

Ghana • le Ghana • Ghana • Ghana • il Ghana

Guinea • la Guinée • Guinea • Guinea • la Guinea

Guinea-Bissau • la Guinée-Bissau • Guinea-Bissau • Guinea-Bissau • la Guinea-Bissau

Ivory Coast • la Côte d'Ivoire • Elfenbeinküste • Costa de Marfil • la Costa d'Avorio

Kenya • le Kenya • Kenia • Kenya • il Kenya

Lesotho • le Lesotho • Lesotho • Lesotho • il Lesotho

Liberia • le Libéria • Liberia • Liberia • la Liberia

Libya • la Libye • Libyen • Libia • la Libia

Madagascar • Madagascar • Madagaskar • Madagascar • il Madagascar

Malawi • le Malawi • Malawi • Malawi • il Malawi

Mali • le Mali • Mali • Malí • il Mali

Mauritania • la Mauritanie • Mauretanien • Mauritania • la Mauritania

Mauritius • l'île Maurice • Mauritius • Mauricio • Mauritius

Morocco • le Maroc • Marokko • Marruecos • il Marocco

Mozambique • le Mozambique • Mosambik • Mozambique • il Mozambico

Namibia • la Namibie • Namibia • Namibia • la Namibia

Niger • le Niger • Niger • Níger • il Niger

Nigeria • le Nigéria • Nigeria • Nigeria • la Nigeria

Rwanda • le Rwanda • Ruanda • Rwanda • il Ruanda

São Tomé and Principe • Sao Tomé-et-Principe • São Tomé und Príncipe • Santo Tomé y Príncipe • São Tomé e Príncipe

Senegal • le Sénégal • Senegal • Senegal • il Senegal

Sierra Leone • la Sierra Leone • Sierra Leone • Sierra Leona • Sierra Leone

Somalia • la Somalie • Somalia • Somalia • la Somalia

South Africa • l'Afrique du Sud • Südafrika • Sudáfrica • il Sud Africa

South Sudan • le Soudan du Sud • Südsudan • Sudán del Sur • il Sudan del Sud

Sudan • le Soudan • der Sudan • Sudán • il Sudan

Swaziland • le Swaziland • Swasiland • Swazilandia • lo Swaziland

Tanzania • la Tanzanie • Tansania • Tanzania • la Tanzania

Togo • le Togo • Togo • Togo • il Togo

Tunisia • la Tunisie • Tunesien • Túnez • la Tunisia

Uganda • l'Ouganda • Uganda • Uganda • l'Uganda

Western Sahara • le Sahara occidental • Westsahara • Sáhara Occidental • il Sahara Occidentale

Zambia • la Zambie • Sambia • Zambia • lo Zambia

Zimbabwe • le Zimbabwe • Simbabwe • Zimbabwe • lo Zimbabwe

Asia • l'Asie • Asien • Asia • l'Asia

Bangladesh

China

India

Japan

Jordan

Philippines

South Korea

Thailand

Turkey

Afghanistan • l'Afghanistan • Afghanistan • Afganistán • l'Afghanistan

Armenia • l'Arménie • Armenien • Armenia • l'Armenia

Azerbaijan • l'Azerbaïdjan • Aserbaidschan • Azerbaiyán • l'Azerbaigian

Bahrain • le Bahreïn • Bahrain • Bahrein • il Bahrain

Bangladesh • le Bangladesh • Bangladecsh • Bangladesh • il Bangladesh

Bhutan • le Bhoutan • Bhutan • Bhutan • il Bhutan

Brunei • le Brunei • Brunei • Brunei • Brunei

Cambodia • le Cambodge • Kambodscha • Camboya • la Cambogia

China • la Chine • China • China • la Cina

Cyprus • Chypre • Zypern • Chipre • Cipro

East Timor • le Timor oriental • Ost-Timor • Timor Oriental • Timor Est

Fiji • Fidji • Fidschi • Fiji • Figi

Georgia • la Géorgie • Georgien • Georgia • la Georgia

India • l'Inde • Indien • India • l'India

Indonesia • l'Indonésie • Indonesien • Indonesia • l'Indonesia

Iran • l'Iran • der Iran • Irán • l'Iran

Iraq • l'Irak • der Irak • Iraq • l'Iraq

Israel • Israël • Israel • Israel • l'Israele

Japan • le Japon • Japan • Japón • il Giappone

Jordan • la Jordanie • Jordanien • Jordania • la Giordania

Kazakhstan • le Kasakhstan • Kasachstan • Kazajstán • il Kazakistan

Kuwait • le Koweït • Kuwait • Kuwait • il Kuwait

Kyrgyzstan • le Kirghizistan • Kirgisistan • Kirguistán • il Kirghizistan

Laos • le Laos • Laos • Laos • il Laos

Lebanon • le Liban • der Libanon • Líbano • il Libano

Malaysia • la Malaisie • Malaysia • Malasia • la Malaysia

Maldives • les Maldives • die Malediven • Maldivas • le Maldive

Mongolia • la Mongolie • die Mongolei • Mongolia • la Mongolia

Myanmar (Burma) • le Myanmar (la Birmanie) • Myanmar (Birma) • Myanmar (Birmania) • il Myanmar (la Birmania)

Nepal • le Népal • Nepal • Nepal • il Nepal

North Korea • la Corée du Nord • Nordkorea • Corea del Norte • la Corea del Nord

Oman • l'Oman • Oman • Omán • l'Oman

Pakistan • le Pakistan • Pakistan • Pakistán • il Pakistan

Papua New Guinea • la Papouasie-Nouvelle-Guinée • Papua-Neuguinea • Papua Nueva Guinea • la Papua Nuova Guinea

Philippines • les Philippines • die Philippinen • Filipinas • le Filippine

Australasia • l'Australasie
• Australien und Ozeanien
• Australasia • l'Oceania

Indonesia

Saudi Arabia

Vietnam

Australia

New Zealand

Qatar • le Qatar • **Katar** • Qatar • il Qatar
Saudi Arabia • l'Arabie Saoudite • **Saudi-Arabien**
   • Arabia Saudita • l'Arabia Saudita
Singapore • Singapour • **Singapur** • Singapur • Singapore
Solomon Islands • les îles Saloman • **die Salomonen**
   • Islas Salomón • le Isole Salomone
South Korea • la Corée du Sud • **Südkorea** • Corea del Sur
   • la Corea del Sud
Sri Lanka • Sri Lanka • **Sri Lanka** • Sri Lanka • lo Sri Lanka
Syria • la Syrie • **Syrien** • Siria • la Siria
Tajikistan • le Tadjikistan • **Tadschikistan** • Tayikistán • il Tagikistan
Thailand • la Thaïlande • **Thailand** • Tailandia • la Tailandia
Turkey • la Turquie • **die Türkei** • Turquía • la Turchia
Turkmenistan • le Turkmenistan • **Turkmenistan** • Turkmenistán
   • il Turkmenistan
United Arab Emirates • les Émirats arabes unis
   • **Vereinigte Arabische Emirate** • Emiratos Árabes Unidos
   • gli Emirati Arabi Uniti
Uzbekistan • l'Ouzbékistan • **Usbekistan** • Uzbekistán
   • l'Uzbekistan
Vanuatu • Vanuatu • **Vanuatu** • Vanuatu • Vanuatu
Vietnam • le Vietnam • **Vietnam** • Viet Nam • il Vietnam
Yemen • le Yémen • **der Jemen** • Yemen • lo Yemen

Australia • l'Australie • **Australien** • Australia • l'Australia
New Zealand • la Nouvelle-Zélande • **Neuseeland**
   • Nueva Zelandia • la Nuova Zelanda
Tasmania • la Tasmanie • **Tasmanien** • Tasmania • la Tasmania

particles and antonyms • particules et antonymes • Partikeln und Antonyme • partículas y antónimos • particelle e antonimi

to	from	through	around
à	de	à travers	autour de
zu, nach	von, aus	durch	um
a, hacia	de, desde	a través de	alrededor de
a	da	attraverso	attorno
over	under	on top of	beside
au-dessus de	sous	sur	à côté de
über	unter	auf	neben
encima de	debajo de	encima de	al lado de
sopra	sotto	in cima	accanto
in front of	behind	between	opposite
devant	derrière	entre	en face de
vor	hinter	zwischen	gegenüber
delante de	detrás de	entre	en frente de
davanti	dietro	tra	di fronte
onto	into	near	far
sur	dans	près de	loin de
auf	in	nahe	weit
sobre	dentro de	cerca	lejos
sopra	dentro	vicino	lontano
in	out	with	without
dans	dehors	avec	sans
in	aus	mit	ohne
en	fuera	con	sin
dentro	fuori	con	senza
above	below	before	after
au-dessus de	au-dessous de	avant	après
über	unter	vor	nach
sobre	bajo	antes	después
sopra	sotto	prima	dopo
inside	outside	by	until
à l'intérieur de	à l'extérieur de	avant	jusqu'à
innerhalb	außerhalb	bis	bis
dentro	fuera	antes de	hasta
all'interno	all'esterno	entro	fino
up	down	for	toward
en haut	en bas	pour	vers
hinauf	hinunter	für	zu
arriba	abajo	para	hacia
su	giù	per	verso
at	beyond	along	across
à	au-delà de	le long de	à travers
an, bei	jenseits	entlang	über
en	más allá de	por	al otro lado de
a	oltre	lungo	attraverso

large	**small**	**hot**	**cold**
grand	petit	chaud	froid
groß	klein	heiß	kalt
grande	pequeño	caliente	frío
grande	piccolo	caldo	freddo
wide	**narrow**	**open**	**closed**
large	étroit	ouvert	fermé
breit	schmal	offen	geschlossen
ancho	estrecho	abierto	cerrado
largo	stretto	aperto	chiuso
tall	**short**	**full**	**empty**
grand	court	plein	vide
groß	kurz	voll	leer
alto	bajo	lleno	vacío
alto	basso	pieno	vuoto
high	**low**	**new**	**old**
haut	bas	neuf	vieux
hoch	niedrig	neu	alt
alto	bajo	nuevo	viejo
alto	basso	nuovo	vecchio
thick	**thin**	**light**	**dark**
épais	mince	clair	foncé
dick	dünn	hell	dunkel
grueso	delgado	claro	oscuro
spesso	sottile	chiaro	scuro
light	**heavy**	**easy**	**difficult**
léger	lourd	facile	difficile
leicht	schwer	leicht	schwer
ligero	pesado	fácil	difícil
leggero	pesante	facile	difficile
hard	**soft**	**free**	**occupied**
dur	mou	libre	occupé
hart	weich	frei	besetzt
duro	blando	libre	ocupado
duro	morbido	libero	occupato
wet	**dry**	**beginning**	**end**
humide	sec	le début	la fin
nass	trocken	der Anfang	das Ende
húmedo	seco	el principio	el final
bagnato	asciutto	l'inizio	la fine
good	**bad**	**strong**	**weak**
bon	mauvais	fort	faible
gut	schlecht	stark	schwach
bueno	malo	fuerte	débil
buono	cattivo	forte	debole
fast	**slow**	**fat**	**thin**
rapide	lent	gros	mince
schnell	langsam	dick	dünn
rápido	lento	gordo	delgado
veloce	lento	grasso	magro

useful phrases • phrases utiles • praktische Redewendungen • frases útiles • frasi utili

essential phrases
- **phrases essentielles**
- **wesentliche Redewendungen**
- **frases esenciales**
- **frasi essenziali**

Yes
Oui
Ja
Sí
Sì

No
Non
Nein
No
No

Maybe
Peut-être
Vielleicht
Quizá
Forse

Please
S'il vous plaît
Bitte
Por favor
Per favore

Thank you
Merci
Danke
Gracias
Grazie

You're welcome
De rien
Bitte sehr
De nada
Prego

Excuse me
Pardon
Entschuldigung
Perdone
Permesso

I'm sorry
Je suis désolé
Es tut mir Leid
Lo siento
Mi dispiace

Don't
Ne... pas
Nicht
No
No

OK
D'accord
Okay
Vale
D'accordo

That's fine
Très bien
In Ordnung
Así vale
Vabbene

That's correct
C'est juste
Das ist richtig
Está bien
È giusto

That's wrong
C'est faux
Das ist falsch
Está mal
È sbagliato

greetings • salutations
- **Begrüßungen**
- **saludos • saluti**

Hello
Bonjour
Guten Tag
Hola
Buongiorno

Goodbye
Au revoir
Auf Wiedersehen
Adiós
Arrivederci

Good morning
Bonjour
Guten Morgen
Buenos días
Buongiorno

Good afternoon
Bonjour
Guten Tag
Buenas tardes
Buon pomeriggio

Good evening
Bonsoir
Guten Abend
Buenas tardes
Buona sera

Good night
Bonne nuit
Gute Nacht
Buenas noches
Buona notte

How are you?
Comment allez-vous?
Wie geht es Ihnen?
¿Cómo está?
Come sta?

My name is...
Je m'appelle...
Ich heiße...
Me llamo...
Mi chiamo...

What is your name?
Vous vous appelez comment?
Wie heißen Sie?
¿Cómo se llama?
Come si chiama?

Whis is his/her name?
Il/Elle s'appelle comment?
Wie heißt er/sie?
¿Cómo se llama?
Come si chiama lui/lei?

May I introduce...
Je vous présente...
Darf ich... vorstellen
Le presento a...
Le posso presentare...

This is...
C'est...
Das ist...
Este es...
Le presento...

Pleased to meet you
Enchanté
Angenehm
Encantado de conocerle
Piacere di conoscerla

See you later
À tout à l'heure
Bis später
Hasta luego
A più tardi

signs • panneaux
- **Schilder • letreros**
- **insegne**

Tourist information
Office de tourisme
Touristen-Information
Información
Ufficio informazioni turistiche

Entrance
Entrée
Eingang
Entrada
Entrata

Exit
Sortie
Ausgang
Salida
Uscita

Emergency exit
Sortie de secours
Notausgang
Salida de emergencia
Uscita di emergenza

Push
Poussez
Drücken
Empuje
Spingere

Danger
Danger
Lebensgefahr
Peligro
Pericolo

No smoking
Défense de fumer
Rauchen verboten
Prohibido fumar
Vietato fumare

Out of order
En panne
Außer Betrieb
Fuera de servicio
Guasto

Opening times
Heures d'ouverture
Öffnungszeiten
Horario de apertura
Orario di apertura

Free admission
Entrée gratuite
Eintritt frei
Entrada libre
Ingresso libero

Knock before entering
Frappez avant d'entrer
Bitte anklopfen
Llame antes de entrar
Bussare prima di entrare

Keep off the grass
Défense de marcher sur la
   pelouse
Betreten des Rasens verboten
Prohibido pisar el césped
Non calpestare l'erba

**help • assistance • Hilfe
   • ayuda • aiuto**

Can you help me?
Pouvez-vous m'aider?
Können Sie mir helfen?
¿Me puede ayudar?
Mi può aiutare?

I don't understand
Je ne comprends pas
Ich verstehe nicht
No entiendo
Non capisco

I don't know
Je ne sais pas
Ich weiß nicht
No lo sé
Non lo so

Do you speak English…?
Vous parlez anglais…?
Sprechen Sie Englisch…?
¿Habla inglés…?
Parla inglese…?

I speak English…
Je parle anglais…
Ich spreche Englisch…
Hablo inglés…
Parlo inglese…

Please speak more slowly
Parlez moins vite, s'il vous
   plaît
Sprechen Sie bitte langsamer
Hable más despacio, por
   favor
Parli più lentamente

Please write it down for me
Écrivez-le pour moi, s'il
   vous plaît
Schreiben Sie es bitte für
   mich auf
¿Me lo puede escribir?
Me lo scriva, per favore

I have lost…
J'ai perdu…
Ich habe… verloren
He perdido…
Ho perso…

**directions • directions
   • Richtungsangaben
   • indicaciones
   • indicazioni**

I am lost
Je me suis perdu
Ich habe mich verlaufen
Me he perdido
Mi sono perso/a

Where is the…?
Où est le/la…?
Wo ist der/die/das…?
¿Dónde está el/la…?
Dov'è il/la…?

Where is the nearest…?
Où est le/la…le/la plus
   proche?
Wo ist der/die/das nächste…?
¿Dónde está el/la… más
   cercano/a?
Dov'è il/la … più vicino/a?

Where is the restroom?
Où sont les toilettes?
Wo sind die Toiletten?
¿Dónde están los servicios?
Dov'è il bagno?

How do I get to…?
Pour aller à…?
Wie komme ich nach…?
¿Cómo voy a…?
Come si arriva a…?

To the right
À droite
Nach rechts
A la derecha
A destra

To the left
À gauche
Nach links
A la izquierda
A sinistra

Straight ahead
Tout droit
Geradeaus
Todo recto
Sempre dritto

How far is…?
C'est loin…?
Wie weit ist…?
¿A qué distancia está…?
Quant'è lontano…?

**accommodation
   • logement • Unterkunft
   • alojamiento • alloggio**

I have a reservation
J'ai réservé une chambre
Ich habe ein Zimmer reserviert
Tengo una reserva
Ho una prenotazione

What time is breakfast?
Le petit déjeuner est à quelle
   heure?
Wann gibt es Frühstück?
¿A qué hora es el desayuno?
A che ora è la colazione?

Where is the dining room?
Où est la salle à manger?
Wo ist der Speisesaal?
¿Dónde está el comedor?
Dov'è la sala da pranzo?

**eating and drinking
   • nourriture et boissons
   • Essen und Trinken
   • comida y bebida
   • cibo e bevande**

Cheers!
À la vôtre!
Zum Wohl!
¡Salud!
Salute!

It's delicious/awful
C'est délicieux/terrible
Es ist köstlich/scheußlich
Está buenísimo/malísimo
È buonissimo/disgustoso

I don't drink/smoke
Je ne bois/fume pas
Ich trinke/rauche nicht
Yo no bebo/fumo
Non bevo/fumo

I don't eat meat
Je ne mange pas de la viande
Ich esse kein Fleisch
Yo no como carne
Non mangio la carne

No more for me, thank you
Je n'en veux plus, merci
Nichts mehr, danke
Ya no más, gracias
Per me basta, grazie

May I have some more?
Encore un peu, s'il vous plaît.
Könnte ich noch etwas mehr
   haben?
¿Puedo repetir?
Posso prenderne ancora?

May we have the check?
L'addition, s'il vous plaît.
Wir möchten bitte zahlen.
¿Me trae la cuenta?
Il conto, per favore.

Can I have a receipt?
Je voudrais un reçu.
Ich hätte gerne eine Quittung.
¿Me da un recibo?
Mi dà una ricevuta?

English index • index anglais • englisches Register • índice inglés • indice inglese

english

english

english

english

english

for 320
forceps 53, 167
forearm 12
forecourt 199
forehand 231
forehead 14
foreign currency 97
foreskin 21
forest 285
fork 65, 88, 207
forklift 186, 216
formal 34
formal garden 84, 262
fortieth 309
forty 308
forty minutes 304
forward 222
foul 222, 226
foul ball 228
foul line 229
foundation 40
fountain 85
four 308
four-door 200
four hundred 308
four-wheel drive 199
fourteen 308
fourteenth 309
fourth 309
fox 290
foxglove 297
foyer 59
fraction 165
fracture 46
fragile 98
fragranced 130
frame 51, 62, 206, 267
frame counter 270
France 316
freckle 15
free 321
free kick 222
free range 118
free-throw line 226
free weights 250
freesia 110
freeway 194
freeze 287
freeze v 67
freezer 67
freight train 208
freighter 215
French bean 122
French fries 154
French Guiana 315
French horn 257
French mustard 135
French press 65
French toast 157
French twist 39
frequency 179
fresh 121, 127, 130
fresh cheese 136
fresh fruit 157
freshwater fishing 245
fret 258
fretsaw 81
Friday 306
fried 159
fried chicken 155
fried egg 157
friend 24
frieze 301
frog 294
from 320
front crawl 239
front door 58

front wheel 196
frontal 16
frost 287
frosting 141
froth 148
frown 25
frozen 121, 124
frozen food 107
frozen yogurt 137
fruit 107, 126, 128
fruit bread 139
fruit farm 183
fruit juice 127, 156
fruit tart 140
fruit yogurt 157
fruitcake 140
fry v 67
frying pan 69
fuel gauge 201
fuel tank 204
full 64, 266, 321
full bed 71
full moon 280
fumble 220
funeral 26
funnel 166, 214
furniture store 115
furrow 183
fuse 60
fuse box 60, 203
fuselage 210

G

gable 300
Gabon 317
Galápagos Islands 315
galaxy 280
gale 286
galley 214
gallon 311
gallop 243
galvanized 79
Gambia 317
game 119, 230, 273
game show 178
games 272
gangway 214
garage 58, 199
garbage can 67
garden 84, 261
garden center 115
garden features 84
garden plants 86
garden styles 84
garden tools 88
gardener 188
gardening 90
gardening basket 88
gardening gloves 89
garland 111
garlic 125, 132
garlic press 68
garnet 288
garter 35
garter straps 35
gas pump 199
gas station 199
gas tank 203
gasket 61
gasoline 199
gate 85, 182, 247
gate number 213
gauze 47, 167
gear lever 207
gearbox 202, 204
gears 206

gearshift 201
gel 38, 109
gems 288
generation 23
generator 60
genitals 12
geography 162
geometry 165
Georgia 318
gerbera 110
Germany 316
get a job v 26
get married v 26
get up v 71
geyser 285
Ghana 317
giant slalom 247
gifts shop 114
gill 294
gin 145
gin and tonic 151
ginger 125, 133
giraffe 291
girder 186
girl 23
girlfriend 24
girth 242
glacier 284
gladiolus 110
gland 19
glass 69, 152
glass bottle 166
glass rod 167
glasses 51, 150
glassware 64
glaze v 139
glider 211, 248
gliding 248
gloss 83, 271
glove 36, 224, 228, 233, 236, 246
glue 275
glue gun 78
go to bed v 71
go to sleep v 71
goal 221, 223, 224
goal area 223
goal line 220, 223, 224
goalkeeper 222, 224
goalpost 220, 222
goat 185
goat cheese 142
goat's milk 136
goggles 238, 247
going out 75
gold 235, 289
goldfish 294
golf 232
golf bag 233
golf ball 233
golf cart 232
golf clubs 233
golf course 232
golf shoe 233
golf trolley 233
golfer 232
gong 257
good 321
good afternoon 322
good evening 322
good morning 322
good night 322
goodbye 322
goose 119, 293
goose egg 137

gooseberry 127
gorge 284
gorilla 291
Gothic 301
gown 169
grade 163
graduate 169
graduate v 26
graduation ceremony 169
graft v 91
grains 130
gram 310
grandchildren 23
granddaughter 22
grandfather 22
grandmother 22
grandparents 23
grandson 22
granite 288
grape juice 144
grapefruit 126
grapeseed oil 134
graphite 289
grass 86, 262
grass bag 88
grasshopper 295
grassland 285
grate v 67
grated cheese 136
grater 68
gratin dish 69
gravel 88
gravity 280
graze 46
greasy 39
Greece 316
green 129, 232, 274
green olive 143
green peas 131
green salad 158
green tea 149
greenhouse 85
Greenland 314
Grenada 314
gray 39, 274
grill pan 69
grilled 159
groceries 106
grocery cart 106
grocery store 114
groin 12
groom 243
ground 60, 132
ground coffee 144
ground cover 87
ground floor 104
ground meat 119
ground sheet 267
group therapy 55
grout 83
guard 236
guardrail 195
Guatemala 314
guava 128
guest 64, 100
guidebook 260
guided tour 260
guilty 181
Guinea 317
Guinea-Bissau 317
guitarist 258
gull 292
gum 50
gumdrop 113
gun 94
gurney 48

gutter 58, 299
guy rope 266
Guyana 315
gym 101, 250
gym machine 250
gymnast 235
gymnastics 235
gynecologist 52
gynecology 49
gypsophila 110

H

hacksaw 81
haddock 120
hemorrhage 46
hail 286
hair 14, 38
hair dye 40
hair straightener 38
hairdresser 38, 188
hairspray 38
Haiti 314
half an hour 304
half-and-half 137
half-liter 311
halftime 223
halibut fillets 120
Halloween 27
halter 243
halter neck 35
ham 119, 143, 156
hammer 80
hammer v 79
hammock 266
hamper 263
hamster 290
hamstring 16
hand 13, 15
hand drill 81
hand fork 89
hand rail 59, 196
hand towel 73
handbag 37
handcuffs 94
handicap 233
handkerchief 36
handle 36, 88, 106, 187, 200, 230
handlebar 207
handles 37
handsaw 81, 89
handset 99
hang v 82
hang-glider 248
hang-gliding 248
hanging basket 84
hanging file 173
happy 25
harbor 217
harbor master 217
hard 129, 321
hard candy 113
hard cheese 136
hard cider 145
hard hat 186
hardboard 79
hardware 176
hardware store 114
hardwood 79
haricot beans 131
harness race 243
harp 256
harvest v 91, 183
hat 36
hatchback 199, 200
have a baby v 26
Hawaii 314

english

english

english

modeling tool 275
moisturizer 41
molar 50
molding 63
Moldova 316
mole 14
Monaco 316
Monday 306
money 97
money order 98
Mongolia 318
monitor 53, 172
monkey 291
monkfish 120
Monopoly 272
monorail 208
monsoon 287
month 306
monthly 307
monument 261
Moon 280
moonstone 288
moor v 217
mooring 217
mop 77
morning 305
Morocco 317
mortar 68, 167, 187
mortgage 96
mosque 300
mosquito 295
mosquito net 267
moth 295
mother 22
mother-in-law 23
motocross 249
motor 88
motorcycle 204
motorcycle racing 249
mountain 284
mountain bike 206
mountain range 282
mouse 176, 290
mousse 141
mouth 14
mouth guard 237
mouthwash 72
move 273
movie set 179
movie theater 255, 299
movies 255
mow v 90
Mozambique 317
mozzarella 142
Mr. 23
Mrs. 23
mudguard 205
muffin 140
muffin pan 69
muffler 203, 204
mug 65
mulch v 91
multigrain bread 139
multiply v 165
multivitamin tablets
    109
mumps 44
mung beans 131
muscles 16
museum 261
mushroom 125
music 162
music school 169
musical 255
musical score 255
musical styles 259

musician 191
mussel 121, 295
mustard 155
mustard seed 131
Myanmar (Burma) 318

N

naan bread 139
nail 15, 80
nail clippers 41
nail file 41
nail scissors 41
nail polish 41
nail polish
    remover 41
Namibia 317
nape 13
napkin 65
napkin ring 65
nappy rash cream 74
narrow 321
nation 315
national park 261
natural 256
natural fiber 31
naturopathy 55
nausea 44
navel 12
navigate v 240
near 320
nearsighted 51
nebula 280
neck 12, 258
neck brace 46
necklace 36
nectarine 126
needle 109, 276
needle-nose
    pliers 80
needle plate 276
needlepoint 277
negative 271
negative electrode
    167
neighbor 24
Neoclassical 301
Nepal 318
nephew 23
Neptune 280
nerve 19, 50
nervous 19, 25
net 217, 222, 226, 227, 231
net v 245
Netherlands 316
nettle 297
network 176
neurology 49
neutral 60
neutral zone 224
new 321
new moon 280
new potato 124
New Year 27
New Zealand 319
newborn baby 53
news 178
newsstand 112
newspaper 112
next week 306
nib 163
Nicaragua 314
nickel 289
niece 23
Niger 317
Nigeria 317
night 305
nightgown 31, 35

nightwear 31
nightstand 70
nightstick 94
nine 308
nine hundred 308
nineteen 308
nineteen hundred
    307
nineteen hundred and one
    307
nineteen ten 307
nineteenth 309
ninetieth 309
ninety 308
ninth 309
nipple 12, 75
no 322
no right turn 195
no stopping 195
nonstick 69
noodles 158
noon 305
normal 39
north 312
North and Central America
    314
North Korea 318
North Pole 283
North Sea 312
Northern
    Hemisphere 283
Norway 316
nose 14, 210
nose clip 238
noseband 242
nosebleed 44
nosewheel 210
nostril 14
notation 256
note 256
notebook 163, 172
notepad 173
notes 191
notions 105
nougat 113
November 306
now 304
nozzle 89
number 226, 308
numerator 165
nurse 45, 48, 189
nursery 74
nursing 53
nursing bra 53
nursing pads 53
nut 80
nutmeg 132
nuts 151
nuts and dried
    fruit 129
nylon 277

O

oak 296
oar 241
oatmeal 157
oats 130
objective lens 167
oboe 257
obsidian 288
obstetrician 52
occupations 188,
    190
occupied 321
ocean 282
ocean liner 215
octagon 164

October 306
octopus 121, 295
odometer 201
off-piste 247
off-ramp 194
office 24, 172, 174
office building 298
office equipment 172
office supplies 173
offside 223
oil 142, 199
oil paint 274
oil tank 204
oil tanker 215
oils 134
oily 41
ointment 47, 109
okra 122
old 321
olive oil 134
olives 151
Oman 318
omelet 158
on-ramp 194
on time 305
on top of 320
oncology 49
one 308
one billion 309
one million 309
one thousand 309
one-way street
    194
one-way system
    298
onesie 30
onion 124
online 177
onto 320
onyx 289
opal 288
open 260, 321
open-faced
    sandwich 155
open-top 260
opening night 254
opera 255
operating room 48
operation 48
operator 99
ophthalmology 49
opponent 236
opposite 320
optic nerve 51
optometrist 51, 189
orange 126, 274
orange juice 148
orangeade 144
orbit 280
orchestra 256
orchestra pit 254
orchestra seats 254
orchid 111
order v 153
oregano 133
organic 91, 118, 122
organic waste 61
origami 275
ornamental 87
orthopedics 49
osteopathy 54
ostrich 292
otter 290
ounce 310
out 225, 228, 320
out of bounds 226
out of focus 271

outboard motor 215
outbuilding 182
outdoor activities
    262
outer core 282
outfield 229
outlet 60, 61
outpatient 48
outside 320
out-tray 172
oval 164
ovary 20
oven 66
oven mitt 69
ovenproof 69
over 320
over par 233
overalls 30
overdraft 96
overexposed 271
overflow pipe 61
overhead bin 210
overpass 194
overture 256
ovulation 20, 52
owl 292
oyster 121
ozone layer 286

P

Pacific Ocean 312
pack 311
pack of cigarettes 112
package 99
packet 311
pad 220, 224
paddle 231, 241
paddock 242
pail 265
painkillers 47, 109
paint 83
paint v 83
paint can 83
paint thinner 83
paint tray 83
painter 191
painting 62, 261, 274
paints 274
pajamas 33
Pakistan 318
palate 19
palette 274
pallet 186
palm 15, 86, 296
palm hearts 122
pan 310
pan fried 159
Panama 314
pancreas 18
panda 291
panties 35
pants 32, 34
panty hose 35, 251
panty liner 108
papaya 128
paper clip 173
paper napkin 154
paper tray 172
papier-maché 275
paprika 132
Papua New
    Guinea 319
par 233
parachute 248
parachuting 248
paragliding 248
Paraguay 315

english

english

english

english

english

French index • index français • französisches Register • índice francés • indice francese

français

français

français

français

français

français

français

français

français

français

français

français

français

français

German index • index allemand • deutsches Register • índice alemán • indice tedesco

deutsch

deutsch

deutsch

deutsch

deutsch

G

Gabel f 65, 207
Gabelstapler m 186, 216
Gabun 317
Gagat m 288
gähnen 25
Galapagos-Inseln f 315
Galaxie f 280
Gallone f 311
Galopp m 243
galvanisiert 79
Gambia 317
Gang m 106, 168, 210, 254
Gänge f 153, 206
Gans f 119, 293
Gänseblümchen n 297
Gänseei n 137
ganz 129, 132
Garage f 58
Gardine f 63
Garn n 276
Garnele f 121
Garten m 84
Garten ornamente f 84
Garten stöcke f 89
Gartenanlagen f 262
Gartenarbeit f 90
Gartencenter n 115
Gartengeräte f 88
Gartenhandschuhe f 89
Gartenkorb m 88
Gartenkürbis m 124
Gartenpflanzen f 86
Gartenschere f 89
Gartenschlauch m 89
Gartentypen f 84
Gärtner m 188
Gasbrenner m 61, 267
Gashebel m 204
Gaspedal n 200
Gasse f 298
Gast m 64, 100
Gästebuch n 100
Gastgeber m 64
Gastgeberin f 64
Gatenummer f 213
Gaumen m 19
Gaze f 47
Gebäck m 140, 149
gebacken 159
Gebärmutter f 20, 52
Gebärmutterhals m 20, 52
Gebäude f 299
Gebäudereiniger m 188
Gebäude und Strukturen f 300
geben 273
Gebiete f 299
Gebirgskette f 282
Gebiss n 242
geboren werden 26
gebraten 159
gebratene Hähnchen m 155
Gebrauchs- anweisung f 109
Gebrauchtwaren-händler m 115
Geburt f 52, 53
Geburt einleiten f 53
Geburtsgewicht n 53
Geburtshelfer m 52
Geburtstag m 27
Geburtstagsfeier f 27

Geburtstagskerzen f 141
Geburtstagskuchen m 141
Geburtsurkunde f 26
Geburtszange f 53
gedämpft 159
Gedeck n 65, 152
Gedränge n 221
Gefahr f 195
Gefängnis n 181
Gefängniswärter m 181
Gefängniszelle f 181
gefärbt 39
Geflügel n 119
Gefrierfach n 67
Gefrier-Kühlschrank m 67
gefrorene Joghurt m 137
Gefühle f 25
gefüllt 159
gefüllte Olive f 143
Gegner m 236
gegrillt 159
Gehalt n 175
gehen lassen 139
Gehirn m 19
Gehirnerschütterung f 46
Gehrungslade f 81
Geige f 256
Geißblatt n 297
gekochte Ei n 137, 157
gekrümmt 165
Gel n 109
geladen 60
Geländemotorrad n 205
Geländewagen m 199
gelangweilt 25
gelb 274
Gelbwurz f 132
Geld n 97
Geldautomat m 97
Geldwirtschaft f 97
Geleebonbon m 113
Gelenk n 17
gemahlen 132
gemahlene Kaffee m 144
Gemälde n 63, 261, 274
gemischte Salat m 158
Gemüse n 107, 122, 124
Gemüsefach n 67
Gemüsegarten m 85, 182
Gemüsehändler m 188
Gemüseladen m 114
Generation f 23
Generator m 60
geöffnet 260
Geometrie f 165
Georgien 318
Gepäck n 100, 198, 213
Gepäckablage f 209
Gepäckabteilung f 104
Gepäckanhänger m 212
Gepäckausgabe f 213
Gepäckband n 212
Gepäckfach n 196, 210
Gepäckröntgen-maschine f 212
Gepäckträger m 204
gepökelt 118, 143
gerade 165
geradeaus 260
geraspelt 132
geräuchert 118, 121, 143, 159
Gerbera f 110
Gerichtsdiener m 180
Gerichtssaal m 180
Gerichtsstenograf m 181
Gerichtstermin m 180

Gerichtsverfahren n 180
geriebene Käse m 136
geröstet 129
Gerste f 130, 184
Gerüst n 186
gesalzen 121, 129, 137
Gesäß n 13
Gesäßmuskel m 16
gesäubert 121
Geschäft n 175
Geschäftsabkommen n 175
Geschäftsfrau f 175
Geschäftsführer m 175
Geschäftsmann m 175
Geschäftspartnerin f 24
Geschäftsreise f 175
geschält 129
geschälten Garnelen f 120
Geschenk n 27
Geschenkartikelladen m 114
Geschichte f 162
Geschirr n 64, 65
Geschlechtskrankheit n 20
Geschlechtsteile f 12
Geschlechtsverkehr m 20
geschlossen 260
Geschwindig- keitsbegrenzung f 195
Geschworenen f 180
Geschworenen bank f 180
Gesicht n 14
Gesichtsbehandlung f 41
Gesichtscreme f 73
Gesichtsmaske f 41
Gesichtspuder m 40
Gesichts-schutzmaske f 225
Gesicht-wasser n 41
Gesims n 300
gestalten 91
Gestänge n 267
Gestein n 288
Gestell n 166, 174
gestern 306
Gesundheit f 44
Gesundheitsfürsorge f 168
geteilt durch 165
getoastete Sandwich m 149
Getränke f 107, 144, 156
Getreidearten und Hülsenfrüchte f 130
Getreide n 130
Getreideflocken f 107, 130, 156
Getriebe n 202, 204
getrocknet 129, 143, 159
getrockneten Erbsen f 131
Gewächshaus n 85
Geweih n 291
Gewichtstange f 251
Gewicht n 166, 244
Gewichte f 250
Gewinnanteile f 97
gewinnen 273
Gewinner m 273
Gewitter n 287
Gewölbe n 15, 300
Gewürze f 132
Gewürzessig m 135
Gewürznelke f 133
Geysir m 285
Ghana 317
Giebel m 300
Giebeldreieck n 301
gießen 67, 90

Gießen n 89
Gießkanne f 89
Gin m 145
Gin Tonic m 151
Gips m 83
Giraffe f 291
Girokonto n 96
Gitarrist m 258
Gitterstäbe f 74
Gladiole f 110
Glanz- 83
Glas- 69
Glas n 51, 134, 152, 311
Gläser f 150
Glasflasche f 166
glasieren 139
Glaskeramik kochfeld m 66
Glasstäbchen m 167
Glaswaren f 65
glatt 39
glätten 39
Glattrochen m 294
gleich 165
Gleichstrom m 60
Gleichung f 165
Gleis n 209
Gleisnummer f 208
Gleitschirmfliegen n 248
Gletscher m 284
Glied m 36
Glimmer m 289
Glimmerschiefer m 288
glücklich 25
Gneis m 288
Gold n 235, 289
Goldbrasse f 120
Goldfisch m 294
Golf n 232
Golfball m 233
Golfplatz m 232
Golfschläger f 233
Golfschuh m 233
Golfspielerin f 232
Golftasche f 233
Golfturnier n 233
Gong m 257
Gorilla m 291
gotisch 301
Gottesanbeterin f 295
GPS-System n 201
graben 90
graduieren 26
Graduierte f 169
Graduierungsfeier f 169
Gramm n 310
Granat m 288
Granatapfel m 128
Granit m 288
Grapefruit f 126
Graphit m 289
Gras m 87, 262
Grasfangsack m 88
Grasland m 285
Gräte f 121
grau 39, 274
Graubrot n 139, 149
graue Star m 51
Gravieren n 275
Greifzange f 167
Grenada 314
Griechenland 316
Grieß m 130
Griff m 36, 88, 230, 237
Griffe f 37
Grill m 267
Grille f 295
grillen 67

Grillpfanne f 69
Grippe f 44
grobe Senf m 135
Grönland 314
Großeltern 23
große Zeh m 15
Großmutter f 22
Großraumlimousine f 199
Großsegel n 240
Großvater m 22
Grübchen n 15
grün 129, 274
Grün n 232
Grundfarbe f 83
Grundfläche f 164
Grundierung f 40, 83
Grundlinie f 230
Grundriss m 261
grüne Bohne f 122
grüne Erbse f 122
grünen Erbsen f 131
grüne Olive f 143
grüne Salat m 158
grüne Tee m 149
Grünkohl m 123
Gruppentherapie f 55
Guatemala 314
Guave f 128
Guinea 317
Guinea-Bissau 317
Gummiband n 173
Gummihöschen n 30
Gummiknüppel m 94
Gummistiefel f 31, 89
Gurke f 125
Gürtel m 32, 36, 236
Gürtelschnalle f 36
Güterzug m 208
gut geschnitten 35
Guyana 315
Gymnastikband n 235
Gymnastikhose f 251
Gynäkologe m 52
Gynäkologie f 49

H

Haar n 14, 38
Haarband n 39
Haarbürste f 38
Haarfärbemittel n 40
Haarfarben f 39
Haargel n 38
Haarglätter m 38
Haarklammer f 38
Haarknoten m 39
Haarreif m 38
Haarspliss m 39
Haarspray n 38
Haarspülung f 38
Hacke f 88
Hackfleisch n 119
Hackmesser n 68
Hafen m 214, 216, 217
Hafenmeister m 217
Hafer m 130
Haferbrei m 157
Haftbefehl m 180
Haftentlassung auf Bewährung f 181
Hagel m 286
Hahn m 61, 185
Hähnchen n 119
Hähnchenstückchen f 155
Hahnenfuß m 297
Hai m 294

deutsch

deutsch

deutsch

deutsch

deutsch

parken 195
Parkett n 254
Parkplatz m 298
Parkuhr f 195
Parmesan m 142
Partner m 23
Partnerin f 23
Pass m 213, 226
Passagierhafen m 216
Passagier m 216
Passah n 27
Passionsfrucht f 128
Passkontrolle f 213
Passwort n 99
Pastellstifte f 274
Pastete f 142, 156, 158
Pasteten f 143
pasteurisiert 137
Pastinake f 125
Patchwork n 277
Pathologie f 49
Patientenstuhl m 50
Patiententabelle f 48
Patientin f 45
Patientzimmer n 48
Patiogarten m 84
Pause f 254, 269
Pausen-zeichen n 256
Pay-Kanal m 269
Pazifische Ozean m 312
Pecannuss f 129
Pedal n 206
Pediküre f 41
Peeling machen 41
Pelikan m 292
Pendler m 208
Penis m 21
Peperoni m 124, 143
Pepperoniwurst f 142
per Luftpost 98
Pergola f 84
Periduralanästhesie f 52
Periodikum n 168
Perlenkette f 36
Personal m 175
Personalabteilung f 175
Personenwaage f 45
persönliche Bestleistung f 234
Peru 315
Perücke f 39
Pessar n 21
Pestizid m 89, 183
Petersilie f 133
Petrischale f 166
Pfannengericht n 158
Pfannenwender m 68
Pfannkuchen f 157
Pfau m 293
Pfeffer m 64, 152
Pfefferkorn n 132
Pfefferminz n 113
Pfefferminztee m 149
Pfeife f 112
Pfeil m 249
Pfeiler m 300
Pferch m 185
Pferd m 185
Pferd m 235, 242
Pferderennen n 243
Pferdeschwanz m 39
Pferdestall m 243
Pfingstrose f 111
Pfirsich m 126, 128
pflanzen 183
Pflanzen f 296
Pflanzenarten f 86

Pflanzenöl n 135
Pflanzenschildchen f 89
Pflanzschaufel f 89
Pflaster n 47
Pflaume f 126
pflücken 91
pflügen 183
pfropfen 91
Pfund n 310
Phantombild n 181
Philippinen f 318
Philosophie f 169
Physik f 162, 169
Physiotherapie f 49
Picknick n 263
Picknickbank f 266
Pick-nickkorb m 263
Pier m 217
Pik n 273
pikante Wurst f 142
Pikkoloflöte f 257
Pilates n 251
Pille f 21
Pilot m 190, 211
Pilz m 125
Piment m 132
PIN-Code m 96
Pinguin m 292
Piniennuss f 129
Pinne f 240
Pinnward f 173
Pinsel m 274
Pint n 311
Pintobohnen f 131
Pinzette f 40, 47, 167
Pipette f 167
Pistazie f 129
Pistole f 94
Pitabrot n 139
Pizza f 154, 155
Pizzabelag m 155
Pizzeria f 154
Plädoyer m 180
Plakat n 255
Plakatfarbe f 274
Planet m 280, 282
Planken f 85
Planschbecken n 263
Plastiktüte f 122
plastische Chirurgie f 49
Plateau n 284
Platin m 289
Platte f 283
Platten f 85
Plattenspieler m 268
Platz m 299
Platzanweiser m 255
Plazenta f 52
plus 165
Pluspol m 167
Pluto m 280
pochieren 67
pochiert 159
Podium n 256
Poker n 273
Pol m 60, 282
Polarlicht n 286
Polaroidkamera f 270
Polen 316
polieren 77
Politologie f 169
Politur f 77
Polizei f 94
Polizeiauto n 94
Polizeiwache f 94
Polizeizelle f 94
Polizist m 94, 189

Poller m 214, 298
Polo n 243
Polster n 224
Polyester n 277
Pommes frites f 154
Poolbillard n 249
Popmusik f 259
Popcorn n 255
Pore f 15
Port m 176
Portefeuille n 97
Portemonnaie n 37
Portion f 64
Portionierer m 68
Portokosten f 98
Portugal 316
Portwein m 145
Porzellan n 105
Posaune f 257
Pose f 244
Post f 98
Postanweisung f 98
Postbeamte m 98
Posteingang m 177
postgraduiert 169
Postkarte f 112
Postleitzahl f 98
Postsack m 98
Poststempel m 98
Posttasche f 190
Potpourri n 111
Praline f 113
Präsentation f 174
Preis m 152
Preiselbeere f 127
Preisliste f 154
Premiere f 254
Presse f 178
Pressluftbohrer m 187
Privatbadezimmer n 100
private Fitnesstrainerin f 250
Privatjet m 211
Unterhaltungselektronik f 268
Privatzimmer n 48
Probleme f 271
Produzent m 254
Profilsäge f 81
Programm n 176, 254, 269
Programm-gestaltung f 178
Promenade f 265
Promotion f 169
Propeller m 211
Prosciutto m 143
Prospekt m 254
Prostata f 21
Protokoll n 174
Protokollführer m 180
Provinz f 315
Provision f 97
Prozentsatz m 165
Prozessor m 176
Prüfung f 163
Psychiatrie f 49
Psychotherapie f 55
Publikum n 254
Puck m 224
Puder m 109
Puderdose f 40
Puderpinsel m 40
Puderquaste f 40
Puderrouge f 40
Puerto Rico 314
Pullover m 33
Puls m 47
Pult n 162
Punk m 259

Punkt m 273
pünktlich 305
Pupille f 51
Puppe f 75
Puppenhaus n 75
püriert 159
Pute f 119
Putter m 233
putzen 77
Puzzle n 273
Pyramide f 164

Q

Qua-dratfuß m 310
Quadrat-meter m 310
Quadrat n 164
Qualle f 295
Quart n 311
Quarz m 289
Quecksilber n 289
quer 271
Querflöte f 257
Querlatte f 222
Querruder m 210
Quiche f 142
Quitte f 128
Quittung f 152

R

Rachen m 19
Racquetball n 231
Rad n 198, 207, 235
Radar m 214, 281
Rad fahren 207
Radfahren n 263
Radicchio m 123
Radiergummi m 163
Radieschen n 124
Radio n 179, 268
Radio einstellen n 269
Radiologie f 49
Radiowecker m 70
Radius m 164
Radkappe f 202
Radmuttern f 203
Radschlüssel m 203
Rafting n 241
Rahmen m 206
Rahmkäse m 136
Rakete f 211
Rallyefahren n 249
RAM n 176
Ramadan m 27
Rap m 259
Raps m 184
Rapsöl n 135
Rasen m 85, 90
Rasenmäher m 88, 90
Rasensprenger m 89
Rasentrimmer m 88
Rasieren n 73
Rasierklinge f 73
Rasierschaum m 73
Rasierwasser n 73
Rassel f 74
Rathaus n 299
Ratte f 290
Rauch m 95
Rauchen n 112
Räucherfisch m 143
Räucherheringe f 157
Rauchmelder m 95
Raumanzug m 281
Raumfähre f 281
Raumforschung f 281
Raumstation m 281

Raupe f 295
Raureif m 287
read 162
Reagenzglas n 166
Rebound m 226
Rechen m 88
Rechnung f 152
Recht n 180
Rechteck n 164
rechte Feld n 229
rechte Spur f 194
rechts 260
rechts abbiegen verboten 195
Rechtsabteilung f 175
Rechtsanwalt m 180
Rechtsanwältin f 190
Rechtsberatung f 180
Rechtssteuerung f 201
Rechtswissenschaft f 169
Reck n 235
Recyclingbehälter m 61
Redakteurin f 191
Reflexzonenmassage f 54
Reformhaus n 115
Regal n 268
Regen m 287
Regenbogen m 287
Regenbogenforelle f 120
Regenhaut f 245, 267
Regenmantel m 31, 32
Regenschirm m 36
Regenwald m 285
Reggae n 259
Region f 315
Regisseur m 254
Reibahle f 80
Reibe f 68
reiben 67
reif 129
Reifen m 198, 205, 206
Reifendruck m 203
Reifenpanne f 203, 207
Reifenprofil n 207
Reifenschlüssel m 207
Reihe f 210, 254
Reihenhaus n 58
Reiki n 55
Reiniger m 41
Reinigung f 115
Reinigungsartikel f 77
Reinigungsmittel n 51, 77
Reinigungstuch n 108
Reis m 130, 158, 184
Reisebüro n 114
Reisebürokauffrau f 190
Reisebus m 196
Reiseführer m 260
Reisekrankheit-stabletten f 109
Reisescheck m 97
Reisetasche f 37
Reiseziel n 213
Reismelde f 130
Reißverschluss m 277
Reißzwecke f 173
Reiten n 263
Reiter m 242
Reitgerte f 242
Reithelm m 242
Reithose f 242
Reitsport m 242
Reitstiefel m 242
Reitweg m 263
Rekord m 234
Relieftapete f 83
Renaissance 301

deutsch

deutsch

deutsch

deutsch

deutsch

Spanish index • index espagnol • spanisches Register • índice español • indice spagnolo

español

español

español

español

español

español

español

español

español

español

español

español

español

español

español

español

Italian index • index italien • italienisches Register • índice italiano • indice italiano

italiano

A

a 320
abat-jour m 70
abbaino m 58
abbigliamento m 205
abbigliamento da donna m 105, 34
abbigliamento da uomo m 105, 32
abboccare 245
abbronzatura f 41
abiti per il bambino m 30
abito m 32
abito da sera m 34
abito da sposa m 35
aborto spontaneo m 52
acacia f 110
accademia di danza f 169
accanto 320
accappatoio m 32, 73
acceleratore m 200, 204
accendere la televisione 269
accendere un fuoco 266
accendino m 112
accensione f 200
accesso per sedie a rotelle m 197
accessori m 36, 38
accessori per la pulizia m 77
acchiappare 227, 229
acciaio inossidabile m 79
acconciatura corta f 39
acconciature f 39
accordo di affari m 175
account di posta elettronica m 177
accusa m 94
accusato m 180
acero m 296
aceto m 135, 142
aceto balsamico m 135
aceto di malto m 135
aceto di sidro m 135
aceto di vino m 135
acetone m 41
acetosa f 123
a chicco corto 130
a chicco lungo 130
acqua f 144, 23
acqua dal rubinetto f 14
acqua di colonia f 4
acqua in bottiglia f 144
acqua minerale m 144
acqua naturale f 144
acqua tonica f 144
acquaio m 61
acquamarina f 288
acquaragia f 83
acquarello m 274
acquascooter m 241
acquavite f 151
acquisti m 104
addebito diretto m 96
addetta alla ricezione f 100, 190
addetto alle pulizie m 188
addome m 12
addominali m 16
addormentarsi 71
adesso 304
adirato 25

adolescente m 23
a due porte 200
adulto m 23
aerare 91
aereo biposto m 211
aereo da caccia m 211
aereo da diporto m 211
aereo di linea m 210, 212
aereo privato m 211
aeroplano m 210
aeroporto m 212
affamato 64
affari m 175
affettare 67
affettatrice f 139
affilacoltelli m 68, 118
affilatore m 81
affittare 58
affitto m 58
affogare 67
affogato 159
affrancatura f 98
affumicato 118, 121, 143, 159
Afghanistan 318
a foglie caduche 86
Africa 317
agata f 289
agenda f 173, 175
agente di viaggio m 190
agente immobiliare f 189
agenzia di viaggi m 114
agenzia immobiliare f 115
aggressione f 94
aggrottare le ciglia 25
aglio m 125, 132
agnello m 118, 185
ago m 109, 276
agopressione f 55
agopuntura f 55
agosto 306
agricoltore m 182, 189
agrifoglio m 296
agro 127
agrumi m 126
aikido m 236
airbag m 201
aiuola f 85, 90
aiuto cuoco m 152
ala f 119, 210, 293
à la carte 152
alambicco m 166
Alaska 314
alba f 305
Albania 316
albergo m 100, 264
albero m 86, 240, 29
albero di trasmissione m 202
albicocca f 126
album fotografico m 271
alchechengi m 128
alesatore m 80
aletta f 210
alettone m 210
alfalfa m 184
alfiere m 272
Algeria 317
al ginocchio 34
aliante m 211, 248
aliscafo m 215

all'esterno 320
all'interno 320
alla caviglia 34
alla griglia 159
allarme antifumo m 95
allarme antifurto m 58
allarme antincendio m 95
allattamento m 53
allattamento al seno m 53
allegato m 177
allenamento m 237
allenamento a circuito m 251
allenarsi 251
allergia f 44
allevamento di maiali m 183
allevamento di pecore m 183
alligatore m 293
allo sciroppo 159
alloro m 133
alluce m 15
alluminio m 289
alpinismo in parete m 248
al sugo 159
alta definizione (HD) 269
altalena f 263
alternatore m 203
altezza f 165
altipiano m 284
alto 98, 321
altoparlante m 176, 209, 258, 268
altre imbarcazioni f 215
altri lavori artigianali m 275
altri negozi m 114
altri sport m 248
altroieri m 307
alluna f 162
al vapore 159
alzarsi 71
alzate con il manubrio f 251
alzatina paraspruzzi f 66
amaca f 266
amaro 124
Amazzonia f 312
ambiente m 280
ambulanza f 94
ambulatorio m 45, 168
America Centrale 314
America del Nord 314
America del Sud 315
ametista f 288
amico m 24
di penna m 24
amministratore delegato m 175
ammorbidente m 76
ammortizzatore m 205
amniocentesi f 52
amo m 244
ampere m 60
amplificatore m 268
anacardi m 151
anacardio m 129
analisi f 49
analisi del sangue f 48
analogico 179
ananas m 128
anatra f 119, 185
anatroccolo m 185
anca f 12
ancora f 214, 240

andare a letto 71
andare in bici 207
andare in pensione 26
Ande f 312
Andorra 316
anelli m 89, 235
anello m 36, 226
anestetista m 48
aneto m 133
anfibi m 294
Angola 317
angolo m 164, 223
angolo della strada m 298
anguilla f 294
anguria f 127
anice stellato m 133
animali m 292, 294
animazione f 255
annaffiare 90
annaffiatoio m 89
annaffiatura f 89
annegare 239
annesso m 58
anniversario m 26
anno m 306
annoiato 25
annotazione f 256
annuale 86
annunciatrice f 179, 191
annuo 307
antenna f 295
antenna della radio f 214
antenna parabolica f 269
antiaderente 69
antidolorifici m 47
antidolorifico m 109
antigelo m 199
Antigua e Barbuda 314
antinfiammatorio m 109
antipasto m 153
antirughe 41
anulare m 15
ape f 295
aperitivo m 153
aperto 260, 321
apice m 164
apoplessia f 44
app m 99
apparecchiare 64
apparecchiature da ufficio f 172
apparecchio a raggi x m 212
apparecchio correttore m 50
appartamento m 59
appellativi m 23
appendice f 18
applaudire 255
applicazione f 176
applique f 62
approdare 217
appuntamento m 45, 175
appunti m 191
apribottiglie m 68, 150
aprile 306
apriscatole m 68
a quattro porte 200
aquila f 292
Arabia Saudita 319
arachide f 129
aragosta f 121, 295
arancio f 126

aranciata f 144
arancino cinese m 126
arancione 274
arare 183
aratro m 182
arbitro m 220, 222, 225, 226, 229, 230
arbusto da fiore m 87
architettare 91
architetto m 190
architettura f 300
architrave m 186, 301
arco m 85, 164, 249, 301
arco plantare m 15
arcobaleno m 287
ardesia f 288
area della porta f 221, 223
area di attacco f 224
area di difesa f 224
area di rigore f 223
area di stazionamento f 199, 212
area neutrale f 224
arena f 243
arenaria f 288
Argentina 315
argento m 235, 289
argilla f 85, 275
aria condizionata f 200
aringhe affumicate f 157
aritmetica f 165
armadietti m 239
armadietto dei medicinali m 72
armadio m 70
armadio a muro m 71
Armenia 318
aromaterapia f 55
arpa f 256
arrabiata 25
arrampicata su ghiaccio f 247
arrangiamenti m 111
arredamento per casa m 105
arresto m 94
arricciacapelli m 38
arringa f 180
arrivederci 322
arrivi m 213
arrostire 67
arrostito 129
arrosto m 158
art déco 301
art nouveau 301
arte f 162
arte e artigianato 274
arteria f 19
arte topiaria f 87
articolazione f 17
articoli da cucina m 105
articoli da toilette m 41, 107
articoli di cancelleria m 173
articoli elettrici m 107
articoli elettronici m 105
articoli sportivi m 105
artigianato m 276
artiglio m 291
arti marziali f 237

italiano

italiano

italiano

italiano

italiano

italiano

italiano

italiano

italiano

italiano

ITALIAN INDEX • INDEX ITALIEN • ITALIENISCHES REGISTER • ÍNDICE ITALIANO • INDICE ITALIANO

italiano

italiano

italiano

acknowledgments • remerciements • Dank • agradecimientos • ringraziamenti

DORLING KINDERSLEY would like to Christine Lacey for design assistance, Georgina Garner for editorial and administrative help, Kopal Agarwal, Polly Boyd, Sonia Gavira, Ankita Gupta, Cathy Meeus, Devangana Ojha, Sandra Prakash, Sai Prasanna, and Priyanka Sharma for editorial help, Claire Bowers for compiling the DK picture credits, Nishwan Rasool for picture research, and Suruchi Bhatia, Miguel Cunha, Mohit Sharma, and Alex Valizadeh for app development and creation. For the 2016 edition, DORLING KINDERSLEY would like to thank Pakshalika Jayaprakash, Antara Moitra, Vineetha Mokkil, Stuart Neilson, Ira Pundeer, and Angela Wilkes for editorial assistance; Meenal Goel, Roshni Kapur, Chhaya Sajwan, Arunesh Talapatra, and Priyanka Tuli for design help; and Nityanand Kumar, Dheeraj Singh, and Jacqueline Street for their help in production of this title.

The publisher would like to thank the following for their kind permission to reproduce their photographs:
Abbreviations key: (a-above; b-below/bottom; c-center; f-far; l-left; r-right; t-top)

123RF.com: Andrey Popov / andreypopov 23bc; Andriy Popov 34tl; Brad Wynnyk 172bc; Daniel Ernst 179tc; Hongqi Zhang 24cla, 175cr; Ingvar Bjork 60c; Kobby Dagan 259c; leonardo255 269c; Liubov Vadimovna (Luba) Nel 39cla; Ljupco Smokovski 75crb; Oleksandr Marynchenko 60bl; Olga Popova 33c; oneblink 49bc; Robert Churchill 94c; Roman Gorielov 33bc; Ruslan Kudrin 35bc, 35br; Subbotina 39cra; Sutichak Yachaingkham 39tc; Tarzhanova 37tc; Vitaly Valua 39tl; Wavebreak Media Ltd 188bl; Wilawan Khasawong 75cb; **Action Plus:** 224bc; **Alamy Images:** 154t; A.T. Willett 287bcl; Alex Segre 105ca, 195cl; Ambrophoto 24cra; Blend Images 168cr; Cultura RM 33r; Doug Houghton 107fbr; Hugh Threlfall 35tl, 176tr; Ian Allenden 48br; Ian Dagnall 270t; Levgen Chepil 250bc; Imagebroker 199tl, 249tc; Keith Morris 178c; Martyn Evans 210b; MBI 175tl; Michael Burrell 213cra; Michael Foyle 184bl; Oleksiy Maksymenko 105tc; Paul Weston 168br; Prisma Bildagentur AG 246b; Radharc Images 197tr; RBtravel 112tl; Ruslan Kudrin 176tl; Sasa Huzjak 258t; Sergey Kravchenko 37ca; Sergio Azenha 270bc; Stanca Sanda (iPad is a trademark of Apple Inc., registered in the U.S. and other countries) 176bc; Stock Connection 287bcr; tarczas 35cr; Vitaly Suprun 176cl; Wavebreak Media Ltd 39cl, 174b, 175tr; **Allsport/Getty Images:** 238cl; **Alvey and Towers:** 209 acr, 215bcl, 215bcr, 241cr; **Peter Anderson:** 188cbr, 271br. **Anthony Blake Photo Library:** Charlie Stebbings 114cl; John Sims 114tcl; **Andyalte:** 98tl; **Arcaid:** John Edward Linden 301bl; Martine Hamilton Knight, Architects: Chapman Taylor Partners, 213cl; Richard Bryant 301br; **Argos:** 41tcl, 66cbl, 66cl, 66br, 66bcl, 69cl, 70bcl, 71t, 77tl, 269tcc, 270tl; **Axiom:** Eitan Simanor 105bcr; Ian Cumming 104; Vicki Couchman 148cr; **Beken Of Cowes Ltd:** 215cbc; **Bosch:** 76tcr, 76tc, 76tcl; **Camera Press:** 38tr, 256t, 257cr; Barry J.

Holmes 148tr; Jane Hanger 159cr; Mary Germanou 259bc; **Corbis:** 78b; Anna Clopet 247tr; Ariel Skelley / Blend Images 52l; Bettmann 181tl, 181tr; Blue Jean Images 48bl; Bo Zauders 156t; Bob Rowan 152bl; Bob Winsett 247cbl; Brian Bailey 247br; Chris Rainer 247ctl; Craig Aurness 215bl; David H. Wells 249cbr; Dennis Marsico 274bl; Dimitri Lundt 236bc; Duomo 211tl; Gail Mooney 277ctcr; George Lepp 248c; Gerald Nowak 239b; Gunter Marx 248cr; Jack Hollingsworth 231bl; Jacqui Hurst 277cbr; James L. Amos 247bl, 191ctr, 220bcr; Jan Butchofsky 277cbc; Johnathan Blair 243cr; Jose F. Poblete 191br; Jose Luis Pelaez.Inc 153tc; Karl Weatherly 220bl, 247tcr; Kelly Mooney Photography 259tl; Kevin Fleming 249bc; Kevin R. Morris 105tr, 243tl, 243tc; Kim Sayer 249tcr; Lynn Goldsmith 258t; Macduff Everton 231bcl; Mark Gibson 249bl; Mark L. Stephenson 249tctl; Michael Pole 115tr; Michael S. Yamashita 247ctcl; Mike King 247cbl; Neil Rabinowitz 214br; Pablo Corral 115bc; Paul A. Saunders 169br, 249ctcl; Paul J. Sutton 224c, 224br; Phil Schermeister 227b, 248tr; R. W Jones 309; Richard Morrell 189bc; Rick Doyle 241ctr; Robert Holmes 97br, 277ctc; Roger Ressmeyer 169tr; Russ Schleipman 229; The Purcell Team 211ctr; Vince Streano 194t; Wally McNamee 220br, 220bcl, 224bl; Wavebreak Media LTD 191bc; Yann Arhus-Bertrand 249tl; **Demetrio Carrasco / Dorling Kindersley (c) Herge / Les Editions Casterman:** 112ccl; **Dorling Kindersley:** Banbury Museum 35c; Five Napkin Burger 152t; **Dixons:** 270cl, 270cr, 270bl, 270bcl, 270bcr, 270ccr; **Dreamstime.com:** Alexander Podshivalov 179tr, 191cr; Alexxl66 268tl; Andersastphoto 176tc; Andrey Popov 191bl; Arne9001 190tl; Chaoss 26c; Designsstock 269cl; Monkey Business Images 26clb; Paul Michael Hughes 162tr; Serghei Starus 190bc; Isselee 292fcrb; Zerbor 296tr; **Education Photos:** John Walmsley 26tl; **Empics Ltd:** Adam Day 236br; Andy Heading 243c; Steve White 249cbc; **Getty Images:** 48bcl, 94tr, 100t, 114cbr, 154bl, 287tr; George Doyle & Ciaran Griffin 22cr; David Leahy 162tl; Don Farrall / Digital Vision 176c; Ethan Miller 270bl; Inti St Clair 179tb; Liam Norris 188br; Sean Justice / Digital Vision 24br; **Dennis Gilbert:** 106tc; **Hulsta:** 70t; **Ideal Standard Ltd:** 72r; **The Image Bank/Getty Images:** 58; **Impact Photos:** Eliza Armstrong 115cr; Philip Achache 246t; **The Interior Archive:** Henry Wilson, Alfie's Market 114tal; Luke White, Architect: David Mikhail, 59bl; Simon Upton, Architect: Phillippe Starck, St Martins Lane Hotel 100bcr, 100br; **iStockphoto.com:** asterix0597 163tl; EdStock 190br; RichLegg 26bc; SorinVidis 27cr; **Jason Hawkes Aerial Photography:** 216t; **Dan Johnson:** 35r; **Kos Pictures Source:** 215cbl, 240tc, 240tr; David Williams 216b; **Lebrecht Collection:** Kate Mount 169bc; **MP Visual.com:** Mark Swallow 202t; **NASA:** 280cr, 280ccl, 281tl; **P&O Princess Cruises:** 214bl; **P A Photos:** 181br; **The Photographers' Library:** 186bl, 186bc, 186t; **Plain and Simple Kitchens:** 66t; **Powerstock Photolibrary:** 169tl, 256t,

287tc; **PunchStock:** Image Source 195tr; **Rail Images:** 208c, 208 cbl, 209br; **Red Consultancy:** Odeon cinemas 257br; **Redferns:** 259br; Nigel Crane 259c; **Rex Features:** 106br, 259tc, 259tr, 259bl, 280b; Charles Ommaney 114tcr; J.F.F Whitehead 243cl; Patrick Barth 101tl; Patrick Frilet 189cbl; Scott Wiseman 287bl; **Royalty Free Images:** Getty Images/Eyewire 154bl; **Science & Society Picture Library:** Science Museum 202b; **Science Photo Library:** IBM Research 190cla; NASA 281cr; **SuperStock:** Ingram Publishing 62; Juanma Aparicio / age fotostock 172t; Nordic Photos 269tl; **Skyscan:** 168t, 182c, 298; Quick UK Ltd 212; **Sony:** 268bc; **Robert Streeter:** 154br; **Neil Sutherland:** 82tr, 83tl, 90t, 118c, 188ctr, 196tl, 196tr, 299cl, 299bl; **The Travel Library:** Stuart Black 264t; **Travelex:** 97cl; **Vauxhall:** Technik 198t, 199tr, 199tcl, 199cr, 199ctccl, 199ctcr, 199tctl, 199tcr, 200; **View Pictures:** Dennis Gilbert, Architects: ACDP Consulting, 106t; Dennis Gilbert, Chris Wilkinson Architects, 209tr; Peter Cook, Architects: Nicholas Crimshaw and partners, 208t; **Betty Walton:** 185br; **Colin Walton:** 2, 4, 7, 10, 28, 40l, 42, 56, 92, 95c, 99tl, 99tcl, 102, 116, 120t, 138t, 146, 150t, 160, 170, 191tcl, 192, 218, 252, 260br, 260l, 261tr, 261c, 261cr, 271cbl, 271ctl, 278, 287br, 302.

DK PICTURE LIBRARY:
Akhil Bahkshi; Patrick Baldwin; Geoff Brightling; British Museum; John Bulmer; Andrew Butler; Joe Cornish; Brian Cosgrove; Andy Crawford and Kit Hougton; Philip Dowell; Alistair Duncan; Gables; Bob Gathany; Norman Hollands; Kew Gardens; Peter James Kindersley; Vladimir Kozlik; Sam Lloyd; London Northern Bus Company Ltd; Tracy Morgan; David Murray and Jules Selmes; Musée Vivant du Cheval, France; Museum of Broadcast Communications; Museum of Natural History; NASA; National History Museum; Norfolk Rural Life Museum; Stephen Oliver; RNLI; Royal Ballet School; Guy Ryecart; Science Museum; Neil Setchfield; Ross Simms and the Winchcombe Folk Police Museum; Singapore Symphony Orchestra; Smart Museum of Art; Tony Souter; Erik Svensson and Jeppe Wikstrom; Sam Tree of Keygrove Marketing Ltd; Barrie Watts; Alan Williams; Jerry Young.

Additional photography by Colin Walton.

Colin Walton would like to thank:
A&A News, Uckfield; Abbey Music, Tunbridge Wells; Arena Mens Clothing, Tunbridge Wells; Burrells of Tunbridge Wells; Gary at Di Marco's; Jeremy's Home Store, Tunbridge Wells; Noakes of Tunbridge Wells; Ottakar's, Tunbridge Wells; Selby's of Uckfield; Sevenoaks Sound and Vision; Westfield, Royal Victoria Place, Tunbridge Wells.

All other images © Dorling Kindersley
For further information see: www.dkimages.com